NON-STATUTORY EXECUTIVE POWERS AND JUDICIAL REVIEW

That non-statutory executive powers are subject to judicial review is beyond doubt. But current judicial practice challenges prevailing theories of judicial review and raises a host of questions about the nature of official power and action. This is particularly the case for official powers not associated with the Royal Prerogative, which have been argued to comprise a "third source" of governmental authority. Looking at non-statutory powers directly, rather than incidentally, stirs up the intense but ultimately inconclusive debate about the conceptual basis of judicial review in English law. This provocative book argues that modern judges and scholars have neglected the very concepts necessary to understand the supervisory jurisdiction and that the law has become more complex than it needs to be. If we start from the concept of office and official action, rather than grand ideas about parliamentary sovereignty and the courts, the central questions answer themselves.

JASON GRANT ALLEN is a Senior Research Fellow at the Humboldt University in Berlin. He read law at the University of Tasmania, the Universität Augsburg, and the University of Cambridge. He has been an Australian Postgraduate Awardee, a DAAD Scholar, a Poynton Scholar, and an Alexander von Humboldt Foundation Postdoctoral Fellow

CAMBRIDGE STUDIES IN CONSTITUTIONAL LAW

The aim of this series is to produce leading monographs in constitutional law. All areas of constitutional law and public law fall within the ambit of the series, including human rights and civil liberties law, administrative law, as well as constitutional theory and the history of constitutional law. A wide variety of scholarly approaches is encouraged, with the governing criterion being simply that the work is of interest to an international audience. Thus, works concerned with only one jurisdiction will be included in the series as appropriate, while, at the same time, the series will include works which are explicitly comparative or theoretical - or both. The series editors likewise welcome proposals that work at the intersection of constitutional and international law, or that seek to bridge the gaps between civil law systems, the US, and the common law jurisdictions of the Commonwealth.

Books in the Series

The Law as a Conversation among Equals
Roberto Gargarella

Micronations and the Search for Sovereignty
Harry Hobbs and George Williams

Fundamental Rights and the Legal Obligations of Business
David Bilchitz

Courting Constitutionalism: The Politics of Public Law and Judicial Review in Pakistan
Moeen Cheema

Ruling by Cheating: Governance in Illiberal Democracy
András Sajó

Local Meanings of Proportionality
Afroditi Marketou

Property Rights and Social Justice: Progressive Property in Action
Rachael Walsh

Carl Schmitt's Early Legal-Theoretical Writings: Statute and Judgment and the Value of the State and the Significance of the Individual
Lars Vinx and Samuel Garrett Zeitlin

Remedies for Human Rights Violations: A Two-Track Approach to Supra-national and National Law
Kent Roach

Europe's Second Constitution: Crisis, Courts and Community
Markus W. Gehring

A.V. Dicey and the Common Law Constitutional Tradition: A Legal Turn of Mind
Mark D. Walters

Administrative Competence: Reimagining Administrative Law
Elizabeth Fisher and Sidney A. Shapiro

Legal Sabotage: Ernst Fraenkel in Hitler's Germany
Douglas Morris

Proportionality in Action: Comparative and Empirical Perspectives on the Judicial Practice
Edited by Mordechai Kremnitzer, Tayla Steiner and Andrej Lang

Constitutional Dialogue: Democracy, Rights, Institutions
Edited by Geoffrey Sigalet, Grégoire Webber and Rosalind Dixon

The Veiled Sceptre: Reserve Powers of Heads of State in Westminster Systems
Anne Twomey

Vigilance and Restraint in the Common Law of Judicial Review
Dean Knight

The Alchemists: Questioning Our Faith in Courts as Democracy-Builders
Tom Gerald Daly

Australia's Constitution after Whitlam
Brendan Lim

Building the Constitution: The Practice of Constitutional Interpretation in Post-Apartheid South Africa
James Fowkes

Dimensions of Dignity: The Theory and Practice of Modern Constitutional Law
Jacob Weinrib

Reason of State: Law, Prerogative, Empire
Thomas Poole

Bills of Rights in the Common Law
Robert Leckey

The Guardian of the Constitution: Hans Kelsen and Carl Schmitt on the Limits of Constitutional Law
Translated by Lars Vinx, with an introduction and notes by Lars Vinx

Parliamentary Bills of Rights: The Experiences of New Zealand and the United Kingdom
Janet L. Hiebert and James B. Kelly

Lawyering for the Rule of Law: Government Lawyers and the Rise of Judicial Power in Israel
Yoav Dotan

Balancing Constitutional Rights: The Origins and Meanings of Postwar Legal Discourse
Jacco Bomhoff

Judges on Trial: The Independence and Accountability of the English Judiciary
Shimon Shetreet and Sophie Turenne

Proportionality and Constitutional Culture
Moshe Cohen-Eliya and Iddo Porat

The Politics of Principle: The First South African Constitutional Court, 1995–2005
Theunis Roux

The New Commonwealth Model of Constitutionalism: Theory and Practice
Stephen Gardbaum

Searching for the State in British Legal Thought: Competing Conceptions of the Public Sphere
Janet McLean

Judging Social Rights
Jeff King

Proportionality: Constitutional Rights and their Limitations
Aharon Barak

Parliamentary Sovereignty: Contemporary Debates
Jeffrey Goldsworthy

Courting Constitutionalism: The Politics of Public Law and Judicial Review in Pakistan
Moeen Cheema

Ruling by Cheating: Governance in Illiberal Democracy
András Sajó

Local Meanings of Proportionality
Afroditi Marketou

Property Rights and Social Justice: Progressive Property in Action
Rachael Walsh

Carl Schmitt's Early Legal-Theoretical Writings: Statute and Judgment and the Value of the State and the Significance of the Individual
Lars Vinx and Samuel Garrett Zeitlin

Remedies for Human Rights Violations: A Two-Track Approach to Supra-national and National Law
Kent Roach

Europe's Second Constitution: Crisis, Courts and Community
Markus W. Gehring

A.V. Dicey and the Common Law Constitutional Tradition: A Legal Turn of Mind
Mark D. Walters

Administrative Competence: Reimagining Administrative Law
Elizabeth Fisher and Sidney A. Shapiro

Legal Sabotage: Ernst Fraenkel in Hitler's Germany
Douglas Morris

Proportionality in Action: Comparative and Empirical Perspectives on the Judicial Practice
Edited by Mordechai Kremnitzer, Tayla Steiner and Andrej Lang

Constitutional Dialogue: Democracy, Rights, Institutions
Edited by Geoffrey Sigalet, Grégoire Webber and Rosalind Dixon

The Veiled Sceptre: Reserve Powers of Heads of State in Westminster Systems
Anne Twomey

Vigilance and Restraint in the Common Law of Judicial Review
Dean Knight

The Alchemists: Questioning Our Faith in Courts as Democracy-Builders
Tom Gerald Daly

Australia's Constitution after Whitlam
Brendan Lim

Building the Constitution: The Practice of Constitutional Interpretation in Post-Apartheid South Africa
James Fowkes

Dimensions of Dignity: The Theory and Practice of Modern Constitutional Law
Jacob Weinrib

Reason of State: Law, Prerogative, Empire
Thomas Poole

Bills of Rights in the Common Law
Robert Leckey

The Guardian of the Constitution: Hans Kelsen and Carl Schmitt on the Limits of Constitutional Law
Translated by Lars Vinx, with an introduction and notes by Lars Vinx

Parliamentary Bills of Rights: The Experiences of New Zealand and the United Kingdom
Janet L. Hiebert and James B. Kelly

Lawyering for the Rule of Law: Government Lawyers and the Rise of Judicial Power in Israel
Yoav Dotan

Balancing Constitutional Rights: The Origins and Meanings of Postwar Legal Discourse
Jacco Bomhoff

Judges on Trial: The Independence and Accountability of the English Judiciary
Shimon Shetreet and Sophie Turenne

Proportionality and Constitutional Culture
Moshe Cohen-Eliya and Iddo Porat

The Politics of Principle: The First South African Constitutional Court, 1995–2005
Theunis Roux

The New Commonwealth Model of Constitutionalism: Theory and Practice
Stephen Gardbaum

Searching for the State in British Legal Thought: Competing Conceptions of the Public Sphere
Janet McLean

Judging Social Rights
Jeff King

Proportionality: Constitutional Rights and their Limitations
Aharon Barak

Parliamentary Sovereignty: Contemporary Debates
Jeffrey Goldsworthy

NON-STATUTORY EXECUTIVE POWERS AND JUDICIAL REVIEW

JASON GRANT ALLEN
Humboldt University of Berlin

CAMBRIDGE
UNIVERSITY PRESS

CAMBRIDGE
UNIVERSITY PRESS

Shaftesbury Road, Cambridge CB2 8EA, United Kingdom

One Liberty Plaza, 20th Floor, New York, NY 10006, USA

477 Williamstown Road, Port Melbourne, VIC 3207, Australia

314–321, 3rd Floor, Plot 3, Splendor Forum, Jasola District Centre, New Delhi – 110025, India

103 Penang Road, #05–06/07, Visioncrest Commercial, Singapore 238467

Cambridge University Press is part of Cambridge University Press & Assessment,
a department of the University of Cambridge.

We share the University's mission to contribute to society through the pursuit of education, learning and research at the highest international levels of excellence.

www.cambridge.org
Information on this title: www.cambridge.org/9781009017725

DOI: 10.1017/9781009039321

First published 2022
First paperback edition 2025

A catalogue record for this publication is available from the British Library

ISBN 978-1-316-51066-7 Hardback
ISBN 978-1-009-01772-5 Paperback

To Stefanie

CONTENTS

ACKNOWLEDGEMENTS

This book is a significantly reworked version of a doctoral thesis submitted in January 2017. Most of the material is new. I have incorporated a number of recent scholarly sources and cases – not least the two landmark decisions on judicial review applications brought in the context of Brexit in 2016 and 2019. I have also reframed the argument to appeal to a broader audience and have expanded my treatment of the Anglo-Commonwealth jurisdictions. I hope it will provide something of interest for students, scholars, and practitioners alike.

I owe a debt of gratitude to many people in the several places this work unfolded. In Cambridge, I would like to thank Professor Trevor Allan for his patience while I found my own way through the thicket. Substantively, his work – and his courage to challenge orthodoxy – has influenced my thinking profoundly. Thanks to my examiners, Professor Mark Elliott and Professor Denis Galligan, for their rigorous scrutiny of the thesis. Professor Kevin Gray first encouraged me to apply to Cambridge, and I would like to thank him for that as well as for his gestures of kindness over the years I was there. I would like to thank my peers, particularly Dr Daniel Clarry and Dr Will Bateman. Together, they have helped to shape my thinking about the law considerably. In Darwin College, I would like to thank the members of an informal group dubbed, after our meeting place, the 'Gazebo Society', and Dr Matteo Corso in particular. Conversations with Dr Isak Herman on the intersection of law and computer science helped me to see my own discipline from another perspective and were instrumental in moving my research in the rewarding direction it has taken since. Although we met late in the piece, Dr Edward Cavanagh was a great source of learning on the history of the Crown.

I would like to thank the Cambridge Australia Trust for supporting me as a Poynton Scholar for the duration of my PhD. Between the happy news of acceptance in 2010 and going up to Cambridge in 2013, I was diagnosed with cancer. I thank the Trust for holding over my offer while

I underwent treatment and for extending my funding for a fourth year in light of continuing difficulties.

In Australia, thanks to Dr Brendan Gogarty for being among the first people to read the thesis and Professor Gino Dal Pont for his supervision and guidance over many years. Mr Michael Stokes led my first steps into jurisprudence. The University of Tasmania provided me with a Burke Scholarship to get established in Cambridge. Professor Justice Paul Finn went out of his way to share his time and knowledge on a visit to Adelaide in 2014 and in a few emails that were, in hindsight, instrumental in helping me stay the course. Dr Robert Moles and Professor Carlos Bernal both helped me to grapple with some of the more complex questions in institutional legal theory and social ontology.

From Canada, Professor Evan Fox-Decent twice arranged for me to visit North America and connect with the community of 'fiduciary public lawyers' working there, once with the active collusion of Professor Lionel Smith.

Shortly before completion of my thesis, I started as Judicial Assistant to (then Chancellor of the High Court of England and Wales) Sir Geoffrey Vos in London. I thank Sir Geoffrey for turning a blind eye to my obvious exhaustion from late nights and early mornings finalising the manuscript. As an equity lawyer at heart, my time with him will stand as a highlight of my legal career, and in personal terms Sir Geoffrey was the model of a supervising judge. In my first weeks in that role, I was billeted as the Assistant to Lord Justice Sales (as he then was) sitting in the Divisional Court in *R (Miller)* v. *Brexit Secretary*. I was incredibly lucky to work on such a landmark case. I thank Lord Sales for being the first person to read the manuscript of this book and for his insightful comments.

This book was written up during my time at the Humboldt University of Berlin Centre for British Studies, initially as an Alexander von Humboldt Foundation postdoctoral fellow. Thanks to Professor Gerhard Dannemann, my host at the Centre, and Professor Patricia Springborg for our tearoom chats on royal personality and for sharing her extraordinary knowledge of the history of political thought. Too little of that has found its way into this already dense book. Dr Tully Rector of the Free University of Berlin was an engaging and challenging conversational partner.

I would like to thank the series editors, Professor David Dyzenhaus and Professor Tom Poole, for helping me bring the book to this final incarnation. David's course on judicial review during his Goodhart

Professorship in Cambridge in 2014–2015 was enlightening in many ways. Both provided very helpful criticism, which improved the text considerably. Thanks to Mr Tom Randall of the Cambridge University Press for his patient guidance.

Supreme thanks go to those closest to home, especially to my mother and father, Peter and Ellen. Above all, however, thanks are due to my wife, Stefanie, who walked with me every step of the way and often carried me. There is more of her in this book than she herself knows.

TABLE OF CASES

Adams *v.* Naylor [1946] 2 All ER 241
Adan *v.* Newham London Borough Council [2001] EWCA Civ 1916
Al-Khawaja *v.* Home Secretary [1984] AC 74
Al-Waheed and Serdar Mohamed *v.* Ministry of Defence [2017] UKSC 2
Allnut *v.* Inglis (1810) 12 East 527
Amalgamated Society of Engineers *v.* Adelaide Steamship Company Limited (1920) 28 CLR 129
Anisminic Ltd *v.* Foreign Compensation Commission [1969] 2 AC 147
Ashby *v.* White (1703) 92 ER 126
Associated Provincial Picture Houses Ltd *v.* Wednesbury Corporation [1948] 1 KB 223
Attorney-General for New South Wales *v.* Perpetual Trustee Co Ltd [1955] AC 457
Attorney-General *v.* Corporation of Leicester [1943] Ch 86
Attorney-General *v.* De Keyser's Royal Hotel Ltd [1920] AC 508
Attorney General *v.* Edison Telephone Co of London Ltd (1880–81) LR 6 QB 244
Attorney-General *v.* Great Eastern Railway Co (1880) 5 App Cas 473
Attorney-General *v.* Great Southern & Western Railway Co of Ireland [1925] AC 754
Attorney-General *v.* Leeds Corporation [1870] LR 5 Ch App 583
Attorney-General *v.* Manchester Corporation [1906] 1 Ch 643
Attorney-General *v.* Mersey Railway Co [1907] AC 415
Attorney General (NSW) *v.* Quin (1990) 170 CLR 1
Attorney-General for New South Wales *v.* Perpetual Trustee Co Ltd [1955] AC 457
Attorney-General of Canada *v.* Cain [1906] AC 542
Attorney-General of Quebec *v.* Labrecque [1980] SCR 1057
Bacchus *v.* Servicio National del Trigo [1957] 1 QB 438
Baxter *v.* NSW Clickers' Association (1909) 10 CLR 114
Begum *v.* Tower Hamlets London Borough Council [2003] UKHL 5
Belhaj and Rahmatullah *v.* Straw [2017] UKSC 3
Bennet *v.* Easedale (1626) 79 Eng Rep 821
Black *v.* Canada (Prime Minister) (2001) 199 DLR (4th) 228
Boddington *v.* British Transport Police [1999] 2 AC 143
Bradley *v.* Jockey Club [2004] EWHC 2164
British Broadcasting Corporation *v.* Johns [1965] Ch 32
British Launderers Association *v.* Borough of Hendon Rating Authority [1949] 1 KB 462
Bromley LBC *v.* Greater London Council [1983] 1 AC 768

Brown *v.* Tasmania (2017) 261 CLR 328
Brown *v.* West (1990) 169 CLR 195
Bugdaycay *v.* Home Secretary [1987] 1 All ER 940
Bugg *v.* DPP [1993] QB 473
Bumper Development Corporation Ltd *v.* Commissioner of Police for the Metropolis [1991] 4 All ER 638
Burmah Oil Co (Burmah Trading) Ltd *v.* Lord Advocate [1965] AC 75
Calvin's Case (1609) 7(5) Co Rep 1a
Canada (Prime Minister) *v.* Khadr [2010] 1 SCR 44
Canadian Doctors for Refugee Care *v.* Canada (2014) FC 651
Carratt *v.* Marley (1841) 1 QB 18
Case of Magdalen College, Cambridge (1572) 11 Co Rep 66b
Case of Proclamations (1611) 12 Co Rep 74
Church of Scientology *v.* Woodward (1982) 154 CLR 25
Clark *v.* University of Lincolnshire and Humberside [2000] EWCA 129
Clough *v.* Leahy (1904) 2 CLR 139
Cocks *v.* Thanet District Council [1983] 2 AC 287
Commonwealth *v.* Baume (1905) 2 CLR 405
Commonwealth *v.* Colonial Combing, Spinning and Weaving Co Ltd (1922) 31 CLR 421
Communications, Electrical, Electronic, Energy, Information, Postal, Plumbing and Allied Services Union of Australia *v.* Queensland Rail (2015) 318 ALR 1
Communist Party of Australia *v.* Commonwealth (1951) 83 CLR 1
Council of Civil Service Unions *v.* Minister for the Civil Service (1985) AC 374
Davis *v.* Commonwealth (1988) 166 CLR 79
Davy *v.* Spelthorne BC [1983] 3 All ER 278
De Portibus Maris (1787) 1 Harg Tr 78
Dickason *v.* Edwards (1910) 10 CLR 243
Dickson *v.* Pharmaceutical Society of Great Britain [1967] Ch 708
Director of Public Prosecutions *v.* Head [1959] AC 83
Duchess of Kingston's Case (1776) 20 St Tr 355
Duchy of Lancaster Case (1561) 1 Plow 212
Durayappah *v.* Fernando [1967] 2 AC 337
E *v.* Home Secretary [2004] 2 WLR 1352
Earl of Shrewsbury Case (1611) 77 Eng Rep 798
Edwards *v.* Bairstow [1956] AC 14
Edwards *v.* Canada (AG) [1930] AC 124 (JBPC)
Edwards *v.* Society of Graphical and Allied Trades [1971] Ch 354
Enderby Town Football Club Ltd *v.* Football Association Ltd [1971] Ch 591
Entick *v.* Carrington (1765) 19 St Tr 1020
Faramis *v.* Film Artistes Association [1964] 1 All ER 25
Farmer *v.* Cotton's Trustees [1925] AC 922
Farnell *v.* Bowman (1887) 12 AC 643
Fowler Developments Limited *v.* The Chief Executive of the Canterbury Earthquake Recovery Authority [2013] NZHC 2173

Gilbert *v.* Corporation of Trinity House (1886) 17 QB 795
Green *v.* Rutherford (1750) 1 Ves Sen 462
Groenvelt *v.* Burwell (1700) 1 Ld Raym 454
Hamed *v.* R [2011] NZSC 101
Haughton *v.* Smith [1975] AC 476
Hazell *v.* Hammersmith and Fulham LBC [1992] 2 AC 1
Henly *v.* The Mayor of Lyme (1828) 130 ER 995
Hocking *v.* Director General of the National Archives of Australia [2020] HCA 19
Hodge *v.* R [1883] UKPC 59
Hoffmann-La Roche *v.* Secretary of State for Trade and Industry [1975] AC 295
Hooper *v.* Lane (1847) 10 QB 546
HTV Ltd *v.* Price Commission [1976] ICR 170
ICC *v.* Union Pacific Rail Road Co (1912) 222 US 541
International Railway Company *v.* Niagara Parks Commission [1941] AC 328
Isbester *v.* Knox City Council [2015] HCA 20
Isle of Ely Case (1609) 10 Co Rep 141a
J. H. Rayner (Mincing Lane) Ltd *v.* Department of Trade and Industry [1990] 2 AC 418
K *v.* K [2007] All ER 202
Katz *v.* United States (1967) 389 US 347
Kinloch *v.* Secretary of State for India in Council (1882) 7 AC 619
Kirk *v.* Industrial Court of New South Wales (2010) 239 CLR 531
Kruse *v.* Johnson [1898] 2 QB 91
Laker Airways *v.* Department of Trade [1976] 1 QB 643
Lavender & Son *v.* Minister of Housing and Local Government [1970] 3 All ER 871
Law *v.* National Greyhound Racing Club [1983] 1 WLR 1302
Lee *v.* Showmen's Guild (1952) 2 QB 329
London & Clydeside Estates Ltd *v.* Aberdeen District Council [1980] 1 WLR 182
M *v.* Home Office [1994] 1 AC 377
Malone *v.* Metropolitan Police Commissioner [1979] Ch 344
Malone *v.* United Kingdom (1984) 7 EHRR 14
McCloy *v.* New South Wales (2015) 257 CLR 178
McDonald *v.* Anishinabek Police Service (2006), 83 OR (3d) 132 (Sup Ct J (Div Ct))
McDonald *v.* Secretary of State for Scotland (1994) SC 234
McInnes *v.* Onslow-Fane [1978] 1 WLR 1520
Meridian Global Funds Management Asia Ltd *v.* Securities Commission [1995] 2 AC 500
Merricks *v.* Heathcote-Amory [1955] Ch 567
Minister for Canterbury Earthquake Recovery *v.* Fowler Investments [2013] NZCA 588
Minister for Immigration and Citizenship *v.* Li [2013] HCA 18
Modahl *v.* British Athletic Federation Ltd [2002] 1 WLR 1192
Moyna *v.* Work and Pensions Secretary [2003] 1 WLR 1929
Mullins *v.* McFarlane and the Jockey Club [2006] EWHC 986
Murphy *v.* Electoral Commissioner (2016) 90 ALJR 1027
Nagle *v.* Feilden [1966] 2 QB 633
New South Wales *v.* Bardolph (1934) 52 CLR 455

Newport Association Football Club Ltd *v.* Football Association of Wales Ltd [1995] 2 All ER 87
O'Reilly *v.* Mackman [1983] 2 AC 237
Osgood *v.* Nelson (1872) LR 5 HL 636
Padfield *v.* Minister for Agriculture, Fisheries and Food [1968] AC 997
Palmer *v.* Crone [1927] 1 KB 804
Pape *v.* Commissioner of Taxation (2009) 238 CLR 1
Pearlman *v.* Keepers and Governors of Harrow School [1979] QB 56
Peat's Case (1704) 6 Mod 228
Percy *v.* Hall [1996] 4 All ER 523
Perkin *v.* Proctor (1768) 2 Wils KB 382
Pharmaceutical Manufacturers Association of Canada *v.* British Columbia (Attorney General) (1997) 149 DLR (4th) 613
Pharmaceutical Society of Great Britain *v.* Dickson [1970] AC 403
Pilbara Infrastructure Pty Ltd *v.* Economic Regulation Authority [2014] WASC 346
Pitt *v.* Holt; Futter *v.* Futter [2012] Ch 132, 204–205
Plaintiff M61/2010E *v.* Commonwealth of Australia; Plaintiff M69/2010 v Commonwealth of Australia (2010) 243 CLR 319
Plaintiff M68/2015 *v.* Minister for Immigration and Border Protection [2016] HCA 1
Plaintiff S157/2002 *v.* Commonwealth (2003) 211 CLR 476
Platt *v.* Lock (1550) 1 Plow 35
Poplar Housing and Regeneration Community Association Ltd *v.* Donaghue [2002] QB 48
Pramatha Nath Mullick *v.* Pradyumna Kumar Mullick (1925) 27 Bom 1064
Quake Outcasts *v.* Minister for Canterbury Earthquake Recovery [2015] NZSC 27
R *v.* Bembridge (1783) 22 How St Tr 1
R *v.* Board of Education (1910) 2 KB 165
R *v.* Campbell [1999] 1 SCR 565
R *v.* Cheltenham Commissioners (1841) 1 QB 467
R *v.* Cichon [1994] Crim LR 918
R *v.* City of London (1682) 8 State Trials 1039
R *v.* Commissioners for Special Purposes of Income Tax (1888) 21 QB 313
R *v.* Earl of Northumberland (1567) 75 ER 472
R *v.* Electricity Commissioners [1924] 1 KB 171
R *v.* Mayor of London (1692) 1 Show KB 274
R *v.* Nat Bell Liquors Ltd [1922] AC 128
R *v.* Ngan [2007] NZSC 105
R *v.* Roupell (1776) 2 Cowp 458
R *v.* Surgeons Company (Master) (1759) 2 Burr 892
R *v.* Wicks [1998] AC 92
R (A) *v.* Criminal Injuries Compensation Board [1999] 2 AC 330
R (Advertising Services plc) *v.* Advertising Standards Authority Ltd [1990] COD 42
R (Aegon Life Assurance Ltd) *v.* Insurance Ombudsman [1994] COD 426
R (Aga Khan) *v.* Disciplinary Committee of the Jockey Club [1993] 2 All ER 853
R (Armah) *v.* Governor of Brixton Prison [1968] AC 192

R (Bancoult) *v.* Foreign Secretary (No 1) [2000] EWHC Admin 413
R (Bancoult) *v.* Foreign Secretary (No 2) [2007] EWCA Civ 498
R (Bancoult) *v.* Foreign Secretary (No 2) [2009] 1 AC 453
R (Barclay) *v.* Secretary of State for Justice (No 2) [2014] UKSC 54
R (Bloom) *v.* London Beth Din (Court of the Chief Rabbi) [1998] COD 131
R (Briggs) *v.* Lloyd's of London [1993] 1 Lloyd's Rep 176
R (Brind) *v.* Secretary of State for the Home Department [1991] 1 AC 696
R (C) *v.* Secretary of State for Health [2000] EWCA Civ 49
R (Carlile) *v.* Home Secretary [2014] UKSC 60
R (Cart) *v.* Upper Tribunal [2008] EWHC Admin 3052
R (Cart) *v.* Upper Tribunal [2010] 2 WLR 1012
R (Cart) *v.* Upper Tribunal [2012] 1 AC 663
R (Datafin) *v.* Take-over Panel [1987] 1 QB 815
R (Evans) *v.* Chief Constable of North Wales [1982] UKHL 10
R (Evans) *v.* Governor of Blockhill Prison [2000] 3 WLR 483
R (Everett) *v.* Foreign Secretary [1989] 1 QB 811
R (Fewings) *v.* Somerset County Council [1995] 3 All ER 20
R (Fire Brigades Union) *v.* Home Secretary [1995] 2 AC 513
R (Flint Town United Football Club) *v.* Football Association of Wales [1991] COD 44
R (Football League Ltd) *v.* Football Association Ltd [1993] 12 All ER 833
R (Gilmore) *v.* Medical Appeal Tribunal [1957] 1 QB 574
R (Heather) *v.* Leonard Cheshire Foundation [2002] All ER 936
R (Holmcroft Properties) *v.* KPMG LLP [2016] EWHC Admin 323
R (Hooper) *v.* Secretary of State for Work and Pensions [2005] UKHL 29
R (HS2 Action Alliance Ltd) *v.* Secretary of State for Transport [2014] UKSC 3
R (Huddlestone) *v.* Lancashire County Council [1986] 2 All ER 941
R (Indian Association of Alberta) *v.* Foreign Secretary [1982] QB 892
R (Khawaja) *v.* Home Secretary [1984] AC 74
R (Kubis) *v.* Panel of the Federation of Communication Services Ltd [1998] COD 56
R (Lain) *v.* Criminal Injuries Compensation Board [1967] 2 QB 864
R (London) *v.* Central London County Court [1993] 3 WLR 1
R (Lumba) *v.* Home Secretary [2011] UKSC 12
R (Mahmood) *v.* Home Secretary [2001] 1 WLR 840
R (March) *v.* Secretary of State for Health [2010] EWHC Admin 765
R (Massingberd-Mundy) *v.* Disciplinary Committee of the Jockey Club [1993] 2 All ER 207
R (Miller) *v.* Brexit Secretary [2016] EWHC 2768
R (Miller) *v.* Brexit Secretary [2017] UKSC 5
R (Miller) *v.* Prime Minister [2019] UKSC 41
R (Mooyer) *v.* Personal Investment Authority Ombudsman Bureau Ltd [2001] EWHC Admin 247
R (New College London Ltd) *v.* Home Secretary [2013] UKSC 51
R (Northumbria Police Authority) *v.* Home Secretary [1988] All ER 556
R (Page) *v.* Lord President of the Privy Council [1993] AC 682
R (Pierson) *v.* Home Secretary [1998] AC 539

R (Preston) *v.* IRC [1985] AC 835
R (Privacy International) *v.* Investigative Powers Tribunal [2019] UKSC 22
R (Professional Counselling Aids Ltd) *v.* British Pharmaceutical Industry Association Code of Practice Committee [1991] COD 228
R (RAM Racecourses Ltd) *v.* Jockey Club [1993] 2 All ER 225
R (Ross) *v.* Life Assurance Unit Trust Regulatory Organisation [1993] QB 17
R (Shaw) *v.* Northumberland CC [1952] 1 KB 338
R (Siborurema) *v.* Office of the Independent Adjudicator [2007] EWCA Civ 1365
R (South Yorkshire Transport) *v.* Monopolies and Mergers Commission [1993] 1 WLR 23
R (Stewart-Brady) *v.* Press Complaints Commission (1997) 9 Admin LR 247
R (Suleiman Ali) *v.* Imam of Bury Park James Masjid Luton [1992] COD 132
R (Sunspell Ltd) *v.* Association of British Travel Agents [2001] ACD 16
R (The Insurance Service plc) *v.* Advertising Standards Authority (1990) 2 Admin LR 77
R (Tucker) *v.* Director General of the National Crime Squad [2003] EWCA Civ 57
R (UNISON) *v.* Lord Chancellor [2017] UKSC 51
R (Vijayatunga) *v.* Judicial Committee of the Privy Council [1988] QB 322
R (Wachmann) *v.* Chief Rabbi of the United Hebrew Congregations of Great Britain and the Commonwealth [1992] 1 WLR 1035
R (Walsh) *v.* East Berkshire Health Authority [1985] QB 152
R (West) *v.* Lloyds of London [2004] EWCA Civ 506
R (Williams) *v.* Provincial Court of the Church in Wales [1999] COD 163
R (Wooller) *v.* The Benchers of Lincoln's Inn (1825) 107 ER 1277
Rahmatullah (No 2) and Serdar Mohamed *v.* Ministry of Defence [2017] UKSC 1
Re Ditfort; Ex parte Deputy Commissioner of Taxation (1988) 19 FCR 347
Re Racal Communications Ltd [1981] AC 374
Re Silver Brothers; AG Quebec *v.* AG Canada [1932] AC 514
Rex *v.* Surgeons Company (1759) 2 Burr 892
Riche *v.* Ashbury Railway Carriage and Iron Co Ltd (1874) LR 9 Ex 224
Ridge *v.* Baldwin [1964] AC 40
Rolled Steel Ltd *v.* British Steel Corporation [1986] 1 Ch 246
Roncarelli *v.* Duplessis [1959] SCR 121
Rooke's Case (1598) 5 Co Rep 99b
Roy *v.* Kensington, Chelsea and Westminster Family Practitioners Committee [1992] 1 AC 624
Ruddock *v.* Vardarlis (2001) 110 FCR 491
Schmidt *v.* Secretary of State for Home Affairs [1969] 2 Ch 149
Scott *v.* Avery (1856) 5 HL Cas 811
Secretary of State for Science and Education *v.* Tameside MBC [1977] AC 1012
Sharp *v.* Wakefield (1891) AC 173
Shergill *v.* Khaira [2014] UKSC 33
Shrewsbury & Atcham BC *v.* Secretary of State for Communities and Local Government [2008] All ER 548

Shrimpton *v.* Commonwealth (1945) 69 CLR 613
Sir George Reynel's Case (1612) 77 Eng Rep 871
Sir James Smith's Case (1692) 4 Mod 258
Sir Thomas Wroth's Case (1572) 1 Plow 455a
Smith *v.* East Elloe Rural District Council [1956] AC 736
Southern Pacific Co *v.* Jensen (1917) 244 US 205
Staatspresident *v.* United Democratic Front (1998) (4) SA 839(A)
Stevenage Borough Football Club Ltd *v.* Football League [1996] WLUK 36
Sutton's Hospital Case (1611) 10 Co Rep 1a
Tailors of Ipswich (1614) 11 Co Rep 53a
Terry *v.* Huntingdon (1668) Hard 480
Tesco Supermarkets Ltd *v.* Nattras [1972] AC 153
The Case of the Company of Horners in London (1642) 2 Roll Rep 481
The Case of the Marshalsea (1612) 10 Co Rep 68b
The Duke of Brunswick *v.* The King of Hanover [1848] 2 HLC 4
Tito *v.* Wadell *(No 2)* [1977] Ch 106
Town Investments Ltd *v.* Department for the Environment [1978] AC 359
United Australia Ltd *v.* Barclays Bank Ltd (1941) AC 1
Verreault & Fils *v.* AG Quebec [1977] 1 RCS 41
Victoria *v.* Australian Building Construction Employees' and Builders' Labourers' Federation (1982) 41 ALR 71
Victoria *v.* Commonwealth (1975) 134 CLR 338
Wandsworth London Borough Council *v.* Winder [1985] AC 461
Weinberger *v.* Inglis [1919] AC 606
Wewaykum Indian Band *v.* Canada [2002] 4 SCR 245
Whitmarsh *v.* Robertson (1845) 1 Coll 571
Wilander *v.* Tobin [1997] 2 Lloyd's Rep 293
William *v.* Berkley (1559) Plowden 233a
Williams *v.* Commonwealth (No 1) (2012) 248 CLR 156
Williams *v.* Commonwealth (No 2) (2014) 252 CLR 416
Willion *v.* Berkley (3 Elizabeth) 1 Plowden 235a
Wilson *v.* Rastall (1792) 100 ER 1286
Wood *v.* Woad (1874) 9 Ex 190
Woodgate *v.* Knatchbull (1787) 2 TR 155
Woolwich Building Society *v.* Inland Revenue Commissioners [1993] AC 70
YL *v.* Birmingham City Council [2008] 1 AC 95
Zamir *v.* Home Secretary [1980] AC 930
Zoernsch *v.* Waldock [1964] 1 WLR 675

1

Introduction

1.1 Introduction

This book is about the judicial review of non-statutory executive powers – the jurisdiction asserted by judges to supervise executive officials (and, sometimes, other people) when they act without reliance on a statutory authorisation. It is the first book to focus on non-statutory executive powers and judicial review in English law.[1] It is also the first book to look at non-statutory executive powers in the first instance and draw conclusions about the law of judicial review *generally* from that perspective. These conclusions relate both to the doctrinal content and to the conceptual and normative basis of the public law supervisory jurisdiction.

The past decades have seen significant changes in the modalities of administration, including the privatisation and 'contracting out' of governmental services and non-statutory executive action in response to financial crises, the 'war on terror', and shifting geopolitical relations. They have also seen developments in the law of judicial review: the judicial practice of reviewing the actions of executive officials taken without reliance on a statutory authorisation is now clearly established. Provided due account is taken of their constitutional systems – particularly things like federation, written constitutions, entrenched rights, and statutory administrative tribunal regimes – similar observations could be made for the Anglo-Commonwealth jurisdictions (i.e., Canada, Australia, and New Zealand), to which I shall also refer to throughout this book.[2]

[1] See also Amanda Sapienza, *Judicial Review of Non-Statutory Executive Action* (Federation Press 2020).

[2] See Amanda Sapienza, 'Judicial Review of Administrative Action: Australia and the United Kingdom Reunited?' (2018) 43(2) *University of Western Australia Law Review* 67; Jennifer A. Klinck, 'Modernizing Judicial Review of the Exercise of Prerogative Powers in Canada' (2017) 54(4) *Alberta Law Review* 998; David Mullan, 'Judicial Review of the Executive – Principled Exasperation' (2010) 8(2) *New Zealand Journal of Public and International Law* 145; Chris Horan, 'Judicial Review of Non-Statutory Executive Powers' (2003) 31(3) *Federal Law Review* 551.

The powers associated with the Royal Prerogative of the British Crown were traditionally immune from the supervisory jurisdiction. Since at least the time of the *Case of Proclamations*,[3] however, the existence and scope of a prerogative power has been recognised as a question of common law that lies prima facie within the province of the judges, even if the manner of its exercise was not. Over the second half of the twentieth century, the immunity of officials exercising the Crown's prerogative powers was diluted. The watershed moment is generally identified with *Council of Civil Service Unions* v. *Minister for the Civil Service*[4] in the mid-1980s. By the mid-1990s, judicial review could be said to be 'as applicable to decisions taken under prerogative powers as to decisions taken under statutory powers'.[5] This trajectory has continued. The House of Lords held in the late 2000s, in *R (Bancoult)* v. *Foreign Secretary*,[6] that primary legislation for a British Overseas Territory made under the Royal Prerogative was subject to the 'ordinary principles' of judicial review 'in the same way as any other executive action'.[7] A spate of cases in the late 2010s, including *R (Miller)* v. *Brexit Secretary*,[8] and *R (Miller)* v. *Prime Minister*,[9] marked a seismic shift in the review of the prerogative powers, cementing their reviewability and possibly replacing the traditional attitude of judicial deference with one of judicial scrutiny.[10]

It is thus absolutely clear *that* non-statutory executive powers are judicially reviewable, and even tolerably clear *how* they are reviewable. There are, of course, disagreements about the grounds of judicial review and the standards applied to a given ground. Non-statutory executive powers are often deployed in contexts in which judges are properly reticent to second-guess executive discretion. The reviewing court determines the intensity of judicial review through the combination of grounds and standards, as well as by reference to the concepts of

3 (1611) 12 Co Rep 74.

4 [1985] AC 374.

5 *R (Fire Brigades Union)* v. *Home Secretary* [1995] 2 AC 513, 553 (Lord Browne-Wilkinson).

6 [2009] 1 AC 453.

7 *R (Bancoult)* v. *Foreign Secretary (No. 2)* [2009] 1 AC 453, 483 (Lord Hoffmann).

8 [2017] UKSC 5.

9 [2019] UKSC 41.

10 Thomas Poole, 'The Strange Death of the Prerogative in England' (2019) 43(2) *University of Western Australia Law Review* 43; *Belhaj and Rahmatullah* v. *Straw* [2017] UKSC 3; *Al-Waheed and Serdar Mohamed* v. *Ministry of Defence* [2017] UKSC 2.

justiciability and deference.[11] But the direction of travel is clear, and it is towards the prima facie amenability of official action to judicial review. The difficulty is rather to articulate *why* this is the case.[12]

1.2 A Gap between Theory and Practice

Debates about amenability, grounds, and standards are hampered in the context of non-statutory powers by confusion surrounding the nature of the powers themselves, their source, and the justification of judicial review more generally. A major theme in this book is the idea of a gap between judicial practice and legal theory that has widened over recent decades. This has potentially enormous implications: the current doctrinal position of the law on the review of non-statutory executive powers suggests that the conventional theories about the law of judicial generally are wrong.

Judicial review is, at core, a process in which official repositories of power are kept within the ambit of the powers reposed in them. Determining the scope of an office's powers is relatively straightforward where they are granted in a written instrument; the court looks to the words of the statutory text, in the relevant context, and determines the scope of the authority granted expressly and by implication. How the scope of lawful authority is determined in the absence of a statutory text is a more complex exercise that requires theoretical groundwork. In my account, the cornerstone of that groundwork is the concept of *office*. As Janet McLean has argued, constitutional law has marginalised the figure of the official,[13] and the 'theoretical turn' taken by British administrative law scholarship since the 1990s has largely drawn on a body of theory unconcerned with the question how individuals act in a corporate capacity for the political community. That is a fundamental problem, because the supervisory jurisdiction is concerned precisely with the official mode of action.

[11] See Dean R. Knight, *Vigilance and Restraint in the Common Law of Judicial Review* (Cambridge University Press 2018); Margit Cohn, 'Legal Transplant Chronicles: The Evolution of Unreasonableness and Proportionality Review of the Administration in the United Kingdom' (2010) 58(3) *American Journal of Comparative Law* 583.

[12] See Sir Philip Sales, 'Crown Powers, the Royal Prerogative and Fundamental Rights' in Hannah Wilberg and Mark Elliott (eds.), *The Scope and Intensity of Substantive Review* (Hart 2015), 378.

[13] Janet McLean, 'The Authority of the Administration' in Elizabeth Fisher, Jeff King, and Alison Young (eds.), *The Foundations and Future of Public Law* (Oxford University Press 2020), 46.

Nowhere is the gap between theory and practice wider than in the context of non-statutory executive powers that are *not* part of the Royal Prerogative. Problems start with disagreement on the nature of non-statutory executive powers themselves. Without begging the question, it is clear that, besides powers classical 'prerogative powers' (such as making treaties), executive officials engage in a wide range of actions without reliance on any obvious statutory basis. These actions include leasing premises, employing staff, making *ex gratia* payments, collecting and disseminating information, and even keeping lists. Many of these actions are mundane, but even the mundane ones can assume critical importance in the right context – imagine reading one's name on a list of suspected terrorists. These powers are called by several names. One influential account has called them a 'third source' of governmental authority, that is, next to statutory powers and prerogative powers.[14] Without adopting the main ideas typically associated with that label, I will use the term because it is pithier than 'non-prerogative non-statutory executive powers'. As we shall see, it is a bone of contention whether third source powers are 'legal powers' at all, where they come from, and why it is the case that officials (high and low) wield them.

The standard explanations of judicial review can broadly be placed into two 'camps'. Both are incapable of explaining the supervisory jurisdiction over non-statutory executive powers satisfactorily. So-called 'ultra vires theories' ground the supervisory jurisdiction in legislative intention. This approach is clearly ill adapted to explain the reviewability of non-statutory executive powers, and as such non-statutory executive powers falsify their claim to being a general theory of judicial review.[15] More disappointing is the failure of the so-called 'common law theories' to explain the supervisory jurisdiction beyond statute. These theories approach non-statutory executive powers on their home turf, but often overlook the crucial questions of empowerment and action. They tend to approach judicial review as a set of common law constraints on governmental 'power' as an amorphous idea, distinct from the set of legal 'powers' implied by the concept of vires, and so ignore the role of the common law in *constituting* offices endowed with specific, *and therefore limited*, powers. Something of value is missed if we abandon the first step

[14] See Bruce V. Harris, 'The "Third Source" of Authority for Government Action' (1992) 108 *Law Quarterly Review* 626.

[15] Janet McLean, 'The Authority of the Administration' in Elizabeth Fisher, Jeff King, and Alison Young (eds.), *The Foundations and Future of Public Law* (Oxford University Press 2020), 46.

of identifying the rules that repose power in executive officials – whether those rules are found in statute or the common law – before turning to the rules that govern the conduct of officials when exercising the powers reposed in them.

1.2.1 Winding Back the Clock

The account of judicial review presented in this book is critical of developments in English public law in the twentieth century. These developments were generally progressive responses to the growth of the welfare state and the encroachment of governmental power into daily life. As Mark Freedland has observed, the traditional problem for English lawyers was less the demarcation of public law and private law than whether a distinct 'public law' existed.[16] Efforts culminated in the 1980s, particularly with the case *O'Reilly* v. *Mackman*,[17] to draw a bright line between judicial review and private law actions, thus relegating older modes of official accountability, which relied on private law, to the past. However, this achievement occurred on the cusp of an epochal shift in the modalities of administration, particularly the rise of outsourcing and privatisation of public functions. Thus, the 'new' public law got off on the wrong foot, and this fact has hampered our ability to understand the changing landscape.

If we look at the ultra vires debate, an 'ironical changing of places' occurred – politically progressive judges and academics had championed the distinctiveness of public law, but their success insulated hybrid modalities of governance from judicial supervision. In response, they came instead to emphasise the continuity between administrative law and the common law as a whole, thereby committing themselves to the 'inherently conservative', casuistic doctrine of the common law. The more politically conservative ultra vires camp, on the other hand, eventually committed itself to the distinctiveness of public law – despite the Diceyan allure of 'ordinary laws' and despite the fact that ultra vires is actually a common law doctrine that governs corporate directors and trustees as well as public officials.[18]

16 Mark Freedland, 'The Evolving Approach to Public/Private Distinction in English Law' in Mark Freedland and Auby Jean-Bernard (eds.), *The Public Law/Private Law Divide: Une entente assez cordiale?* (Hart 2005), 97.

17 [1983] 2 AC 237.

18 Mark Freedland, 'The Evolving Approach to Public/Private Distinction in English Law' in Mark Freedland and Auby Jean-Bernard (eds.), *The Public Law/Private Law Divide: Une*

This book is a plea to consider these developments afresh, with the benefit of hindsight. Counter-intuitively, perhaps, it pleads for the reinstatement of some doctrinal fixtures that prevailing opinion would suggest we are better off without – for example, the traditional doctrine of jurisdictional error, and a more rigid conceptual approach to 'voidness' and 'voidability'.

1.2.2 *The Purpose of This Book*

This book has three closely related aims. First, it aims to provide a definitive conceptual and terminological clean-up, such that we can debate questions of amenability, grounds, and standards of review in the context of non-statutory executive powers without talking at cross purposes. This involves, first and foremost, deciding what the term 'non-statutory executive powers' means, and describing the relationship between the 'Royal Prerogative' and the 'third source'. Secondly, it aims to provide an explanation of how the ordinary mechanisms of judicial review apply to non-statutory executive powers of both types. Finally, it aims to explain the conceptual basis of the supervisory jurisdiction and to ground that jurisdiction in a plausible normative theory of the rule of law.

In pursuing these aims, I set out a conceptual framework that is carried by the following features: (i) a *concept of office* as an impersonal, institutionalised role separate to its incumbent from time to time, which is the repository of powers amenable to judicial review; (ii) an account of the *Crown* as a corporation sole, which is a particular type of office, in which common law and statutory powers repose; (iii) *rules of competence* that confer those powers and set the scope of the office's vires in the narrow sense; (iv) *rules of conduct* which impose restrictions on the manner in which, and purposes for which, an official uses her powers *virtute officii*; and (v) a *logic of official action*, by which we can understand how the actions of a (human) individual are attributed to an office – and thence to the Crown that sits at the centre of the British constitutional tradition.

At the broadest level, both prerogative-type and third source-type powers (as I shall call them) comprise 'powers' in the sense of vires. These powers are reposed in the Crown and its officials by rules of competence that are unwritten, but just as capable of judicial

entente assez cordiale? (Hart 2005), 106, citing Sir Stephen Sedley, 'Public Power and Private Power' in Christopher F. Forsyth (ed.), *Judicial Review and the Constitution* (Hart 2000), 296; see also C. F. Forsyth, 'Beyond *O'Reilly v Mackman*: The Foundations and Nature of Procedural Exclusivity' (1985) 44(3) *Cambridge Law Journal* 415.

determination as their statutory counterparts. This should not be a challenging notion. The common law always imposes rules of conduct that govern the exercise of powers, whether those powers are conferred by statutory or non-statutory rules of competence. Combined with a logic of action, acting in excess of a rule of competence produces a nullity, a 'non-action', whereas breaches of a rule of conduct yield a prima facie valid but voidable (or perfectible) official action. This raises difficult questions of attribution and liability, and it is necessary to develop the conceptual framework of official action that embraces official wrongdoing as such. For largely historical reasons, not least because the authority claims of government officials have been understood through very different lenses over the centuries, there is insufficient clarity around the personal *versus* official accountability of officials before the law.[19]

I will argue that there is no reason to identify different conceptual bases for the supervisory jurisdiction over statutory and non-statutory executive powers, let alone for different categories of non-statutory executive powers. Both statute and the common law are *always* relevant to determine the limits of an office's vires, understood as a product of rules of competence (statutory and/or common law) with inherent limits and rules of conduct (often statutory and always common law). While legislative intention is clearly important, *where it exists*, there is no reason to impute it counterfactually to explain the common law powers of an institution (i.e., the court) that predates the modern institution of Parliament. It is the legitimate role of judges, within the British constitutional tradition, to supervise the limits of valid official action. The normative justification for this is a concept of the *rule of law* as the *rule of officials acting lawfully*. The repository of a power is always subject to the inherent limits of that power, and that power it always conjoined with duties. It is the judges' unique and inalienable constitutional role to

[19] Janet McLean describes four broad periods of development. In the seventeenth century, emphasis was on proprietary tenure of office as a bulwark of independence against royal power. In the eighteenth century, criminal law was used to control officials' incentives towards self-service. In the nineteenth century, governmental authority moved from an office-based justification to one based on the implicit rationality of bureaucratic organisation. In the twentieth century, the narrative shifted to democracy and the legislative intent (a.k.a. ultra vires) theory of judicial review. See Janet McLean, 'The Authority of the Administration' in Elizabeth Fisher, Jeff King, and Alison Young (eds.), *The Foundations and Future of Public Law* (Oxford University Press 2020), 55 discussing *Woodgate* v. *Knatchbull* (1787) 2 TR 155.

determine those limits and to determine how duty conditions the exercise of power.

Compared to the existing literature on the English law of judicial review, this represents a novel departure point in at least two respects. The first has already been noticed, namely the decision to look at the supervisory jurisdiction over non-statutory powers as the primary case, and to draw conclusions about the supervisory jurisdiction generally from that. The second is to focus on the role of officials in administration and the concept of office as the central concept in public law. As judicial review is concerned with official action, the logic of action in this mode provides the conceptual footings of the supervisory jurisdiction on which we can construct a rational doctrinal structure.

The approach that emerges implies a sustained critique of the so-called ultra vires theories, with a particular focus on the latest and most sophisticated such theory presented in the early 2000s by Mark Elliot.[20] However, while I present a kind of 'common law theory' of judicial review, my approach also implies a critique of leading common law theories, in particular their reliance on outcome-driven judicial discretion in the development of the supervisory jurisdiction. If successful, my critique will reignite interest in the conceptual basis of judicial review and break the ground for a 'third way' that circumvents the impasse reached in the historical ultra vires debate. At the least, I believe it is well-founded enough to warrant the reappropriation of the language of ultra vires for my theory of judicial review, which is based on the logic of ultra vires and is capable of application across the whole spectrum of statutory and non-statutory executive powers. This would lead to the rebranding of the ultra vires theories as 'legislative intent theories' of judicial review.[21] If accepted, my approach would also lead to the definitive rejection of the 'third source' as it is understood by the majority of its proponents.

1.2.3 The Scope and Focus of This Book

This book addresses two clusters of questions. The first cluster sits squarely in 'administrative law' proper: What non-statutory executive powers repose in the Crown and its officials? What is their source? What are their extent and limits? How are they supervised by the judicial

[20] See generally Mark Elliott, *The Constitutional Foundations of Judicial Review* (Hart 2000).

[21] As suggested by Dean R. Knight, *Vigilance and Restraint in the Common Law of Judicial Review* (Cambridge University Press 2018), 58.

branch? Are all the same doctrines of judicial review applicable, and what special considerations apply in this context? Why is this the case?

These questions raise a cluster of preliminary questions in constitutional law, constitutional theory, and legal theory. As we will see, the cases and scholarly literature on the 'third source', for example, force us to ask whether Ministers and Secretaries of State can make contracts on behalf of the Crown because (i) the Crown is a natural person; (ii) the Crown is a corporation (a) sole or (b) aggregate with the same, open-ended capacities as a natural person; or (iii) the Crown is a placeholder for the organised 'polity' or 'state' that has some inherent capacity to perform acts-in-the-law (like making contracts). There are, unfortunately, no pre-packed answers to these questions. They raise technical issues of deontic logic and of the logic of action. These preliminary questions cannot be avoided – if we attempt to do so we turn in circles. The literature is full of basic errors on precisely these points, many of them born of an understandable but fatal desire to avoid 'academic' and 'technical' problems. In writing this book, I have made the intentional decision to confront them squarely. Certain chapters are therefore quite technical. However, my theoretical investigations always serve some practical purpose, either by shedding light on a specific doctrinal question (usually by identifying the way to *frame* it properly), by connecting administrative law with its constitutional context, or by identifying a fundamental error in the cases and commentary.

My analysis is, in the first instance, of the law of England and Wales. This is for the rather accidental reason that I undertook the research for this book in England, but it is also for a deeper one. English law is the root from which the other branches of the Commonwealth legal family have grown. In my view, there is great value in reflecting on the English position from a 'colonial' perspective – in my view, that perspective is often more interesting, particularly when it comes to working out the juristic nature of the Crown, for the simple reason that federation has forced Australian and Canadian scholars and judges to engage with problems like suits between states or between a state and the federal centre. Such questions are still fudged in the United Kingdom through insistence on a unitary state under a unitary Crown. There seems to be an irresistible, if glacial, shift regarding the appropriateness of discussing 'federalism' in the United Kingdom; however, that is not the focus of this book.[22]

[22] See, e.g., Martin Laffin and Alys Thomas, 'The United Kingdom: Federalism in Denial?' (1999) 29(3) *Publius: The Journal of Federalism* 89; Michael Keating, 'Why No Federalism

I have, wherever possible, incorporated both English and Commonwealth perspectives. However, the main focus remains on English law, for the simple reason that a comprehensive survey of Anglo-Commonwealth administrative law is beyond the scope of this book. There are too many jurisdictional differences to account for without detracting from my core focus. My reference to authorities from Australia, Canada, and New Zealand is limited to those that illustrate a difference between jurisdictions that is important to my argument or, just as often, to those that are particularly illustrative of a general point. There are a number of authorities in the latter category, especially in the opening chapters.

My argument should not be uninteresting from a Commonwealth perspective, however. There is great value in adopting an Anglo-Commonwealth, rather than an Anglocentric, perspective.[23] That perspective also suggests that we have, at times, perhaps made too much of the obvious divergences that exist. Australian constitutional jurisprudence since the 1980s, for example, seems to be characterised by a project of establishing the independence of Australian constitutional law. This is as it should be, but there is a strand of Australian exceptionalism that doth protest too much. I have always found the shared assumptions and commonalities across the jurisdictions just as interesting than the differences between them.

Given the substantive features of its constitutional system and historical separation from the United Kingdom, the New Zealand branch perhaps lies closest to the English root. But the Australian and Canadian positions are also derivative. The Australian Constitution Act 1900 (Imp) section 61, for example, provides that the executive power of the Commonwealth is vested in the Queen and is exercisable by the Governor General as the Queen's representative. This has been interpreted by modern Australian judges to mean that executive power flows from the federal compact in the Constitution, and should not be seen as a species of the Royal Prerogative.[24] But, as D. G. Morgan observed in the Irish context, provisions like this are 'barren ground for any analytical

in the United Kingdom?' in Alain G. Gagnon, Soeren Keil, and Sean Mueller (eds.), *Understanding Federalism and Federation* (Routledge 2016), Ch 11.

[23] See also Stephen Gardbaum, *The New Commonwealth Model of Constitutionalism* (Cambridge University Press 2013); Anne Twomey, *The Veiled Sceptre: Reserve Powers of Heads of State in Westminster Systems* (Cambridge University Press 2018).

[24] See *Re Ditfort; Ex parte Deputy Commissioner of Taxation* (1988) 19 FCR 347, 369 (Gummow J); *Ruddock* v. *Vardarlis* (2001) 110 FCR 491, 540 (French J).

approach'.[25] Although section 61 might be argued to mean that even non-statutory executive powers are 'statutory', the actual scope of those powers has to be read from the common law because the Australian Constitution says nothing particularly helpful about the powers' source or scope. And even if we accept that the ultimate source of the Queen's executive power is in the federal compact, section 61 seems to refer to the state of affairs that pre-existed the grant. Likewise, the opening words of the British North America Act 1867 (Imp) declare the desire of the original Provinces to be 'federally united into One Dominion under the Crown' and that Canada be endowed with 'a Constitution similar in Principle to that of the United Kingdom'. Section 9 provides that '[t]he Executive Government and Authority of and over Canada is hereby declared to continue and be vested in the Queen'.

Howsoever one cuts it, therefore, the English position must be of considerable historical and comparative interest. Thus, while being careful to avoid doctrinal inaccuracy, my focus in this book will be on the unwritten elements and assumptions shared across the whole legal tradition, particularly those surrounding the Crown.

1.3 The Structure of This Book

My common law ultra vires theory of judicial review is developed over twelve substantive chapters. Chapter 2 reviews the traditional learning on the taxonomy of non-statutory executive powers. It reviews the most important historical approaches to the Royal Prerogative in English political and legal thought and presents the modern notion of the 'third source'. This introduces a major theme in the book, which is the concept of 'legal power' and its relationship to concepts like 'capacities' (factual and legal) and 'residual liberties'. It also introduces the conventional terms on which this sort of question is asked, which turn on the juristic nature of the Crown and the relationship of the Crown to the human beings that act for it.

Chapter 3 reviews the modern cases on the putative 'third source'. This review illustrates that the law is in an unsatisfactory state and that further theory is needed if we are to reach a settled position within any of the jurisdictions in question, let alone between or across them. This chapter

[25] Davis G. Morgan, *The Separation of Powers in the Irish Constitution* (Sweet & Maxwell 1997), 272, cited in Leslie Zines, 'The Inherent Executive Power of the Commonwealth' (2005) 16 *Public Law Review* 279.

is one of the most comparative, as it seeks to establish a basic taxonomy of non-statutory executive powers. Chapter 3 opens much new ground and charts a course for the chapters to follow.

Chapter 4 sets out my approach to non-statutory executive powers. The distinction between statutory and non-statutory powers is important,[26] but the distinction between different sub-types of the latter is less so. The 'third source' really comprises two categories: (i) private law powers reposing in Crown (e.g., the power to make contracts) and (ii) factual abilities of Crown *officials* (e.g., the ability to make enquiries) the exercise of which can be attributed to the Crown. All this really shows is that analysis of the concept of legal power and of the logic of action is necessary; once this analysis is undertaken, the 'third source' as it is currently understood simply falls away. For the purposes of judicial review – both its conceptual basis and doctrinal structure – there is no meaningful difference between what I call 'prerogative-type' and 'third source-type' non-statutory executive powers.

Chapters 5 to 7 each supply an essential building block to fill the gap between theory and practice. Chapter 5 provides an account of the Crown and its officials. The idea of the 'third source' pulls us, inexorably, into conceptual debates about the nature of the Crown. 'The Crown' is an ambiguous term and it is important to specify what we actually mean when we use it to refer to the Queen, Her Majesty's Government, and what we might call the 'commonwealth'. This entails cracking some old chestnuts, including whether the Crown is a 'natural person' or a corporation, and, if the latter, whether it is a corporation 'sole' or 'aggregate' (and why that matters). The person who occupies the office of the Monarch is a natural person, but the Crown is no such thing. However, the 'corporation sole' has been described as 'nonsense' by none less than F. W. Maitland.[27] I argue that such concepts should be taken as an expression of the sound principle that there is a separation between the *office* of the Monarch and its *incumbent*.

Chapter 6 builds on that discussion, presenting a general concept of office as the organising concept in public law. I explore the reasons for

[26] Historically, this distinction was less important, as statutes were seen as declaratory of the common law: see Janet McLean, 'The Authority of the Administration' in Elizabeth Fisher, Jeff King, and Alison Young (eds.), *The Foundations and Future of Public Law* (Oxford University Press 2020), 52.

[27] 'Metaphysiological nonsense': see Frederick W. Maitland, 'The Crown as Corporation' in David Runciman and Magnus Ryan (eds.), *State, Trust and Corporation* (Cambridge University Press 2003), 35.

which the concept of office was abandoned in public law scholarship, which had mainly to do with the suppression of traditional offices in the nineteenth century and the reformation of the civil service along managerialist lines. However, I argue that office is unavoidable as the central category of public law. An office is an institutionalised social role that a person fills from time to time, but which is always separate from its occupant. Public law just is the 'law of public offices'.

Chapter 7 introduces the central technical apparatus to explain the mechanics of the supervisory jurisdiction. Officials wield powers because of rules that imbue their office with powers, which I call *rules of competence*. They are also subject to rules that regulate the manner in which that competence is exercised, which I call *rules of conduct*. As mentioned earlier, these two types of rules 'box out' the space in which an official can act lawfully, which I call *Spielraum*. The account is not complete with an analysis of empowerment, however; judicial review is concerned with official *action*. Judicial review is never concerned with the individuals (who happen to be officials) acting as private citizens directly, but with officials acting in their official capacity. If we take this truism seriously, a rational conceptual scheme naturally unfolds.

Chapter 8 explores the different ways of approaching judicial review. Providing a critical review of the ultra vires debate, which began in the context of non-statutory powers but largely talked past the problem of official action beyond statute, this chapter argues for a return to the concept of jurisdiction as an organising category and the reconceptualisation of judicial review based as a common law doctrine that has only a contingent relationship to legislative intent. Legislative intention is important, where it exists, and in the modern law (which is almost saturated with statute law), legislative intention seems ubiquitous. But the common law is also omnipresent, for example, imposing rules of conduct on statutory grants of power. There is no inherent connection between the concept or the language of ultra vires and legislative intention, and there is no reason not to describe the review of non-statutory executive powers as 'vires based'.

Chapter 9 explores the relationship between rules of competence, rules of conduct, and validity. Rules of competence determine what an official *can* do and set the bounds of the office's *ability-space*. Rules of conduct, reflecting the 'principles of good administration' developed by the common law, set the bounds of what the official *may* do, her *liberty-space*. The conjunction of ability-space and liberty-space yields an office's *Spielraum*. The narrow limb of the ultra vires rule relates to ability-space and the broad limb to liberty-space. This approach avoids the pain points in relation to powers, capacities, and residual liberties, and introduces some analytical rigour to the discussion. Most importantly, because the logic is based on office, rules of competence, and rules of conduct (instead of legislative intention), this account can apply to statutory and non-statutory executive powers alike.

Chapter 10 provides a redux of the ultra vires debate and argues that we must abandon its terms. The ultra vires debate started with a common law challenge that framed its enquiry in terms of a 'traditional' ultra vires theory which saw the courts, in their supervisory jurisdiction, as agents of legislative intent translated through statutory law. While correctly arguing that legislative intent was not the basis of judicial review, however, the common law challengers acquiesced in a cramped frame of reference and in the false appropriation of the ultra vires label by the legislative intent theorists. Ultra vires should be dissociated with those theories and developed as a common law theory that reflects the logic of office.

Chapter 11 presents my own theory of ultra vires. It provides a brief review of the leading cases that establish the amenability of non-statutory executive powers to judicial review, and probes the historical association of ultra vires with legislative intent. The common law ultra vires theory applies straightforwardly to prerogative-type and third source-type powers in both its limbs. I draw indirect support from recent UK Supreme Court jurisprudence, despite the apparent preoccupation with parliamentary sovereignty in the judges' reasoning. These cases also demonstrate the proper, surprisingly limited, role that 'justiciability' and 'deference' play in the judicial supervision of even highly politicised exercises of non-statutory executive powers.

Chapter 12 probes the borders of the supervisory jurisdiction, which helps us to determine who is and who is not amenable – and to understand the conceptual structure of judicial review itself. I provide a brief survey of the cases in which nominally private bodies, often called 'domestic tribunals', have been held amenable to a supervisory jurisdiction that is generally accepted to be distinct from public law judicial review but is, for all intents and purposes, identical in structure and content. The traditional jurisdiction to supervise economic monopolies, too, has featured in the literature but its connection to judicial review 'proper' is not completely clear. Although I do not argue that they are one and the same, looking at the supervisory jurisdictions together, and searching for a common basis of principle, is helpful.

Chapter 13 explores the normative foundations of judicial review, rounding back on the concept of office and the importance of rules of competence and rules of conduct. The characteristic feature of office, I argue, is the *coupling of power with duty*. The purpose of judicial review is to ensure that officials exercise the powers entrusted to them consistently with the conditions on which it was entrusted to them. The rule of law means *the rule of officials acting lawfully*, that is, discharging the trust reposed in them by the political community. The normative foundation of the supervisory jurisdiction is, then, what might be called a public law fiduciary principle that is given concrete expression through the mechanisms of judicial review. This principle can serve as a touchstone for the further development of the law, for example in connecting grounds of judicial review with abstract concepts like the rule of law and resolving debates about the standards of review applicable to different types of official powers.

2

Official Action beyond Statute

2.1 Introduction

The first step is to define with more precision what exactly this book is about. To that end, this chapter explores the taxonomy of non-statutory executive powers.[1] I have chosen this generic term because it clearly embraces, but is broader than, those powers associated with the Royal Prerogative without begging too many questions about their source or nature. The taxonomy of non-statutory executive powers that we adopt defines the nature and scope of the challenge posed by the expansion of judicial review. In particular, it is only with such a taxonomy that we can usefully address the question whether existing theories of the conceptual basis of the supervisory jurisdiction are adequate to explain the availability of judicial review beyond statute, and whether we need a different set of doctrines for different 'species' of non-statutory executive power.

Mark Elliott, for example, has argued that the review of statutory and prerogative powers is 'vires-based', while the judicial review of what he calls 'de facto governmental power' is 'rules-based'.[2] These forms of review, according to Elliott, are about different things: in the first case, judges enforce the limits of an actor's vires in the sense of legal powers; in the second, judges apply a set of rules which regulates the exercise of (assumed) power.[3] Already, the difficulties of non-statutory executive powers for legislative intent theories of judicial review begin to appear. If review the Royal Prerogative is 'vires-based', why is ultra vires not a common law doctrine? Further, the doctrines through which 'vires-based' and 'rules-based' judicial review is achieved are identical, and

[1] Thanks to Max Harris of All Souls College for our exchanges on non-statutory executive powers, which increased my understanding considerably.

[2] Mark Elliott, *The Constitutional Foundations of Judicial Review* (Hart 2001), 194.

[3] Mark Elliott, *The Constitutional Foundations of Judicial Review* (Hart 2001), 194.

Elliott concedes that 'the core principle which underlies review of both de jure and de facto power of government is the rule of law', anyway.[4]

Elliott's distinction follows from more or less tacit views he holds about the personality of the Crown, the relation between the Crown and its officers, and the logic of official empowerment and action:

> Rather than accepting that it requires legal power to commit the action in question and arguing that it acted within the scope of such power, it is sometimes open to the government to contend that it does not, in the first place, need to demonstrate any legal authority in support of the decision under review. This follows from the fact that the Crown, *as a natural person,* may do all that other natural persons may do; and the government may, in the Crown's name, do those things, too.[5]

This passage contains the germ of many ideas against which this book argues. The Crown is, emphatically, not a natural person.[6] There is no such thing as 'de facto governmental power'. The fact that an official – a mortal being of flesh and blood – wields governmental power is *always* a product of rules that confer power, and that kind of power is always reposed in officials as limited bundles of 'legal powers' in the sense of vires. The supervisory jurisdiction is concerned with identifying the contents of the relevant 'bundle' and making sure that the official in question does not purport to perform an action unsupported by the rules that govern his office. Judicial review is therefore always 'vires-based'. For the purposes of judicial review, at least, there is no meaningful difference between different forms of non-statutory executive power; the supervisory jurisdiction extends, with the same doctrines and for the same conceptual and normative reasons, to all forms of non-statutory executive power.

In this chapter and the ones that follow, I return to the questions of Crown personality, office, and deontic and operational logic. I do not provide an exhaustive catalogue of the powers that have existed historically under the Royal Prerogative or that subsist in any of the Crown's Realms today.[7] Others

[4] Mark Elliott, *The Constitutional Foundations of Judicial Review* (Hart 2001), 195.

[5] Mark Elliott, *The Constitutional Foundation Judicial Review* (Hart 2001), 168. Emphasis mine.

[6] See Jason G. Allen, 'The Office of the Crown' (2018) 77(2) *Cambridge Law Journal* 298; John Howell, 'What the Crown May Do' (2010) 15(1) *Judicial Review* 36.

[7] See in particular Joseph Chitty, *A Treatise on the Law of the Prerogatives of the Crown: And the Relative Duties and Rights of the Subject* (Butterworths 1820); Christopher Vincenzi, *Crown Powers, Subjects and Citizens* (Pinter 1998).

have compiled catalogues, and others again regard that task as impossible.[8] My goal is to rather define what have traditionally been called 'prerogative powers' in relation to (i) powers granted in statute and (ii) powers (or, to avoid question-begging, apparent powers) that are neither based in statute nor typically listed in such catalogues. Various names have been suggested for these non-prerogative, non-statutory powers, including 'capacities', 'de facto governmental powers', 'secondary prerogative powers', 'common law powers', 'common law discretionary powers', 'common law personified powers', and 'pretended prerogatives'.[9] In an influential series of articles, B. V. Harris has called them a 'third source of governmental authority'.[10] That terminology has not been generally accepted, and I reject the major tenets of the 'third source theory' in its various versions. However, the terminology has percolated through much of the debate, and as it is pithier than 'non-prerogative non-statutory powers', it serves as a useful shorthand. Pre-empting Chapter 4, I will speak of *non-statutory executive powers* as the general term and of *prerogative-type* and *third source-type* powers as heuristics.

This chapter reviews the classical approaches to classifying non-statutory executive powers. Section 2.2 starts with the notion of the Royal Prerogative following John Locke, Sir William Blackstone, A. V. Dicey, and Sir William Wade. Section 2.3 then turns to B. V. Harris' presentation of the third source theory in the 1990s, and to a historical memorandum written by Sir Granville Ram in the 1940s that adopts a similar approach. This survey reveals a fundamental disagreement between those who see executive power in *binary* and in *ternary* terms. Blackstone, Wade, Ram, and Harris all adopt a ternary conception of executive power. While not all 'ternary' theories are identical, they tend to share a number of features that I will argue compromise our ability to understand non-statutory executive powers and the judges' power to review them.

[8] See Anthony W. Bradley, Keith D. Ewing, and Christopher J. S. Knight, *Constitutional and Administrative Law* (16th ed., Pearson 2015), 253; Andrew Le Sueur and Maurice Sunkin, *Public Law* (Longman 1997), 271.

[9] See Bruce V. Harris, 'The "Third Source" of Authority for Government Action Revisited' (2007) 123 *Law Quarterly Review* 225, 226.

[10] Bruce V. Harris, 'The "Third Source" of Authority for Government Action' (1992) 108 *Law Quarterly Review* 626; B. V. Harris, 'The "Third Source" of Authority for Government Action Revisited' (2007) 123 *Law Quarterly Review* 225.

2.2 Three Accounts of the Royal Prerogative

The Royal Prerogative is a broad term that embraces not only the powers but also the traditional property rights and immunities of the Crown – for example, rights to precious minerals and immunities from being sued. In this book, I am concerned with non-statutory executive powers in the sense of *authorisation for positive action* by Crown officials.

Not everybody thinks that it is necessary or desirable to use a constrained vocabulary to distinguish legal concepts such as 'right', 'duty', 'power', 'immunity', 'liberty', and so forth. Leslie Zines, for example, argued over many years that the reference to 'the executive power of the Commonwealth' in s. 61 of the Australian Constitution should not be understood to include the Crown's traditional 'privileges and immunities',[11] but the High Court of Australia did exactly that in *Re Residential Tenancies Tribunal of NSW; Ex parte Defence Housing Authority*.[12] Although one can use often-used terms loosely without any grave difficulties, there will be situations when precision is vital, and in my view the case of non-statutory executive powers is such a situation. I shall return to the 'privileges and immunities' of the Crown from time to time, particularly in relation to the liability of the Crown's officials for wrongdoing, but I am concerned chiefly with capacity for action rather than immunities from liability.

I am less concerned with which specific powers can be exercised by Her Majesty's Government of any Realm today and more concerned with the nature of non-statutory powers and the relation between those that belong to the Royal Prerogative and those that do not. The Royal Prerogative conventionally includes powers to do such things as making treaties, appointing prime ministers, calling and proroguing parliaments, and minting coins. Many of these powers concern matters of high state, and some still bear the lustre of a medieval monarchy. Others, such as management of the civil service, are more workaday, almost approximating mundane managerial powers. (Indeed, given the trend towards bureaucratic organisation of the civil service since the nineteenth century and the infiltration of the language of 'customer service' since the 1980s,

[11] Leslie Zines, *The High Court and the Constitution* (Butterworths 1981), 214. Section 61 provides: 'The executive power of the Commonwealth is vested in the Queen and is exercisable by the Governor-General as the Queen's representative, and extends to the execution and maintenance of this Constitution, and of the laws of the Commonwealth.'

[12] (1997) 190 CLR 410. See Leslie Zines, 'The Inherent Executive Power of the Commonwealth' (2005) 16 *Public Law Review* 279, 283.

it is difficult to perceive the unique nature of civil service at all.) All of the prerogative powers are of ancient provenance; it is clear that they can be nibbled (or swept) away by statute, somewhat clear that they lapse through disuse (though not entirely clear whether they can spring back to life),[13] and fairly certain that no new ones can be created.[14]

A preliminary question is whether we are concerned with a singular or plural phenomenon – with 'the Royal Prerogative' or 'the prerogative powers' of the Crown. The question has been dismissed as academic,[15] but in fact it represents the first major turning point in the definition of our category. Is it a residual source of power, subject to encroachment by statute, or a *numerus clausus* of discrete, specific powers? As Christopher Vincenzi has argued, the choice is fundamental: 'If there is a general power to act for the public good, of which the recognised prerogatives are but a part, then the scope for lawful action by the Crown will be immeasurably greater.'[16] Indeed, the properties of residuality, generality, and responsiveness to contingency can be seen to play out in the classical conceptions of prerogative powers.

2.2.1 Locke: Reserve Power to Act for the Public Good

John Locke was one of the most influential political theorists of the Glorious Revolution of the late seventeenth century, and his account of the prerogative provides a good starting point for two reasons. First, it expresses the ancient principle[17] that the sovereign can act outside (and against) the law in emergencies *within* a broadly liberal constitutional framework; as Thomas Poole observes, Locke's theory is 'juristic in its willingness to articulate how the prerogative might fit within the legal, institutional and normative architecture of the modern state patterned along English lines'. Locke conceived of the prerogative as a set of *reserve powers* – an essentially formless wellspring of power that is activated and

[13] See, e.g., *Burmah Oil* v. *Lord Advocate* [1965] AC 75, 101 (Lord Reid), 122 (Viscount Radcliffe).

[14] *British Broadcasting Corporation* v. *Johns* [1965] Ch 32, 79 (Diplock LJ). Cf Thomas Poole, 'The Strange Death of Prerogative in England' (2018) 43(2) *University of Western Australia Law Review* 42, 55.

[15] See *R (Northumbria Police Authority)* v. *Home Secretary* [1988] All ER 556, 564 (Croome LJ).

[16] See Christopher Vincenzi, *Crown Powers, Subjects and Citizens* (Pinter 1998), 7.

[17] See Michael Wilks, *The Problem of Sovereignty in the Later Middle Ages: The Papal Monarchy with Augustinus Triumphus and the Publicists* (Cambridge University Press 1964).

takes shape in the contingencies of political life.[18] These powers are, however, never without limits – they are powers held 'in trust'. Nor are those limits unenforceable, or enforceable only by God, as some of his rivals argued. The trust is subject to forfeiture if its terms are breached, under Locke's doctrine of justified resistance. Although Locke is generally identified as a social contract theorist, the notion of trust between ruler and ruled does most of the heavy lifting.[19] The significance of this will appear in Chapter 13 when we come to consider the normative foundations of judicial review.

The terms of Locke's trust are not, however, exactly coterminous with the bounds of the positive law, and the implicit power to act for the public good in this 'grey zone' is important for Locke's definition. The prerogative is 'nothing but the power of doing public good without a rule' to support it.[20]

It is important to keep Locke's conception of prerogative in mind because emergency powers have a tendency to crop up again and again. The power of the executive government to act outside the law for the good of the community is both difficult to resist and also difficult to contain within liberal theory. The 'state of exception' has, for example, been used in the hands of modern political theorists like Carl Schmitt to launch a fundamental challenge to liberal democracy,[21] and shades of Schmitt emerge in contemporary critiques of liberalism from both Left and Right.[22]

Timothy Endicott, for example, has argued for a 'positive conception' of public power that includes an open-ended power in the executive (and the other branches of government) to act 'lawfully' in pursuit of legitimate public ends without any identifiable 'legal' authorisation.[23]

[18] Thomas Poole, 'The Strange Death of Prerogative in England' (2018) 43(2) *University of Western Australia Law Review* 42, 48.

[19] See Peter Laslett, 'Introduction' in John Lock (Peter Laslett ed.), *Two Treatises of Government* (Cambridge University Press 1960), 112.

[20] John Locke (Peter Laslett ed.), *Two Treatises of Government* (Cambridge University Press 1988), II:XIV §160.

[21] See Carl Schmitt (George Schwab trans.), *Political Theology: Four Chapters on the Concept of Sovereignty* (University of Chicago Press 2005).

[22] See also John P. McCormick, *Carl Schmitt's Critique of Liberalism: Against Politics as Technology* (Cambridge University Press 1999). The post-modern Left, in particular, seems enamoured of Schmitt: Matthew G. Specter, 'What's "Left" in Schmitt? From Aversion to Appropriation in Contemporary Political Theory' in Jens Meierhenrich and Oliver Simons (eds.), *The Oxford Handbook of Carl Schmitt* (Oxford University Press 2017), 426–454

[23] Timothy A. O. Endicott, 'Lawful Power' (2017) 15 *New Zealand Journal of Public and International Law* 1.

Emergencies are, by their nature, difficult for constitutions, and they raise difficult questions about the justiciability of executive discretion regarding the existence of an emergency and what response is called for. Few would seriously argue that executive officials should be bound by positive laws during times when the existence of the political community (and its legal order) is under existential threat, for example; extraordinary circumstances sometimes demand extraordinary action. But this does not threaten the ideal of a liberal constitution so fundamentally. Crown officials, when faced with a conflict between the dictates of the positive law and the duty to preserve the republic, should look to the equity of the law (in the older, Aristotelian sense) for the bounds of their trust.[24] This seems to me to be the most consistent with Locke's approach and the generally fiduciary nature of his scheme of thought.

As for the prerogative in quotidian circumstances, I would read Locke as proposing an open-ended reserve power to pursue the public interest conditioned by both the positive law and 'fiduciary' duties of loyalty to that interest. Provided that we adopt the right conception of official power and action, there is nothing inherently problematic about such an approach. Prerogative powers are bundled up and apportioned as vires to discrete offices, subject to implicit duties in the manner of their exercise. This undermines the notion that prerogative powers are not 'legal' because (as I will argue) official acts are actions by individuals that inherently and necessarily purport to be something more than actions by individuals; they purport to be authorised by the legal rules that constitute an office in which some of this 'sovereign' power is reposed.

In sum, then, Locke teaches both the importance of emergencies and the challenges they raise for constitutionalism and points to the need for a deeper understanding of power and the limits inherent in its generation within a politico-legal system that exists for the ultimate benefit of its membership, not its organs. His account suggests to me (although Locke would not accept it on such terms) that the courts might play a role in policing the borders of prerogative action based on the notion of a 'public trust'; if a breach of that trust justified armed resistance in Locke's England, perhaps it should be taken (in the context of a mature parliamentary democracy in the twenty-first century) to justify some appropriate scope of judicial review.

[24] See, e.g., James Edelman, 'The Equity of the Statute' in Dennis Klimchuk, Irit Samet, and Henry E. Smith (eds.), *Philosophical Foundations of the Law of Equity* (Oxford University Press 2020), 352.

2.2.2 *Blackstone: Singular and Eccentrical*

Writing in the latter eighteenth century, Blackstone approached prerogative powers as a unique incident of the royal dignity. He seems at times to conflate the office of the Crown with the person of the King, and to give perhaps too much credence to ideas that were, already in his day, anachronous; at other times, however, he appears rather candid about the fact that the trappings of regal power are just 'bells and smells'.[25]

Shades of Locke are evident in Blackstone's treatment of the prerogative. But Poole identifies a very important difference. Blackstone insists, on the one hand, that the prerogative is a special type of *claim to legal authority*. The prerogative is not legally unconstrained; it is based in, and sanctioned by, law. 'For Blackstone, prerogative power comes nested within law and institutional structures more firmly and squarely than Locke's theory seems to allow.'[26] But, on the other hand, Blackstone insists that the sovereign is free to act within the bounds of that authority *as he sees fit*. 'I shall not (I trust) be considered as an advocate for arbitrary power, when I lay it down as a principle, that in the execution of lawful prerogative, the king is and ought to be absolute', or at least immune to resistance from any other institution of government.[27] Blackstone then lists a number of *distinct actions* under the prerogative – rejecting bills, making treaties, coining, creating peers, and pardoning offences. This suggests that the power is absolute only within carefully delimited spheres of action.

Blackstone also makes allowance for states of emergency but seems most concerned with the kind of emergency that calls for resistance *against* the Crown. In the 'ordinary course of law', he says, there is no man or body of men that can resist the Crown, but he brackets out 'those *extraordinary* recourses to first principles, which are necessary when the contracts of society are in danger of dissolution'.[28] Blackstone essentially glosses Locke's theory of resistance against constituted authority for breach of the trust on which sovereignty is held; however, he draws somewhat different implications for the concept of the prerogative. We

[25] See Sir William Blackstone, *Commentaries on the Laws of England* (Clarendon Press 1765), Book I:7, 234.

[26] Thomas Poole, 'The Strange Death of Prerogative in England' (2018) 43(2) *University of Western Australia Law Review* 42, 51.

[27] Sir William Blackstone, *Commentaries on the Laws of England* (Clarendon Press 1765), Book I:7, 243.

[28] Sir William Blackstone, *Commentaries on the Laws of England* (Clarendon Press 1765), Book I:7, 244.

have seen that Locke's conception of the prerogative de-emphasises the *specific* prerogative powers and emphasises an open-ended, reserve power to act *contra legem* (subject to duties of fiduciary loyalty enforced by the sanction of popular resistance). Blackstone, by way of contrast, casts the prerogative as a set of definitely circumscribed empowerments that are generally free of constraining duties in the manner of their exercise (subject also to an overriding proviso of popular resistance).

Of importance to the taxonomic question is Blackstone's characterisation of prerogative powers as *singular and eccentric* – as something unique and limited to the Crown:

> By the word prerogative we usually understand that special pre-eminence, which the king hath, over and above all other persons, and out of the ordinary course of the common law, in right of his royal dignity. It signifies, in its etymology, from *pre* and *rogo*, something that is required or demanded before, or in preference to, all others. And hence it follows, that it must be in its nature singular and eccentrical; that *it can only be applied to those rights and capacities which the king enjoys alone, in contradistinction to others, and not to those which he enjoys in common with any of his subjects;* for if once any one prerogative of the crown could be held in common with the subject, it would cease to be prerogative any longer.[29]

Blackstone thus presents a ternary view of non-statutory executive powers, opening space for the idea of a 'third source'. As we shall see, this space has provided fertile ground for modern scholars and judges to theorise the changing modalities of government in our own day.

Early modern accounts of the Royal Prerogative such as those of Locke and Blackstone are interesting for two further reasons. First, in the seventeenth and eighteenth centuries, the Crown still exercised a number of prerogatives that were more 'legislative' than 'executive'. Today, most of the Crown's legislative prerogative powers are hold-overs in British Overseas Territory law, and even in that preserve they are recognised to be amenable to the supervisory jurisdiction on a basis substantially identical to the executive prerogatives.[30] As noted, these legislative prerogative powers were held to be subject to ordinary judicial

[29] Sir William Blackstone, *Commentaries on the Laws of England* (Clarendon Press 1765), Book I:7, 223. Emphasis mine.

[30] See Ian Hendry and Susan Dickson, *British Overseas Territories Law* (2nd ed., Hart 2018); Sir Philip Sales, 'Crown Powers, the Royal Prerogative and Fundamental Rights' in Hanna Wilberg and Mark Elliott (eds.), *The Scope and Intensity of Substantive Review* (Hart 2015), 367.

review by the House of Lords in *R (Bancoult)* v. *Secretary of State for Foreign and Commonwealth Affairs*.[31] In this book, I will not distinguish between the legislative and executive prerogative powers of the Crown.

Second, what modern commentators often miss is that, just as eighteenth-century lawyers did not distinguish so strictly between the common law and statute, Blackstone did not distinguish strictly, or even consistently, between 'statutory' and 'prerogative' powers.[32] This departs from the modern understanding of prerogative powers as being inherently non-statutory and rather suggests that Blackstone saw 'prerogative powers' as being discretionary powers, statutory or non-statutory, which the Crown and its officials could exercise as they saw fit.

2.2.3 *Dicey: Residual and Comprehensive*

Dicey's view of the Royal Prerogative, developed in the late nineteenth and early twentieth century, was the preferred view for much of the last century. It is to Dicey, for example, that we owe the common impression that 'prerogative' is inherently 'non-statutory'. Dicey defines the prerogative as 'the residue of discretionary power left at any moment in the hands of the Crown'.[33] One theme in Dicey's account is the translation of prerogative powers from the King to the Crown and the evolution of the Crown into one organ in a mixed government.[34] One way of reading Dicey is to see him as fundamentally critical of the concept of prerogative powers as the vestiges of a political universe structured around outmoded political values.[35] For present purposes, Dicey's *binary* view of executive powers is important. The prerogative is a comprehensive, single category: '[e]very act which the executive government can lawfully do without the

[31] [2009] 1 AC 453.

[32] He labels some statutory powers as 'prerogative', such as 'the power vested in his majesty . . . of prohibiting the exportation of arms or ammunition out of this kingdom', and mentions statutory 'improvements' made to the prerogative power to oversee justice by statute, under which judges remain in office through an *interregnum*. See Sir William Blackstone, *Commentaries on the Laws of England* (Clarendon Press 1765), Book I:7, 255, 258.

[33] Albert V. Dicey, *Introduction to the Study of the Law of the Constitution* (8th ed., Liberty Fund 1982), 282.

[34] See A. V. Dicey (John W. F. Allison ed.), *The Law of the Constitution* (Cambridge University Press 2013), 39, 190–191.

[35] See Thomas Poole, 'The Strange Death of Prerogative in England' (2018) 43(2) *University of Western Australia Law Review* 42, 47.

authority of an Act of Parliament'.[36] These 'discretionary powers of the Crown' cover the field, representing 'every kind of action which can be taken by the Crown, or its servants, without the necessity of applying to Parliament for new statutory authority'.[37]

Significantly, Dicey accepts that the HM Government might find itself unable to act, given that it must rely on *either* a statutory or a prerogative head of power, even where this is to the detriment of the public interest:

> The rigidity of the law constantly hampers (and sometimes with great injury to the public) the action of the executive, and from the hard-and-fast rules of strict law, as interpreted by the judges, the government can escape only by obtaining from Parliament the discretionary authority which is denied to the Crown by the law of the land.[38]

Emergency is never far away in this quarter, and the state of exception proves Dicey's rule:

> There are times of tumult or invasion when for the sake of legality itself the rules of law must be broken. The course which the government must then take is dear. The Ministry must break the law and trust for protection to an Act of Indemnity. A statute of this kind is (as already pointed out) the last and supreme exercise of Parliamentary sovereignty. It legalises illegality; it affords the practical solution of the problem which perplexed the statesmanship of the sixteenth and seventeenth centuries, how to combine the maintenance of law and the authority of the Houses of Parliament with the free exercise of that kind of discretionary power or prerogative which, under some shape or other, *must at critical junctures be wielded by the executive government* of every civilised country.[39]

In this passage, Dicey is responding to a long tradition of thinking about executive power and emergency. His preferred mechanism is for the executive to act illegally, and then to benefit from an Act of Indemnity. This limits the illegality in time – it subsists only until such an Act is passed, and the authority to act 'beyond the law' is granted by Parliament, not attributed to the inherent powers of the Crown. As David Dyzenahaus argues, Dicey's views on the personal liability of officials

[36] A. V. Dicey, *Introduction to the Study of the Law of the Constitution* (8th ed., Liberty Fund 1982), 282.
[37] A. V. Dicey, *Introduction to the Study of the Law of the Constitution* (8th ed., Liberty Fund 1982), 282.
[38] A. V. Dicey, *Introduction to the Study of the Law of the Constitution* (8th ed., Liberty Fund 1982), 272.
[39] Albert V. Dicey, *Introduction to the Study of the Law of the Constitution* (8th ed., Liberty Fund 1982), 272. Emphasis mine.

acting illegally also goes some way to curing the rupture with legality caused by exigencies; if an official successfully argues the defence of necessity, it is not a case of legalising illegality but of finding that the action was not illegal in the first place.[40] It is noteworthy, if not necessarily material, that Dicey himself seems to have abandoned this approach when it came to the perceived 'catastrophe' of Irish independence.[41]

Dicey casts a long shadow in English public law, and his legacy is not always judged favourably.[42] There is much of value in Dicey's thought, but he had an undeniable blind spot when it came to the existence of 'administrative law';[43] some of his pre-commitments precluded him from describing the juristic nature of the Crown (and its relationship to officials) properly. Dicey's conception of the British constitutional tradition will crop up repeatedly in this book, and I will have a good deal to say about his ideas of official action and liability as well as his influence on our comprehension of public law today and how that squares with the notion of a corporate Crown.[44]

However, this takes us outside the present question of the taxonomy of non-statutory executive powers. What I take from Dicey is the proposition that executive power is binary: What is not statutory is prerogative, and what is not prerogative is statutory. There is no *tertium quid*. Ultimately, I will argue for a binary view that owes some debt to Dicey. However, I will also argue for movement away from the language of the Royal Prerogative and towards a category of 'non-statutory executive powers' that embraces both prerogative-type and third source-type powers. The touchstone for my categorisation is the amenability to all forms of non-statutory executive power to judicial review, on the same grounds.

2.2.4 *Wade: Blackstone, with a Hohfeldian Gloss*

Blackstone's account was given a rather unfortunate gloss by Sir William Wade in the latter twentieth century. Wade wrote at a time when the

40 See David Dyzenhaus, 'The Compulsion of Legality' in Victor Ramraj (ed.), *Emergencies and the Limits of Legality* (Cambridge University Press 2008), 33, 54.

41 See Iain McLean, *What's Wrong with the British Constitution?* (Oxford University Press 2010), Ch 6.

42 Mark Walters, *A. V. Dicey and the Common Law Constitutional Tradition* (Cambridge University Press 2020), 2.

43 Mark Walters, *A. V. Dicey and the Common Law Constitutional Tradition* (Cambridge University Press 2020), 299.

44 Janet McLean, 'Personality and Public Law Doctrine' (1999) 49 *University of Toronto Law Journal* 123.

twentieth-century administrative state had reached its zenith, when the frontiers of judicial review were steadily advancing beyond statute, and when the Diceyan view was (still) predominant. Wade took Blackstone's conception of the prerogative as something 'singular and eccentrical' to the Crown, but narrowed it with a further requirement. Only 'legal powers', as Wade defined them, belong to the prerogative, properly so called:

> [W]hat does 'prerogative' mean? . . . If prerogative power is to be brought under judicial control, and if ministers are to be condemned for abusing it unlawfully, it is worth finding out what it really is. In the first place, the prerogative consists of legal power – that is, *the ability to alter people's rights, duties or status under the laws of this country which the courts of this country enforce*. Thus, when Parliament is dissolved under the prerogative it can no longer validly do business. When a man is made a peer, he may no longer lawfully vote in a parliamentary election. When a university is incorporated by royal charter, a new legal person enters the world. All these legal transformations are effected in terms of rights, duties, disabilities, etc, which the courts will acknowledge and enforce. The power to bring them about is vested in the Crown by the common law, so it clearly falls within the definition of the royal prerogative as 'the common law powers of the Crown'.[45]

Wade's concept of 'legal power' seems to draw inspiration from W. N. Hohfeld's classical scheme of fundamental legal conceptions, in which a 'power' is defined as the ability to alter one's own or another's legal position.[46] Wade opined that many of the conventional powers of the Crown, exercised by officials in HM Government, are not 'legal powers', and therefore not accurately described as 'prerogative', at all. He referred critically to a number of (then recent) leading cases. *Laker Airways Ltd* v. *Department of Trade*,[47] for example, concerned an act of designation by HM Government under an international agreement. This was not an exercise of prerogative power, argued Wade, because '[w]hatever powers the government may have had under the Bermuda Agreement were powers in the sphere of international law, and capacity to make the Agreement came not from common law but from status in international law as an international person'.[48] *R (Lain)* v. *Criminal*

[45] H. W. R. Wade, *Constitutional Fundamentals* (Stevens 1980), 46. Emphasis mine.

[46] See in particular Wesley N. Hohfeld, 'Fundamental Legal Conceptions as Applied in Judicial Reasoning' (1913) 23 *Yale Law Journal* 16 and W. N. Hohfeld, 'Fundamental Legal Conceptions as Applied in Judicial Reasoning' (1917) 27 *Yale Law Journal* 710.

[47] [1977] 2 All ER 182.

[48] H. W. R. Wade, *Constitutional Fundamentals* (Stevens 1980), 47. Emphasis mine.

Injuries Compensation Board[49] was mistaken because, in setting up a Compensation Board and making *ex gratia* payments, the Crown, 'so far as it came into the picture at all', 'was exercising its ordinary powers *as a natural person*, which of course include power to transfer property, make contracts, and so on'.[50] As for the power to appoint and dismiss Ministers, Wade said that the action was 'nothing else than the power which all legal persons have at common law to employ servants or agents'; in short, the judges had 'fallen into the habit of describing as "prerogative" any and every sort of action which is not statutory'.[51] Wade blamed the influence of Dicey for this trend, particularly Dicey's failure to make a distinction between the Crown's 'natural' and 'regal' capacities.

In this, Wade sowed various seeds of confusion regarding non-statutory executive powers in English law. The main features of Wade's position could be summarised as follows. The prerogative consists only of legal powers, defined (following Hohfeld, albeit loosely) as the ability to alter rights and duties in the domestic legal system. The prerogative includes only those legal powers that are unique to the Crown, and excludes mundane powers, for example, the power to make contracts. The apparent power to make treaties comes not from the common law but from international law, and is not actually a true prerogative, despite its traditional treatment as a paradigm example of the prerogative. The Crown possesses mundane powers as a natural person, rather than in a 'regal capacity'. Finally, *contra* Dicey, the prerogative does not embrace every executive power (or 'non-power' capacity) that is non-statutory.

2.3 A 'Third Source' of Governmental Authority?

The space left by a ternary approach defines the boundaries of what has come to be called the 'third source' of governmental authority. The leading case for the third source (*avant la lettre*) is *Malone* v. *Metropolitan Police Commissioner*.[52] In that case, the Police Commissioner had instructed the Post Office to tap a criminal suspect's telephone line under a warrant issued by the Home Secretary. The suspect challenged the lawfulness of the Commissioner's act on the basis that it was an unauthorised search, in reliance on the rule in *Entick* v. *Carrington*.[53] There, the Secretary of State

49 [1967] 2 QB 864.
50 H. W. R. Wade, *Constitutional Fundamentals* (Stevens 1980), 48. Emphasis mine.
51 H. W. R. Wade, *Constitutional Fundamentals* (Stevens 1980), 49.
52 [1977] Ch 344.
53 (1765) 2 Wils KB 275.

had issued a warrant purporting to authorise his messengers to break into Entick's house, prompting the latter to bring an action in trespass. Carrington argued that he was protected by the Constables Protection Act 1750 because he had acted under a warrant. The King's Bench asked (i) whether Carrington was acting under a warrant issued by Lord Halifax; (ii) whether Lord Halifax was a 'Secretary of State'; and (iii) whether Secretaries of State had the power to issue warrants of this kind. This involved a historical review of the office of Secretary of State and the powers associated with it.[54] Secretaries of State generally had the power to issue legal instruments including warrants, but the Secretary lacked the competence to issue this kind of warrant. As the warrant was 'wholly void',[55] all that remained was a forced entry, which amounted to a trespass (i.e., a private law wrong) at common law.

Sir Robert Megarry VC distinguished the case, however. In *Entick* v. *Carrington*, Entick (as an occupier of property) had a common law right against trespass. It was the tort that subsisted after the apparent authority of the warrant fell away. According to Megarry VC, Carrington would simply have done no wrong in the absence of a duty to stay off the property correlative to that right. By analogy, so long as Malone had no right to telephonic privacy, neither the Postmaster nor the Commissioner had any duty *not* to wiretap his phone; they could not, therefore, have done any actionable wrong by installing one. I shall return to Megarry VC's decision in Chapter 7 with a detailed critique. What is noteworthy about it now is that it takes a conventionally Diceyan approach to the private nature of official wrongs, and combines it with a Blackstonian notion of the prerogative. This opens up a kind of grey area for official action that seems logically robust – indeed, inevitable – but is really a conceptual rut difficult to escape.

The terminology of a 'third source' was suggested by B. V. Harris to explain cases like *Malone* v. *Metropolitan Police Commissioner*. Harris adopts a ternary approach to executive power somewhat akin to Wade's. The 'prerogative' includes not only the prerogative in the narrow, Blackstonian sense, 'but also the freedom which the government has to do anything that is not prohibited by law'.[56] Harris, like Wade, defines

[54] 'We must know what a Secretary of State is, before we can tell whether [the Constable] is within the [statutory defence]'. *Entick* v. *Carrington* (1765) 2 Wils KB 275, 288.

[55] *Entick* v. *Carrington* (1765) 2 Wils KB 275, 292.

[56] Bruce V. Harris, 'The "Third Source" of Authority for Government Action' (1992) 108 *Law Quarterly Review* 626, 626.

'power' in a loosely Hohfeldian manner.[57] Both actions that are apparently not an exercise of a power at all (such as publishing information) and actions that are the exercise of a private law power (such as contracting) are examples of the 'third source' in action.[58] Despite his apparently technical approach to 'power', however, Harris uses the term 'authority' in an ambiguous manner; as Adam Perry has observed, Harris treats an absence of prohibition as a source of authority, which is a *non sequitur*.[59] Harris posits various limits on the ambit of the third source. These include the limits of what is 'physically possible', but Harris does not specify what is physically possible for 'the government' as such to do; apparently, he presumes that any action that is physically possible for an *official* is physically possible for HM Government.[60] Limits also include judicial review, the general law of tort, and legislation.

Harris revisited the 'third source' in a second paper in 2007, commenting on a number of judicial decisions since he first presented his argument. In particular, he discusses the (then) recent House of Lords decision in *R (Hooper)* v. *Secretary of State for Work and Pensions*.[61] Although he cites that case as tentative judicial endorsement of his 'understanding of the third source', Harris criticises the House of Lords for speaking of 'common law powers'; that language, he claims, 'obfuscates the necessary distinction between the government's freedom to act when not prohibited and the prerogative, the latter also being a common law power', and 'gives the impression that the government is acting pursuant to specific authority in positive law' where in fact it is using 'a residuary freedom to do that which does not conflict with what other persons are permitted to do by the authority of positive law'.[62] The major features of his account remain unchanged.

I shall use the 'third source' label to refer to a family of theories that share a family resemblance based on three primary features: (i) a ternary approach to executive power; (ii) a tendency to locate the source of the third source powers in the nature of the Crown (or the Queen, or HM

57 Bruce V. Harris, 'The "Third Source" of Authority for Government Action' (1992) 108 *Law Quarterly Review* 626, 629.

58 Bruce V. Harris, 'The "Third Source" of Authority for Government Action' (1992) 108 *Law Quarterly Review* 626, 645.

59 Adam Perry, 'The Crown's Administrative Powers' (2015) 131 *Law Quarterly Review* 652.

60 Bruce V. Harris, 'The "Third Source" of Authority for Government Action' (1992) 108 *Law Quarterly Review* 626, 633.

61 [2005] UKHL 29.

62 Bruce V. Harris, 'The Third Source Authority for Government Action Revisited' (2007) 123 *Law Quarterly Review* 225, 226.

Government) as a type of acting subject, usually a 'natural person' or 'corporation sole'; and (iii) a tendency to distinguish legal powers (in loosely Hohfeldian terms) from 'capacities' and to stress the 'liberty' or 'freedom' of the Crown (or the Queen, or HM Government) to act without formal vires. Theories diverge on (ii) and (iii), in particular. Elliott, we have seen, endorses a 'natural person' approach to (ii) and a 'residual liberties' approach to (iii). Nevertheless, I would call Elliott's a 'third source theory'. Harris, for his part, does not base his arguments on the fact that the Crown is a natural person. In fact, in contrast to the majority of commentators,[63] Harris expressly disclaims (iii), that is, the idea that the third source of authority for governmental action exists in virtue of the Crown's personality at all.[64] However, he does not actually offer any alternative explanation for what 'the government' is, or why it has the ability to act.

2.3.1 Ram: Non-statutory and Open-ended

In the English context, the so-called 'Ram Memorandum' is also relevant as evidence of administrative practice. In 2003, a memorandum of government legal advice was disclosed in a parliamentary written answer at the instigation of Lord Anthony Lester. The memorandum, incorporating a kind of third source approach, had been written by Sir Granville Ram in 1945, and was apparently relied on routinely by Whitehall in the intervening decades.[65] The specific question addressed by the memorandum arose in the context of money and appropriations, namely whether legislation is always necessary to extend the existing powers of a Government Department. The memorandum turns first to the legal position and then to the practice concerning money questions. Sir Granville started from the premise that the office of a Minister is non-statutory and that, by virtue of the relationship between the Crown and its Ministers, the latter exercises the powers of the Crown at common law:

> A Minister of the Crown is not in the same position as a statutory corporation. A statutory corporation (whether constituted by special statute as, for instance, a railway company is, or constitution under Companies Acts in the case of an ordinary company) is entirely

[63] Harris lists T. C. Daintith, Dawn Oliver, H. W. R. Wade, George Winterton, and Leslie Zines.

[64] Bruce V. Harris, 'The "Third Source" of Authority for Government Action' (1992) 108 *Law Quarterly Review* 626, 635.

[65] Lord Anthony Lester and Matthew Weait, 'The Use of Ministerial Powers without Parliamentary Authority: The Ram Doctrine' (2003) *Public Law* 415.

> a creature of statute and has no powers except those conferred upon it by statute, but a Minister of the Crown, even though there may have been a statute authorising his appointment, is not a creature of statute and may, as an agent of the Crown, *exercise any powers that the Crown has power to exercise*, except so far as he is precluded from doing so by statute. In other words, in the case of a Government Department, one must look at the statutes to see what it may not do not as in the case of a company to see what it may do. There are, of course, innumerable instances in which statutory powers have been conferred on Ministers and there are frequently questions whether an express statutory provision conferring particular power does not by implication have a restrictive effect in the field in which those powers have been granted. Whether or not such an implication ought to be drawn in any particular case must always be a question of construction to be determined on the wording of the relevant statutes, *but the governing principle is that express statutory provision is not necessary to enable a Minister to exercise functions.*[66]

In answer to Lord Lester's written questions, then Justice Minister Baroness Scotland cited a supposed 'Ram Doctrine' to the following effect:[67]

> The Ram doctrine reflects a well-established principle of constitutional law. Like many other persons, Ministers and their departments *have common law powers which derive from the Crown's status as a corporation sole.* Ministers and their departments also exercise prerogative powers of the Crown. Common law and prerogative powers may be limited by statute either expressly or by necessary implication and in this respect are subject to direct parliamentary control. The courts have recognised the legitimacy of these principles.[68]

The Ram Memorandum does not actually say so much in terms; it says only that a Minister can exercise 'any powers that the Crown has power to exercise' – a circular statement that merely restates the question in terms of the Crown's non-statutory executive powers. But the Minister's claim was not baseless. As we shall see in the next chapter, this proposition is found in a number of the cases. The idea that a non-statutory corporation has open-ended legal capacities, analogous to those of a natural person, goes back to

[66] See Lord Anthony Lester and Matthew Weait, 'The Use of Ministerial Powers without Parliamentary Authority: The Ram Doctrine' (2003) *Public Law* 415; *HL Debates*, vol. 643, cols. WA 98–99 (22 January 2003); S. H. Bailey, *Bailey, Jones and Mowbray Cases, Materials and Commentary on Administrative Law* (4th ed., Sweet & Maxwell 2005), 64. Emphasis mine.

[67] See Sir Stephen Sedley, *Lions under the Throne: Essays on the History of Public Law* (Cambridge University Press 2015), 135.

[68] Cited in Lord Anthony Lester and Matthew Weait, 'The Use of Ministerial Powers without Parliamentary Authority: The Ram Doctrine' (2003) *Public Law* 415, 416.

the seminal *Sutton's Hospital Case*,[69] at least as interpreted by Blackstone and the nineteenth-century railway cases.[70] Blackstone posited that every corporation implicitly acquired a set of 'powers, rights, capacities, and incapacities', including the capacity to sue and be sued, implead or be impleaded, grant or receive in the corporate name, and 'do all other things as natural persons may'.[71] This did not survive as a general rule; the price of simplified incorporation by registration under modern corporations legislation led to the rise of the corporate ultra vires rule for registered corporations to keep these new persons within the bounds of their corporate purposes. But the old position remained for chartered and common law corporations, such that the latter are still said to have powers analogous to those of a natural person, in the sense of being open-ended.[72] When the Ram Memorandum came to light, the 4th Edition of *Halsbury's Laws of England* stated that '[a]t common law the Crown, as a corporation possessing legal personality, has the capacities of a natural person and thus the same liberties as an individual'.[73]

The Ram Memorandum thus represents a third source theory deriving the Crown's capacities from its personality as a common law corporation. But it has also been the subject of some controversy. The House of Lords Select Committee on the Constitution, which produced a Report on the pre-emption of Parliament in 2013,[74] was troubled by the assertion of a doctrine that ministers can do whatever a natural person can do (unless prohibited by legislation). This was, according to the Committee, plainly wrong. It cited evidence to the effect that the true proposition to be drawn from the Ram Memorandum is a more limited one, namely 'that government can do anything reasonably ancillary to its explicit functions'; this is 'nowhere near the proposition' that HM Government 'can do anything that a private individual can do'.[75] Sir Jeffrey Jowell gave evidence to the

69 (1612) 77 Eng Rep 960.

70 See, e.g., *Riche* v. *Ashbury Railway Carriage and Iron Co Ltd* (1874) LR Ex 224.

71 Sir William Blackstone, *Commentaries on the Laws of England Book I* (Clarendon Press 1765), 463.

72 Henry Rajak, 'Judicial Control: Corporations and the Decline of Ultra Vires' (1995) 26 *Cambrian Law Review* 9, 11; John Howell, 'What the Crown May Do' (2010) 15(1) *Judicial Review* 36, 45.

73 See. e.g., Lord Hailsham (ed.), *Halsbury's Laws of England*, Vol. 8(2) (4th ed., Butterworths 1998), §101, n6. This has been omitted from the 5th edition.

74 House of Lords Select Committee on the Constitution, *The Pre-emption of Parliament: 13th Report of Session 2012–13* (HL Paper 165, 1 May 2013).

75 House of Lords Select Committee on the Constitution, *The Pre-emption of Parliament: 13th Report of Session 2012–13* (HL Paper 165, 1 May 2013), [56] citing evidence by Sir Stephen Sedley.

effect that equating the powers of ministers with those of private individuals was 'constitutional heresy'.[76] The then Attorney General, Dominic Grieve, supported a more limited reading of the Memorandum:

> I think that Sir Granville Ram was emphasising that the Crown is not a creature of statute. Therefore, it has inherent powers that it can exercise, apart from prerogative powers, *as if* it were a natural person. But . . . it is circumscribed by public law; by propriety; by human rights . . . I do not think that Whitehall thinks the Government can do everything a private individual can do, because it is circumscribed by those very things I have just listed.[77]

The Committee concluded that the description of the scope of Government power posited by the supposed doctrine was 'unhelpful and inaccurate', did not reflect important restrictions on ministerial powers under the common law, and created an impression that Ministers possess greater legal authority than was the case. 'It also fails to recognise that, whereas lawful expenditure incurred by a private person involves his or her own money, expenditure by the Government does not: *it is public money*'.[78] The Ram Memorandum should, perhaps, never have been used as it was.[79] It had no 'inherent legal authority', and, as a piece of legal advice from 1945, does not reflect the law today; the evidence was that Ministers' ability to exercise common law powers is 'constrained by the public law limitations on Government action as enforced through judicial review', among various other sources of constraint.[80] Throughout the report, the Committee refers consistently to 'common law powers'. The best current reading of the Ram Memorandum is therefore probably as a historically relevant 'common law corporation' theory of non-statutory executive powers subject to appropriate limits.

2.4 Conclusion

This chapter has introduced the most important approaches to the categorisation of executive powers in the literature, noting a significant degree of uncertainty about how the category of executive

[76] House of Lords Select Committee on the Constitution, *The Pre-emption of Parliament: 13th Report of Session 2012–13* (HL Paper 165, 1 May 2013), [57].

[77] House of Lords Select Committee on the Constitution, *The Pre-emption of Parliament: 13th Report of Session 2012–13* (HL Paper 165, 1 May 2013), [58]. Emphasis mine.

[78] House of Lords Select Committee on the Constitution, *The Pre-emption of Parliament: 13th Report of Session 2012–13* (HL Paper 165, 1 May 2013), [59]. Emphasis mine.

[79] See Lord Anthony Lester and Matthew Weait, 'The Use of Ministerial Powers without Parliamentary Authority: The Ram Doctrine' (2003) *Public Law* 415, n1.

[80] House of Lords Select Committee on the Constitution, *The Pre-emption of Parliament: 13th Report of Session 2012–13* (HL Paper 165, 1 May 2013), [54].

powers carves up. The first question is the 'Dicey *versus* Blackstone question', that is, whether we should adopt a binary or a ternary view of executive powers. In other words, does the category of 'prerogative powers' embrace all non-statutory executive powers, or do we need a third category? Beyond this, a raft of questions relates to the nature of the third source, if it exists. Does the 'third source' comprise a set of 'common law powers', a set of 'capacities', and/or a set of 'residual liberties'? The third question relates to the source of those powers, capacities, and/or liberties. Does the third source arise from the 'natural person' capacities of the Queen, from the natural person capacities of the (other) officers of the Crown, or from the legal personality of the Crown itself? If the latter, what kind of corporation is the Crown? I will address these questions in the next chapter.

I have chosen not to approach the definition of non-statutory executive powers from the problem of emergencies. While important, I do not think that the problem of emergency powers should be the primary determinant of the concept of non-statutory power for the law of judicial review in ordinary times. What I take from my discussion of emergency power is that there is, in the British constitutional tradition, an open-ended non-statutory power in HM Government to do what is needful in an emergency. In short, it is better to examine emergency action against the background of a well-formed theory of judicial review than to approach the question of judicial review against the background of emergencies. Whatever powers the Crown possesses in an emergency are subject to duties, and not all of these duties are suspended even in genuine emergencies. In fact, I think there is a case to be made that *some* public law duties are *especially* important in emergency situations – the duty to act reasonably when disbursing public resources, for example, must assume heightened importance when those resources are so scarce that the survival of the community is on the line. (Consider the allocation of vaccines in a pandemic). Nor do I think that the spurious assertion of an emergency by HM Government can constitute a bar to judicial review. The justification for my approach will become clearer in light of the distinction I draw in Chapter 7 between rules of competence and rules of conduct; in effect, I take 'emergency powers' to be open-ended rules of competence circumscribed by strict rules of conduct, and I take the latter to be enforceable by the courts in at least some exigent circumstances. That being the case, I will focus on non-emergency situations in this book.

3

The 'Third Source' in the Courts

3.1 Introduction

The last chapter brought us to the 'Dicey *versus* Blackstone' question and its spin-off, namely whether the notion of a 'third source' of authority for government action must be accommodated within a theory of judicial review. This chapter reviews the more recent cases to identify the current state of the law on each of these questions, which also serves to frame some of the more technical discussion in following chapters. The kind of fact scenarios that arise in judicial review applications are, themselves, instructive.

A number of courts in England and Wales and in the Anglo-Commonwealth jurisdictions have now considered the notion of a 'third source'. To the extent that generalisations can be made, the balance of authorities seem rather critical of the 'residual liberties' approach and suggest a 'common law powers' approach based in the corporate personality of the Crown. But there is nothing that could safely be called a consensus; it is not even possible to reconcile all the authorities within any given jurisdiction. There are too many conflicting opinions, too much *obiter*, and too many references to technical and fundamentally contestable notions that are not fully developed. The most that we can say is that there is non-trivial support for the third source notion, but that further theoretical effort is required to settle some basic questions relating to the personality of the Crown, the concept of office, and the deontic and operational logic of official action. That unsatisfactory *status quo* effectively sets the stage for the major contribution of this book.

This chapter presents a more comprehensive survey of the Anglo-Commonwealth jurisdictions than the rest of the book. Section 3.2 begins with England and Wales. Section 3.3 turns to New Zealand. Section 3.4 covers Canada and Australia.

3.2 England and Wales

It is well established in the English cases that the Crown has certain powers that are, to some extent, conceptually distinct from the Royal Prerogative.[1] However, the leading cases leave the current position less than clear. The first, *R (C)* v. *Secretary of State for Health*,[2] concerned a list kept by the Department of Health containing the names of individuals whose suitability to work with children was doubtful. At the time, there was no statutory basis for the Department's keeping the list. After a number of internal and tribunal proceedings, a decision was taken to include C's name on the list, on the basis of proven allegations of sexual misconduct. C sought judicial review of this decision on the basis that the Crown could not maintain such a list without statutory authority. He was unsuccessful at first instance, but leave to appeal was ultimately granted. Hale LJ delivered the unanimous judgment of the Court of Appeal.

Some years earlier, in *R (Fewings)* v. *Somerset County Council*,[3] the Court of Appeal had held that a public body could *only* act in reliance on its legal powers. Sir Thomas Bingham MR had approved the speech of Laws J, at first instance, that the permissive rule for private persons (i.e., 'you may do anything you choose which the law does not prohibit') was inverted for public bodies, including the Crown (i.e., 'any action taken you take must be justified by positive law'.)[4] Hale LJ distinguished the case from *R (Fewings)* v. *Somerset County Council* because that case concerned a local government body – a creature of statute – rather than a Secretary of State, and pointed in the first instance to the prerogative (citing Blackstone and Wade) as an alternative source of power. As there was 'no suggestion of a specific prerogative power in this case', however, Hale LJ relied on the Fourth Edition of *Halsbury's Laws of England* for the proposition that the Crown (i) is a corporation sole and thus (ii) has the same powers as a natural person and thus (iii) has the same liberties as an individual.[5] On this basis, she affirmed the rule in *Entick* v. *Carrington*[6] but distinguished it, applying *Malone* v. *Police*

[1] See Sir Philip Sales, 'Crown Powers, the Royal Prerogative and Fundamental Rights' in Hanna Wilberg and Mark Elliott (eds.), *The Scope and Intensity of Substantive Review* (Hart 2015), 376, 380.

[2] [2000] 1 FLR 627.

[3] [1995] 1 All ER 513.

[4] See *R (Fewings)* v. *Somerset County Council* [1995] 3 All ER 20, 25 (Sir Thomas Bingham MR) citing *R (Fewings)* v. *Somerset County Council* [1995] 1 All ER 513, 524 (Laws J).

[5] *R (C)* v. *Secretary of State for Health* [2000] 1 FLR 627, [16]–[17].

[6] (1765) 2 Wils KB 275.

Commissioner[7] instead. Although being named on a list affected C's chances of getting a job, it did not affect his legal rights, and it was within the residual liberties of the Crown to name him on the list.[8]

R (C) v. *Secretary of State for Health* thus provides support for the notion of a third source, albeit in a somewhat convoluted fashion. Specifically, it is authority for the proposition that the Crown is a common law corporation and can act in reliance on its corporate capacities, whatever they are. (I shall have more to say on the question whether it is ever helpful to determine the powers of a corporation by straightforward analogy with an individual.) The judgment adopts a residual liberties approach to the third source but says little about how the actions of officials within the relevant Department of HM Government constitute actions of the Crown. Importantly, however, Hale LJ also qualified the proposition in *Halsbury's Laws of England*. However far the analogy could be pushed, it was only an analogy. The Crown is subject to duties that reflect the position of the Department of Health, as opposed to the position of a private individual:

> Its status as a public authority brings consequences which would not apply to a private citizen. A private citizen would find it difficult to maintain such a list. He would not have access to the necessary information and he would not have the power, as the Department has, to give guidance both to former and prospective employers which will make its operation so much more effective. The appellant may not have a right to be provided with a job, nor is the Department expressly prohibiting his employment. Nevertheless he is placed in a position where he will find it extremely difficult to get a job in child care: indeed it is the declared object of the Index to secure that he does not do so. The impact of a list such as this maintained by a Government Department or public authority is that much more powerful because they are generally so much more powerful.[9]

The case chimes with a general trend, over the 1980s and 1990s, to focus on the 'function' rather than the 'source' of powers for the purposes of determining their amenability to judicial review.[10] However, it implicitly speaks to the importance of an *official mode of action*. As Leslie Zines observed, the salient feature of *R (C)* v. *Secretary of State for Health* is that

[7] [1977] Ch 344.

[8] *R (C)* v. *Secretary of State for Health* [2000] 1 FLR 627, [18], [20], [30].

[9] *R (C)* v. *Secretary of State for Health* [2000] 1 FLR 627, [22].

[10] Dawn Oliver, 'Is the Ultra Vires Rule the Basis of Judicial Review?' in C. F. Forsyth (ed.), *Judicial Review and the Constitution* (Hart 2000), 3.

'the Department's list is seen as an "official" one'.[11] Precisely this point, however – what it means to be an 'official' list – remains undeveloped in both the judgment and the subsequent literature.[12]

The next case, *R (Hooper)* v. *Secretary of State for Work and Pensions*,[13] concerned a non-statutory pension scheme that was challenged on the basis that it discriminated between widows and widowers. The aspect of present interest is the treatment of the Secretary of State's submissions on the third source. They are tortuously stated in terms of the compatibility of the non-statutory scheme with statute in the context of the Human Rights Act 1998. Stripping as much of that away as possible, the thrust was that the Secretary of State held a common law power to make non-statutory payments *alongside* a statutory scheme. This was accepted by Moses J at first instance. The Court of Appeal rejected the submission, however. The existence of a statutory provision stipulating payments to widows (and not widowers) would trigger the rule in *Attorney General* v. *De Keyser's Royal Hotel Ltd*,[14] by which the Royal Prerogative may not be used to pre-empt or undermine a statute covering the relevant field. It would be an abuse of power to operate a non-statutory scheme giving the same benefits to widowers in parallel to a statutory scheme that stipulated widows only.

In the House of Lords, the Secretary of State argued in reliance on the third source: 'as a corporation sole, the Crown has the same right to deal with its property as any other legal person [and] needs no statutory authority to do so'.[15] As Lord Hoffmann summarised the submission:

> The principle in the *De Keyser's Royal Hotel* case is, says Mr Sales, nothing to the point because it deals with an implied statutory extinction or restriction of the historic prerogative powers which belong to the Crown as supreme executive authority. *The right to spend money is not a power which the Crown enjoys as executive but simply by virtue of being a legal person like any other.* A statute would have to be a good deal more explicit before it could be interpreted as extinguishing such a commonplace power. Mr Sales added that it would be unfortunate if the dicta in the Court of Appeal cast doubt upon the validity of extra-statutory schemes such as the

[11] Leslie Zines, 'The Inherent Executive Power of the Commonwealth' (2005) 16 *Public Law Review* 279, 285.

[12] Cf *Hocking* v. *Director General of the National Archives of Australia* [2020] HCA 19; see also Chapter 5 and Chapter 6.

[13] [2005] UKHL 29.

[14] [1920] AC 508.

[15] *R (Hooper)* v. *Secretary of State for Work and Pensions* [2005] UKHL 29, [46] (Lord Hoffmann).

> Criminal Injuries Compensation Scheme, which was originally established without any statutory authority.[16]

There seemed, Lord Hoffmann noted, 'a good deal of force in these submissions', but His Lordship did not express a concluded opinion 'because, if they are right, they lead to the same conclusion as that reached by the Court of Appeal'.[17] Lord Hoffmann's *obiter* speech again seems to accept a third source that is based in the corporate personality of the Crown, which includes the 'right' to spend money distinct from the powers which the Crown holds 'as executive'. It is noteworthy, however, that all the judgments in the House of Lords refer to the powers in question only as 'common law powers'.

Shrewsbury & Atcham Borough Council v. *Secretary of State for Communities and Local Government*[18] concerned actions taken by the Secretary of State in the lead-up to a reform of local government authorities. This case is noteworthy for a disagreement between Carnwath LJ and Richards LJ on the third source point. The relevant actions included issuing invitations and making decisions that the Secretary was 'minded to' pursue a certain course of action, once the relevant legislative framework was passed. They were challenged on a number of grounds, including want of vires.[19] At first instance, the judge applied *R (C)* v. *Secretary of State for Health* to the effect that there was no relevant limit on the powers of the Secretary of State to do what she had done. With reference to *R (Hooper)* v. *Secretary of State for Work and Pensions*, Underhill J adopted 'common law powers' as the 'most workmanlike description' of this third category of powers that did not form part of the traditional prerogative.[20] The actions of the Secretary of State in *R (C)* v. *Secretary of State for Health*, however, were not totally mundane, 'like renting office accommodation or buying paperclips'; keeping the list was a 'governmental act':[21]

> [T]he fact that the Crown enjoys legal personality means that it is *prima facie* entitled – so far as *vires* in the strict sense are concerned – to do

[16] *R (Hooper)* v. *Secretary of State for Work and Pensions* [2005] UKHL 29, [46] (Lord Hoffmann). Emphasis mine.

[17] *R (Hooper)* v. *Secretary of State for Work and Pensions* [2005] UKHL 29, [47] (Lord Hoffmann).

[18] [2008] EWCA Civ 148.

[19] [2008] EWCA Civ 148, [17] (Carnwath LJ).

[20] *Shrewsbury and Atcham Borough Council* v. *Secretary of State for Communities and Local Government* [2007] EWHC 2279 (Admin), [16] (Underhill J).

[21] *Shrewsbury and Atcham Borough Council* v. *Secretary of State for Communities and Local Government* [2007] EWHC 2279 (Admin), [16] (Underhill J).

> any lawful act, even if the act in question is plainly governmental. I say '*prima facie*' because such power is limited in a number of important ways. In particular: [(i)] It does not, as discussed above, extend to any act involving interference with the rights and liberties of the subject. [(ii)] Its exercise is reviewable on ordinary public law grounds. [(iii)] It does not operate in any 'field' in which Parliament has chosen to legislate.[22]

This view casts the 'third source' as a set of common law vires that is subject to certain limits derived from statute and the common law, including the protected rights of subjects. In the Court of Appeal, Carnwath LJ noted the significant degree of scholarly disagreement on the topic, alerting to the 'so-called Ram doctrine' and critiques of it. For both the judge at first instance and the Court of Appeal, however, *R (C)* v. *Secretary of State for Health* was binding authority. That case, he said, 'confirm[ed] that the powers of the Secretary of State are not confined to those conferred by statute or prerogative, but extend, subject to any relevant statutory or public law constraints, and to the competing rights of other parties, to anything which could be done by a natural person'.[23] Expressing some degree of sympathy with the impulse to 'unwind the clock to a time when the accepted wisdom was that Ministers had only two sources of power', Carnwath LJ observed that the examples of 'common law power' or 'third source power' given by Hale LJ in *R (C)* v. *Secretary of State for Health* were of limited assistance because 'they are in the nature of ancillary powers, necessary for the carrying on of any substantive governmental (or indeed non-governmental) function, whether statutory, corporate, or common law'.[24] However, these ancillary powers threw 'no light on what, if any, non-statutory substantive functions the Crown retains beyond the scope of the "prerogative" as traditionally understood'.[25]

Carnwath LJ also expressed doubts about the usefulness of references to the status of a Minister as a corporation sole or to analogies with the

[22] *Shrewsbury and Atcham Borough Council* v. *Secretary of State for Communities and Local Government* [2007] EWHC 2279 (Admin), [17] (Underhill J).

[23] *Shrewsbury and Atcham Borough Council* v. *Secretary of State for Communities and Local Government* [2008] EWCA Civ 148, [44] (Carnwath LJ).

[24] *Shrewsbury and Atcham Borough Council* v. *Secretary of State for Communities and Local Government* [2008] EWCA Civ 148, [45] (Carnwath LJ).

[25] *Shrewsbury and Atcham Borough Council* v. *Secretary of State for Communities and Local Government* [2008] EWCA Civ 148, [45] (Carnwath LJ).

powers of natural persons. This concluded with an important rider on the valid exercise of these powers:

> In the case of an artificial person, it may be important to distinguish between the *power to act*, as a matter of corporate capacity, and the legal *constraints limiting the exercise of the power*. Unlike a local authority, the Crown is not a creature of statute. As a matter of capacity, no doubt, it has power to do whatever a private person can do. But as an organ of government, it can only exercise those powers for the public benefit, and for identifiably 'governmental' purposes within limits set by the law.[26]

This expresses two of the central ideas in my account of the judicial review of non-statutory executive powers. First, notwithstanding analogies between the Crown and individuals, special considerations always apply to the Crown and its officials. Second, a proper analysis of the lawfulness of official actions always embraces an enquiry into the actor's 'power to act, as a matter of capacity' *and* the constraints that operate on that power.

Richards LJ, on the other hand, preferred a more typical 'third source' approach:

> I agree with Carnwath LJ's conclusions and with much of his reasoning. I do not, however, share his reservations about the extent of the common law powers of the Crown. As the first instance judge whose decision was upheld by the Court of Appeal in [*R (C)* v. *Secretary of State for Health*] I took a broad view of those powers, and nothing in the materials deployed before us in the present case has caused me to change my mind. The Court of Appeal's judgment in that case is not only determinative of the issue at this level [. . .] but was in my view correct.[27]

Explicit reference to the 'third source' was necessary to 'explain the basis on which that ordinary business of government is conducted', and the most straightforward explanation of that was the 'powers (or capacities and freedoms) of a corporation with legal personality' outside the traditional prerogative.[28] Crucially, Richards LJ accepted that 'such powers cannot override the rights of others and, when exercised by government, are subject to judicial review on ordinary public law grounds'; however, he disagreed with Carnwath LJ's addition of the

[26] *Shrewsbury and Atcham Borough Council* v. *Secretary of State for Communities and Local Government* [2008] EWCA Civ 148, [48] (Carnwath LJ). Emphasis mine.

[27] *Shrewsbury and Atcham Borough Council* v. *Secretary of State for Communities and Local Government* [2008] EWCA Civ 148, [72] (Richards LJ).

[28] *Shrewsbury and Atcham Borough Council* v. *Secretary of State for Communities and Local Government* [2008] EWCA Civ 148, [73] (Richards LJ).

qualification that they can only be exercised for the 'public benefit' and for 'identifiably governmental purposes'.[29]

For his part, Waller LJ opined that, once one accepts capacity, the limits of that capacity for the purposes of judicial review can only be by reference to the limits 'set by the law'; he declined to comment on the concrete question of constraints formulated in terms of 'public benefit' and 'identifiably governmental purposes'.[30] Again, all of this discussion between the Lords Justices was *obiter*. The Court of Appeal was in any case bound by its previous decision *R (C)* v. *Secretary of State for Health*; the controversy would have to wait for a House of Lords decision, as the resolution of the case did not require a firm answer one way or the other.[31]

Most recently, the Supreme Court considered the third source in *R (New London College Ltd)* v. *Home Secretary*.[32] This case concerned the conferral and removal of status of a higher education provider under the applicable Immigration Rules. Lord Sumption (with whom Lord Hope, Lord Clarke, and Lord Reed agreed) said that it had been 'long established that the Crown possesses some general administrative powers which are not exercises of the prerogative and do not require statutory authority'; however, Lord Sumption introduced a twist by advancing a novel theory of powers incidental to statutory powers as his preferred view:

> If the Secretary of State is entitled (as she plainly is) to prescribe and lay before Parliament rules for the grant or leave to enter or remain in the United Kingdom which depend on the migrant having a suitable sponsor, then she must also be entitled to take administrative measures for identifying sponsors who are and remain suitable, *even if these measures do not themselves fall within section 3(2) of the [Immigration Act 1971]*.[33]

Echoing arguments made about the third source, Lord Sumption opined that these incidental powers could not be used to impose coercive measures nor to infringe the legal rights of others or to act irrationally or unfairly 'or otherwise in conflict with the general constraints on

[29] *Shrewsbury and Atcham Borough Council* v. *Secretary of State for Communities and Local Government* [2008] EWCA Civ 148, [74] (Richards LJ).

[30] *Shrewsbury and Atcham Borough Council* v. *Secretary of State for Communities and Local Government* [2008] EWCA Civ 148, [80] (Waller LJ).

[31] *Shrewsbury and Atcham Borough Council* v. *Secretary of State for Communities and Local Government* [2008] EWCA Civ 148, [48] (Carnwath LJ).

[32] [2013] UKSC 51.

[33] *R (New London College Ltd)* v. *Home Secretary* [2013] UKSC 51, [29] (Lord Sumption).

administrative action imposed by public law'.[34] Lord Sumption's speech presents a novel category of non-statutory executive power, namely powers *incidental to* but not *implied from* statute.

Lord Carnwath agreed with the majority's ruling, but gave his own reasons. In essence, he reiterated his scepticism towards the 'third source' theory as set out in his speech in *Shrewsbury and Atcham Borough Council* v. *Secretary of State for Communities and Local Government.*[35] But he seemed rather more concerned with Lord Sumption's novel contrivance. Rightly, in my view, Lord Carnwath cited a line of authorities to the effect that incidental powers must be derived, if at all, from the construction of the statutory language said to confer and limit them.[36] In all the relevant cases, 'the source of the incidental power was found in a specific provision conferring specific functions'.[37] Some commentators have supported Lord Sumption's innovations;[38] with respect, while the Crown obviously has some implied statutory powers, the development of another category of non-statutory executive powers should be aborted.

For better or worse, both speeches in *R (New London College Ltd)* v. *Home Secretary* were, again, *obiter*, leaving English law in a state of uncertainty. On balance, we can say that the only binding English authority on the matter endorses the existence of a third source but takes a 'corporate common law powers' rather than a 'residual liberties' approach to non-prerogative non-statutory powers.

3.3 Home of the Third Source: New Zealand

The most direct support for the third source approach to non-statutory executive powers not associated with the Royal Prerogative is found in New Zealand. Two recent New Zealand Supreme Court cases, *R* v. *Ngan*[39] and *Hamed* v. *R*,[40] both dealing with video surveillance made

34 *R (New London College Ltd)* v. *Home Secretary* [2013] UKSC 51, [29] (Lord Sumption).

35 *R (New London College Ltd)* v. *Home Secretary* [2013] UKSC 51, [34] (Lord Carnwath).

36 *R (New London College Ltd)* v. *Home Secretary* [2013] UKSC 51, [35] (Lord Carnwath), citing *Hazell* v. *Hammersmith London Borough Council* [1992] 2 AC 1 and *Attorney General* v. *Great Eastern Railway Co* (1880) 5 App Cas 473.

37 *R (New London College Ltd)* v. *Home Secretary* [2013] UKSC 51, [36] (Lord Carnwath).

38 See, e.g., Paul Daly, 'Royal Treatment: The Crown's Special Status in Administrative Law' (2017) 22(1) *Review of Constitutional Studies* 81.

39 [2007] NZSC 105; [2008] 2 NZLR 48.

40 [2011] NZSC 101; [2012] 2 NZLR 305.

without statutory authorisation, provide support for the approach taken in *Malone* v. *Metropolitan Police Commissioner*.[41]

Hamed v. *R* is a long and complex case about police surveillance on Maori-owned land. Much of the case turned on the law governing warrants for search and seizure and the admissibility of improperly gathered evidence. There are numerous separate judgments, two of which deal with the third source question directly, albeit in *obiter* because the appeal was disposed of on admissibility grounds. Tipping J, citing *R* v. *Ngan*, opined that 'the police are entitled to do what any member of the public can lawfully do in the same circumstances'.[42] This amounts to a fairly clear endorsement of the third source as presented by B. V. Harris. Elias CJ's dissenting judgment is, in my view, more instructive, as it engages with the broader context of the question. Again, we see questions about the appropriateness of drawing conclusions from the liberties of private persons and the applicability of the reasoning in *R (Fewings)* v. *Somerset County Council* (about whether the default rule for public officials should be restrictive or permissive) in the context of non-statutory executive powers.

In short, Elias CJ opined that it was unlawful to undertake secret filming of people in the absence of lawfully prescribed authority.[43] The Chief Justice based her reasoning on the existence of a right against unreasonable search and seizure protected by s. 21 of the Bill of Rights Act 1990 (NZ). This statutory right goes further than the property-based common law rights that preceded it, thus distinguishing the situation from *Malone* v. *Police Commissioner* and making it analogous to *Entick* v. *Carrington*. Importantly, the statutory provision protects not only the privacy of the individual but also the 'constitutional balance between the State and citizen by preserving space for individual freedom and protection against unlawful and arbitrary intrusion by state agents'.[44] Elias CJ opined that a search must be authorised by law before it can be deemed 'reasonable' or not, and rejected the notion that police officers may 'act reasonably outside the law'.[45] The search would have been an 'actionable wrong' if undertaken by a private person.[46] However, she also stated

41 See *R* v. *Ngan* [2008] 2 NZLR 48, [46] (McGrath J).
42 *Hamed* v. *R* [2012] 2 NZLR 305, [217] (Tipping J).
43 *Hamed* v. *R* [2012] 2 NZLR 305, [9] (Elias CJ).
44 *Hamed* v. *R* [2012] 2 NZLR 305, [10] (Elias CJ).
45 *Hamed* v. *R* [2012] 2 NZLR 305, [19] (Elias CJ).
46 *Hamed* v. *R* [2012] 2 NZLR 305, [22] (Elias CJ). Her Honour cited in support *R* v. *Jefferies* [1994] 1 NZLR 290.

a wider principle, namely that the common law 'withholds from State agents the liberties preserved for individual citizens':[47]

> Public officials do not have freedom to act in any way they choose unless prohibited by law, as individual citizens do. The common law position in New Zealand and in the United Kingdom is that, except in matters within the prerogative or as is purely incidental to the exercise of statutory or prerogative powers, the executive and its servants must point to lawful authority for all actions undertaken. That constitutional principle of legality applies to the police surveillance undertaken here ... The principle is, as successive editions of *Halsbury's Laws of England* recognised, a necessary condition for the liberties of the subject ...[48]

Echoing Hale LJ's concerns in *R (C)* v. *Secretary of State for Health*, Elias CJ continued that where the subject is free to do anything not prohibited by law, 'public authorities (including the Crown) may do nothing but what they are authorised to do by some rule of common law (including the Royal Prerogative) or statute'.[49] The basic lack of equivalence between the subject and public authorities is a necessary condition of the liberties of the subject: 'Equivalent liberty for public authorities would destroy individual liberty'.[50]

Quake Outcasts v. *Minister for Canterbury Earthquake Recovery*[51] concerned the scope of lawful executive action in parallel to a special statutory regime.[52] Acting without reliance on any of the powers granted in the Canterbury Earthquake Recovery Act 2011 (NZ), the Prime Minister declared into existence a number of different 'zones', including a 'red zone' in which reconstruction was unlikely to be possible. The Chief Executive of the Canterbury Earthquake Reconstruction Authority, acting in the name of the Crown under a statutory authority, made offers to purchase properties in the red zone on differential terms, for example, depending on whether the land was developed or vacant.

A group of disgruntled red zone landowners challenged the decision to declare the zones; the 2011 Act contained a power to suspend the normal planning law zoning process, but that statutory power had not been

[47] *Hamed* v. *R* [2012] 2 NZLR 305, [23] (Elias CJ).

[48] *Hamed* v. *R* [2012] 2 NZLR 305, [24] (Elias CJ).

[49] *Hamed* v. *R* [2012] 2 NZLR 305, [24], [27]–[28] (Elias CJ). Citations omitted.

[50] *Hamed* v. *R* [2012] 2 NZLR 305, [28] (Elias CJ). Citations omitted.

[51] [2015] NZSC 27.

[52] Following an earthquake in 2010, the Canterbury Earthquake Response and Recovery Act 2010 (NZ) was passed and the Canterbury Earthquake Recovery Authority was established. A second earthquake in 2011 led to the Canterbury Earthquake Recovery Act 2011 (NZ).

exercised. The Prime Minister argued that the red zone was created in the exercise of the Crown's common law powers to 'publish information', for which no statutory authority was needed. The judicial review of the decision thus turned on (i) whether the red zone decision was a 'government decision authorised by common law or in terms of the so-called third source of power' and (ii) whether the 2011 Act covered the field. At first instance, Panckhurst J held that the creation and announcement of the red zone was much more than an exercise of the Crown's 'undoubted power to publish information'.[53] Thus, without needing to enter into the debate about the third source, he applied the test in *Attorney General* v. *De Keyser's Royal Hotel Ltd*, which governs the interaction of statute and non-statutory executive powers on the same field, and held that the decision ought to have been taken under the statutory regime.[54] The Court of Appeal reversed Pankhurst J's decision.[55] O'Regan P (with whom Ellen, France, and Stevens JJ agreed) held that the Crown could rely on a residual freedom as the juridical basis of the creation of the red zone.[56] The zoning decisions were merely the dissemination of information, did not affect the rights of the individuals and did not contravene the provisions of the 2011 Act or any other law.

The New Zealand Supreme Court upheld the judge's decision on appeal, but without necessarily contradicting the Court of Appeal's holding on the third source. Glazebrook J (with whom McGrath and Arnold JJ agreed) rejected the submission that the zoning decisions merely provided information to the public; they were *governmental decisions* on a number of important matters.[57] On the proper construction of the Act, and the proper characterisation of the decisions, they should have been taken under the Act following the *De Keyser* principle.[58] Elias CJ found that the matter could be disposed of without addressing the third source question,[59] and did not

[53] *Fowler Developments Limited* v. *The Chief Executive of the Canterbury Earthquake Recovery Authority* [2013] NZHC 2173, [60] (Panckhurst J).

[54] *Fowler Developments Limited* v. *The Chief Executive of the Canterbury Earthquake Recovery Authority* [2013] NZHC 2173, [68] (Panckhurst J).

[55] *Quake Outcasts* v. *Minister for Canterbury Earthquake Recovery* [2013] NZCA 588.

[56] *Quake Outcasts* v. *Minister for Canterbury Earthquake Recovery* [2013] NZCA 588, [108] (O'Regan P).

[57] *Quake Outcasts* v. *Minister for Canterbury Earthquake Recovery* [2013] NZCA 588, [106]–[107] (O'Regan P).

[58] *Quake Outcasts* v. *Minister for Canterbury Earthquake Recovery* [2013] NZCA 588, [146] (O'Regan P).

[59] *Quake Outcasts* v. *Minister for Canterbury Earthquake Recovery* [2013] NZCA 588, [275]–[276] (Elias CJ).

provide much further discussion of the existence or scope of the third source in this context. William Young J, in dissent, held that the Act covered only part of the relevant field, and that the Minister could therefore lawfully act in parallel.[60]

This leaves New Zealand law in a curious position. The New Zealand authorities lend considerable direct support for the third source theory as argued by Harris. The third source has been accepted to exist and to comprise a set of residual liberties, not legal powers. It is said to be impotent to affect the 'rights and liberties' of individuals, and is not derived from the Crown's nature as either a 'natural person' or a 'corporation sole'. Its limits are traced by common law and statutory constraints, it is subject to the *De Keyser* principle about the pre-emption of statute, and actions taken in reliance on it are amenable to judicial review on the ordinary grounds.

However, Elias CJ's dissent in *R* v. *Hamed* is somewhat at odds with the 'residual liberties' approach, and the majority's approach in *Quake Outcasts* v. *Minister for Canterbury Earthquake Recovery* restricts the scope of the third source by identifying the relevant action as 'taking a decision' rather than merely 'publishing information'.[61] Taking a decision would seem always to entail the exercise of a legal power, and any action that a Minister might pursue under the Crown's 'residual liberties' could be argued to rest on a decision. Elias CJ also laid emphasis on the background of potentially coercive legislative powers, which made the putative provision of information rather a statement of 'formally and announced Government policy'.[62] What scope for action the third source can really be said to provide in New Zealand law is therefore not clear.

3.4 Federations with a Written Constitution: Canada and Australia

Turning to the Canadian and Australian law, it is first necessary to note that the Crown is federated in both legal systems, but in slightly different ways, and that this can complicate the task of comparison.[63] For present

[60] *Quake Outcasts* v. *Minister for Canterbury Earthquake Recovery* [2013] NZCA 588, [340] (Elias CJ).

[61] *Quake Outcasts* v. *Minister for Canterbury Earthquake Recovery* [2013] NZCA 588, [190]–[191] (O'Regan P).

[62] *Quake Outcasts* v. *Minister for Canterbury Earthquake Recovery* [2013] NZCA 588, [283] (Elias CJ).

[63] '[W]ith questions arising in federal jurisdiction, one looks not to the content of the prerogative in Britain but rather to s. 61 of the Constitution'. *Re Ditfort; Ex parte Deputy Commissioner of Taxation* (1988) 19 FCR 347, 369 (Gummow J).

purposes, however, it is the nature of executive power *generally*, and not the distribution of executive power within a federal system, that is of interest. To the extent it is possible, therefore, I will bracket out the federal aspects of Australian and Canadian law to explore the taxonomy of non-statutory executive powers.

3.4.1 Canada

The first thing to observe is a degree of tension between the binary and ternary approaches to non-statutory executive powers in Canadian law. A number of the older cases endorse a kind of third source reasoning. In *Attorney General of Quebec* v. *Labrecque*,[64] for example, the Canadian Supreme Court identified 'the Crown' with the human being who is King or Queen and posited his or her natural capacities as a source of capacity to engage in private law acts such as contracting:

> [I]n Anglo-Canadian law, the relationship between a civil servant and his employer is not, strictly speaking, a relationship with an abstract being, the State: it is a relationship with a relatively more concrete entity, the Crown, which 'personifies the state' [...] but exercises only executive authority: s. 9 of the British North America Act, 1867. *The Crown is also the Sovereign, a physical person* who, in addition to the prerogative, enjoys a general capacity to contract in accordance with the rule of ordinary law. This general capacity to contract, like the prerogative, is also one of the attributes of the Crown in right of a province: [*Verreault & Fils v Attorney General of Quebec*]. Modern English law, hostile to the extension of the royal prerogative, is unwilling to use it to explain a legal situation which can just as well be explained by the general capacity of the Crown.[65]

A number of provincial appellate courts have adopted this 'natural person' approach to non-statutory executive powers, including the British Columbia Court of Appeal in *Pharmaceutical Manufacturers Association of Canada* v. *British Columbia (Attorney General).*[66] The Ontario Superior Court of Justice, on the other hand, has held that only the binary approach is consistent with the modern position that all of non-statutory executive powers are reviewable. In *McDonald* v. *Anishinabek Police Service*,[67] Lane, Greer and Lax JJ referred to the

[64] [1980] SCR 1057.

[65] *Attorney General of Quebec* v. *Labrecque* [1980] SCR 1057, 1082 (Beetz J), citing [*Verreault & Fils* v. *Attorney General of Quebec* 1977] 1 SCR 41. Emphasis mine.

[66] *Pharmaceutical Manufacturers Association of Canada* v. *British Columbia (Attorney General)* (1997) 149 DLR (4th) 613, [47] (Newbury J).

[67] (2006) 83 OR (3d) 132 (Sup Ct J (Div Ct)).

Supreme Court case of *Black* v. *Canada (Prime Minister)*,[68] which had clearly established that the prerogative power was subject to judicial review. The reviewability of 'prerogative' and non-prerogative non-statutory executive powers meant that Blackstone's distinction was one without a difference.

McDonald v. *Ashinabek Police Service* concerned the status and employment of a police officer whose training had been terminated with an apparent breach of natural justice. The decision by the public authority could plausibly have been characterised as an exercise of prerogative power or the 'natural person powers' of the Crown (as an employer). Holding that the 'employment' of a public official is inherently a matter for judicial review, the Superior Court of Justice noted the disagreement in the literature:

> Some commentators take the view that prerogative powers consist only of powers that are unique to the Crown and do not include powers that are equally enjoyed by private persons – such as the power to enter into contracts. Other commentators take the view that every executive act taken without the authority of an Act of Parliament is done pursuant to Crown prerogative. It is the latter view that is compatible with [*R (Lain) v Criminal Injuries Compensation Board*] where a criminal injuries compensation board was treated as established by prerogative powers, despite the fact that a private citizen is equally empowered to make gratuitous payments to victims of crime.[69]

This speech highlights a fact that some judges elsewhere appear to have overlooked; *R (Lain)* v. *Criminal Injuries Compensation Board*, which established the reviewability of non-statutory executive powers, was implicitly taken by the judges to have been an exercise of the Crown's prerogative powers.[70] (Given what we now know about the Ram Memorandum, it is possible that HM Government considered it rather a scheme taken under the 'Ram Doctrine', i.e., under the 'third source'.) The more important point is that the amenability of both prerogative-type and third source-type powers to judicial review undermines the whole point of the ternary approach:

> Ultimately ... the distinction between prerogative powers and natural person powers may be of little import, as in the view of Lord Diplock in

[68] (2001) 199 DLR (4th) 228.

[69] *McDonald* v. *Anishinabek Police Service* (2006) 83 OR (3d) 132 (Sup Ct J (Div Ct)), [65]–[67].

[70] See also Philip Sales, 'Crown Powers, the Royal Prerogative and Fundamental Rights' in Hanna Wilberg and Mark Elliott (eds.), *The Scope and Intensity of Substantive Review* (Hart 2015), 369.

> *Council of Civil Service Unions v Minister for the Civil Service*, there is no practical significance to the distinction between prerogative powers and natural person powers since, in either case, the power is reviewable by the court.[71]

In the more recent *Canada (Prime Minister)* v. *Khadr*,[72] the Supreme Court expressly endorsed a Diceyan definition: 'The prerogative power is the "residue of discretionary or arbitrary authority, which at any given time is legally left in the hands of the Crown" . . . It is a limited source of non-statutory administrative power accorded by the common law to the Crown'.[73] From this, it would seem that the modern position in Canada must be that there is only one category of non-statutory executive powers, which is called the prerogative.

However, the Supreme Court did not rule expressly on the 'general capacity' question. In *Canadian Doctors for Refugee Care* v. *Canada*,[74] the Federal Court (taking note of *Canada (Prime Minister)* v. *Khadr*) Mactavish J adopted a kind of ternary approach, citing *Pharmaceutical Manufacturers Association of Canada* v. *British Columbia (Attorney General)* and a scholarly treatise endorsing the 'natural person powers' approach.[75] Thus, Paul Daly, despite disclaiming any attempt to 'lay out a taxonomy of Crown powers',[76] has argued that 'it is clear that the Crown in Canada benefits from some inherent powers that are not granted by statute and do not necessarily reside in the royal prerogative' because the Crown 'has the capacities of a natural person and, as such, can do those things that a natural person can do'.[77] However, Mactavish J in that case also endorsed the reasoning that there is no practical difference between prerogative and 'natural person powers', and the

[71] *McDonald* v. *Anishinabek Police Service* (2006) 83 OR (3d) 132 (Sup Ct J (Div Ct)), [65]–[67], citing *Council of Civil Service Unions* v. *Minister for the Civil Service* [1984] 3 All ER 935.

[72] [2010] 1 SCR 44.

[73] *Canada (Prime Minister)* v. *Khadr* [2010] 1 SCR 44, [34] (McLachlin CJ, Binnie, LeBel, Deschamps, Fish, Abella, Charron, Rothstein, and Cromwell JJ) citing *Reference as to the Effect of the Exercise of the Royal Prerogative of Mercy Upon Deportation Proceedings* [1933] SCR 269, 272 (Duff CJ).

[74] (2014) FC 651.

[75] See *Canadian Doctors for Refugee Care* v. *Canada* (2014) FC 651, [392], citing Peter Hogg, *Constitutional Law of Canada* (5th ed., Carswell 2007).

[76] Paul Daly, 'Royal Treatment: The Crown's Special Status in Administrative Law' (2017) 22 *Review of Constitutional Studies* 81, 83.

[77] Paul Daly, 'Royal Treatment: The Crown's Special Status in Administrative Law' (2017) 22 *Review of Constitutional Studies* 81, 86.

balance of the judgment actually speaks of 'natural person powers' as part of the Crown's 'prerogative powers'.[78]

The position in Canada is thus not completely straightforward, but could be summarised as follows. Powers outside the historical 'high' prerogative powers are accepted to exist in Canada, but there is disagreement regarding how they fit within the broader scheme. A tension between Dicey and Blackstone is frequently noted, and most Canadian judges seem to prefer Dicey's binary approach. In fact, this would seem to be the irresistible effect of Canadian Supreme Court authority. Whatever echoes of Blackstone remain, 'natural person powers' are treated rather more like 'common law powers' than 'residual liberties' and are effectively assimilated to the Royal Prerogative because nothing turns on the distinction for the purposes of judicial review.

3.4.2 Australia

In Australia, s. 61 of the Australian Constitution Act 1900 (Imp) provides that '[t]he executive power of the Commonwealth is vested in the Queen and is exercisable by the Governor General as the Queen's representative, and extends to the execution and maintenance of this Constitution, and of the laws of the Commonwealth'. The exact meaning of this provision is not always clear, may depend on the context, and has probably changed over time. Australian jurisprudence has cut its own path, particularly since the 1980s, and references to the Crown are less frequent now than they were in the past.[79] For present purposes, the main import of s. 61 is that 'the executive power of the Commonwealth extends to the execution and maintenance of [the] Constitution, and of the laws of the Commonwealth' rather than the federal aspects of the role of the Governor General.[80] In this respect, Isaacs J observed in *Commonwealth* v. *Colonial Combing, Spinning and Weaving Co Ltd*[81] that s. 61 'marks the external boundaries of the Commonwealth executive power, so far as it is conferred by the Constitution, but it leaves entirely untouched the definition of that power and its ascertainment in any

[78] See *Canadian Doctors for Refugee Care* v. *Canada* (2014) FC 651, [392].

[79] Cheryl Saunders, 'The Concept of the Crown' (2015) 38 *Melbourne University Law Review* 873, 890–892.

[80] See Martin Hinton and Sue Milne, 'The Executive Power' in Martin Hinton and J. M. Williams (eds.), *The Crown: Essays on its Manifestation, Power and Accountability* (University of Adelaide Press 2018), 153.

[81] (1922) 31 CLR 421.

case'.[82] That is largely a matter of the common law against the background of which the Australia Constitution was drafted.[83] According to Gageler J in *Plaintiff M68/2015* v. *Minister for Immigration and Border Protection*:[84]

> The nature of Commonwealth executive power can only be understood within that historical and structural constitutional context. It is described – not defined – in s. 61 of the Constitution, in that it is extended – not confined – by that section to the 'execution and maintenance' of the Constitution and of laws of the Commonwealth. It is therefore 'barren ground for any analytical approach'. Alfred Deakin said of it in a profound opinion which he gave as Attorney-General in 1902 that 'it would be dangerous, if not impossible, to define', emphasising that it 'is administrative, as well as in the strict sense executive; that is to say, it must obviously include the power not only to execute laws, but also to effectively administer the whole Government'.[85]

Earlier Australian High Court decisions endorsed a narrow concept of 'the prerogative' nested within a broader category of executive powers. This reflects a broadly Blackstonian view, without, however, the requirement of 'legal effect'.[86] The early case of *Clough* v. *Leahy*,[87] for example, turned on the lawfulness of a Royal Enquiry into a matter that had already been the subject of an adjudication in an industrial Arbitration Commission. Griffith CJ reasoned that it was within the powers of an individual to make what enquiries he can, and that '[t]hat which is lawful to an individual can surely not be denied to the Crown'.[88] In *New South Wales* v. *Bardolph*,[89] Evatt J observed that the King had doubtless enjoyed

[82] *Commonwealth* v. *Colonial Combing, Spinning and Weaving Co Ltd* (1922) 31 CLR 421, 437.

[83] See Peter Gerangelos, 'Section 61 of the *Commonwealth Constitution* and an "Historical Constitutional Approach": An Excursus on Justice Gageler's Reasoning in the *M68* Case' (2018) 43(2) *University of Western Australia Law Review* 103.

[84] [2016] HCA 1.

[85] *Plaintiff M68/2015* v. *Minister for Immigration and Border Protection* [2016] HCA 1, [129], citing Leslie Zines, 'The Inherent Power of the Commonwealth' (2005) 16(4) *Public Law Review* 279 and Sir Alfred Deakin, 'Channel of Communication with Imperial Government: Position of Consuls: Executive Power of Commonwealth' in Patrick Brazil and Bevan Mitchell (eds.), *Opinions of Attorneys-General of the Commonwealth of Australia, Vol. 1: 1901–14* (Australian Government Publishing Service 1981), 130.

[86] Cheryl Saunders, 'The Concept of the Crown' (2015) 38 *Melbourne University Law Review* 873, 891.

[87] (1904) 2 CLR 139.

[88] *Clough* v. *Leahy* (1904) 2 CLR 139, 157.

[89] (1934) 52 CLR 455.

'special powers, privileges, immunities and prerogatives' but that 'he never seems to have been regarded as being less powerful to enter into contracts than one of his subjects'.[90] In *Victoria* v. *Australian Building Construction Employees' and Builders Labourers' Federation*,[91] Brennan J expressed agreement with Griffith CJ's approach in *Clough* v. *Leahy*, citing Blackstone,[92] but harboured doubts about the appropriateness of the analogy between the citizen's rights to ask questions and the Crown's rights to appoint a commission of inquiry. Nevertheless, in *Davis* v. *Commonwealth*[93] Brennan J accepted a distinction between prerogative powers as such and the 'capacities' of the Commonwealth Government that are also held by ordinary citizens. This distinction has been described as 'orthodox' in Australian law.[94]

However, to the extent that the third source is recognised in the Australian cases, it is generally grounded not by references to the Crown or to the Queen as a natural person, but to the nature of the Commonwealth of Australia as a political community.[95]

The leading modern case is *Williams* v. *Commonwealth (No 1)*.[96] Before turning to that case, however, it is convenient to notice another unique feature of the Australian jurisprudence, which is the introduction of an additional subcategory of non-statutory executive powers. In the *Communist Party of Australia* v. *Commonwealth*,[97] *Victoria* v. *Commonwealth*,[98] and *Pape* v. *Commissioner of Taxation*,[99] Australian judges have advanced the idea of a 'nationhood power' as a category of Commonwealth executive power. Expressed in various ways, the idea is one of an inherent power to do the kind of thing necessary for the maintenance of an organised political community. For reasons I explain

90 *New South Wales* v. *Bardolph* (1934) 52 CLR 455, 475.

91 (1982) 152 CLR 25.

92 *Victoria* v. *Australian Building Construction Employees' and Builders Labourers' Federation* (1982) 152 CLR 25, [17]. Brennan J criticized the 'wide and potentially-question begging' definition of prerogative set out in Andrew Inglis Clark, *Studies in Australian Constitutional Law* (2nd ed., Maxwell 1905), 235.

93 (1988) 166 CLR 79.

94 Simon Evans, 'Continuity and Flexibility: Executive Power in Australia' in Paul Craig and Adam Tomkins (eds.), *The Executive and Public Law: Power and Accountability in Comparative Perspective* (Oxford University Press 2006), 89, 93.

95 Cheryl Saunders, 'The Concept of the Crown' (2015) 38 *Melbourne University Law Review* 873, 892.

96 (2012) 248 CLR 156.

97 (1951) 83 CLR 1.

98 (1975) 134 CLR 338.

99 (2009) 238 CLR 1.

in Chapter 4, however, to the extent it exists, the nationhood power should be assimilated to the overarching category of 'non-statutory executive powers'.

Pape v. *Commissioner for Taxation* is also important for its impact on the understanding of executive powers generally. The case concerned *ex gratia* payments made as part of an economic stimulus package in response to the 2008–2009 global financial crisis. French CJ provided a kind of taxonomy of the non-statutory executive powers embraced by s. 61. The 'executive power of the Commonwealth' vested by that section in the Queen encompassed (i) statutory powers;[100] (ii) the prerogative (on a Blackstonian definition); (iii) the legal capacities of the Commonwealth, such as the power to contract; and (iv) some 'inherent' power to respond to exigent circumstances.[101] The spending in question was upheld under the fourth category.

Williams v. *Commonwealth (No 1)* concerned a set of contracts between the Commonwealth Government and a company offering school chaplaincy services. These contracts were challenged on the basis that they were ultra vires the Commonwealth Government. The Commonwealth made two primary submissions relating to s. 61, one broader and one narrower.[102] The broad submission will, by now, be familiar: the capacities of the executive were analogous to the juristic powers of an ordinary legal person, and were therefore effectively unlimited in scope, provided only that they did not interfere with the legal rights and duties of others. The narrower submission was that the scope of the Commonwealth Government's executive power under s. 61 extended at least to things covered by express grants of legislative power in the Constitution, even if legislation had not actually been passed under those heads of power. The latter submission was addressed primarily in terms of federal concerns,[103] rather than in more general terms of pre-emption of the legislature (as we have seen in the United Kingdom

[100] In particular, powers conferred on the Commonwealth Government by the Commonwealth Parliament; whether the State Parliaments can confer powers on the Commonwealth Government goes beyond the present enquiry.

[101] See *Pape* v. *Commissioner for Taxation* (2009) 238 CLR 1, [126] and following.

[102] See Shipra Chordia, Andrew Lynch, and George Williams, '*Williams v Commonwealth*: Commonwealth Executive Power and Australian Federalism' (2013) 37 *Melbourne University Law Review* 189, 199.

[103] See Shipra Chordia, Andrew Lynch, and George Williams, '*Williams v Commonwealth*: Commonwealth Executive Power and Australian Federalism' (2013) 37 *Melbourne University Law Review* 189, 203–207.

and New Zealand). The broad submission is more relevant to the taxonomic question.

The multiple judgments in *Williams* v. *Commonwealth (No 1)* are long and complex. They have been summarised elsewhere.[104] It is perhaps telling that the court in *Williams* v. *Commonwealth (No 2)*,[105] considering saving legislation for impugned scheme, did not clearly state the *ratio* of *Williams* v. *Commonwealth (No 1)*.[106] Generally, the reasons are bound up with the structure of the Australian Constitution and the federal system. In my summary, I will focus on the 'third source question', even at the risk of missing issues such as the relation between legislative heads of power and executive power in the Australian Constitution.[107]

In short, the High Court generally endorsed a non-binary approach to executive power, but none of the judges accepted that the Commonwealth Government could 'do anything a natural person could do', and all judgments characterised non-prerogative non-statutory executive powers as 'powers' rather than 'residual liberties'.[108] French CJ elaborated on his scheme in *Pape* v. *Commissioner of Taxation*, holding that s. 61 embraces (i) powers necessary or incidental to the execution and maintenance of a law of the Commonwealth; (ii) powers conferred on the Commonwealth by statute; (iii) powers defined by reference to such of the prerogatives of the Crown as are properly attributable to the Commonwealth; (iv) powers defined by the capacities of the Commonwealth common to legal persons; (v) inherent authority derived from the character and status of the Commonwealth as the national government.[109] Gummow and Bell JJ criticised 'assimilation of the executive branch to a natural person and other entities with legal

[104] See also Geoffrey Lindell, 'The Changed Landscape of the Executive Power of the Commonwealth after the *Williams* Case' (2013) 39(2) *Monash University Law Review* 348.

[105] (2014) 252 CLR 416.

[106] See Will Bateman, *Public Finance and Parliamentary Constitutionalism* (Cambridge University Press 2020), Ch 8.

[107] The questions are entangled if one approaches them from the perspective of an entrenched federal distribution of powers: See *Williams* v. *Commonwealth (No 1)* (2012) 248 CLR 156, [373] (Kiefel J).

[108] *Williams* v. *Commonwealth (No 1)* (2012) 248 CLR 156, [193] (French CJ), [238] (Gummow and Bell JJ), [253] (Hayne J) [320] (Heydon J, in dissent), [352] (Crennan J), [373] (Kiefel J).

[109] See *Williams* v. *Commonwealth (No 1)* (2012) 248 CLR 156, [184] (French CJ); Cameron Moore, *Crown and Sword: Executive Power and the Use of Force by the Australian Defence Force* (Australian National University Press 2017), 35.

personality'.[110] This does not exclude a 'third source' based otherwise than on the analogy to natural persons, however. Crennan J endorsed a trichotomy of statutory, prerogative, and third source powers, the latter comprising 'powers which derive from the capacities of the Commonwealth as a juristic person, such as the capacities to enter a contract and to spend money'.[111]

The most interesting judgment, in my view, is that of Hayne J. The Commonwealth submission implied that, because the Commonwealth has 'some *contractual* and *dispositive* "capacity," it had power to act as it did in this case'; this argument 'conflated the question of contractual and dispositive capacity (in the sense of absence of disability) with the question of whether there was power [in the Commonwealth] to enter into the contract and make the payments in issue'.[112] It was unhelpful to talk about 'capacities' except in the sense of 'powers'. Hayne J went on to criticise the straightforward analogy with individuals in forceful terms:

> It is not to be assumed, and was not demonstrated, that the Executive Government of the Commonwealth has all of the capacities – in the sense of powers – to contract and spend that a natural person has. There is no basis in law for attributing human attitudes, form, or personality either to the federal polity that was created by the Constitution or, as the Commonwealth parties sought to do, to one branch of the government of that polity – the Executive. The argument asserting that the Executive Government of the Commonwealth should be assumed to have the same capacities to spend and make contracts as a natural person was no more than a particular form of anthropomorphism writ large. It was an argument that sought to endow an artificial person with human characteristics. The dangers of doing that are self-evident.[113]

Hayne J also provided an instructive gloss on the classical Australian case of *Clough* v. *Leahy*. That case was concerned with the action of an 'officer of the State', and Griffith CJ's judgment was merely recognising that an organised polity acts through individuals; an officer of the Commonwealth Government was not somehow prevented, when 'acting for the Crown', from undertaking something he was otherwise free to do. So much was evident, according to Hayne J, from the reference to 'the advisers of the Crown' getting information. In short, '[c]ontrary to the submissions of the Commonwealth parties and the fourth defendant,

110 *Williams* v. *Commonwealth (No 1)* (2012) 248 CLR 156, [237].
111 *Williams* v. *Commonwealth (No 1)* (2012) 248 CLR 156, [342].
112 *Williams* v. *Commonwealth (No 1)* (2012) 248 CLR 156, [203]. Emphasis mine.
113 *Williams* v. *Commonwealth (No 1)* (2012) 248 CLR 156, [204].

Clough does not stand for a general proposition that a polity, or the Commonwealth in particular, has the same powers or capacities as a natural person'.[114] While Hayne J's analysis does not, with respect, advance a sufficient concept of office and official action, it points to the role that office *could* play in reasoning through difficult questions of 'power' and 'capacity' in the context of an abstract entity that 'acts' with human hands and feet.

Most recently, in *Plaintiff M68/2015* v. *Minister for Immigration and Border Protection*, Gageler J presented an extensive review of the nature of executive power in Australian law, and introduced a variant of the ternary approach. Starting from the need to understand s. 61 of the Australian Constitution, he expressly endorsed Brennan J's approach in *Davis* v. *Commonwealth* by which executive power falls into three categories: (i) statutory powers, (ii) 'non-statutory prerogative powers', and (iii) non-statutory, non-prerogative powers or 'capacities':[115]

> The tripartite categorisation posited by Brennan J has utility in highlighting, in relation to acts done in the exercise of a non-statutory power or capacity, the essential difference between an act done in the execution of a prerogative executive power and an act done in the execution of a non-prerogative executive capacity. An act done in the execution of a prerogative executive power is an act which is capable of interfering with legal rights of others. An act done in the execution of a non-prerogative executive capacity, in contrast, involves nothing more than the utilisation of a *bare capacity or permission*, which can also be described as ability to act or as a 'faculty'. Such effects as the act might have on legal rights or juridical relations result not from the act being uniquely that of the Executive Government but from the application to the act of the same substantive law as would be applicable in respect of the act had it been done by any other actor. In this respect, the Executive Government 'is affected by the condition of the general law'. Subject to statute, and to the limited extent to which the operation of the common law accommodates to the continued existence of 'those rights and capacities which the King enjoys alone' and which are therefore properly to be categorised as prerogative, the Executive Government must take the civil and criminal law as the Executive Government finds it, and must suffer the civil and criminal consequences of any breach.[116]

[114] *Williams* v. *Commonwealth (No 1)* (2012) 248 CLR 156, [257]–[258].

[115] *Plaintiff M68/2015* v. *Minister for Immigration and Border Protection* (2016) 257 CLR 42, [132], citing *Davis* v. *The Commonwealth* (1988) 166 CLR 79, 108 (Brennan J).

[116] *Plaintiff M68/2015* v. *Minister for Immigration and Border Protection* (2016) 257 CLR 42, [135]–[136]. Citations omitted, emphasis mine.

The absence of a prohibition does not equate to the existence of a capacity; there is a *deontic* and a *capacitative* question to be answered before any proposition can be made about the range of lawful actions open to a Crown official in any given situation. This point is complicated by the frame of analysis in Australian law, following George Winterton, of the 'breadth' and 'depth' of s. 61.[117] In Gageler J's words, 'breadth' refers to the subject matters of Commonwealth (i.e., federal executive government) competence in the Australian system, and 'depth' refers to type of actions which the Commonwealth is empowered to undertake in relation to those subject matters.[118] I am not concerned with the federal question here, and I will introduce my own 'spatial metaphor' in due course, so this is not a frame of analysis that I will adopt.

In summary, then, the modern Australian position can be taken to accept some kind of 'third source' besides statute and the traditional prerogative, albeit generally couched in terms of 'powers' rather than 'capacities' and couched in terms of the juristic qualities of an organised political community ('polity'), not the Crown as a natural person or corporation sole. The notion of a set of 'residual liberties' analogous to those of an individual appears not to be part of Australian law.

3.5 Conclusion

This review of the authorities has shown that the courts have not settled on a stable position – in any jurisdiction – regarding the taxonomy of non-statutory executive powers. Even in Australia and New Zealand, where there seems to be a greater degree of judicial consensus, a number of basic questions subsist. However, we can see a broadly similar set of questions being worked out in all the jurisdictions. These questions could be posed as follows under four heads.

First, do we adopt a binary or a ternary conception of the category of 'non-statutory executive power'? We have seen that many judges, in particular, seem to prefer a binary approach, but that the notion of a third source is resilient – in certain contexts it is perhaps irresistible.

Secondly, how do we accommodate non-prerogative non-statutory powers into our scheme? This question is closely related to the first. In particular, we are concerned with (i) exercises of mundane, general law

117 George Winterton, *Parliament, the Executive and the Governor-General* (Melbourne University Press 1983), 29, 111.

118 *Plaintiff M68/2015* v. *Minister for Immigration and Border Protection* (2016) 257 CLR 42, [130] (Gageler J).

legal powers (such as the power to contract) and (ii) actions that are not obviously the exercise of a legal power at all (such as disseminating information). If a ternary conception of executive power is adopted, these legal powers and 'capacities' present a third source; if a binary conception as adopted, they would appear as a subcategory of 'prerogative powers' (to the extent that category is useful as a descriptor itself).

Thirdly, accepting that something outside the historical prerogative exists, is it properly seen as a set of 'common law powers' or 'residual liberties'?

Fourthly, whether a binary or ternary view is adopted, and agnostic to the question of 'powers' *versus* 'liberties', what is the source of this category of executive powers? In particular, are they a consequence of the fact that (i) the Queen is a natural person; (ii) officers of the Crown other than the Queen are natural persons; (iii) the Crown is a corporation ('sole' or 'aggregate'); or (iv) the organs of an organised political community have some kind of inherent capacities?

These questions, so posed, can form quite a thicket. If one chooses the wrong entry-point, analysis can be strangled by technical foreclosures. In my view, they are most usefully addressed by asking three preliminary questions. *First*, what kind of entity is the Crown, and how do we take it as an acting subject? *Secondly*, what is the relationship between the Crown, its officials, and the organised political community (what I shall call the 'small c' commonwealth.) *Thirdly*, how does the Crown act (through its officials)?

Questions relating to the personality of the Crown, the concept of office, and the deontic and operational logic necessary to explain official action are highly technical. For this reason, perhaps, they are often lost by the wayside. The challenge for this book is to adopt a taxonomy of executive power that does not presuppose too much at the outset, such that these questions can be reasoned through systematically. It is to that task that I now turn. The overriding question in constructing that taxonomy is: What (if anything) makes a difference to the grounds, or to the conceptual and normative justification, of the judicial review of non-statutory executive powers?

4

A Unified Category of 'Non-Statutory Executive Powers'

4.1 Introduction

Statutory powers are by nature clearly enumerated and conceptually rooted in the representative nature of our democratic legislatures. Non-statutory executive powers are more troublesome – they raise difficult questions about the personality of the Crown, the concept of office, and the logic of official action and suffer a kind of democratic deficit. We have surveyed a number of divergent approaches, but no clear position emerges from the cases. This underlines the existence of a gap between theory and practice in the law of judicial review, and demonstrates that it is important to define our subject-matter carefully to avoid question-begging and talking at cross purposes. To bridge this gap, we need a framework to explain how the Crown and its officials act beyond statute that (i) reflects the modern judicial practice of universal amenability on unified grounds and (ii) does not beg any of the basic questions identified in the previous chapter.

This chapter sets out the very simple taxonomy that will frame discussion in the rest of this book. Some commentators have lamented the cleavage of theories about non-prerogative non-statutory powers into a 'third source' camp and a 'common law powers' camp.[1] Ultimately, I will argue that the third source camp, as understood by its adherents, should be abandoned. It is an unhelpful category that misdirects analysis and so hinders debate about a vitally important head of governmental power. Further, the distinction between the Royal Prerogative and the Crown's (other) 'common law powers' is not as important as it first appears – at least for the law of judicial review. In other words, the structure of our taxonomy must be driven by the *how* and *why* of judicial review.

[1] See Jeff Simpson, 'The Third Source of Authority for Government Action Misconceived' (2012) 18 *Auckland University Law Review* 86, 87.

My taxonomy comprises (i) statutory executive powers and (ii) non-statutory executive powers. Some non-statutory executive powers are associated with the historical prerogative, others are not. The 'third source' is a set of common law legal powers, based in the Crown's legal personality as a common law corporation. It is sometimes helpful to distinguish these common law powers from the common law powers associated with the Royal Prerogative heuristically, and I will therefore continue to use 'prerogative-type powers' and 'third source-type powers' as labels of convenience, but they are reviewable on the same grounds for the same reasons.

Section 4.2 frames the problem and argues that the touchstone must be how and why non-statutory executive powers are reviewable. Section 4.3 explains the limited importance of the Royal Prerogative in the exercise that lies before us, and why we should rather describe the common law powers of the Crown as simply 'non-statutory executive powers'. Section 4.4 sets out some criticisms of the ternary view, with a focus on the influential account of Sir William Wade, which introduces the major themes in Chapter 5, Chapter 6, and Chapter 7.

4.2 A Unified Category of Non-statutory Executive Powers

Taxonomies are schemes of classification that organise complex phenomena, ultimately choosing heuristic cleavage points for some given purpose. The purpose of this book is to develop a theory of the judicial review of non-statutory executive powers. In this, the criterion of amenability to review must be the driving consideration in developing a taxonomy of executive powers. In *MacDonald* v. *Ashinabek Police Service*,[2] Lane, Greer, and Lax JJ of the Ontario Superior Court of Justice rightly held that Blackstone's distinction between 'prerogative powers' and 'natural person powers' was of little import in light of the fact that, following *Council of Civil Service Unions* v. *Minister for the Civil Service*,[3] both categories of power are clearly amenable to judicial review.[4]

A similar position emerges, in the end, from Wade's various writings. Wade seems to have been pulled in different directions over the decades. Prior to *Council of Civil Service Unions* v. *Minister for the Civil Service*, the label of 'prerogative' was a bar to judicial review. At that time, a restrictive

[2] (2006) 83 OR (3d) 132.
[3] [1984] 3 All ER 935.
[4] *MacDonald* v. *Ashinabek Police Service* (2006) 83 OR (3d) 132, [67].

definition to the 'true' prerogative entailed a more expansive supervisory jurisdiction, so Wade's narrow definition of the 'prerogative' might well have been motivated by a desire for the broadest possible doctrine of amenability. On the other hand, Wade adhered to the 'traditional' ultra vires theory throughout his career; he thought judicial review was only justifiable by reference to legislative intent, and that developments in the latter twentieth century had brought the supervisory jurisdiction outside its logical boundaries.[5] In any case, a clear shift is observable in his position. Initially, Wade argued that the 'genuine' prerogative powers should *not* be reviewable, but that the Crown's non-prerogative non-statutory powers *should* be.[6] Some years later, Wade argued that it might be easier to extend the supervisory jurisdiction 'to the few genuine prerogative powers' if the court were not, by the same token, committed to review 'all sorts of pretended prerogatives'.[7]

Ultimately, Wade conceded the point that, for the purposes of judicial review, there is no meaningful difference between the 'prerogative' (defined in his narrow terms) and the Crown's other non-statutory executive powers. Alerting to the sympathetic, if non-committal, judicial reception of his gloss on Blackstone, Wade observed in the late 1990s:

> My comments were made purely for the purposes of terminological accuracy, *without any suggestion that they had legal consequences.* The House of Lords' [*Council of Civil Service Unions v Minister for the Civil Service*] decision may, indeed, be regarded as ruling out the distinction Blackstone made, particularly in its insistence on the irrelevance of the source of the power.[8]

Terminological accuracy is indeed crucial, but terminological distinctions are important *only because* they have consequences for the conceptual foundations and/or doctrinal structure of the supervisory jurisdiction. It is surely the case that prerogative-type and third source-type non-statutory executive powers are reviewable for the same reasons and on the same grounds. Reviewing the historical development of non-statutory executive powers, Sir Philip Sales has rightly observed the tendency of the different

[5] H. W. R. Wade, 'Judicial Review of Ministerial Guidance' (1986) 102 *Law Quarterly Review* 173, 175, commenting on *Gillick* v. *West Norfolk and Wisbech Area Health Authority* [1986] AC 112.

[6] H. W. R. Wade, 'Procedure and Prerogative in Administrative Law' (1985) 101 *Law Quarterly Review* 180, 198.

[7] H. W. R. Wade, *Constitutional Fundamentals* (Rev. ed., Stevens 1989), 62.

[8] Sir William Wade, 'The Crown, Ministers and Officials: Legal Status and Liability' in Maurice Sunkin and Sebastian Payne (eds.), *The Nature of the Crown* (Oxford University Press 1998), 31. Emphasis mine.

forms of Crown powers to run into each other and overlap in their function and effect: 'It makes it difficult to sustain an argument that there should be any radically different approach to the standards of control to be applied by the courts in relation to the different powers'.[9] The various types of power are, increasingly, seen as different aspects of public power wielded by the Crown as a 'cipher for the state'. Indeed, although the theoretical basis for their application has not been spelled out, there is 'no serious suggestion' that the 'general ordinary principles of judicial review' do not apply to third source-type powers.[10]

The *summa divisio* in my conceptual scheme is therefore the distinction between powers reposed in the Crown and its officials by *parliamentary legislation* and powers reposed in the Crown by the *common law*. The 'general law powers', 'capacities', and apparent 'liberties' of the Crown fall naturally into the latter category. How they relate to the Royal Prerogative is a secondary question with few implications for the theory or practice of their judicial review.

The characterisation of 'powers', 'capacities', 'residual liberties', etc., requires a logic of deontic relations and legal operations (i.e., acts-in-the-law) that applies across all categories of executive power. As we have seen, however, the logic implicit in discussions of 'power' and 'liberty' in the cases and commentary are generally deficient. I will argue that the Crown can only act through its human officials; every action by (that is, *attributed to*) the Crown is the exercise of a 'legal power' by some official.

4.2.1 Bracketing Out the 'Nationhood Power'

It is convenient to bracket out one strand of thought that I will not develop further in this book – the Australian 'nationhood power'. As we have seen, there is a tendency in the Australian cases and literature to approach non-statutory executive powers as an incident of the Commonwealth of Australia as an 'organised polity', rather than as an incident of the Crown's legal personality. In *Williams* v. *Commonwealth (No 1)*,[11] for example, French CJ distinguished 'that aspect of the executive power

[9] Sir Philip Sales, 'Crown Powers, the Royal Prerogative and Fundamental Rights' in Hanna Wilberg and Mark Elliott (eds.), *The Scope and Intensity of Substantive Review* (Hart 2015), 369.

[10] Sir Philip Sales, 'Crown Powers, the Royal Prerogative and Fundamental Rights' in Hanna Wilberg and Mark Elliott (eds.), *The Scope and Intensity of Substantive Review* (Hart 2015), 378.

[11] (2012) 248 CLR 156.

which derives its content from the prerogatives of the Crown' from 'that aspect defined by reference to the capacities which the Commonwealth has in common with juristic persons'.[12] The Commonwealth Government should not be treated as a separate legal actor, however: 'the executive power of the Commonwealth is to be understood as a reference to that power exercised by the Commonwealth as a polity through the executive branch of its government'; it would be 'an error to treat the Commonwealth Executive as a separate juristic person'.[13]

With respect, I can see no way that the 'Commonwealth Executive' could be understood to wield the power of the 'Commonwealth as a polity' without treating it as a separate juristic person, and I see no authentic way of describing the powers of that juristic person without reference to the legal conceptions of the Crown that Australian law has received. My reasons will emerge over the course of this chapter and Chapter 5. As with so many modern approaches, this analysis does not incorporate an adequate concept of office.

Recent authorities may signal a decline in the fortunes of the doctrine.[14] Either way, the nationhood power can be bracketed out because it makes little difference for the law of judicial review: subject to considerations of justiciability and deference, exercises of the 'nationhood power' must be amenable to judicial review. In a similar vein, Anne Twomey has challenged the cogency of the arguments used to justify the existence of this supposed category.[15] In line with this analysis, my references to 'prerogative-type powers' should be taken to include the nationhood power by those who endorse it.

4.3 The Problematical Prerogative

The resilience of non-statutory executive powers not associated with the historical prerogative is a problem for my binary approach I am

12 *Williams* v. *Commonwealth (No 1)* (2012) 248 CLR 156, 185 (French CJ).

13 *Williams* v. *Commonwealth (No 1)* (2012) 248 CLR 156, 184 (French CJ).

14 See Peter Gerangelos, 'Section 61 of the *Commonwealth Constitution* and an "Historical Constitutional Approach": An Excursus on Justice Gageler's Reasoning in the *M68* Case' (2018) 43(2) *University of Western Australia Law Review* 103, 107. In *Plaintiff M68/2015* v. *Minister for Immigration and Border Protection* (2016) 257 CLR 42, Gageler J provided the first detailed analysis of non-statutory executive power since the leading cases *Williams* v. *Commonwealth (No 1)* (2012) 248 CLR 156 and *Pape* v. *Federal Commissioner of Taxation*(2009) 238 CLR 1, but made no mention of the nationhood power.

15 See Anne Twomey, 'Pushing the Boundaries of Executive Power: Pape, the Prerogative and Nationhood Powers' (2010) 34 *Melbourne University Law Review* 313, 336.

advocating if the category of non-statutory executive powers is associated too closely with the Royal Prerogative. Margit Cohn has argued that leaving the concept of non-statutory powers tied to the prerogative is conducive to error because the prerogative (i) evokes the idea of royal dignity in inappropriate contexts, (ii) conflates immunities and powers associated with the prerogative, and (iii) deflects attention from the 'de facto scope of non-statutory executive action, broadly-so-called, and inhibit[s] systemic treatment of the exercise of such powers'.[16] While I agree with the first two points, the idea of 'de facto governmental powers' only confounds the analysis. Cohn should be taken to mean that we should not shoe-horn the 'third source' into the 'Royal Prerogative' as traditionally understood. If, however, we are concerned with 'non-statutory executive powers' rather than 'Royal Prerogative', no difficulty arises. Again, the defining feature of all non-statutory executive powers is that the rules granting vires to the office in which the powers are reposed are found in the common law, while the rules that regulate the exercise of those vires may be found in the common law and/or in statute.

The Royal Prerogative is an important historical category, and demoting it in this way may seem counter-intuitive. However, Thomas Poole has rightly argued that the preponderance of recent United Kingdom Supreme Court jurisprudence is actually inconsistent with any of the conventional accounts of the Royal Prerogative. Judicial review has marched onward – particularly since 2017 – such that these powers are treated with judicial suspicion rather than the traditional deference. The English courts now recognise only a nominal core of non-justiciable executive action, even in high-stakes contexts like acts of state in war zones abroad.[17] This being the case, the term 'prerogative' obscures more than it elucidates, and Poole suggests that it may be time to 'talk instead about the general executive powers of government'.[18]

Ministers, Secretaries of State, and other officials within HM Government exercise powers that are reposed in the Crown in statute and by the common law. While the historical prerogatives of the Crown

[16] See Margit Cohn, 'Medieval Chains, Invisible Inks: On Non-Statutory Powers of the Executive' (2005) 25(1) *Oxford Journal of Legal Studies* 97, 105.

[17] Thomas Poole, 'The Strange Death of Prerogative in England' (2018) 43(2) *University of Western Australia Law Review* 42, 65 discussing *Rahmatullah (No 2) and Serdar Mohamed* v. *Ministry of Defence* [2017] UKSC 1, [37] (Lady Hale).

[18] Thomas Poole, 'The Strange Death of Prerogative in England' (2018) 43(2) *University of Western Australia Law Review* 42, 65.

are an essential component of any enquiry into what those common law powers are, and how widely they range, the hallmark of these powers is that they are based in rules of competence that are found in the unwritten law as opposed to statute.

Jennifer Klinck has argued against such an approach on the basis that it hinders the determination of the existence and scope of the relevant power. By itself, she argues, Dicey's definition of the Royal Prerogative does not provide any device for identifying and limiting the scope of prerogative powers.[19] Although she admits that Blackstone's definition furnishes no such device, either, Klinck prefers Blackstone's distinction because it determines which criteria apply and so provides a starting point to the enquiry.[20] This starting point is the analogy to a natural person (in the case of the third source) and historical enquiry (in the case of the prerogative). Clearly, the Royal Prerogative cannot be understood without historical enquiry, but analogies with natural persons are possibly the worst starting point for the exercise of identifying and limiting the scope of third source-type powers. The analogy displaces the very enquiry we need to make into the juristic nature of the Crown (which is *not* a natural person), the relationship of the Crown to its officials, and how officials act for and on behalf of the Crown in their capacity as such.

As we have seen, neither the conventional wisdom surrounding the Royal Prerogative nor prevailing accounts of the Crown's personality and its third source-type powers are really up to the task at hand, so we need to develop new conceptual tools.

4.3.1 The Personal Prerogatives

Another tricky question concerns what we might call the 'personal prerogatives'. In most cases, the official who formally exercises the Crown's non-statutory executive powers is a Minister or Secretary of State. In some cases, however, the official who exercises the power is the Queen herself (or the Vice-Regent in Realms outside the United Kingdom).[21] There are potentially difficult questions of the Monarch's amenability to suit in her own courts in the context of these non-statutory executive powers. Prima

[19] Jennifer Klinck, 'Modernising Judicial Review of the Exercise of Prerogative Powers in Canada' (2017) 54(4) *Alberta Law Review* 997, 1004.

[20] Jennifer Klinck, 'Modernising Judicial Review of the Exercise of Prerogative Powers in Canada' (2017) 54(4) *Alberta Law Review* 997, 1005.

[21] On these 'reserve powers', see generally Anne Twomey, *The Veiled Sceptre: Reserve Powers of Heads of State in Westminster Systems* (Cambridge University Press 2018).

facie, then, it would seem arguable that some special considerations might apply, or even that a unique set of 'prerogative powers' exists that speaks against the binary view I propose.

This problem is less serious than it seems. The prorogation of Parliament, for example, is a power that must be exercised by the Queen personally; to allow the Prime Minister to exercise it would allow the current executive to capture Parliament to an unacceptable extent. However, this power is still exercised on ministerial advice, and this advice, as Mark Walters has argued, provides a target for judicial review.[22] Such an approach was indeed taken by the Supreme Court in *R (Miller)* v. *Prime Minister*.[23] The application in that case was for a declaration that the advice given to Her Majesty to prorogue Parliament at a certain time, and for certain reasons, was unlawful. Lady Hale and Lord Reed gave the judgment of the court:

> The logical approach to [the question of the lawfulness of the prorogation] is to start at the beginning, with the advice that led to it. That advice was unlawful. It was outside the powers of the Prime Minister to give it. This means that it was null and of no effect ... It led to the Order in Council which, being founded on unlawful advice, was likewise unlawful, null and of no effect and should be quashed. This led to the actual prorogation, which was as if the Commissioners had walked into Parliament with a blank piece of paper. It too was unlawful, null and of no effect.[24]

The act of *advising the Queen* was an official act, amenable to review. The Queen can do no wrong, perhaps, but HM Prime Minister can.[25] This reasoning speaks, yet again, to the need for a better concept of office and of the relationship between the Crown and its officials. *The Crown always acts through an official*, and, even in the cases where that official is the Queen, the Queen is acting on the advice on another official who can be brought before Her Majesty's courts. In the rare case that the Queen – acting without advice – should actually perform some actionable wrong, the republican in me would sooner abolish the ancient rules against suing the Monarch in her own courts than accepting a *damnum sine injuria*.

[22] See Mark Walters, 'Judicial Review of Ministerial Advice to the Crown' (2016) 25(3) *Constitutional Forum* 33.

[23] [2019] UKSC 41.

[24] *R (Miller)* v. *Prime Minister* [2019] UKSC 41, [69] (Lady Hale and Lord Reed, with whom Lord Kerr, Lord Wilson, Lord Carnwath, Lord Hodge, Lady Black, Lord Lloyd-Jones, Lady Arden, Lord Kitchin, and Lord Sales agreed).

[25] Mark Walters, 'Judicial Review of Ministerial Advice to the Crown' (2016) 25(3) *Constitutional Forum* 33, 37.

Sometimes, the Crown needs to be protected from the King himself. I would see no inherent problem in determining whether Elizabeth Windsor exercised her official functions for an improper purpose, for example, beyond a political scandal. Whether that should occur through ordinary judicial review or some special process of impeachment is, however, beyond the scope of analysis.

4.4 The Way Forward

The way forward is to adopt a binary view of executive power, which entails rejection of the idea of a third source per se. My reasons for doing this will become clear over the course of Chapters 5, 6, and 7, which deal with the Crown's juristic personality, the concept of office, and the logic of official action respectively. In this section, I will trace out some of these themes as a kind of roadmap for what lies ahead.

The need for that analysis appears from the problems with the ternary view, which gives too much importance to the supposed uniqueness of the powers associated with the Royal Prerogative, and, more seriously, rests on a faulty technical conception of legal power. Wade, as we have seen, started with Blackstone's definition of the prerogative as something 'singular and eccentrical' to the Crown and *then* super-added the stipulation that the prerogative comprises only 'legal powers' (in a technical sense). There is a certain logic to this. As John Howell explains, it is obvious that there are things that Ministers and Secretaries of State can do which are not authorised by statute, which ordinary individuals can also do. If a 'singular and eccentrical' conception of the Royal Prerogative is assumed, we are forced either (i) to say that such actions are unlawful, or (ii) to accept that there is some 'third source' of power for government action other than Parliament and the prerogative, or (iii) to argue that there is no requirement for a source of power as such (i.e., to adopt a 'residual liberties' approach).[26] The problem is that, while the latter two approaches to non-statutory executive powers seem based on a robust concept of legal power, they operate with a faulty one.

With his discussion of *Laker Airways Ltd* v. *Department of Trade*,[27] Wade stepped into a particularly difficult area – the interaction of the treaty making power and domestic law in a dualist legal system. Because treaties are not automatically incorporated into United Kingdom domestic law, argued Wade, they do not 'alter people's rights and duties' and are

[26] John Howell, 'What the Crown May Do' (2010) 15(1) *Judicial Review* 36, 39.
[27] [1977] 2 All ER 182.

therefore not the product of a (domestic) legal power. '[T]here was much talk about prerogative in the judgments. But if there was no power, in the correct legal and constitutional sense, there was no prerogative either'.[28]

This area is so difficult because it is framed by three propositions that are not always easy to reconcile. The first, drawn from the *Case of Proclamations*,[29] is that the King cannot use the Royal Prerogative to change statute, the common law, or (possibly) take away rights. The second is that, in a dualist system, actions on the international plane do not directly change the domestic law. The third is Wade's notion that the prerogative, properly so called, must by definition 'alter people's rights and duties'. The second and third, in particular, stand in some degree of tension; at the very least, if different notions of 'changing the law' and 'taking away rights' are adopted, one finds oneself talking at cross purposes. For example, it is unclear whether Wade's approach can be said to have survived *R (Miller)* v. *Brexit Secretary*,[30] where the emphasis was on the impotence of the Crown, acting under the prerogative, to take away rights. This ground was effectively treated as sufficient in the Divisional Court, where Lord Thomas CJ, Sir Terence Etherton MR and Sales LJ accepted the argument that 'the Crown could not change domestic law and nullify rights under the law unless Parliament had conferred upon the Crown authority to do so either expressly or by necessary implication by an Act of Parliament'.[31] In the Supreme Court, the point was accepted by the majority but drove their reasoning to a lesser extent.[32] This has been a major point of contention in the secondary literature.[33]

The tension between the propositions that the Crown (i) cannot change the law but (ii) can make binding treaties is conventionally reconciled in dualist systems by reference to the institutional spheres of competence of Parliament and the Crown.[34] According to Lord Oliver in *J.H. Rayner (Mincing Lane) Ltd* v. *Department of Trade and Industry*:[35]

> A treaty is not part of English law unless and until it has been incorporated into the law by legislation. So far as individuals are concerned, it is *res inter*

[28] H. W. R. Wade, *Constitutional Fundamentals* (Stevens 1980), 47.
[29] [1610] EWHC KB J22.
[30] [2017] UKSC 5.
[31] *R (Miller)* v. *Brexit Secretary* [2016] EWHC 2768 (Admin), [95]–[96].
[32] See *R (Miller)* v. *Brexit Secretary* [2017] UKSC 51, [122], [177] (Lord Reed).
[33] See Timothy A. O. Endicott, 'Lord Reed's Dissent in Gina Miller's Case and the Principles of Our Constitution' (2016–2017) 8 *UK Supreme Court Yearbook* 259.
[34] See Campbell McLachlan, *Foreign Relations Law* (Oxford University Press 2014), [5.20].
[35] [1990] 2 AC 418.

> *alios acta* [i.e. something done between others], from which they cannot derive rights and by which they cannot be deprived of rights or subjected to obligations; and it is outside the purview of the court not only because it is made in the conduct of foreign relations, which are a prerogative of the Crown, but also because, as a source of rights and obligations, it is irrelevant.[36]

One might ask whether this position is entirely satisfactory. However, it is all orthogonal to the present question, which is the taxonomy of non-statutory executive powers. Even if we accept Wade's argument that the prerogative ought to be cast narrowly as a set of 'legal powers' that change subjects' legal position, this neither precludes us from seeing the treaty making power as a 'prerogative-type power' nor does it require us to cleave non-statutory executive powers into 'true' and 'false' prerogatives. Even an unincorporated treaty has legal effects 'somewhere along the line'.[37] In *R (Miller)* v. *Brexit Secretary*, Lord Neuberger (for the majority of the Supreme Court) held that '[t]he fact that the exercise of prerogative powers cannot change the domestic law does not mean that such an exercise is always devoid of domestic legal consequences'.[38] Domestic legal consequences would follow 'where it is inherent in the prerogative power that its exercise will affect the legal rights or duties of others', such as in the case of the prerogative to manage the civil service. In such cases, '[w]hile the exercise of the prerogative power … may affect individual rights, the important point is that it does not change the law, because the law has always authorised the exercise of the power'.[39] Domestic legal consequences would also follow, however, 'where the effect of an exercise of prerogative powers is to change the facts to which the law applies', such as where a declaration of war changes the status of aliens to 'enemy aliens'.[40] There are indeed a number of ways in which a treaty might alter subjects rights and duties, even prior to incorporation.[41]

[36] *J. H. Rayner (Mincing Lane) Ltd* v. *Department of Trade and Industry* [1990] 2 AC 418, 500 (Lord Oliver).

[37] Sebastian Payne, 'The Royal Prerogative' in Maurice Sunkin and Sebastian Payne (eds.), *The Nature of the Crown* (Oxford University Press 1998), 84.

[38] *R (Miller)* v. *Brexit Secretary* [2017] UKSC 5, [52].

[39] *R (Miller)* v. *Brexit Secretary* [2017] UKSC 5, [52].

[40] *R (Miller)* v. *Brexit Secretary* [2017] UKSC 5, [53].

[41] Anne Twomey, '*Miller* and the Prerogative' in Mark Elliott, Jack Williams, and Alison Young (eds.), *The UK Constitution after Miller: Brexit and Beyond* (Hart 2018), 77–78.

The narrowness of Wade's 'legal powers' is evident from some of the other examples on which he drew, such as the act of issuing a passport. The traditional position is that the issue of a passport is the exercise of a prerogative power. Wade argued that a passport is an 'administrative document' with no status or legal effect at common law; the British citizen's legal rights are unaffected by the grant or refusal of a passport, as these rights 'are a matter of common and statute law, which the Crown has no power to alter'; since there is no effect on legal rights, the act of issuing a passport does not qualify as an exercise of a legal power and 'cannot therefore represent the exercise of prerogative power'.[42] Again, it is perhaps significant that Wade first made this argument when the prerogative was non-reviewable, such that a restrictive reading of 'prerogative' confined the scope of administrative impunity to the minimum. His approach was, at any rate, at odds with that taken by the Court of Appeal in *R (Everett)* v. *Secretary of State for Foreign and Commonwealth Affairs*,[43] in which Taylor LJ said that 'the grant or refusal of a passport . . . is a matter of administrative decision, affecting the rights of individuals and their freedom of travel'.[44] Writing after the case, Wade moved the goal-post, characterising the decision to grant or refuse a passport as 'within the sphere of positive acts of power by the government'[45] and falling back to another category of actions, including publishing information, as examples of actions which 'though acts of government, [are] not positive acts of power'.[46]

Fundamentally, it is necessary to disambiguate 'affecting rights' and 'changing the law', and to connect both of these ideas to the concept of legal power. We need to distinguish between changing the law, in the sense of (i) legislating per se, (ii) taking away rights that are vested in such a way that they might be said to be immune from interference (such as 'fundamental' or 'constitutional' rights), (iii) changing the factual scenario to which the law (as it exists) applies, and (iv) changing the subject's legal position in the regular way through an act-in-the-law (such as a contract). Our definition of 'affecting rights and duties' has to be

[42] H. W. R. Wade, *Constitutional Fundamentals* (Stevens 1980), 51.

[43] [1988] EWCA Civ 7.

[44] *R (Everett)* v. *Secretary of State for Foreign and Commonwealth Affairs* [1988] EWCA Civ 7, [25].

[45] H. W. R. Wade, 'Beyond the Law: A British Innovation in Judicial Review' (1991) 43 *Administrative Law Review* 559, 565.

[46] H. W. R. Wade, 'Beyond the Law: A British Innovation in Judicial Review' (1991) 43 *Administrative Law Review* 559, 565.

technical and accurate. Even a gift changes the donor's and the donee's legal position in the fourth sense, by eliminating and creating property rights in the subject matter of the gift, for example, and therefore constitutes the exercise of a 'legal power' on the Hohfeldian view.

The difficult case of treaty-making and treaty demission might, therefore, not be the best entry-point into this problematic. In Chapter 7, I spell out the apparent influence of Hohfeld's schematic logic on Wade, and on the seminal decision of Wade's collaborator[47] Sir Robert Megarry VC in *Malone* v. *Metropolitan Police Commissioner*,[48] and present the schema of deontic and operational logic with which I approach the supervisory jurisdiction.

4.4.1 The Importance of Office

The question of legal power naturally bleeds into the concept of office. Wade advanced a shaky conception of what actually occurs when an official acts (or purports to act) under a non-statutory power. Again choosing the trickiest example, Wade attributed the treaty-making power to a rule of international law rather than to a rule of the domestic constitution; not only was the pseudo-power to 'designate' under the Bermuda Agreement a product of international law, '[HM Government's] power to make the Agreement came not from the common law but from their status as an international person'.[49]

Grammatically, there is an obvious problem with this proposition. If HM Government is an 'international person', HM Government must be an 'it', not a 'they'. Wade does not explain how 'their' acts – 'they' are presumably individuals within HM Government – count as the acts of this international person. There is also a logical problem, which surely motivates Wade's use of the plural pronoun. As Alf Ross explains, 'the United Kingdom' can be the *grammatical* subject of the proposition that 'the United Kingdom has signed a treaty', but the United Kingdom cannot be the *logical* subject of this proposition because the United Kingdom is not the kind of entity that can 'sign' anything.[50] Signing is an action that requires hands and volition, which the United Kingdom

[47] See Robert E. Megarry and H. W. R. Wade, *The Law of Real Property* (Stevens 1957).
[48] [1979] Ch 344.
[49] H. W. R. Wade, *Constitutional Fundamentals* (Stevens 1980), 47.
[50] Alf Ross, 'On the Concepts "State" and "State Organs" in Constitutional Law' (1961) 5 *Scandinavian Studies in Law* 112, 125.

lacks. Rather, what we mean is that some individual(s) empowered to *represent* the United Kingdom signed a treaty:

> When the legislative organ has enacted a statute we do not attribute this act to the physical persons – the King and the members of Parliament – who have contributed to the enactment, but regard the legislative act as a State act performed through the legislative organ. In the same way we say that the State, with the King as its instrument or organ, enters into treaties with foreign powers, or that it delivers judgments through judges, or constructs railways, builds hospitals, and runs schools through its ministers. The common feature is this usage is that certain *acts that are in reality performed by definite individuals* – and who else could perform an act? – *are spoken of as being performed not by the physical person in question but by a subject called 'the State'*. The act, one can also say, is *attributed* to 'the State'.[51]

Although the physical act of appending a signature (or seal) is conventionally part of the process, what we really mean to say is that the United Kingdom as an organised political community, through the act of an official organ, has entered into an international agreement. But, *contra* Wade, this is clearly the exercise of a legal power in the domestic law of the United Kingdom *by the relevant official.* It must be the case that the Foreign Secretary can sign a treaty because a rule of the *domestic* constitution empowers her to represent the United Kingdom abroad. Even though a treaty changes the legal position of the United Kingdom as such on the plane of international law in the first instance, the Minister's ability to perform an 'act of the nation' is, and can only be, the product of a rule of the domestic constitution investing her with legal power to act for and on behalf of whole political community.[52]

A shade of Diceyan logic, indeed, is prefigured in Blackstone's own treatment: '[w]hat is done by the royal authority, with regard to foreign powers, is the act of the whole nation; what is done without the king's concurrence is the act only of private men'.[53] In other words, one exercising the power to make treaties has to act in conformity with the relevant legal rule that stipulates how one performs an act of treaty-making for and on behalf of the United Kingdom. In reality, *every* official action is an

[51] Alf Ross, 'On the Concepts "State" and "State Organs" in Constitutional Law' (1961) 5 *Scandinavian Studies in Law* 112, 115. Emphasis mine.

[52] See also Campbell McLachlan, *Foreign Relations Law* (Oxford University Press 2014), [4.40], [4.41]. In Canada, a note of the Legal Bureau stipulates clearly that authorisation to sign and ratify a treaty 'takes the form of an Order in Council (OIC), signed by the Governor General, on the basis of a Submission to the Special Committee of the Council prepared by the Minister of Foreign Affairs': See (1999) 37 Can YIL 342.

[53] Sir William Blackstone, *Commentaries on the Laws of England* (Clarendon Press 1765), Book I, 245.

exercise of legal power, because there is no way for an official to act *as an official* except in the valid exercise of her office's vires. All of this presupposes a concept of office that explains how the capacities of individuals are harnessed and put to work for an abstract institution like HM Government or the Crown. Dicey was undeniably right that a wholly unauthorised act by an official had, logically, to be a private one – what he failed to grasp was the corporate nature of the Crown and HM Government and the kernel of '*droit administratif*' that is inherent in the concept of office.

4.4.2 *The Crown as Corporation*

This brings us to the Crown's juristic personality. Wade's various references to the Crown 'as a natural person' have encouraged all kinds of error, compounding with the errors outlined above. We have seen that nothing really turns on whether the Crown's abilities to enter into contracts and perform other mundane legal acts belong to the Royal Prerogative. However, Wade's identification of the Crown with a natural person (presumably the person who is Queen) has inspired arguments such as that made by Mark Elliott, that the 'statutory', 'prerogative' or 'third source' nature of executive action *does* entail consequences for the why, if not the how, of judicial review.[54] If we adopt this position at the outset of an enquiry such as the present, an overly convoluted picture of the supervisory jurisdiction is a foregone conclusion and we will naturally gravitate towards the terms of the ultra vires debate (i.e., legislative intention) instead of focussing on the actual problems of non-statutory executive power.

The 'natural person' approach is superficially attractive because it grounds both (i) exercises of factual abilities (including physical and mental actions that require a biological organism, such as an act of *signing*, *considering*, or *taking a decision*) and (ii) exercises legal abilities (i.e., *making a contract*, *making a gift*, or *signing a treaty*) in a juristic category – the 'natural person'. However, that category is totally inappropriate to the Crown. As we have seen, not all third source theories cast the Crown as a natural person, or even rely on the legal personality of the Crown at all. But non-personality based third source theories, such as those presented by B. V. Harris or indeed by French CJ in *Williams* v. *Commonwealth (No 1)*, say nothing about how the Crown possess the abilities that the residual liberties approach presumes. This explains why

[54] Mark Elliott, *The Constitutional Foundation Judicial Review* (Hart 2001), 168.

the courts have generally adopted a personality-based conception of third source-type powers.

The personality problem really boils down to two questions, both of which underline the important of office. First, is it ever accurate to speak of the *factual abilities* of the Crown at all? Put another way, how can the factual abilities of individual human beings produce actions that are attributed to the Crown? Secondly, should the Crown be accepted to hold *general law powers*, including private law powers such as the power to contract? If so, how should we treat them in public law? Put another way, when the Crown exercises private law powers in the course of administration, should it be treated as just another private law acting subject, or should its public character translate into judicially enforceable duties on those powers? The paradigm case of this is, of course, a contract in which the Crown is a contracting party.[55]

Here, we can loop back to the concept of legal power. Wade argued, for example, that in 'placing its contracts as and how it wishes the government is exercising the ordinary liberty possessed by anyone (and I hope no one will call it prerogative). The government's duty not to abuse that liberty is constitutional rather than legal'.[56] But the *liberty* to make contracts presupposes a *power* to make contracts, which Wade – for all his insistence on technical precision – simply ignored. He could only say that it is a 'liberty' (i.e., the freedom of action implied by the absence of a duty) because he made a distinction between 'legal' and 'constitutional' duties, whatever that means. The manoeuvre reflects the shuffle performed in the context of the treaty-making power, i.e., hiving off domestic from international legal powers. For my part, a Minister's duty not to make corrupt contracts, for example, is strictly 'legal'. This being the case, the picture that emerges is of a legal power reposed in an official to make contracts on behalf of the organised political community subject to common law duties of integrity and fidelity to public purposes.

4.5 Conclusion

This chapter has set the stage for a substantive analysis of the concept of office and the mechanics of official empowerment and accountability, so it

[55] See Janet McLean, 'For a Law of Public Contract *Per Se*: An Intervention from Liberal Contract Theory' (2019) 39(4) *Oxford Journal of Legal Studies* 856.

[56] H. W. R. Wade, *Constitutional Fundamentals* (Rev. ed., Stevens 1989), 71. On the distinction between 'law' and 'convention', see Mark Walters, *A. V. Dicey and the Common Law Constitutional Tradition* (Cambridge University Press 2020), 145.

is convenient briefly to recap the core tenets of the view that is emerging. 'Non-statutory executive powers' comprise a single category that exists in a dichotomous relation to 'statutory executive powers'. This is based on the simple fact that 'prerogative-type' and 'third source-type' powers are amenable to judicial review on the same grounds and, all else being equal, on the same standards. While there may be historical or even conceptual distinctions to draw between them in some contexts, the labels cannot be more than labels of convenience for a theory of judicial review.

The category of 'non-statutory executive powers' comprises every power reposed by an unwritten rule of competence in the Crown and its officials. In particular, it includes those general law powers that the Crown possesses as a common law corporation. Some of these powers repose in the Crown in virtue of its legal personality as a corporation sole. All the Crown's powers are exercised, as in the case of any corporation, by its human organs – Ministers, Secretaries of State, and other public officials.[57]

Above all, public law theory needs to explain how and why a *certain action by a certain official* is subject to judicial review. Simply taking this problem seriously sets us upon a path in which the important questions quite naturally arise, in a more or less logical order. First, it demands an explanation of the Crown as a legal institution and of the institutions around it – the agglomeration that we conventionally call 'HM Government'. Whether a 'natural person', 'corporate', or 'nationhood' approach is taken, a good concept of non-statutory executive powers must provide an account of the nature of the Queen, the Crown, and the organised political community. Secondly, it demands an explanation of the relationship between the Crown and its officials within HM Government, whose actions are deemed, in law, to be actions of the Crown. This requires us to study the rules attributing actions to the Crown and also determining the liability of the Crown and/or the official (in a personal capacity) for unlawful action. Thirdly, it demands a sophisticated deontic logic and operational logic – that is, a scheme of *legal relations* (rights, duties, powers, etc.) and *legal actions* that we can use to analyse the position of a given repository of power *vis-à-vis* a given subject of power. The lack of such a scheme, after all, rests at the heart of disagreements about the non-statutory executive powers.

[57] Sometimes, nominally private actors carry out an essentially public function. This scenario is best addressed once armed with a concept of office and official action.

5

The Crown as Corporation

5.1 Introduction

'The Crown' holds central importance in our tradition of public law, providing the symbolic focal point for organising the various powers associated with the state and its government.[1] In the context of non-statutory executive powers, the Crown is only more important because they are generally derived from (i) the Royal Prerogative or (ii) the common law powers of the Crown and/or (iii) the supposed factual abilities and legal liberties of the Crown. As we have seen, a false apprehension of the Crown can set a whole theory of judicial review off on the wrong tack.

Unfortunately, there is no clear concept of what the Crown really *is* – despite being perhaps the most important of our political institutions, it is one of the least understood.[2] 'The Crown' is used to refer to the Queen in her private and her public capacity, as well as to the executive branch of government, potentially including the Queen, ministers, and civil servants within the administration,[3] and is often used as a stand-in for the concept of the 'state'.[4] Disambiguating the various usages of the term is the first step to establishing a coherent framework for identifying those actions that are the province of judicial review. As we have seen, the failure to develop an adequate concept of *office* has hampered efforts to understand the Crown, too. It is ill-advised – perhaps impossible – to examine the Crown in isolation from the officials who act for it. Put

1 See Nick Seddon, 'The Crown' (2000) 38 *Federal Law Review* 245; Martin Loughlin, 'The State, the Crown, and the Law' in Maurice Sunkin and Sebastian Payne (eds.), *The Nature of the Crown* (Oxford University Press 1999), 58.

2 D. E. Smith, *The Invisible Crown: The First Principle of Canadian Government* (University of Toronto Press 2013), ix.

3 Cheryl Saunders, 'The Concept of the Crown' (2015) 38 *Melbourne University Law Review* 873, 875.

4 Janet McLean, *Searching for the State in British Legal Thought* (Cambridge University Press 2012).

another way, 'what the Crown may do' is a question of what *officials* may do in the name of the Crown, which in turn becomes a question of what acts by officials ought to be *attributed* to the Crown. That is where changing preconceptions about the nature of public law itself, and the long shadow of A. V. Dicey in English legal pedagogy, need critical revision.

The Crown remains shrouded in mystery, often described with archaic concepts such as the 'two bodies' doctrine. There is fundamental disagreement about whether the Crown is a 'natural person' or some kind of corporation, and uncertainty about what consequences follow from this fact. When speaking about the liability of officials for wrongdoing, one is faced with unattractive categories such as 'emanations of the Crown' and distracted by maxims such as 'the King can do no wrong' that obviously do not mean what they once meant. The liability of officials for wrongdoings has conventionally relied on the notions of an idealised Crown to which no wrongdoing can be attributed, but that view – despite its appeal – is out of touch with the modern approach to state liability for the actions of its officials.

The modern impulse is to avoid all of this by approaching questions on the premise of a bureaucratic apparatus of government organised by the employment relationship and managerial control. However, it is necessary to engage with the corporate nature of the Crown because it is unlikely to be abandoned any time soon, and because it expresses, at base, concepts that are both essential and fundamentally sound. In the haunted castle of British public law, running from ghouls leads us into blind passages. In studying abstractions, artifices, and fictions, we discover something about the essential structure of law, legal power, and political organisation. If we keep our wits about us, we might find a more mundane explanation for the 'clanking of medieval chains'.[5]

This chapter explains the traditional doctrine that the Crown is a common law corporation, namely a 'corporation sole'. As John Howell has rightly observed, the Crown's nature as a corporation sole is clear as a matter of doctrinal (including statute) law, so must form the starting point (if not the destination) of our analysis.[6] Although the idea of a corporate Crown presents some conceptual difficulties, it also holds the germ of a sophisticated logic of office and action in an 'official

[5] *United Australia Ltd* v. *Barclays Bank Ltd* (1941) AC 1, 29 (Lord Atkin), cited in *Council of Civil Service Unions* v. *Minister for the Civil Service* (1985) AC 374, 417 (Lord Roskill).

[6] John Howell, 'What the Crown May Do' (2010) 15(1) *Judicial Review* 36, 42–43, referring *inter alia* to the Law of Property Act 1925.

capacity' that is vital to any proper understanding of public law. The Crown's corporate nature explains the source of third source-type powers and provides the conceptual framework for thinking about how individuals – officials – act for and on behalf of the Crown. Section 5.2 explores the relationship between the Queen and the Crown. Section 5.3 explores the relationship between the Crown and HM Government, Section 5.4 explores the relationship between the Crown and the organised political community, and Section 5.5 concludes.

5.2 The Queen and the Crown

The first question to arise is the relation between 'the Crown' and 'the Queen', the woman Elizabeth, the Ministers advising it (or her, or Her), the other officials executing that advice. Whenever one reads of the Crown acting, one suspects a metaphor at work. F.W. Maitland warned his students of the 'metaphysiological nonsense' implicit in the notion of an acting hat.[7] Instead, he said they should focus on the actual apparatus of government – an apparatus which was, at the time, rapidly growing in size and sophistication, largely due to statutory innovations and an employment-based turn in the organisation of the various bodies comprising HM Government:

> You will certainly read that the crown does this and the crown does that. As a matter of fact we know that the crown does nothing but lie in the Tower of London to be gazed at by sight-seers ... the crown is a convenient cover for ignorance: it saves us from asking difficult questions ... do not be content until you know who legally has the power – is it the king, is it one of his secretaries: is this power a prerogative power or is it the outcome of statute?[8]

Maitland's proposed way out of the mess – 'for mess it is'[9] – was to reject the traditional doctrine that the Crown is a corporation sole and to describe it rather as a 'corporation aggregate of many'; 'I see no great harm in calling this corporation a Crown. But a better word has lately returned to the statute book. That word is Commonwealth'.[10] Maitland's

[7] F. W. Maitland, 'The Crown as Corporation' in David Runciman and Magnus Ryan (eds.), *State, Trust, and Corporation* (Cambridge University Press 2003), 35.

[8] F. W. Maitland, *The Constitutional History of England* (Cambridge University Press 1908), 418.

[9] F. W. Maitland, 'The Crown as Corporation' in David Runciman and Magnus Ryan (eds.), *State, Trust, and Corporation* (Cambridge University Press 2003), 35.

[10] F. W. Maitland, 'The Crown as Corporation' in David Runciman and Magnus Ryan (eds.), *State, Trust, and Corporation* (Cambridge University Press 2003), 35.

solution sounds eminently sensible, but it actually jumps a step. While using 'the commonwealth' to refer to the constituted body politic is surely right, I have reservations about using the Crown to refer to the commonwealth, and none of this undermines the core idea expressed by the doctrine that the Crown is a corporation sole.

Maitland was critical of the corporation sole itself. It is a peculiar English contrivance: the *persona ficta* of the 'corporation aggregate' evolved to enable the group ownership of property and perpetual succession.[11] Medieval jurists began to treat certain personages as a 'company of one', especially ecclesiastical offices. Maitland punned on the 'parsonification' of the King,[12] and found the idea oxymoronic. However, in my view, the corporation sole can be understood as an apt expression of the *concept of office*. If we understand it correctly, it is quite useful, actually, as a category of modern public law.

5.2.1 The Crown as a Natural Person

As we have seen, some really do appear to think that the Crown just is a natural person. Of course, the person who occupies the office of Queen is a natural person. But even where King and Crown have been held 'inseparable', they have always been recognised as distinct bearers of rights and duties and distinct authors of acts-in-the-law.[13] Conflating the two undermines centuries of legal development from personal rule by a feudal landowning monarch to the constitutional monarchy of today,[14] 'antiquarianism masquerading as contemporary legal analysis'.[15]

At base, what probably motivates proponents of the natural person argument is the imperative to animate the institution of the Crown with the actions of human beings. Fundamentally, institutions (like corporations and states) require human agents. However, there are much better ways of explaining this than positing that the Crown is a natural person. Conflating the person who is Monarch with the institution of the Crown, in fact, *elides* the mechanics of office and representation that actually

[11] See Maximilian Koessler, 'The Person in Imagination or Persona Ficta of the Corporation' (1949) 9(4) *Louisiana Law Review* 435.

[12] F. W. Maitland, 'The Crown as Corporation' in David Runciman and Magnus Ryan (eds.), *State, Trust, and Corporation* (Cambridge University Press 2003), 33.

[13] Ernst Kantorowicz, *The King's Two Bodies* (Princeton University Press 1997), 21.

[14] *Town Investments* v. *Department of Environment* [1978] AC 359, 380 (Lord Diplock); *Council of Civil Service Unions* v. *Minister for the Civil Service* [1985] AC 374, 417 (Lord Roskill).

[15] John Howell, 'What the Crown May Do' [2010] *Judicial Review* 36, [38].

achieve this result; in so doing, the natural person account renders the Crown concept inutile at best, and obstructive at worst, and attributes the same mode and scope of action to very different classes of entity.

5.2.2 *Legal Personality and the Office of the Sovereign*

Not only is the concept of 'legal' as opposed to 'natural' personality important in a doctrinal sense; corporate legal personality plays a significant conceptual role in our tradition of political philosophy, especially in English social contract thought. In his classical work on the 'Matter, Forme, and power of a Common-wealth', for example, Thomas Hobbes adopted a schematic of three types of persons – natural, artificial, and fictitious. I will return to Hobbes from time to time throughout this book because he is illustrative of the genre and, in my view, ontologically very sophisticated. There are complexities to Hobbes' scheme, on which I shall not elaborate, which Hobbes probably introduced to avoid the potentially republican implications of his account of political organisation.[16] For now, the feature to notice is his distinction between 'natural' and 'artificial' persons.

For Hobbes, a person is someone 'whose words or actions are considered, either as his own, or as representing the words or action of another man, or of any other thing to whom they are attributed'. A 'person' is an entity capable of action. In Hobbes' conceptual scheme, action can be attributed to a person 'truly' or 'by fiction'. A person who acts for himself Hobbes calls a 'natural person'; a person who acts through another is a 'feigned' or 'artificial' person. 'Personation', in Hobbes' usage, is itself a synonym for 'representation':

> The word Person is latine: insteed whereof the Greeks have πρόσωπον, which signifies the *Face*, as *Persona* in latine signifies the *disguise*, or *outward appearance* of a man, counterfeited on the Stage; and sometimes

[16] See Patricia Springborg, 'Quentin Skinner and Hobbes' Artificial Person of the State Redux' (2019) *Global Intellectual History*, http://doi.org/10.1080/23801883.2019.1677282; Quentin Skinner, 'Hobbes and the Purely Artificial Person of the State' (1999) 7(1) *Journal of Political Philosophy* 1; David Runciman, 'What Kind of Person is Hobbes' State? A Reply to Skinner' (2000) 8(2) *Journal of Political Philosophy* 268; Daniel Lee, *Popular Sovereignty in Early Modern Constitutional Thought* (Oxford University Press 2016), 74; J. P. Canning, 'Corporation in the Political Thought of the Jurists of the Thirteenth and Fourteenth Centuries' (1980) 1(1) *History of Political Thought* 9; Laurens van Apeldorn, 'On the Person and Office of the Sovereign in Hobbes' Leviathan' (2020) 28(1) *British Journal for the History of Philosophy*, 49, http://doi.org/10.1080/09608788.2019.1613632.

> more particularly that part of it, which disguiseth the face, as a Mask or Visard: And from the Stage, hath been translated to any Representer of speech and action, as well in Tribunalls, as Theaters. So that a *Person*, is the same that an *Actor* is, both on the Stage and in common Conversation; and to *Personate*, is to *Act*, or *Represent* himselfe, or another; and he that acteth another, is said to beare his Person, or act in his name; [. . .] and is called in diverse occasions, diversly; as a *Representer*, or *Representative*, a *Lieutenant*, a *Vicar*, an *Attorney*, a *Deputy*, a *Procurator*, an *Actor*, and the like.[17]

The 'Common-wealth' itself is an artificial person for Hobbes, and requires the agency of human individuals to act; the state has no capacity on its own to do anything, being 'but a word, without substance, [that] cannot stand'.[18] The existence and action of an institutional entity, that is, one instituted by human beings pursuant to shared intentions and understandings, implicitly relies on human agents to 'personate' it. Thus, Hobbes argued (pre-empting Hart's 'King Rex' giving private orders[19]) that the sovereign must make his will known through the medium of promulgated laws: '[F]or the King, though as a father of children, and a master of domestic servants command many things which bind those children and those servants yet he commands the people in general never but by a precedent law, and as a politic, not a natural person'.[20]

This brings us to the core of the personality problem. The person who is King is a natural person, but he acts as a 'political, not a natural person' when acting as King. In other words, there is at least one degree of separation between the Crown and the nearest natural person.

Arguments about persons and corporations are difficult because disagreements exist along several axes, going to basic metaphysical and ontological questions. If we take our departure point a little later, with Blackstone, '[n]atural persons are such as the God of nature formed us: artificial are such as created and devised by human laws for the purposes of society and government; which are called corporations or bodies politic'.[21] For a long time, and especially in the latter nineteenth century, debate raged between those who saw corporations as something 'real'

17 Thomas Hobbes (Richard Tuck ed.), *Leviathan* (Cambridge University Press 1996), 111–112.

18 Thomas Hobbes (Richard Tuck ed.), *Leviathan* (Cambridge University Press 1996), 245.

19 H. L. A. Hart, *The Concept of Law* (Rev. ed., Clarendon Press 1982), 68.

20 Thomas Hobbes (Ferdinand Tönnies ed.), *Behemoth or the Long Parliament* (Frank Cass 1969), 51.

21 William Blackstone, *Commentaries on the Laws of England*, Vol. 1 (Clarendon Press 1765), 119.

that arose 'by the nature of things' and those who saw them as a fiction.[22] The latter split in their view of the author of the fiction. The facts of early modern life suggested that corporations were the product of bottom-up custom; royalist and, later, parliamentarian theorists vehemently countered that the existence of group entities was a concession of the sovereign.[23]

The 'fiction' *versus* 'organic' debate was the context in which Maitland wrote, and he was rather influenced by the German Idealists on the organic side. While of great historical importance, this debate can be set to one side for present purposes. It turns on one of those dichotomies which, although not per se useless, becomes entrenched and continues to impress and inform debates even after it has provided them with useful structure. According to John Searle, we are concerned with real aspects of a 'mind dependent, but not totally mind determined, social reality'; social structure is a 'real' enough feature of our world, continuously reproduced and transformed through our individual practices in total – however unaware or even mistaken we may be about what is going on.[24] When it comes to things like Crowns, states, and corporations, we are *clearly* dealing with conventional entities, that is, products of human 'artifice', but their conventional nature is not really problematic. Ontologically, they are mind-dependent phenomena, but this does not make them fictional in the pejorative sense. The debate was anyway of more political than analytical significance.[25]

As Neil MacCormick rightly argues, the personality of human beings in law 'is neither less nor more "juristic" than that of any other entity that the law recognises'.[26] A person – a recognised bearer of legal rights, duties, and powers – is a legal, not a natural kind. 'Natural person' is just the status that modern legal systems attribute to adult human beings of full capacity. According to W. J. Brown, a natural person is a legal

22 A. V. Dicey, 'The Combination Laws as Illustrating the Relation between Law and Opinion during the Nineteenth Century' (1903) 17 *Harvard Law Review* 511, 513; F. W. Maitland, 'Moral Personality and Legal Personality' in David Runciman and Magnus Ryan (eds.), *State, Trust, and Corporation* (Cambridge University Press 2003), 63.

23 *R* v. *Mayor of London* (1692) 1 Show KB 274, 275 (Holt CJ).

24 John Searle, 'The Limits of Emergence: Reply to Tony Lawson' (2016) 46(4) *Journal for the Theory of Social Behaviour* 357; Tony Lawson, 'Comparing Conceptions of Social Ontology: Emergent Social Entities and/or Institutional Facts?' (2016) 46(4) *Journal for the Theory of Social Behaviour* 359.

25 See H. L. A. Hart, 'Definition and Theory in Jurisprudence' in *Essays in Jurisprudence and Philosophy* (Clarendon Press 1983), 25.

26 Neil MacCormick, *Institutions of Law* (Oxford University Press 2007), 83.

conception, a physical entity, and an organism; a 'corporation' is a legal conception but neither a physical entity nor an organism.[27] Not all legal systems recognise all human beings as persons for all purposes.[28] However, the institution of the 'natural person' is so well established that it appears self-evident, and the denial of personality to adult human beings by a legal system on the basis of sex or race, for example, shocks the modern conscience. It is perhaps helpful to distinguish *personhood* (i.e., a status implied by a normative theory about which entities attract the full suite of rights and powers associated with adult human beings) from *personality* (i.e., a status implied by a theory about what kind of entities can be recognised as acting subjects of the law).

If both 'artificial' and 'natural' persons are legal institutions, why should we avoid calling the Crown a natural person? The reason is simple. As Maitland taught, they are both 'persons' in the eyes of the law, but 'not all the propositions that are true of a man will be true of a corporation'.[29] The personality of human beings and business corporations are posited, by a legal system, for different reasons.[30] Generally, the legal capacities incidental to individual legal personality reflect the regard given to the social creatures that bear it, while those of private business corporations reflect the associative freedom that our legal system affords to individuals to pursue economic plans. Different justifications again undergird the legal personality of public bodies. The capacities given to a natural person or private corporation can generally be used in that subject's own interests, and at its own whim (although possibly subject to some supervisory jurisdiction, such as the monopolies rule or the corporate ultra vires rule). 'Public' corporations such as the Crown, on the other hand, hold powers that can only be used for legitimate public purposes, reflecting the reasons for which they are recognised by the community.[31] The existence of the Crown is, like every legal institution, conditional on its service of 'a purpose recognised to be in the common interest'.[32] Thus, it will never do

[27] W. J. Brown, 'The Personality of the Corporation and the Personality of the State' (1905) 21 *Law Quarterly Review* 365, 372.

[28] See *Edwards* v. *Canada (AG)* [1930] AC 124 (JBPC).

[29] F. W. Maitland, 'Moral Personality and Legal Personality' in H. A. L. Fisher (ed.), *Collected Papers*, Vol. 3 (Cambridge University Press 1911), 307.

[30] Ngaire Naffine, 'Who are Law's Person? From Cheshire Cats to Responsible Subjects' (2003) 66(3) *Modern Law Review* 346; Neil MacCormick, *Institutions of Law* (Oxford University Press 2007), 83.

[31] See Alf Ross, *Directives and Norms* (Humanities Press 1968), 130–133.

[32] Edmund Bernatzik, *Über den Begriff der juristischen Person* (Springer 1996 [1890]), 26, fn 135. Translation mine.

just to posit that the Crown has legal personality and *therefore* has all the powers and freedoms of the private citizen, as several third source proponents do. According to Roscoe Pound:

> Instead of a single category of legal 'persons' . . . we have to consider a variety of legal units in a scale from some with but one potential right (in the broader sense) to others which by reason of greater social or economic importance have many rights, powers, liberties, and privileges attributed to them and duties imposed on them . . . Whatever is treated as a legally significant entity by attributing or giving to it any of the juristic conceptions involved in the term 'a right' in its broadest sense is a legal unit.[33]

This captures something very important about the law of judicial review. In effect, the supervisory jurisdiction is the deliberative context in which the legal position of the Crown is set down – particularly, the powers reposed in the office of the Crown and the offices beneath it, and the duties imposed upon them that condition the exercise of those powers.

All 'legal units' have some capacities, but these must be *sui generis* for *sui generis* persons such as the Crown.[34] So much was observed by Stuart Kyd in his eighteenth century treatise on the law of corporations. A corporation is 'merely a political institution', so it can have no capacities other than those necessary to effect the purposes for which it was established; it cannot be considered as a 'moral agent subject to moral obligation', nor as a 'single person capable of personal action'; this explains the incapacities attributed to corporations 'without having recourse to the quaint observation frequent in the old books, "that [a corporation aggregate] exists merely in idea, and that it has neither soul nor body."'[35] The claim that corporations 'may do all other acts as natural persons may' was, according to Seward Brice, author of a nineteenth century treatise on the law of ultra vires, 'manifestly wrong if taken in its full sense'.[36]

5.2.3 The Corporate Crown

The Crown was thus traditionally described not as a natural person at all but as a corporation. However, far from putting all our questions to bed,

33 Roscoe Pound, *Jurisprudence*, Vol. 1 (West 1959), 269; Alexander Nékám, *The Personality Conception of Legal Entity* (Cambridge University Press 1938), 218.

34 See Sir Francis Bacon (James Spedding, R. L. Ellis, and D. D. Heath eds.), *The Works of Sir Francis Bacon* (Longman 1892), 667.

35 Stuart Kyd, *Treatise on the Law of Corporations*, Vol. 1 (Butterworths 1793), 70–71.

36 Seward Brice, *A Treatise on the Doctrine of* Ultra Vires (Stevens & Haynes 1874), 10. See also Chapter 11.

accepting the corporate nature of the Crown raises a host of new problems. One of the leading modern cases, *Town Investments* v. *Department of Environment*,[37] concerned a lease 'for and on behalf of Her Majesty', prompting an enquiry into the identity of the tenant. Treasury Counsel (Nicolas Browne-Wilkinson QC) submitted that the Crown was 'an amorphous, abstract concept' and was 'impossible to define'.[38] Happily, the House of Lords attempted the impossible. Although the nature of the Crown was an essential premise, the case turned on the relationship between the Crown and its Ministers and Secretaries of State. This raised difficult questions, such as whether the Crown (i.e., a Minister as an 'emanation of the Crown') could hold a lease 'on trust for' the Crown (i.e., the Queen, or some other entity), and whether Crown immunities attached to Ministers (as 'emanations of the Crown'), given that the Crown is said to be 'one and indivisible'.

The case is known for Lord Diplock's attempt to cut the Gordian knot with the suggestion that although the Crown is a corporation sole, we should avoid such terminology where possible and speak of 'the government' instead:[39]

> Where, as in the instant case, we are concerned with the legal nature of the exercise of executive powers of government, I believe that some of the more Athanasian-like features of the debate in your Lordships' House could have been eliminated if instead of speaking of 'the Crown' we were to speak of 'the government' – a term appropriate to embrace both collectively and individually all the ministers of the Crown and parliamentary secretaries under whose direction the work of government is carried on by the civil servants employed in the various government departments.[40]

This suggestion has much to commend it but, the problem cannot be so easily circumvented. In short, 'the government' is no less complex an entity than 'the Crown', and even if we try to follow Lord Diplock's suggestion we end up more or less where we started.

Lord Simon took a different tack, which, despite initial appearances, is ultimately more promising. With a nod to Maitland, the Crown was 'a

[37] [1978] AC 359.

[38] *Town Investments* v. *Department of Environment* [1978] AC 359, 376.

[39] *Town Investments Ltd* v. *Department of Environment* [1978] AC 359, 381 (Lord Diplock).

[40] *Town Investments Ltd* v. *Department of Environment* [1978] AC 359, 381 (Lord Diplock). The Athanasian creed in effect says that the Father, Son, and Holy Ghost are all 'God' but are not each other. See, for example, 'On the Logical Problem of the Trinity' in Richard Cartwright, *Philosophical Essays* (MIT Press 1990), 187.

piece of bejewelled headgear under guard at the Tower of London'.[41] However, he noted that 'the Crown' symbolises the powers of government that were originally wielded by its wearer:

> The term 'the Crown' is therefore used in constitutional law to denote the collection of such of those powers as remain extant (the royal prerogative), together with such other powers as have been expressly conferred by statute on 'the Crown'. So too 'the Queen' indicates the person who by right of succession is entitled to wear the crown. *But 'Her Majesty' is evidently a symbolic phrase, betokening the power, the 'mana', which is embodied in the person entitled to wear the crown – as 'His Holiness', 'His Beatitude' or 'Mr Justice' are descriptive of the power believed to inspire and characterise the person so entitled.* 'Her Majesty' in constitutional legal usage thus generally personifies the powers of 'the Crown' – powers the nucleus of which legally and historically are those of The Queen, but which by constitutional convention (i.e. in political reality) are exercised in the name of The Queen by those who are nominally and legally her servants and agents.[42]

He continued that, if terms such as 'emanations of the Crown' be 'too cloudy for legal usage', the most fitting legal concept is to consider the Crown 'a corporation aggregate headed by the Queen'.[43] Departments of State and the Ministers at their head are 'themselves members of the corporation aggregate of the Crown', and we should conceive of their actions as we conceive of the parts of a body acting with and on each other. This 'legal substratum', however, was still overlaid by the fact that the Queen does not command her Ministers today, but instead acts on *their* advice; as such, references to 'Her Majesty' usually refer to the entire apparatus. Lord Simon couched the principle in the traditional idiom: 'This distinction between "The Queen" and "Her Majesty" reflects the ancient distinction between "the King's two bodies," "natural," and "politic"'.[44]

Note how, in order to explain the nature of the Crown, the powers it exercises, and its relation to human actors, Lord Simon lapsed into the terminology of supernatural forces, referring to religious offices in order

41 *Town Investments Ltd* v. *Department for the Environment* [1978] AC 359, 397–398 (Lord Simon). Emphasis mine.
42 *Town Investments Ltd* v. *Department for the Environment* [1978] AC 359, 397–398 (Lord Simon). Emphasis mine.
43 *Town Investments Ltd* v. *Department for the Environment* [1978] AC 359, 399 (Lord Simon).
44 *Town Investments Ltd* v. *Department for the Environment* [1978] AC 359, 400 (Lord Simon).

to explain the nature of a (now) secular, political one.[45] Both of these devices are superficially problematic, but actually highly instructive. Our challenge is to explain how an inert *object* becomes an acting *subject* to which the actions of real human beings are attributed – ideally without resorting to concepts such as *mana*. We have no shortage of conceptual material, but it mainly comprises ancient doctrines with a theological cant. These heirlooms are logically and historically difficult; they do find modern application, but they do not meet with enthusiastic support and they have not, generally, been put to good use. They are, however, absolutely crucial to working our way out of the mess that Maitland observed. While some diffidence towards juridical metaphysics is healthy, it is not possible to understand the Crown without deliberately grappling with its history, and with the assumptions we inevitably make about its nature.

5.2.4 *The King's 'Two Bodies'*

Perhaps the most difficult, but the most essential, doctrine is that the King has 'two bodies'. Surprisingly, we can even look to a modern illustration. In *Cross* v. *Information Commissioner*[46] the First Tier Tribunal had to decide whether the Duchy of Lancaster was a public authority for the purposes of the Environmental Information Regulations 2004.[47] The Duchy comprises lands seized by Henry III in 1256 and hived off from the royal demesne in 1351 by Edward III for his son, John of Gaunt, who had inherited them through marriage. After deposing Richard II, John's son became Henry IV in 1399. On becoming King, Henry declared that the Duchy should be treated 'as if we had never assumed the ensign of royal dignity'.[48] Feudal franchises were tantamount to 'petty kingdoms' affording their feudal lord some independence and unaccountability.[49] Henry so retained the private powers of a territorial magnate separate from the rights of the Crown acquired by

[45] See R. M. Keesing, 'Rethinking *Mana*' (1984) 40(1) *Journal of Anthropological Research* 137; R. H. Codrington, 'Religious Beliefs and Practices in Melanesia' (1881) 10 *Journal of the Royal Anthropological Institute* 261.

[46] *Case No. EA/2010/0101* (First Tier Tribunal, 21 December 2010).

[47] *Case No. EA/2010/0101* (First Tier Tribunal, 21 December 2010), [30].

[48] William Hardy (trans.), *The Charters of the Duchy of Lancaster* (Bentley, Wilson & Fley 1845), 137.

[49] A. F. Pollard, *The Evolution of Parliament* (Longmans, Green 1920), 7.

accession to the throne. The Duchy's separation from the royal demesne was confirmed by subsequent Acts of Parliament and Royal Charters.

In The *Duchy of Lancaster Case*,[50] the King's Bench considered a lease granted by Henry VIII before his death, and renewed by Edward VI as a minor, which Elizabeth I sought to avoid. The case confirmed that the Duchy was held by the sovereign reigning from time to time, but in a separate capacity: Elizabeth I held certain rights *qua* Duke of Lancaster and others *qua* Queen;[51] these remained separate, even though she held the former status in virtue of the latter. On this basis, the First Tier Tribunal in *Cross* v. *Information Commissioner* held that the Duchy was 'distinctly separate' from the Crown, that the Duchy's powers were 'matters of private law' deriving from the relevant charters, and the Duchy was not a 'public authority' under the relevant statutory tests.[52] The holding is generally dubious, but interesting as a modern application of the doctrine that 'the king has in him two bodies, *viz.* a body natural, and a body politic'.[53]

In his earlier writings, Hobbes identified the sovereign with the natural person of the King (or an assembly of natural persons). However, as we have seen, in *Leviathan* he seems to have taken seriously the point that the King acts in a different capacity when acting in his own right and when acting in right of the commonwealth. The sovereign 'representeth two persons, or (as the more common phrase is) has two Capacities, one Naturall, and another Politique'.[54] Despite the antiquated language, this expresses the fundamentally sound idea that kingship itself is a kind of office.

Hobbes ultimately argued, somewhat inconsistently, that the King is sovereign in *both* his personal and political capacities, probably to avoid arguments that Parliament could resist the King.[55] Elizabethan judges

[50] (1561) 1 Plow 212.

[51] It is customary to refer to the Duke of Lancaster irrespective of the sex of the Monarch.

[52] The Duchy was not a 'government department', despite its Chancellor being *ex officio* a member of Cabinet appointed by the Prime Minister; nor a 'publicly owned company', despite being a chartered corporation kept for the maintenance of the current head of state; nor a 'body that carries out functions of public administration', despite administering *bona vacantia* within the Duchy and holding palatine courts: *Case No. EA/2010/0101* (First Tier Tribunal, 21 December 2010), [30]–[43].

[53] *The Duchy of Lancaster Case* (1561) 1 Plow 212, 213.

[54] Thomas Hobbes (Richard Tuck ed.), *Leviathan* (Cambridge University Press 1996), 376.

[55] See Laurens van Apeldorn, 'On the Person and Office of the Sovereign in Hobbes' Leviathan' (2020) 28(1)*British Journal for the History of Philosophy*, 49, http://doi.org/10.1080/09608788.2019.1613632.

had mixed the bodies' respective capacities woefully. *Willion* v. *Berkley*,[56] for example, held that they were 'conjoined' and 'consolidated into one'; the natural person of the King 'partake[s] of the Effects of Body politic' such that it 'wipes away every Imperfection of the other Body'.[57] In *Calvin's Case*,[58] a Scot became an Englishman in virtue of James I's accession to the English throne, although the King wore the Crowns 'by dint of a different office'.[59] Lord Diplock was correct to describe the law as Athanasian; in these cases, a resemblance to the Trinitarian doctrine of three 'consubstantial' persons is one of many debts to Christology and papal theory.[60] Ernst Kantorowicz observed the judges' difficulty in defining their relationship: 'It was anything but a simple task to remain consistent when one had to defend at once the perfect union of the King's Two Bodies and the very distinct capacities of each body alone'.[61]

As it was held in the *Duchy of Lancaster Case*, while the King has a natural body like anybody else's, 'his body politic is a body that cannot be seen or handled, consisting of policy and government, and constituted for the direction of the people, and the management of the public weal'.[62] The principle was established earlier – in sounder terms – that those things '*que appertaine al corone*' must be distinguished from those things which appertain to '*son duchie de Lancaster*' held '*come auter person*'.[63] I have some sympathy for the modernizing impulse to rid political and legal theory of devices that are 'heuristics, or metaphors, rather than observable features of the world'.[64] But we are not dealing with natural kinds here. Behind a shroud of mysticism, the two bodies doctrine

[56] (3 Elizabeth) 1 Plowden 235a.

[57] *Willion* v. *Berkley* (3 Elizabeth) 1 Plowden 235a, 238.

[58] (1608) 77 ER 377.

[59] See Richard Ekins, 'Facts, Reasons and Joint Action: Thoughts on the Social Ontology of Law' (2014) 45 *Rechtstheorie* 313, 318–319.

[60] See Ernst Kantorowicz, *The King's Two Bodies* (Princeton University Press 1997), 16–19.

[61] Ernst Kantorowicz, *The King's Two Bodies* (Princeton University Press 1997), 12.

[62] *The Duchy of Lancaster Case* (1561) 1 Plow 212, 213.

[63] See S. B. Chrimes, *English Constitutional Ideas in the Fifteenth Century* (Cambridge University Press 1936), 352. It was also applied to mundane questions, for example, whether an attendant followed the heir on accession. *Sir Thomas Wroth's Case* (15 Elizabeth) 1 Plowden 455 held that the office of Physician appertained to the natural body of the heir, and followed it; other offices (such as a Privy Councillor to the heir *qua* heir) did not follow him to the kingship.

[64] Martin Loughlin, *Foundations of Public Law* (Oxford University Press 2010), 446, citing Edward L. Rubin, *Beyond Camelot: Rethinking Politics and Law for the Modern State* (Princeton University Press 2005), 15.

advances the sensible proposition that the King must be distinguished from the *office* of the Crown, along with their respective patrimonies.

5.2.5 *The Corporation Sole*

The idea should, by now, be emerging that ideas of office, personality, and corporation are conceptually related and that they serve a special purpose in the associational life of human beings.[65] To reconcile the self-binding character of legislation with the fact that an order is something given to others, for example, John Austin described legislators 'as *one* person ordering *others* who include themselves in their private capacities'.[66] This entails the split personality of officials. Assumption of an office involves the official acting 'outside himself'.[67] The 'two bodies' doctrine, at its core, simply recognises that one individual sometimes acts as two separate subjects. Each capacity comprises a bundle of legal relations, which enables an individual to act in each of her capacities *suo jure*.

At base, this is what the idea of 'personality' is all about. Although we sometimes associate 'personality' with 'personhood', that is, what it means to be human, this is not the core of the technical concept of personality at all. Roman law – which never developed a concept of the true *persona ficta* as a stand-alone legal subject in its own right[68] – provides an instructive starting point. As Bartosz Brozek explains:

> One man could, from the legal perspective, be many persons. As it was termed: *unus homo sustinet plures personas*. It functioned thus so that *persona* identified (some) legal status of a man, independent of their other statuses. Romans could thus be one person as a Roman citizen, another as *pater familias*, yet other if they performed certain public offices . . . [F]or the law, a man – depending on the legal context – wore different 'masks'.[69]

[65] See Marie-France Fontin, 'The King's Two Bodies and the Crown a Corporation Sole: Historical Dualities in English Legal Thinking' (2021) *History of European Ideas*, https://doi.org/10.1080/01916599.2021.1914934.

[66] See H. L. A. Hart, *The Concept of Law* (Clarendon Press 1982), 78.

[67] Meyer Fortes, 'Ritual and Office in Tribal Society' in Max Gluckman (ed.), *Essays on the Ritual of Social Relations* (Manchester University Press 1962), 57.

[68] This was a later contrivance of Romano-Canon law: Joshua Getzler, 'Personality and Capacity: Lessons from Legal History' in Tim Bonyhady (ed.), *Finn's Law* (Federation Press 2016), 160, 163.

[69] Bartosz Brozek, 'The Troublesome Person' in V. A. J. Kurki and Tomasz Pietrzykowski (eds.), *Legal Personhood: Animals, Artificial Intelligence and the Unborn* (Springer 2017), 4.

The Duke of Brunswick v. *The King of Hanover*[70] provides a fascinating illustration. The case concerned the internal administration of affairs following unrest in the Kingdom of Hanover. Decisions taken in the German Imperial Diet and by William IV (the previous King of Hanover) had the consequence that Charles Frederick, Duke of Brunswick, became disentitled, and his wealth was put into guardianship. The parties both held titles in Great Britain and Ireland as well as on the Continent. Eventually, after some successions of guardian, the Duke of Brunswick sued in the English Court of Chancery for declarative relief. The case is most well known for its ruling on the justiciability of foreign acts of state in English courts, a question not distant from the topic of non-statutory executive power. But it is equally interesting for its implicit ruling on the split personality of the King of Hanover.

The King was, according to the House of Lords, *both* a foreign sovereign *and* an English subject; acts done in his sovereign capacity were not amenable to the jurisdiction of Her Majesty's (English) courts, while acts done in his private capacity as a subject of Her Majesty were.[71] The latter point is *obiter*, because the bill did not reveal any allegation of a private action. But the implication of the ruling, despite the difficult question of 'how far a foreign Sovereign, coming into this country, is amenable at all', is that a foreign King who is also a local Duke and Earl acts in several capacities, with different consequences in English law. In fact, we apply this logic all the time in more mundane circumstances. An average lawyer in private practice might, on any given day, act as executor of a will, guardian of an incompetent ward, secretary of a limited liability company, and trustee of a charitable organisation. In distinct capacities, he performs legal acts (such as signing contracts, buying and selling property, hiring employees, or even committing torts) that generate legal consequences for that *persona* only, without affecting his personal legal position at all.

At least since the early seventeenth century, the King's political *persona* has been identified as the 'corporation sole' of the Crown.[72] The corporation sole was used to describe clerical offices from about the mid-fifteenth century to solve problems of succession within religious orders.[73] Legal forms did not exist to devise real property to a church

[70] [1848] 2 HLC 4

[71] *The Duke of Brunswick* v. *The King of Hanover* [1848] 2 HLC 4, 17 (Pepys LC).

[72] *Sutton's Hospital Case* (1611) 10 Co Rep 1a, 29b; *Case of Magdalen College, Cambridge* (1572) 11 Co Rep 66b, 70a.

[73] F. W. Maitland, 'The Corporation Sole' in David Runciman and Magnus Ryan (eds.), *State, Trust, and Corporation* (Cambridge University Press 2003), 12.

in fee simple absolute, so property was devised to the Saint after whom a parish was named, or to the four walls of a church building, with the local bishop or priest as agent or administrator.[74] Against this background, 'incorporating' the administrator involved a lesser fiction; property rights and powers were transferred on the death of an incumbent to her successor-in-office directly, not to her heirs or through executors.[75] With the normal vagaries and inconsistencies of history, by the eighteenth century Kyd observed 'many instances' of revenues being taken for the maintenance of a single person 'filling some particular station', which belonged to the person 'not in his natural capacity, but in his public character'. There were also persons who held particular offices, being 'vested with the power of acting, in their public character, as trustees for others', which required a separate patrimony, succession, and the capacity for suing and being sued 'in their public character, as far as their trust is concerned'.[76]

Despite Maitland's antipathy, the corporation sole is a useful way of conceptualising these legal constellations. Where a corporation aggregate is lateral, treating many *contemporaneously* as one, a corporation sole is 'vertical in time'. Its members are each 'one of a series of single persons succeeding one another in some official position'; a corporation sole incorporates a single person, being 'really composed of a number of persons who, *one after another*, hold the same office', and emphasis is on the 'series itself and the *seriatim* succession'.[77] Elizabeth II is identical to Victoria; the present Archbishop of Canterbury, in his corporate form, is one with his predecessors. Frederick Pollock described corporate personality as a way of 'constituting the official character of the holders for the time being of the same office . . . into an artificial person or ideal subject of legal capacities and duties'.[78] Hobbes remarked that 'natural capacity, and politick Capacity, signifie no more than private and public right'.[79]

'Office' is pervasive throughout medieval and early modern thought. It was presumed that proper official conduct was by the office as a *persona*; conversely, improper conduct was conceptualised as abuse of office. *In extremis*, abuse of an office 'sloughed off' the *persona*, erasing the moral

[74] J. B. O'Hara, 'The Modern Corporation Sole' (1988) 93 *Dickinson Law Review* 23, 26.
[75] Stuart Kyd, *Treatise on the Law of Corporations*, Vol. 1 (Butterworths 1793), 77.
[76] Stuart Kyd, *Treatise on the Law of Corporations*, Vol. 1 (Butterworths 1793), 19–20.
[77] J. B. O'Hara, 'The Modern Corporation Sole' (1989) 93 *Dickinson Law Review* 23, 25.
[78] Frederick Pollock, *Principles of Contract at Law and in Equity* (6th ed., Stevens 1881), 107.
[79] Thomas Hobbes (Joseph Cropsey ed.), *A Dialogue between a Philosopher and a Student of the Common Laws of England* (University of Chicago Press 1971), 162.

identity and social standing generated by association with it.[80] These are themes which we see play out in the context of judicial review, for example, in the question whether a wrongdoing under colour of official authority is an act of the office or of the official as a private individual, and there is a basic symmetry in the fact that a corporation would forfeit its franchise for acting without authorisation ultra vires. As Seward Brice observed, 'this is but the germ of the doctrine of ultra vires'.[81]

5.2.6 Office and Corporate Personality

The ancient and early modern law on the office of the Crown is of value because it illustrates a deep logical structure that is a general feature of constituted political leadership. Whatever the unique incidents (e.g., rights, powers, and duties) associated with the *particular* offices found in a given social order, *office itself* is essential to the management of the social relations of persons and groups, and is present in all social systems in some form.[82] A particularly vivid account of office is found in the anthropology of Meyer Fortes, who worked on kingship and chiefship, primarily in West African societies.

In Fortes' account, 'office' is characterised by six features. First, office and office holder are seen as distinct; secondly, offices are perpetual and entail succession – an unoccupied office presents a potentially dangerous rupture in the fabric of the institutional order;[83] thirdly, offices have outward, visible regalia and insignia, which objectify their powers and their perpetuity; fourthly, office holders must conform to certain modes of behaviour connected with the office; fifthly, offices have a mandate from society, through its other organs and institutions, giving each office a moral and jural sanction to exercise its stipulated function; finally, offices are conferred on individuals by means of ritual, usually involving ritualised objects and symbols.[84]

80 Conal Condren, *Argument and Authority in Early Modern England* (Cambridge University Press 2006), 6.

81 Seward Brice, *A Treatise on the Doctrine of* Ultra Vires (Stevens & Haynes 1874), 10.

82 Meyer Fortes, 'Ritual and Office in Tribal Society' in Max Gluckman (ed.), *Essays on the Ritual of Social Relations* (Manchester University Press 1962), 58–59.

83 Norman Chester, *The English Administrative System 1780–1870* (Oxford University Press 1981), 6; see also Larissa Katz, 'Offices and Ownership: Possession as a Default Procedure for Appointment' (2020) 70(2) *University of Toronto Law Journal* 267.

84 Burkhard Schnepel, 'Corporations, Personhood, and Ritual in Tribal Society: Three Interconnected Topics in the Anthropology of Meyer Fortes' (1990) 21(1) *Journal of the Anthropological Society of Oxford* 1, 8.

Using this lens, Fortes makes some comparisons back to the British Crown. Ashanti kingship is referred to with the term *akonnua*, generally translated as 'stool', 'in the same way we use "crown" and "throne" to stand for Kingship'.[85] The rite of passage into the office culminates with the solemn seating of the King-Elect on the Stool, after which he is 'obliged to observe a number of rigorous taboos', that is, duties, disabilities, and proscriptions, and is regarded as 'invested with sanctity'. Crucially, the distinction between the incumbent and the office is the key feature of the institution of the *akonnua*. The incoming King swears a public oath of fidelity to the people, and his loyalty to the whole group is acknowledged to be superior to his loyalty to his personal lineage. Any treasure, territory, persons, or other things of value gained during his tenure accrues to the 'Stool property'. During the rite, his senior councillors admonish him to remember never to act without their advice, and to rule with justice and impartiality. He may be 'de-stooled' for breach of the conditions of his office, on which he loses his official dignity and reverts to his common lineage.[86] The coronation oath,[87] political elites' claim to consultation and co-decision,[88] and the separation of the monarch's personal patrimony from the royal demesne all track to the ritual and conventions surrounding the office of the British Crown:[89]

> A jurist, I would take it, would say that *office is none other than the corporation sole in another guise* ... [I]n connection with issues that are closely parallel to the conflicts of status illustrated by Ashanti chiefship, [Pollock and Maitland] discuss the difficulties of sixteenth-century lawyers over the king's status. Was he to be regarded as 'merely a natural person' or also as an 'ideal person', a 'corporation sole'? They conclude that the 'personification of the kingly office in the guise of a corporation sole' was, in the then state of the law, almost a 'necessary expedient'. And they refer back to a much earlier state of affairs when there was no clear-cut distinction between the king's proprietary rights as king and those he had in a private capacity.[90]

85 Meyer Fortes, 'Ritual and Office in Tribal Society' in Max Gluckman (ed.), *Essays on the Ritual of Social Relations* (Manchester University Press 1962), 59.

86 Meyer Fortes, 'Ritual and Office in Tribal Society' in Max Gluckman (ed.), *Essays on the Ritual of Social Relations* (Manchester University Press 1962), 59; R. S. Rattray, *Ashanti Law and Constitution* (Clarendon Press 1929), 60.

87 See Margaret Kelly, 'The Queen of the Commonwealth of Australia' (2001) 16(1) *Australasian Parliamentary Review* 150.

88 See J. C. Davies, *The Baronial Opposition to Edward II* (Cambridge University Press 2014), 15.

89 See Ernst Kantorowicz, *The King's Two Bodies* (Princeton University Press 1997), 342. On the device of royal 'twinning' in a much broader historical context, see Patricia Springborg, *Royal Persons: Patriarchal Monarchy and the Feminine Principle* (Unwin Hyman 1990).

90 Meyer Fortes, 'Ritual and Office in Tribal Society' in Max Gluckman (ed.), *Essays on the Ritual of Social Relations* (Manchester University Press 1962), 60–61, citing

As 'juristic persons', corporations sole are autonomous, enduring, structural units that enable political organisation over time; they persist as institutions despite changing generations of human beings in their membership. From the external point of view, the construct of the juristic person ensures that the community's network of politico-jural statuses persists through time; from the internal point of view, it provides authoritative rules of succession for actors within that web.[91]

This allows us to reflect on modern debates with new clarity. Joshua Getzler has suggested that the corporation sole is a redundant part of our legal history that can be abandoned, as the law has 'so many other tools to create right- and duty-bearing groups and entities'.[92] In a similar vein, David Heaton has argued that we can explain the nature of the Crown without reference to the corporation sole by using concepts such as 'trust, status, or office'.[93] In my view, these arguments rest on a distinction without a difference. To say that the Queen acts in an 'official capacity' is to say that the office of the Queen is a separate legal personality, which is tantamount to acting as a 'corporation sole'. This emphasises the independence and endurance of offices as entities in their own right, for example, through changes of incumbent or even periods of vacancy.

These are good conceptual reasons to retain, and renovate, the conventional doctrine that the Crown is a corporation sole, and that is the approach I will take in this book. To that extent, the notion that the Crown and its officials can perform actions without statutory empowerment on the basis of the Crown's legal personality is robust. The ambit of these third source-type powers, however, should not be determined by analogy with natural persons or indeed necessarily private business corporations.[94]

Frederick Pollock and F. W. Maitland, *History of the Laws of England before Edward I*, Vol. 1 (Cambridge University Press 1923), 495, 502–503. Emphasis mine.

91 Burkhard Schnepel, 'Corporations, Personhood, and Ritual in Tribal Society: Three Interconnected Topics in the Anthropology of Meyer Fortes' (1999) 21(1) *Journal of the Anthropological Society of Oxford* 1, 7; citing Meyer Fortes, 'The Structure of Unilineal Descent Groups' in *Time and Social Structure, and Other Essays* (Athlone Press 1970), 83.

92 Joshua Getzler, 'Personality and Capacity: Lessons from Legal History' in Tim Bonyhady (ed.), *Finn's Law* (Federation Press 2016), 169–170.

93 D. O. F. Heaton, *The Power of Government to Make Contracts* (MPhil Thesis,University of Oxford 2015), 112.

94 See Janet McLean, 'Personality and Public Law Doctrine' (1999) 49 *University of Toronto Law Journal* 123.

5.3 The Crown and HM Government

Town Investments v. *Department of Environment* turned on the identity of the tenant in a lease entered into 'for and on behalf of Her Majesty'. Earlier, I said that although Lord Diplock's suggestion to focus on 'the government' was superficially attractive, following that advice leads in circles.[95] For example, if we focus our attention on HM Government, and assume that all civil servants are 'employees', who is their employer? Ultimately, we come to a variant of the very question we started with.[96] Formally, the employer is the Crown, acting through one of its Ministers. Even if we say that the employer is the Minister, it is obviously the Minister in her ministerial, rather than personal, capacity. Thus, to the extent that the employment paradigm displaces many *offices* in the civil service, it actually bolsters the *importance of office.*

5.3.1 Corporations Sole in a Corporation Aggregate?

We also need a framework to express the connection between the civil servant, his legal employer, and the public, which the employment paradigm cannot do alone.[97] This is the impulse behind the tendency to describe the Crown as a corporation aggregate, rather than a corporation sole. The better view, however, is to see the Crown as one corporation sole of many that together comprise HM Government.

In *M* v. *Home Office*,[98] for example, the question was whether a Minister was amenable to contempt proceedings and, by analogy, injunctions. This occasioned a lengthy enquiry into the traditional immunities of the Crown, before and after the Crown Proceedings Act 1947, and the modern application of the doctrine that 'the King can do no wrong'. Lord Woolf equivocated on the question of corporation sole *versus*

[95] See H. W. R. Wade, 'The Crown, Ministers and Officials: Legal Status and Liability' and Peter Rowe, 'The Crown and Accountability for the Armed Forces', both in Maurice Sunkin and Sebastian Payne (eds.), *The Nature of the Crown* (Oxford University Press 1999), 27 and 267, respectively.

[96] See Robert Watt, 'The Crown and its Employees' in Maurice Sunkin and Sebastian Payne (eds.), *The Nature of the Crown* (Oxford University Press 1999), 293; Mark Freedland, 'Contracting the Employment of Civil Servants – A Transparent Exercise' [1995] *Public Law* 224, 230.

[97] See *Henly* v. *The Mayor of Lyme* (1828) 130 ER 995, 1001 (Best CJ); P. D. Finn, 'The Forgotten "Trust": The People and the State' in Malcolm Cope (ed.), *Equity Issues and Trends* (Federation Press 1995); P. D. Finn, 'A Sovereign People, a Public Trust' in P. D. Finn (ed.), *Essays on Law and Government*, Vol. 1 (Law Book 1995).

[98] [1994] 1 AC 377.

aggregate, for which he has been criticised.[99] Granted, both are 'autonomous and enduring structural units' occupying 'structural places' in political organisations.[100] But, ultimately, we do need to make a choice. If we describe the Crown as a corporation sole, and then equate the Crown with the whole of HM Government, we run into the problems of *Town Investments* v. *Department of Environment*. In my view, it is preferable to see the Crown as a corporation sole and HM Government as a corporation aggregate formed of many offices with the Crown at its head.[101] Indeed, in *Town Investments* v. *Department of Environment*, Lord Morris characterised a Minister acting on behalf of the Crown as a corporation sole, comprising a part of 'HM Government', presumably a corporation aggregate.[102]

Adopting such a position, however, requires a more advanced concept of office than we currently have. *M* v. *Home Office* itself illustrates the problem. Lord Woolf predicated his enquiry with the remark that, although the distinction between the Crown and an officer of the Crown is of great importance 'in the theory which clouds the subject', 'in reality' it was 'of no practical significance in judicial review proceedings'.[103] But questions of an agent's liability are logically secondary to the question whether she acted within or without her vires, and to determine an agent's vires we need to identify the agent.

As Janet McLean argues, these cases illustrate the tendency of English administrative lawyers to 'disaggregate' the government. The focal beam of judicial review naturally centres on the powers and duties of some official in terms of *his particular* office, as defined by statute and augmented by the common law principles of judicial review, not by reference to the Crown or

[99] See Martin Loughlin, 'The State, the Crown and the Law' in Maurice Sunkin and Sebastian Payne (eds.), *The Nature of the Crown* (Oxford University Press 1999).

[100] Burkhart Schnepel, 'Corporations, Personhood, and Ritual in Tribal Society: Three Interconnected Topics in the Anthropology of Meyer Fortes' (1999) 21(1) *Journal of the Anthropological Society of Oxford* 1, 7.

[101] See F. W. Maitland, 'The Crown as Corporation' in David Runciman and Magnus Ryan (eds.), *State, Trust, and Corporation* (Cambridge University Press 2003), 34, citing the speech of Fineux CJ (YB 14 Henry VIII) that the Parliament of the King and Lords and Commons is a corporation by common law.

[102] *Town Investments Ltd* v. *Department for the Environment* [1978] AC 359, 395; see also *Bacchus* v. *Servicio National del Trigo* [1957] 1 QB 438, 472 (Parker LJ); F. A. Mann, *Foreign Affairs in English Courts* (Oxford University Press 1986), 4.

[103] *M* v. *Home Office* [1994] 1 AC 377, 406, 407; S. A. de Smith, Sir Harry Woolf, and Jeffrey Jowell, *Judicial Review of Administrative Action* (5th ed., Sweet & Maxwell 1995), 204; see Martin Loughlin, 'The State, the Crown, and the Law' in Maurice Sunkin and Sebastian Payne (eds.), *The Nature of the Crown* (Oxford University Press 1999), 72–73.

HM Government as a corporate entity.[104] Contract law, by way of contrast, presupposes a single corporate actor and treats all the individuals who make up HM Government as a 'single entity that bears rights and duties that are distinct from the rights and duties of the individuals who comprise it'.[105] Thus, the Crown appears as a common law corporation with all the incidents of corporate personality we might expect, such as perpetuity and contractual capacity. Dicey's dogged defence of the idea that ultra vires action was personal, rather than corporate, and that the 'ordinary courts' were the only proper forum in which to hold officials to account, exemplifies the 'disaggregating view'. However, that position is impossible to maintain in the modern context where the Crown is liable in a corporate capacity, and in which the Crown's assumed contractual capacities have become a systemic modality of public administration.[106] It is particularly unhelpful in the context of third source-type powers, in which officials within HM Government exercise, for example, the contractual capacity that inures in the Crown's corporate legal personality.

A recurrent issue in English public law is the tendency to focus on remedies in the first instance, reason backwards, and call it theory.[107] As McLean observes, Dicey's view seems to have been formed with the law of tort almost exclusively in mind – given its vital historical role in executive accountability – and seems to have left contract out.[108] He ignored contemporary work, for example, by Ernest Barker and F. W. Maitland, on the juristic personality of the Crown.[109] But the curtailment of Crown immunities raised questions:

> An agent in contract can only act on behalf of a principal. The Prime Minister could not be the principal because he (like the agent) was also legally a servant of the Crown. For an official to be acting as an agent, the

[104] Janet McLean, 'The Crown in Contract and Administrative Law' (2004) 24(1) *Oxford Journal of Legal Studies* 129, 132.

[105] Janet McLean, 'The Crown in Contract and Administrative Law' (2004) 24(1) *Oxford Journal of Legal Studies* 129, 136.

[106] See Andreas Abegg, 'The Evolution of the Contracting State and Its Courts' (2011) 59(3) *The American Journal of Comparative Law* 622.

[107] See *Davy* v. *Spelthorne Borough Council* [1983] 3 All ER 278, 285 (Lord Wilberforce); Thomas Poole, 'Judicial Review at the Margins: Law, Power, and Prerogative' (2010) 60 *University of Toronto Law Journal* 81, 93; Mark Walters, *A.V. Dicey and the Common Law Constitutional Tradition* (Cambridge University Press 2020), 151.

[108] Janet McLean, 'The Crown in Contract and Administrative Law' (2004) 24(1) *Oxford Journal of Legal Studies* 129, 141.

[109] See Janet McLean, 'The Crown in Contract and Administrative Law' (2004) 24(1) *Oxford Journal of Legal Studies* 129, 141, citing Ernest Barker, 'The Rule of Law' (1914) 1 *Political Quarterly* 118.

> principal must exist. Once the principal is no longer immune, a great deal of work is required to be done to shape what kind of legal person that principal is and should be.[110]

Holding the official to account does not work in the context of contract. In terms of subsequent development, the application of the ordinary law of contract to Government has prevailed over a Diceyan vision of the state.[111] The whole field is a little confused because a good deal of conventional administrative law theory (which disaggregates the Crown) cleaves to Dicey's conception of the state even while introducing a 'separate public law' towards which Dicey was originally so hostile.[112] The fallback position for Dicey was to concede the development of 'something like the *droit administratif* of France' but maintain 'the fact that the ordinary law courts can deal with any actual and provable breach of the law committed by a servant of the Crown still preserves that rule of law which is fatal to the existence of true *droit administratif*.[113] As Mark Walters explains:

> Dicey saw the light (or at least *a* light): it is possible to have administrative power and the rule of law if there is judicial review by the ordinary common law courts to ensure power is exercised consistently with the principle of legality ... Dicey's willingness to accept that public officials were increasingly like business managers and needed some additional room to manoeuvre, including the ability to exercise judicial-like powers, is a far cry from his account of the rule of law in *Law of the Constitution*. Of course, his willingness to entertain these new administrative modes of decision-making was contingent upon the exercise by the ordinary courts of a supervisory review function to ensure compliance with legal standards of fairness. Thus, Dicey seems finally to have made the link between an English-style of administrative law and the prerogative writs.[114]

I shall present my own views about the rule of law, executive power, and judicial review in Chapter 12. For now, it suffices to say that the concept

[110] See Janet McLean, 'The Crown in Contract and Administrative Law' (2004) 24(1) *Oxford Journal of Legal Studies* 129, 142.

[111] See Mark Walters, *A.V. Dicey and the Common Law Constitutional Tradition* (Cambridge University Press 2020), 315, citing A. V. Dicey, 'The Development of Administrative Law in England' (1915) *Law Quarterly Review* 148(31).

[112] Janet McLean, 'The Crown in Contract and Administrative Law' (2004) 24(1) *Oxford Journal of Legal Studies* 129, 154.

[113] A. V. Dicey, 'The Development of Administrative Law in England' (1915) *Law Quarterly Review* 148, 152.

[114] Mark Walters, *A.V. Dicey and the Common Law Constitutional Tradition* (Cambridge University Press 2020), 315–316.

of office is an implicit piece of the puzzle of English public law that has been missing for too long.

5.3.2 The Legal Personality of Officials

It is thus essential not only to theorise the legal personality of the Crown, but also of officials such as Ministers, and to explain their relationship. We are caught between conflicting approaches. The ghost of Dicey continues to disaggregate the Crown and look for a personal wrongdoing at private law by one of its officials wherever something goes wrong. Twentieth century reformers like Lord Diplock admonish us to look past the Crown and its 'emanations' and to look at the modern apparatus of public sector employees and their managers – implicitly relying on Ministers' ultimate responsibility to Parliament, but not answering the question 'Who signed the lease for these premises?'. But that question has become only more important in the contracting state that has emerged since the 1980s, which makes it obvious that the Crown does, indeed, contract in a corporate capacity.

The administrative state is a 'network of offices',[115] and it seems fair characterise this network as a corporation aggregate of so many corporations sole, including the Crown, Ministers, Secretaries of State, and other officials which derive their powers formally (if not always historically[116]) from the Crown.[117] This requires us to take more seriously the nature of HM Government as a corporate actor, which may entail a more restricted sphere of application for the conventional immunities of the Monarch within HM Government, and it demands more efforts to conceptualise the mechanics of attributed action within that framework.[118]

[115] Bradley Selway, 'Of Kings and Officers – The Judicial Development of Public Law' (2005) 33 *Federal Law Review* 1, 6; M. J. Braddick, *State Formation in Early Modern England c 1550–1700* (Cambridge University Press 2000), 11, 45.

[116] See F. W. Maitland, *The Constitutional History of England* (Cambridge University Press 1908), 39–54.

[117] Lord Morris suggested that Ministers be seen as corporations sole in *Town Investments Ltd* v. *Department of Environment* [1978] AC 359, 395. In *Kinloch* v. *Secretary of State for India in Council* (1882) 7 AC 619 the Secretary of State was called expressly 'a body corporate, or something in the nature of a body corporate', and 'not the individual who now happens to fill that office [but] the officer bearing that description' for the purposes of contracting, suing, and being sued – but not for the purposes of holding property.

[118] The personality of officials was also thrashed out in a Germanophone debate of the late nineteenth century: see Edmund Bernatzik, *Über den Begriff der juristischen Person und über die juristische Persönlichkeit der Behörden insbesondere* (Springer 1996 [1890]) (*On*

5.3.3 *The Attribution of Official Action to the Crown*

Legal institutions can only act through human beings. Categorically, an office without an office holder is inert. How, then, are actions by human beings attributed to an entity like the Crown? In *Meridian Global Funds Management Asia Ltd* v. *Securities Commission*,[119] Lord Hoffmann observed that any proposition about a corporation necessarily refers to a *set of rules*. These rules provide that a *persona ficta* shall be deemed to exist and to have certain powers, rights, and duties, but also what acts are to count as acts of the *persona ficta*. This is as true of a political corporation, such as the Crown, as it is of a private business organisation. 'To say that a company cannot do something means only that there is no one whose doing of that act would, under the applicable rules of attribution, count as an act of the [corporation]'.[120]

The powers of a Minister are formally derived from the Crown, and they are exercised in its name. We can say 'emanation' if we must, but we should not take this to mean that the Minister is *actually part of* the Crown in its narrower sense. Rather we mean that the Crown, an office at the centre of a network of offices called HM Government, is the nominal actor to whom actions by officials within HM Government are attributed. These *rules of attribution* provide that any (valid) act by a Minister shall count as an act of the Crown. But there need not be a relation of identity between the entities, nor perfect symmetry between rules of attribution of valid actions (whether exercising the Crown's private law or 'sovereign' powers) and liability for invalid actions (whether in tort or in public law). The point is not easy, but may appear a little more clearly in the mundane light of private law:

> [T]he fact that a company's employee is authorised to drive a lorry does not in itself lead to the conclusion that if he kills someone by reckless driving, the company will be guilty of manslaughter. There is no inconsistency. Each is an example of an attribution rule for a particular purpose, tailored as it always must be to the terms and policies of the substantive rule.[121]

the Concept of the Juristic Person and on the Juristic Personality of Public Authorities in Particular, not yet available in English), written in the context of the late Hapsburg Empire.

119 [1995] 3 All ER 918 (JCPC).

120 *Meridian Global Funds Management Asia Ltd* v. *Securities Commission* [1995] 2 AC 500, 506–507.

121 *Meridian Global Funds Management Asia Ltd* v. *Securities Commission* [1995] 2 AC 500, 512.

Really it boils down to a fairly simple question. Given that the Crown acts (only) through its officers, should the relevant rules attribute wrongdoing to the relevant official in his *personal* or *official* capacity? If the latter, what ideas about the Crown and HM Government do we need to adjust?

Traditionally, the special status of the Crown was reconciled with the rule of law by insisting on the personal liability of officials acting ultra vires.[122] As the Crown could do no wrong, it could not be taken (by a court) to have authorised wrongdoing; the wrongdoing must have been an act of the official *qua* individual, not *qua* official. This is consistent with the 'disaggregating' tendency noted earlier, and worked tolerably well as long as private law actions in tort were the primary mechanism of official accountability. As Lord Woolf observed in *M* v. *Home Office*, as long as the plaintiff sued the 'actual wrongdoer' personally, they were unable to 'hide behind the immunity of the Crown'.[123] However, it was not always possible to sue the actual wrongdoer personally,[124] and in practical terms this depended on the government indemnifying the hapless official, who in many cases would have been acting pursuant to instructions.[125] Conceptually, it has been criticised for allowing private law (i.e., tort) to do all the heavy lifting in constitutional and administrative law.

It was rather ingenious of English lawyers to reinterpret the absolutist doctrine that the King can do no wrong to reflect the notion that every actor in our legal system, from the Prime Minister to Valuation Officer, is responsible for every act done without legal justification like any other citizen.[126] There is also an undeniable logic to the approach, because if rules empower me to perform an action subject to certain conditions, and I breach the conditions, no valid action has occurred.

However, the conception of administrative law to which that view leads is too far out of touch with the realities that the Crown and its officials comprise a complex organisational entity that can, in fact, commit wrongs in a 'corporate' capacity, and that the supervisory

[122] Martin Loughlin, 'The State, the Crown, and the Law' in Maurice Sunkin and Sebastian Payne (eds.), *The Nature of the Crown* (Oxford University Press 1999), 72.

[123] *M* v. *Home Office* [1994] 1 AC 377, 409.

[124] See Dennis Thompson, *Political Ethics and Public Office* (Harvard University Press 1987), 40.

[125] See *Adams* v. *Naylor* [1946] 2 All ER 241, which led to the passage of the Civil Proceedings Act 1947.

[126] A. V. Dicey, *Introduction to the Study of the Law of the Constitution* (10th ed., Macmillan 1959), 193; *The Case of the Marshalsea* (1612) 10 Co Rep 68b; *Terry* v. *Huntingdon* (1688) Hard 480; *Perkin* v. *Proctor* (1768) 2 Wils KB 382; *Palmer* v. *Crone* [1927] 1 KB 804.

jurisdiction is about more than just suing rogue officials in tort. In *M* v. *Home Office*, for example, it was held that officials could be the subject of an injunction in their official capacity; as Lord Templeman observed, to hold otherwise would lead to the position that 'the executive obey the law as a matter of grace and not as a matter of necessity', which would 'reverse the result of the Civil War'.[127]

The conventional, private law constitutionalist approach also puts us on the horns of a dilemma noticed by Sir Raymond Evershed MR in *Harper* v. *Secretary of State for the Home Department*.[128] If an act is a nullity and I seek to restrain a particular individual 'who happens at the moment' to be a Minister, I should sue her in her personal capacity as for an ordinary wrong; however, it would not be clear what breach of duty she would have committed in that personal capacity, for the relevant duties attach to her *office*. On the other hand, if she is sued in her capacity as Minister, she would be protected by the traditional Crown immunities,[129] and to the extent this is not the case we must admit the development of an 'administrative law' that is distinct, in certain respects at least, from the ordinary law of tort.

Further, the traditional approach often put the cart before the horse, inspiring submissions like the following:

> In the last resort the question whether the Minister is or is not acting in a representative capacity depends on whether the scheme is or is not ultra vires, for as the Crown can do no wrong, if the scheme is ultra vires and unlawful, the Minister cannot be acting in his representative capacity.[130]

Again, identifying the defendant incidentally to the question of remedies invites confusion. Our three candidates are the Crown, the Minister in his official capacity, and the Minister in his personal capacity. In the former two cases, problems of Crown immunity arise, as well as 'Evershed's Dilemma'. In the third case, we are vulnerable to the critique that 'private law' concepts of liability do the heavy lifting in public law.

In any case, governmental immunity has been abolished, or at least seriously diminished, for some time,[131] and questions of sovereign

[127] *M* v. *Home Office* [1994] 1 AC 377, 395.

[128] *The Times*, 18 December 1954.

[129] *Harper* v. *Secretary of State for the Home Department*, *The Times*, 18 December 1954, cited in *Merricks* v. *Heathcote-Amory* [1955] Ch 567, 574.

[130] *Merricks* v. *Heathcote-Amory* [1955] Ch 567, 577.

[131] In colonial Australia, the question of personal versus official liability of government officials turned on whether the tortious act was authorised by (superior officers within) the government, done on the government's behalf, and subject to the government's

immunity can be reserved for those cases *actually* involving the Queen.[132] The matter is truly simplified by recognising the Queen as distinct from the Crown, and recognising each of HM Ministers and Secretaries of State as a corporation, an acting subject separate from the Crown, within HM Government. This may well diminish the actual relevance of 'the Crown' to a formal, or indeed formalistic, *locus* of attribution.

In Australia, nineteenth century colonial legislation enabled claims against the government as of right, using the device of a nominal defendant to hold the relevant colonial government to account in a corporate capacity.[133] Maitland approved: it was a 'wholesome sight to see "the Crown" sued and answering for its torts'.[134] But there, too, legislatures shrank from naming the Crown expressly, instead (pre-empting Lord Diplock) using various formulations incorporating 'the Government', and Finn has described how judges construed the statutes 'under the shadow of the Crown prerogative'.[135] In other words, while the legislation demanded a conceptual effort to theorise the new landscape – in which officers of the Crown were stripped of their historical immunities and HM Government entered the 'liability calculus' as a player in its own right[136] – the necessary theoretical efforts did not eventuate. Nor did they eventuate in the England following the passage of the Crown Proceedings Act 1947; cases like *Town Investments* and *M* v. *Home Office* show that 'contradictions and loose ends' subsist.[137] Tying up those loose ends is

control: P. D. Finn, *Law and Government in Colonial Australia* (Oxford University Press 1987), 141, 152.

132 See H. W. R. Wade, 'The Crown, Ministers, and Officials: Legal Status and Liability' in Maurice Sunkin and Sebastian Payne (eds.), *The Nature of the Crown* (Oxford University Press 1999), 28.

133 See P. D. Finn, *Law and Government in Colonial Australia* (Oxford University Press 1987), 141–155.

134 F. W. Maitland, 'The Crown as Corporation' (1901) 17 *Law Quarterly Review* 131, 142.

135 P. D. Finn, *Law and Government in Colonial Australia* (Oxford University Press 1987), 145, 148.

136 P. D. Finn, *Law and Government in Colonial Australia* (Oxford University Press 1987), 145, 153.

137 H. W. R. Wade, 'The Crown, Ministers, and Officials: Legal Status and Liability' in Maurice Sunkin and Sebastian Payne (eds.), *The Nature of the Crown* (Oxford University Press 1999), 24. The situation, he argued, was even more dire in Scotland where *McDonald* v. *Secretary of State for Scotland* 1994 SC 234 interpreted the Act as prohibiting certain injunctive relief against Crown officers. On the Scots position see also Adam Tomkins, 'Crown Privileges' in Maurice Sunkin and Sebastian Payne (eds.), *The Nature of the Crown* (Oxford University Press 1999), 174.

greatly assisted by adopting the terminology I have suggested, and embracing the liability of HM Government as a corporate actor.

5.4 The Crown and the Commonwealth

'The Crown' is not just used to refer to the Queen and HM Government, however; it is also used as a kind of placeholder for the organised political community itself. When creating the Duchy of Lancaster, Henry IV asserted that the Crown was a 'public body'.[138] The *Duchy of Lancaster Case* duly held that the King and his subjects 'together compose the corporation'; 'he is incorporated with them and they with him, he is the head and they the members'.[139] According to Michael Wilks, 'when the whole community is in its corporate nature represented by one man, that one man becomes himself a corporation'; this is was a 'direct transference to the papacy of the Roman law theory of the corporation sole' later borrowed by royalists and republicans.[140] We have seen a secularised version of this device in Hobbes' *Leviathian.* Ernst Kantorowicz explained, in his seminal study of the two bodies doctrine, that the 'community of the realm' swore fealty to the Crown in medieval England: 'king, councillors, officials, and lords spiritual and secular took consonantly the same oath to maintain the rights of the Crown', and together represented the political *universitas.*[141] The relationship was conceived as a double bond of obedience and protection. Significantly, an oath sworn by the King himself to maintain the rights of the Crown show that the Crown was distinct from the King, at once something superior to all and something all had in common.[142]

It is convenient now to return to Maitland's 'metaphysiological problem'. The way out of the mess, he argued, was to see the King as the head of a 'complex and highly organised' corporation aggregate that embraces not only the government but also the people, which he called the 'commonwealth'.[143] Maitland was compelled to this kind of conclusion because he thought that corporations were real, organic

[138] See Helen Castor, *The King, the Crown, and the Duchy of Lancaster: Public Authority and Private Power, 1399–1461* (Cambridge University Press 2000), 3.

[139] *The Case of the Duchy of Lancaster* (1561) 1 Plowd 212.

[140] Michael Wilks, *The Problem of Sovereignty in the Later Middle Ages* (Cambridge University Press 1964), 32.

[141] Ernst Kantorowicz, *The King's Two Bodies* (Princeton University Press 1997), 360.

[142] Ernst Kantorowicz, *The King's Two Bodies* (Princeton University Press 1997), 360.

[143] F. W. Maitland, 'The Crown as Corporation' in David Runciman and Magnus Ryan (eds.), *State, Trust, and Corporation* (Cambridge University Press 2003), 35.

entities.[144] A corporation could *only* be aggregate, for Maitland, because he thought that corporate personality was merely the law's recognition of facts in the real world: '[I]f *n* men unite themselves in an organised body, jurisprudence, unless it wishes to pulverise the group, must see *n*+1 persons'.[145] Maitland lamented that instead of personifying the 'state', the English sought to 'parsonify' the Crown:

> What we see in England … is not that the State is personified or that the State's personality is openly acknowledged, but … that the king is 'parsonified'. Since that feat was performed, we have been, more or less explicitly, trying to persuade ourselves that our law does not recognise the personality or corporate character of the State or Nation or Commonwealth, and has no need to do anything of the sort if only it will admit that the king, or, yet worse, the Crown, is not unlike a parson.[146]

Maitland's concern was that 'Crown' had, historically, eclipsed 'republic' and 'commonwealth'. Elizabeth I's Secretary could write of '*De republica Anglorum*' with no contradiction, but after the constitutional struggles of the seventeenth century these terms 'implied kinglessness and therefore treason'.[147] Terminological confusion had proliferated. The Pensions (Colonial Service) Act 1887, for example, declared that the terms 'permanent civil service of the State', 'permanent civil service of Her Majesty', and 'permanent civil service of the Crown' were to have the same meaning.

The absence of a 'state' concept and the tendency to disaggregate the Crown into so many officials in cases of wrongdoing informed a common law tradition that Martin Loughlin has argued was 'unable to accommodate the idea of government as a category of juristic thought' and which, instead, either 'elevate[d] government beyond the law' or 'press[ed] official action into the categories of private law'.[148] These problems are due to a failure to distinguish the office of the Monarch from the complex

144 F. W. Maitland, 'The Corporation Sole' in David Runciman and Magnus Ryan (eds.), *State, Trust, and Corporation* (Cambridge University Press 2003), 14.

145 See F. W. Maitland, 'Moral Personality and Legal Personality' in David Runciman and Magnus Ryan (eds.), *State, Trust, and Corporation* (Cambridge University Press 2003); Janet McLean, *Searching for the State in British Legal Thought* (Cambridge University Press 2012), 72, 82; F. W. Maitland, 'Translator's Introduction' in Otto von Gierke (F. W. Maitland trans.), *Political Theories of the Middle Age* (Cambridge University Press 1911), xi.

146 F. W. Maitland, 'The Crown as Corporation' in David Runciman and Magnus Ryan (eds.), *State, Trust, and Corporation* (Cambridge University Press 2003), 33.

147 F. W. Maitland, 'The Crown as Corporation' in David Runciman and Magnus Ryan (eds.), *State, Trust, and Corporation* (Cambridge University Press 2003), 38.

148 Martin Loughlin, 'The State, the Crown, and the Law' in Maurice Sunkin and Sebastian Payne (eds.), *The Nature of the Crown* (Oxford University Press 1999), 75.

network of offices that together comprise HM Government. The key, in my view, is (again) the concept of office, the importance of which Loughlin himself describes aptly. Hobbes' attempt to build a system of public law on the idea of an artificial, representative personality demonstrates the 'critical importance to public law of the concept of office'; it is office that distinguishes between the post and the post-holder, on the basis of which 'the public can be differentiated from the private'.[149] In my view, the concept of office is even more important than the concept of state for public law, especially in a constitutional tradition in which the Crown (still) stands in for the state.

5.4.1 *The Importance of Saying What We Actually Mean*

A recent Australian case illustrates the importance (and difficulty) of theorising the relation between Crown, official, and body politic. In *Hocking* v. *Director General of the National Archive*,[150] it fell to be determined whether certain letters between HM the Queen and the Australian Governor-General were the property of the Commonwealth of Australia, which turned on whether they were 'official' or 'personal'.

All judgments advanced some analysis of the nature of the Commonwealth of Australia and its relationship to the organised political community, the Crown, the Vice-Regent, and the other officers that animate its various organs. Edelman J, for example, began his analysis with a reference to Jean-Jacques Rousseau's political theory before moving to Australian law.[151] 'The Commonwealth' in its primary sense refers to a body politic that is a 'legal entity or right-holder', which 'has a legal body or corpus like a body corporate' and represents its membership. He referred to the speech of Griffith CJ in an older case which distinguished the Australian body politic from ordinary corporations but said that it 'stands for the Crown as representing the whole community'.[152] The body politic referred to as 'the Commonwealth' has the usual triad of governmental functions, and the expression 'Crown in right of the

[149] Martin Loughlin, *The Idea of Public Law* (Oxford University Press 2003), 157–158. Emphasis mine.

[150] [2020] HCA 19.

[151] *Hocking* v. *Director General of the National Archive of Australia* [2020] HCA 19, [212] (Edleman J).

[152] *Commonwealth* v. *Baume* (1905) 2 CLR 405, 413 (Griffith CJ).

Commonwealth' was generally used to describe the exercise of executive power by the Commonwealth as a body politic.[153] However:

> The primary sense of 'the Commonwealth' as a body politic is not its only connotation ... For instance, the Commonwealth has also been extended beyond its character as a body politic to include all legal entities within the description of Commonwealth agencies and instrumentalities. This includes the creation of a new body corporate from that which would otherwise have fallen within the conception of the Commonwealth as a body politic ... Another meaning of the Commonwealth is a secondary, or instrumental, conception, also used in the *Constitution*, to describe the 'central organs of government', and particularly the executive. In this secondary sense, the Commonwealth connotes the 'organizations or institutions of government in accordance with the conceptions of ordinary life' including 'government owned and controlled instrumentalities'. Such organisations can be, but need not be, entities with a legal corpus or body.[154]

While all judgments in *Hocking* v. *Director General of the National Archive* take seriously the problem of official action, the analysis is complicated by the lack of a coherent concept of office. In particular, it is important to remember that even an 'organisation of government' with legal personality relies, categorically, on human agents to act. My preference is to use a 'small c' commonwealth to capture Edelman J's first sense. Much of the 'big c' Commonwealth (in the Australian context) can be captured by reference to 'Commonwealth Government' (or 'HM Government').[155]

5.4.2 *The Divisible Crown*

One last set of questions relates to the traditional doctrine that the Crown is 'one and indivisible'. As we have seen, this maxim complicates the analysis of the relationship between the Crown and its officials and, makes analysis of things like Government Business Enterprises and Quasi Non-Governmental Organisations more complex, as well.

153 *Hocking* v. *Director General of the National Archive of Australia* [2020] HCA 19, [213] (Edelman J).

154 *Hocking* v. *Director General of the National Archive of Australia* [2020] HCA 19, [214]–[215] (Edelman J). Citations omitted.

155 There is possibly a residual space not covered by either of these terms, which may explain the persistence of 'the Crown' in legal usage. Sebastian Hartford Davis argues for speaking of the 'Commonwealth' (in the sense of 'Commonwealth of Australia', traditionally 'the Crown in right of the Commonwealth of Australia') as a 'constitutional person' conceptually distinct from both the 'nation' and the 'government'. I do not think that is necessary. See Sebastian Hartford Davis, 'The Legal Personality of the Commonwealth of Australia' (2019) 47(1) *Federal Law Review* 3.

There is an external aspect to the doctrine, which is that the Crown is indivisible 'throughout the Empire'. For example, in *Amalgamated Society of Engineers* v. *Adelaide Steamship Company Limited*,[156] the High Court of Australia rejected suggestions that there was an 'Imperial King', a 'Commonwealth King' and a 'State King'.[157] This doctrine has not survived twentieth century developments, but the role of the Crown in structuring the constitutional relations that subsist between the United Kingdom and its former colonies is a question for another day.

Of more immediate concern to the law of judicial review is the Crown's divisibility *within* any given constitutional order. Here, the federal jurisdiction authorities are most helpful. Lionel Smith has observed that the Province of Ontario can make a contractual agreement or have a legal dispute with Canada, of which Ontario forms a part. 'If we wish to insist that the Crown remains one and indivisible', he concludes, 'we have no longer any choice but to acknowledge that it is made up of a multitude of patrimonies (or, if we prefer, capacities)'.[158] The Privy Council has said that while there is only one Crown, it has multiple 'purses',[159] and in *Wewaykum Indian Band* v. *Canada*,[160] Binnie J of the Canadian Supreme Court pushed the headdress metaphor even further: the Crown 'wears many hats'.[161] Maitland, for his part, praised American opinions treating the states of the United States as bodies corporate: 'This seems to be the result to which English law would naturally have come, had not that foolish parson led it astray'. The Australian states, while they did not use the term, adopted a similar posture in their agreement to 'unite in one indissoluble Federal Commonwealth under the Crown'; a body politic, after all, 'may be a member of another body politic'.[162] If devolution follows its current trajectory, it may well be that the Crown in right of the United Kingdom may have to be reconceptualised as a federated Crown, as well.[163] In my account, the distinctions between different officials within HM Government

[156] (1920) 28 CLR 129.

[157] *Amalgamated Society of Engineers* v. *Adelaide Steamship Company Limited* (1920) 28 CLR 129, 153 (Knox CJ, Isaacs, Rich, and Stark JJ).

[158] Lionel Smith, 'Scottish Trusts in the Common Law' (2013) 17 *Edinburgh Law Review* 283.

[159] *Re Silver Brothers; A-G Quebec* v. *A-G Canada* [1932] AC 514, 524.

[160] [2002] 4 SCR 245.

[161] *Wewaykum Indian Band* v. *Canada* [2002] 4 SCR 245, [96].

[162] F. W. Maitland, 'The Crown as Corporation' in David Runciman and Magnus Ryan (eds.), *State, Trust, and Corporation* (Cambridge University Press 2003), 46.

[163] Anne Twomey has observed that Scotland has a better claim to a separate Crown than some British Overseas Territories, having an executive government responsible to

and between HM Governments in different territorial communities can be accommodated, leaving the relations between the 'Imperial Crown', the 'Crown in right of the United Kingdom', and the Crown in right of the other realms to one side.

5.5 Conclusion

This chapter has attempted a kind of conceptual and terminological 'clean up' of the central figure in the story of non-statutory executive powers, the Crown. The most important point is that the Crown must never be described as a 'natural person'. The conventional doctrine that the Crown is a corporation sole, on the other hand, has been shown to be sounder than it first appears. The 'metaphysiological nonsense' that Maitland criticised is a consequence of medieval people articulating a concept in their proper idiom. The problem was the idiom, not the concept itself. Indeed, with respect, this is not one of Maitland's better arguments. If we couch the concept in more analytical terms, many of the problems evaporate.

Thus, nothing speaks per se against deriving third source-type powers from the Crown's common law powers as a corporation sole. However, doing so makes the concept of office essential – both to understand the Crown itself and to the exercise of its powers by individuals. Office explains how acts, in reality performed by human beings, are attributed to an ideal subject, taken as representative of the community.[164] The key to understanding the relation between Crown and commonwealth, therefore, is the former's role as a *representative*. When officials (including the Queen) act within their roles, they act for the commonwealth.[165] This helps to sharpen our focus to the task at hand – the conception of the Crown and its officials maintaining a lawful state of affairs by keeping officials within their proper bounds.

a representative legislature, the First Minister of which advises the Queen on some Scottish matters and keeps the Scottish Seal by which acts under the prerogative are certified. See Anne Twomey, 'Responsible Government and the Divisibility of the Crown' [2008] *Public Law* 742, 765, 768. On statutory language in the Scotland Act 1998 to the effect that there is a 'Crown in right of the Scottish Administration' separate from the 'Crown in right of Her Majesty's Government in the United Kingdom', see the explanatory notes to The Scotland Act 1998, Schedule 8, Paragraph 7: www.legislation.gov.uk/ukpga/1998/46/notes/division/5/8/7.

164 Alf Ross, 'On the Concepts "State" and "State Organs" in Constitutional Law' (1961) 5 *Scandinavian Studies in Law* 112, 115.

165 See Arthur Ripstein, *Force and Freedom* (Harvard University Press 2009), 195.

6

Public Law as the Law of Public Offices

6.1 Introduction

Mark Elliott has rightly argued that 'developed societies employ power-allocation methodologies which are based in law and which regulate the distribution of power to the various branches of government'.[1] As a participant in the ultra vires debate, Elliott directed this separation of powers argument against the so-called common law theorists, who argued that judicial review rested on the judges' inherent power of controlling governmental action. Elliott argued that the constitutional allocation of powers between the branches of government placed untrammelled legislative power in Parliament, and that the common law theorists' view of the constitutional allocation of powers challenged this notion too openly. Thus, even though an inherent supervisory function in the judicial office was a more plausible interpretation of the historical record and current court practice, as the common law theorists argued, Elliott was resolute that the principle of parliamentary supremacy require one to ground the supervisory jurisdiction in an attenuated theory of legislative intent.

For this reason, the theories of judicial review argued in the historical ultra vires debate are of limited assistance to understanding the review of non-statutory executive powers today.[2] If we want to understand how and why prerogative-type and third source-type powers are reviewed, we should start with the mechanics of Elliott's 'power-allocation methodology' rather than with assumptions about legislative *versus* judicial supremacy. In effect, English public lawyers took the 'constitutional

[1] Mark Elliott, 'The Ultra Vires Doctrine in a Constitutional Setting: Still the Central Principle of Administrative Law' in C. F. Forsyth (ed.), *Judicial Review and the Constitution* (Hart 2000), 86; Sir John Laws, 'Illegality: The Problem of Jurisdiction' in Michael Supperstone and James Goudie (eds.), *Judicial Review* (2nd ed., Hart 1997), 51.

[2] See Chapter 11 and Chapter 12, in particular.

turn' too early, that is, before they had engaged with the foundational question of how 'administration' actually works.[3]

Leaving the ultra vires debate to one side, Elliott is correct that every legal system endows certain individuals with authority to make and apply norms over its membership. But taking this point seriously raises a more basic question. How can an institution, whose 'offices are filled with ordinary fallible people', be empowered to do things that none of those human beings are entitled to do as individuals?[4] The whole point of judicial review *is just* to ensure that officials act only in the ways determined by legal rules. As Brennan J of the Australian High Court said in *Church of Scientology* v. *Woodward*:[5] 'Judicial review is neither more nor less than the enforcement of the rule of law over executive action; it is the means by which executive action is prevented from exceeding the powers and functions assigned to the executive by law and the interests of the individual are protected accordingly'.[6]

We are concerned with the powers and functions assigned to executive officials by law. In due course, we will have to ask whether it makes a difference that assignment takes place by words in a constitutional text, in an ordinary statute (as construed by a court), or by judicial pronouncement on the basis of common law principles. In the first instance, however, we need to determine how it is that the law assigns powers and functions to individuals at all. Section 6.2 states the problem of official action. Section 6.3 looks at the traditional concept of office, some of the problems that led to its abandonment as a category of modern public law, and why it remains necessary. Section 6.4 provides the building blocks of a modern concept of office around which a theory of judicial review could be constructed.

6.2 The Problem of Official Action

Chapter 5 discussed legal personality as a device to enable individual actions to be attributed to an organised group. This process is essential to the kind of group life we often take for granted, but, as we have seen in cases like

[3] See Jacob Weinrib, 'Maitland's Challenge for Administrative Law Theory' (2021) 84(2) *Modern Law Review* 207.

[4] Arthur Ripstein, *Force and Freedom* (Harvard University Press 2009), 145; Scott Shapiro, *Legality* (Belknap 2011), 79; Harold Laski, *The Foundations of Sovereignty* (Routledge 1921), 108.

[5] (1982) 154 CLR 25.

[6] *Church of Scientology* v. *Woodward* (1982) 154 CLR 25, 70 (Brennan J).

Hocking v. *Director General of the National Archive*,[7] cases touching on questions of office often require engagement with fundamental principles of political philosophy to lay the groundwork for the doctrinal law.

Again, the social contract theory presented by Thomas Hobbes in *Leviathan* provides an apt starting point. Hobbes posited that two forms of commonwealth exist: those established by 'natural force' (i.e., paternal power or conquest) and those established by agreement, which are 'Commonwealths by institution'.[8] While humans are naturally associative animals, he argued, we are not like bees or ants; the individual will of a bee is naturally directed to the good of the colony, whereas human nature is competitive and self-interested. However, we are also rational, language possessing, covenant-making animals. Therefore, human nature requires a common power instituted by force or agreement to maintain the 'civil state' and prevent a lapse into the natural state in which we interact on a plane of natural force.[9]

Humans have never really lived in a pre-social 'state of nature',[10] and Hobbes was probably too pessimistic about it.[11] But he was quite correct that the associative behaviour of bees and ants can be explained by reference to their physiological characteristics.[12] Not even small scale, homogeneous human societies operate like bee colonies.[13] We are at once rationally self-interested and altruistic; we cooperate with non-kin on a scale unknown in any other species,[14] but never quite lose the impulse

[7] See *Hocking* v. *Director General of the National Archive of Australia* [2020] HCA 19, [214] (Edelman J), citing Jean-Jacques Rousseau on the nature of a 'body politic'.

[8] Thomas Hobbes (Richard Tuck ed.), *Leviathan* (Cambridge University Press 1996), 119.

[9] Thomas Hobbes (Richard Tuck ed.), *Leviathan* (Cambridge University Press 1996), 121.

[10] See Jeremy Bentham (Ross Harrison ed.), *Fragment on Government* (Cambridge University Press 1988), 36; David Hume, 'Of the Original Contract' in H. D. Aiken (ed.), *Hume's Moral and Political Philosophy* (Hafner 1948), 358.

[11] Steven Pinker, *The Better Angels of Our Nature* (Penguin 2011), Ch 5; Bernard Gert, 'Introduction' in Thomas Hobbes (Bernard Gert (ed.), *Man and Citizen* (Anchor 1972), 10.

[12] The chromosomal structure of the haplodiploid insects means that individual reproductive fitness is enhanced by colony hierarchy – a worker bee's sister is a closer genetic relative than her own daughter, so it is her interests to serve the queen rather than reproduce herself: See Robert Trivers (ed.), *Natural Selection and Social Theory* (Oxford University Press 2002), 173–177.

[13] Humans do not outsource reproduction, and, compared to the other great apes, are quite egalitarian: see Christopher Boehm, *Hierarchy in the Forest* (Harvard University Press 1999), 64, 90. We are not divided into 'castes' by epigenetic expression during early development. Our hierarchy is complex and fluid.

[14] See Matt Ridley, *The Origins of Virtue* (Penguin 1997), Ch 2; Marc Hauser, *Moral Minds* (Harper Collins 2006); Herbert Gintis, 'Strong Reciprocity and Human Sociality' (2000) 206(2) *Journal of Theoretical Biology* 169.

to defect for selfish purposes.[15] We form coalitions in a field of tension between individual and group interest, hierarchy and egalitarianism, cooperation and defection. Perhaps most importantly, all of this occurs through the medium of language, through which we create a 'common weal' and organise a 'common will'.

We have seen the role that representation (in his language, 'personation') plays in Hobbes' conceptual scheme. In describing how a system of government is established 'by Art',[16] Hobbes stipulated that he was speaking 'not of the men, but (in the Abstract) of the Seat of Power' personified in the 'sovereign'.[17] The Commonwealth 'is no Person, nor has capacity to doe any thing, but by the Representative (that is, the Sovereign)'.[18] The office of the sovereign representative is created by a mutual covenant between the individuals forming the organised political community, namely that they will 'own' her actions and adopt her will as the 'public conscience' to govern their relations for the purposes of mutual aid and security.[19]

Hobbes' familiar account, even if we reject the obvious fiction of a 'social contract', expresses something basic about the nature of social organisation. However, it presents us with somewhat of a paradox. The complex social forces that make up an organised political society are, in fact, always exerted by individuals; while we can see the men and women who rule, and the physical means they use, Hobbes' 'Abstract Seat of Power' is invisible. Indeed, '[o]n a purely factual plane, the State does not "exist": it is nowhere to be found, a real person of flesh and blood'.[20] Only individuals can be found, whose decisions and actions are *attributed* to the collective because of some special qualification. True, there are special garments, symbols, forms of address, Great Seals and rubber stamps – but these are all just trappings. If it is *individuals* that exercise legal authority, who are they, and how do they come to rule?

15 See Bryan Skyrms, *The Stag Hunt and the Evolution of Social Structure* (Cambridge University Press 2003); Jean-Jacques Rousseau (Maurice Cranston trans.), *A Discourse on Inequality* (Penguin 1984).

16 Martin Loughlin, *The Idea of Public Law* (Oxford University Press 2003), 157–158.

17 Thomas Hobbes (Richard Tuck ed.), *Leviathan* (Cambridge University Press 1996), 3, 184.

18 Thomas Hobbes (Richard Tuck ed.), *Leviathan* (Cambridge University Press 1996), 184.

19 See David Dyzenhaus, 'The Public Conscience of the Law' (2014) 2 *Netherlands Journal of Legal Philosophy* 115.

20 Alexander Passerin d'Entreves, *The Notion of the State* (Oxford University Press 1961), 19.

This paradox is solved by the concept of office, which for that reason is the central category of public law. Modern constitution makers and reformers, however, have tended to neglect a constitution's role in creating and conferring authority, instead focussing on the apparatus of administration it establishes.[21] Nineteenth century legislative reforms (e.g., the consolidation of cabinet government, ministerial responsibility, and public service legislation) encouraged the view that the regulation of officials was a matter of political, parliamentary, and employment accountability; the legal aspects of office fell from view.[22] This was encouraged by the fact that traditional offices themselves hampered efforts to centralise power and rationalise public administration.[23] This all has implications for our understanding of judicial review today. If Weberian 'rational-legal' bureaucratic structures are taken for granted, public law becomes little more than a body of norms regulating their power.

This is, unfortunately, the view adopted by many of the common law theorists in the ultra vires debate. Dawn Oliver, for example, emphasised the importance of understanding power for a proper understanding of judicial review, but she argued that judicial review is concerned not with 'powers' in the sense of vires but with subjecting 'power' in a broader sense to principles of good administration.[24] In other words, despite correctly identifying the nature of 'power' as a central concern, her seminal contribution in fact left the concept of 'power' under-theorised.[25] The very idea of judicial review over 'power' is incoherent without the concept of 'vires': the only way that we can speak cogently of reviewable power is by expressing it as a set of 'official powers', in the sense of vires, recognised by the legal system. That makes the concept of ultra vires essential to a proper theory of judicial review.

[21] Michael Oakeshott, *On Human Conduct* (Clarendon Press 2003), 194.

[22] Paul Finn, 'The Forgotten "Trust": The People and the State' in Malcome Cope (ed.), *Equity: Issues and Trends* (Federation Press 1995), 134; Roscoe Pound, 'Fifty Years of Jurisprudence' (1937) 50(4) *Harvard Law Review* 557, 559.

[23] Janet McLean, *Searching for the State in British Legal Thought* (Cambridge University Press 2012), 27.

[24] Dawn Oliver, 'Is the Ultra Vires Rule the Basis of Judicial Review?' in C. F. Forsyth (ed.), *Judicial Review and the Constitution* (Hart 2000), 3.

[25] Oliver discussed Max Weber on *Macht* and *Herrschaft* and J. K. Galbraith on 'condign', 'compensatory', and 'conditioned' powers. See Max Weber, 'Politik als Beruf' in Max Weber *Geistige Arbeit als Beruf: Vier Vorträge vor dem Freistudentischen Bund* (Duncker & Humblot 1919); J. K. Galbraith, *The Anatomy of Power* (Hamish Hamilton 1984).

6.2.1 *The Importance of Office in the Modern Law*

The recent Australian High Court decision in *Hocking* v. *Director General of the National Archive of Australia* illustrates the importance of office in the context of a practical, contemporary question. This judicial review action concerned an application for an order of *mandamus* to compel the delivery of correspondence between former Australian Governor General Sir John Kerr and the Queen. The correspondence was deposited with the National Archives by the Official Secretary to the Governor General in his 'official capacity'.[26] Sir John noted, in a letter to HM's Private Secretary, that these letters 'were in a separate category' to letters that were 'exclusively [his]'.[27] They were deposited with the predecessor to the National Archive under the Queen's 'wishes' and the Governor General's 'instructions' that the documents remain sealed for a certain period, while later legislation provided for a lesser period. At the time of the application, that lesser period had elapsed.

On the passage of the National Archives Act 1983 (Cth), the letters became 'materials', namely 'records', forming part of the 'archival resources of the Commonwealth' within the 'care and management' of the National Archives. The majority of the Full Federal Court held that the letters were private to Sir John.[28] The appeal to the High Court turned on the construction of the statutory definition of 'Commonwealth records', namely whether the letters amounted to records under the power of control of the 'official establishment of the Governor-General' as a 'Commonwealth institution'.[29]

As mentioned in Chapter 5, all of the judges examined the concept of 'the Commonwealth' and its relation to the Crown and to the Australian 'body politic'. The next step in most of the judgments was to concretise what is meant by the various terms in s. 3(1) of the Act, and the relationship between them.

26 The finding that the Official Secretary deposited the letters 'as Sir John [Kerr's] agent and not as the agent of the incumbent Governor General [at the time]' was not challenged in the appeal; this point can be left to one side for now. See *Hocking* v. *Director General of the National Archive of Australia* [2020] HCA 19, [13] (Kiefel CJ, Bell, Gageler, and Keane JJ).

27 *Hocking* v. *Director General of the National Archive of Australia* [2020] HCA 19, [16] (Kiefel CJ, Bell, Gageler, and Keane JJ).

28 *Hocking* v. *Director-General of the National Archives of Australia* [2019] FCAFC 12 (Allsop CJ and Robertson J, Flick J dissenting).

29 *Hocking* v. *Director General of the National Archive of Australia* [2020] HCA 19, [7] (Kiefel CJ, Bell, Gageler, and Keane JJ).

The plurality judgment (Kiefel CJ, Bell, Gageler, and Keane JJ) turned to the key terms after a detailed description of the correspondence and the legislative framework. The Act applies to 'Commonwealth records' that are defined as 'record[s] that [are] the property of the Commonwealth or of a Commonwealth institution', which is in turn defined by reference to a closed list that includes 'the official establishment of the Governor-General'. Further, 'a record that is the property of the Commonwealth' is defined as including 'records of which the Commonwealth or a Commonwealth Institution has, or is entitled have, possession'.

The operative concept of 'property' was said to be wider than private law ownership *stricto sensu*,[30] but that is not the point of immediate concern.[31] The terms 'Commonwealth' and 'Commonwealth of Australia' are used in different senses in the Constitution and other statutes.[32] The Commonwealth of Australia is a 'distinct legal entity' with legislative, executive, and judicial powers, and the executive power includes the power to own property that is 'vested in the Commonwealth as a body politic'. Executive power is vested in the Queen and exercised by the Governor General, 'functionally exercisable by the Executive Government'. This 'distinct legal personality' is generally referred to with the phrase 'the Crown in right of the Commonwealth'. In other contexts, 'the Commonwealth' refers to the central government, including the 'agencies and instrumentalities of the central government which have their own legal personalities'.[33] That is a broader sense, and encompasses the 'constitutional offices of the Commonwealth as a body politic and of statutory offices created by the Commonwealth Parliament in their official capacities'.[34] The Act uses the former, narrower sense. Therefore, the judges reasoned, not all holders of constitutional and statutory offices should be taken to be 'the Commonwealth' for the purposes of the Act; Ministers, Members of Parliament, Judges, and indeed the Governor General are named by

[30] *Hocking* v. *Director General of the National Archive of Australia* [2020] HCA 19, [64]–[67] (Kiefel CJ, Bell, Gageler, and Keane JJ).

[31] Apart from the point that 'ownership' is categorically a relation between *persons* vis-à-vis *things*; ownership implies legal personality of the 'owner'.

[32] *Hocking* v. *Director General of the National Archive of Australia* [2020] HCA 19, [75] (Kiefel CJ, Bell, Gageler, and Keane JJ).

[33] *Hocking* v. *Director General of the National Archive of Australia* [2020] HCA 19, [76] (Kiefel CJ, Bell, Gageler, and Keane JJ).

[34] *Hocking* v. *Director General of the National Archive of Australia* [2020] HCA 19, [77] (Kiefel CJ, Bell, Gageler, and Keane JJ).

way of example.[35] Further, holders of these offices are not automatically within the statutory category of 'Commonwealth institutions' either: '[A] Minister who is a member of the Federal Executive Council is not "the Executive Council"; a Senator is not "the Senate" [and] the Governor General is not "the official establishment of the Governor-General."'[36]

By taking this approach, the plurality avoided the conclusion that *every* document ever produced or received by an official automatically becomes a 'Commonwealth record'. The 'official establishment of the Governor-General' was said to be used 'in the arcane sense of an organised staff provided at public expense for the assistance of the holder of an office'.[37] In the instant case, this was essentially the office of the Official Secretary: 'The Official Secretary *acting in his or her official capacity* could always have been expected to have had responsibility for keeping records created or obtained by the Governor General *in his or her official capacity*'.[38]

This analysis, perhaps necessarily by reason of the nature of the statutory scheme analysed, is complex. It draws a distinction between (i) the person who holds the office (Sir John Kerr), (ii) the office itself (Governor-General), and (iii) the 'institution' that the office comprises (the 'official establishment' of the Governor- General), which effectively refers to (iv) the office of the Official *Secretary* occupied by (v) the incumbent of that office (a Mr Smith). With respect, I think it might have been better for the legislature to treat the relevant 'institution' as the office of the Governor General itself, and to enquire further into action in a personal *versus* official capacity.

Applying this analysis to the property question, the plurality judges held that the inclusion of 'Departments of State of the Commonwealth and other functional units of government which lack legal personality [within the statutory definition of "Commonwealth institution"] necessarily means that the connoted relationship cannot be confined to the holding of rights'; the relationship is rather one of 'a legally endorsed

35 *Hocking* v. *Director General of the National Archive of Australia* [2020] HCA 19, [79] (Kiefel CJ, Bell, Gageler, and Keane JJ).

36 *Hocking* v. *Director General of the National Archive of Australia* [2020] HCA 19, [80] (Kiefel CJ, Bell, Gageler, and Keane JJ).

37 *Hocking* v. *Director General of the National Archive of Australia* [2020] HCA 19, [86] (Kiefel CJ, Bell, Gageler, and Keane JJ).

38 *Hocking* v. *Director General of the National Archive of Australia* [2020] HCA 19, [88] (Kiefel CJ, Bell, Gageler, and Keane JJ). Emphasis mine.

concentration of power' irrespective of whether the true owner is the Commonwealth as a body politic or another legal person.[39] In the end, the question of ownership was subordinate to the operative question of the capacity in which the relevant officeholders acted at the relevant time:

> The very actions of Mr Smith in making and fulfilling in his capacity as Official Secretary the arrangement by which the correspondence came to be deposited with the Australian Archives are sufficient to demonstrate that lawful power to control the physical custody of the correspondence then lay with Mr Smith *in his capacity as Official Secretary*. The quality of that power to control the physical custody of the correspondence is not affected by the finding that Mr Smith acted on the instructions of Sir John Kerr in making the deposit in his capacity as Official Secretary just as it is unaffected by the inference that the arrangement was entered into by Mr Smith in his capacity as Official Secretary with the knowing approval of Sir John when he was still Governor-General.[40]

The concurring judgments also rely more or less expressly on the concept of office and official capacity. Edelman J construed the Act to refer to 'property' in the strict sense, and held that the rights-holder would either be a subordinate functional unit of government with legal personality, or the Commonwealth as a body politic if the relevant functional unit of government lacked legal personality.[41] Gordon J construed the key terms in the Act differently, but the same basic concepts drive the reasoning. A 'Commonwealth institution' is defined by means of a list of eight institutions including the 'official establishment of the Governor-General'.[42] However, not all of these institutions have legal personality in their own right. In consequence, 'like artificial persons, the interests of the named institutions can be pursued and protected only by natural persons appointed to act for an institution'.[43] In the case of the official establishment of the Governor-General, the relevant natural person was Mr Smith, the Official Secretary. With respect, even institutions with separate legal personality will have human organs, that is, officials, to act for them. The chain of attribution

[39] *Hocking* v. *Director General of the National Archive of Australia* [2020] HCA 19, [94]–[98] (Kiefel CJ, Bell, Gageler, and Keane JJ).

[40] *Hocking* v. *Director General of the National Archive of Australia* [2020] HCA 19, [116] (Kiefel CJ, Bell, Gageler, and Keane JJ). Emphasis mine.

[41] *Hocking* v. *Director General of the National Archive of Australia* [2020] HCA 19, [225], [228] (Edelman J).

[42] *Hocking* v. *Director General of the National Archive of Australia* [2020] HCA 19, [169] (Gordon J).

[43] *Hocking* v. *Director General of the National Archive of Australia* [2020] HCA 19, [170] (Gordon J).

is slightly different, with another 'layer' of analysis, but the basic mechanics of official empowerment, action, and attribution are the same. Nettle J, in a dissenting judgement, also agreed on the basic principle:

> For Commonwealth institutions that have no separate legal personality or collective power over chattels (such as the power to compel production of documents on pain of contempt), possession in law – like any other legally endorsed concentration of power over things – must be exercised by one or more natural persons comprising the Commonwealth institution. To avoid the absurd consequence that every record in the lawful possession of any such natural person is a 'Commonwealth record', the references to such Commonwealth institutions must be taken to require that the person lawfully possess the record *in his or her capacity* as one of the persons comprising the Commonwealth institution.[44]

The scheme of the Act was to 'distinguish records officially possessed by organs of government from records in the personal possession of office holders'.[45] In Nettle J's judgement, however, the facts of the case showed that the documents were personal, rather than official.

Really, the difference between the majority and Nettle J boils down to the approach used to determine which actions by the official should be treated as done in her official capacity and which in her personal one. In evidence, the practical difficulty was noted that 'there was a grey area between personal and official'.[46] Each of the judgments presents a different analysis of when actions are in a (sufficiently) 'official' capacity, and the judgements all give examples of different officials producing documents that might go either way.

6.3 The Traditional Concept of Office

The term 'office' appears in *Hocking* v. *Director General of the National Archive of Australia* 118 times, on 43 of 111 pages, without any explicit attempt at a definition by any of the judges. This is not uncommon. Despite the frequency of its use, the term 'office' itself has no generally accepted legal denotation.[47] In his seminal work on fiduciary obligations,

[44] *Hocking* v. *Director General of the National Archive of Australia* [2020] HCA 19, [130] (Nettle J). Emphasis mine.

[45] *Hocking* v. *Director General of the National Archive of Australia* [2020] HCA 19, [132] (Nettle J).

[46] *Hocking* v. *Director General of the National Archive of Australia* [2020] HCA 19, [63] (Kiefel CJ, Bell, Gageler, and Keane JJ).

[47] P. D. Finn, *Fiduciary Obligations* (Law Book 1977), 8.

P. D. Finn surveyed the range of offices in ecclesiastical, public, and private associations over the centuries. As a working definition, he suggested that an 'office' is to be found where a position exists, carrying with it certain powers and duties, which exists for another's benefit, and often independently of the person who happens to be the incumbent for the time being.[48]

The term derives from Latin *officium*,[49] which became the preferred signifier of organisational status as medieval hierocratic theory was modified to explain the increasing institutionalisation of political power.[50] Ecclesiastical institutions, drawing on the Romano-canon tradition of disinterested service to a common good, used office to confer specific administrative tasks on individuals.[51] Kingship itself was increasingly seen as an office, conferred on a person by grace in a manner analogous to church office, rather than an emanation of the personal attributes of the king himself. Initially interchangeable with terms such as *dignitas* and *ministerium*, during the middle ages *officium* came to express the juristic nature of public officers and their powers, coming to signify a position of some permanence.[52] In particular, 'office' expresses the *institutionalisation* of a social role, akin to a status or separate legal personality in the sense of an acting, and rights and duties holding, unit of legal analysis.[53] Thus, the concept constitutionally grounds administrative law and has a critical role to play in limiting the power of the sovereign and keeping its agencies accountable before the law.[54]

6.3.1 *The Traditional Common Law View*

It is impossible to set out a modern concept of office, and its relative neglect in modern public law, without understanding why it has come to

[48] P. D. Finn, *Fiduciary Obligations* (Law Book 1977), 8.

[49] Probably a contraction of *opificium*, from *opifex*, 'one who works' and ultimately from *opus* ('work') + *facere* ('to do').

[50] See Martin Loughlin, *Foundations of Public Law* (Oxford University Press 2010), 26.

[51] Hélène Millet and Peter Moraw, 'Clerics in the State' in Wolfgang Reinhard (ed.), *Power Elites and State Building* (Clarendon Press 1996), 179.

[52] Martin Loughlin, *Foundations of Public Law* (Oxford University Press 2010), 26.

[53] See Burkhard Schnepel, 'Corporations, Personhood, and Ritual in Tribal Society: Three Interconnected Topics in the Anthropology of Meyer Fortes' (1990) 21(1) *Journal of the Anthropological Society of Oxford* 1, 8.

[54] Janet McLean, 'Between Sovereign and Subject: The Constitutional Position of the Official' (2020) 70(2) *University of Toronto Law Journal* 167.

occupy a marginal place in English public law theory. Until the late eighteenth century, public authority in England was exercised through a decentralised and dispersed system of local officials, especially in the regions.[55] By consolidating royal power early, England had avoided the strong political feudalism that provoked the development of centralised, bureaucratic states on the Continent. As a result, the centre was able to leave much to ancient, local institutions.[56] Thus, although Blackstone conveyed the notion that all public power emanated from the Crown, public power in his day had much more to do with local customs.[57] Many of these offices derived their status from acts of the Crown (e.g., by Letters Patent) or an Act of Parliament, but a substantial number exercised their functions under the common law.

In this period officials held office as a matter of proprietary right, drew emoluments and fees from the office, owed legally enforceable duties to the public whom they served, freely deputised the performance of their duties, but operated independently of managerial control.[58] Accordingly, Blackstone catalogued offices as a species of property – 'incorporeal hereditaments', in the same genus as rights of way:[59] 'Offices, which are a right to exercise a public or private employment, and the fees and emoluments thereunto belonging, are also incorporeal hereditaments: whether public, as those of magistrates; or private, as of bailiffs, receivers, and the like'.[60]

From a modern perspective, it seems suspect that a political office should be a form of property. Max Weber, for example, categorised political orders according to whether their officials possessed the means of administration in their private capacity, or whether the administrative

[55] Norman Chester, *The English Administrative System 1780–1870* (Clarendon Press 1981), 12, 52.

[56] Martin Loughlin, 'The State, the Crown, and the Law' in Maurice Sunkin and Sebastian Payne (eds.), *The Nature of the Crown* (Oxford University Press 1999), 44. Max Weber noticed that the gentry and the urban bourgeoisie had largely been left to engage in 'self-government' in England: Max Weber (W. J. Mommsen, Wolfgang Schleuchter, and Birgit Morgenbrod eds.), *Wissenschaft als Beruf; Politik als Beruf* (Mohr Siebeck 1994), 75.

[57] Janet McLean, *Searching for the State in British Legal Thought* (Cambridge University Press 2012), 24.

[58] Norman Chester, *The English Administrative System 1780–1870* (Clarendon Press 1981), 26.

[59] Willian Blackstone, *Commentaries on the Laws of England* (Clarendon Press 1766), Book II, 21.

[60] Willian Blackstone, *Commentaries on the Laws of England* (Clarendon Press 1766), Book II, 37.

personnel was separated from the administrative apparatus 'as employees within the capitalist firm'; the advent of the 'modern state' was brought about by the dispossession of those who owned the means of administration by private right.[61]

In the course of the nineteenth century, the preponderance of ancient offices was suppressed and the administration reformed along 'Weberian' lines. By the 1870s, the civil service was largely free of traditional offices, and most civil servants were employees, rather than officers, of the Crown. Modernisation proceeded in fits and bursts, effected by restricting the performance of official duties by deputy, prohibiting purchase and sale of offices and their use for political bribes, abolishing the inheritance of offices in reversion, removing the 'banking' function (whereby officials were entitled to draw on official receipts and retain interest), and replacing fee income with salaries. The new civil service that emerged was one of hierarchically organised, salaried, and meritocratically selected employees.[62]

We need not celebrate the *arcana* of ancient offices in English law, let alone revivify the structures of pre-modern administration.[63] But, as we have seen from cases like *Town Investments* v. *Department of Environment*[64] and *M* v. *Home Office*,[65] modernisation did not actually remove the need for a concept of office. Every employee is the *employee of someone*, and office is still necessary to describe who that someone is and how they act. As McLean explains, nineteenth century developments – again epitomised in the work of A. V. Dicey – denuded the concept of its inherent, and historical, public law controls: 'the central thrust of Dicey's invocation of the rule of law is that there should be no special category of law for officials'.[66] But in so doing, Dicey and those that followed him obscured the relation between sovereign and subject and obscured the conceptual foundations of the law of judicial review. This is, in large part,

[61] Max Weber (W. J. Mommsen, Wolfgang Schluchter, and Birgitt Morgenbrod eds.), *Wissenschaft als Beruf; Politik als Beruf* (Mohr Siebeck 1994), 40.

[62] Norman Chester, *The English Administrative System 1780–1870* (Clarendon Press 1981), 122, 131.

[63] House of Commons Information Office, *Factsheet P11: The Chiltern Hundreds* (April 2011) provides an overview of the procedure for resigning from the House of Commons, which involves taking up a paid sinecure so as to disqualify the new holder of a 'paid office under the Crown' from membership in Parliament.

[64] [1978] AC 359.

[65] [1994] 1 AC 377.

[66] Jane McLean, 'Between Sovereign and Subject: The Constitutional Position of the Official' (2020) 70(2) *University of Toronto Law Journal* 167, 180.

the reason why modern debates about the conceptual foundations of the supervisory jurisdiction have been confused and ultimately sterile.

While the early modern concept of office clearly needs adjustment, it reveals two persistent structural elements that are perfectly valid today. First, the similarity between a right of way and an office is that both are standardised 'bundles' of rights and powers to which a person accedes. The bundle is pre-packaged in the sense that the *content* of the bundle is independent of the personal attributes of he who possesses it. A right of way remains the same irrespective of the personal attributes of the dominant tenement-holder; a franchise remains the same irrespective of the personal attributes of the franchisee; an office remains the same irrespective of the personal identity of the official.[67] The essence of an office is the standardised, institutionalised nature of the role played by its incumbent. The feudal and the modern officeholder alike are the bearers of an institutionalised role. Different powers inure in the bundles, but they bear a similar logical structure.

Secondly, the proprietarian concept of office provided the context for the development of one of the major concepts in political thought up to the eighteenth century – the idea of offices as a 'public trust'.[68] Offices, like other hereditaments, could be the subject of various estates – for life, at pleasure, in reversion, and so forth.[69] However, offices of public trust could not be granted for a term of years, 'especially if they concern the administration of justice, for then they might perhaps vest in executors or administrators'. Judicial offices could not be granted in reversion, 'because, though the grantee may be able to perform it at the time of the grant, yet before the office falls he may become unable and insufficient'. Ministerial offices, on the other hand, could be so granted, 'for those may be executed by deputy'.[70] The Sale of Offices Act 1551 stipulated that no public office be sold, under pain of disability to dispose of or hold it, '[f]or the law presumes that he, who buys an office, will by

[67] On the conceptual parallels between ownership and office, see Christopher Essert, 'The Office of Ownership' (2013) 63(3) *University of Toronto Law Journal* 418; Larissa Katz, 'Ownership and Office: The Building Blocks of a Legal Order' (2020) 70(2) *University of Toronto Law Journal* 267.

[68] See John Gough, *John Locke's Political Philosophy: Eight Studies* (Oxford University Press 1964), 138; P. D. Finn, 'The Forgotten "Trust": The People and the State' in Malcolm Cope (ed.), *Equity: Issues and Trends* (Federation Press 1995), 131.

[69] William Blackstone, *Commentaries on the Laws of England*, Vol. 2 (Clarendon Press 1766), Book II, 37.

[70] William Blackstone, *Commentaries on the Laws of England*, Vol. 2 (Clarendon Press 1766), Book II, 37.

bribery, extortion, or other unlawful means, make his purchase good, to the manifest detriment of the public'.[71] This is, again, one of the ideas that has been lost in modern public law theory – although, as I explain in Chapter 12, there is currently somewhat of a revival underway.[72]

6.3.2 *Office and Employment*

Perhaps the major challenge is disambiguating the category of office from the category of employment. Until the early nineteenth century, digests and abridgements generally contained a title on the law of offices.[73] For example, working from the English and American cases, Floyd Mechem defined office as a status, role, or position conferred on an individual in virtue of which she can perform functions for the group as a whole, for a common objective or benefit:

> A public office is the right, authority and duty, created and conferred by law, by which for a given period, either fixed by law or enduring at the pleasure of the creating power, an individual is invested with some portion of the sovereign functions of government, to be exercised by him for the benefit of the public.[74]

But then, too, it was difficult to distinguish 'office' from 'employment':

> The most important characteristic which distinguishes an office from an employment or contract is that the creation and conferring of an office involves a *delegation to the individual of some of the sovereign functions of government, to be exercised by him for the benefit of the public;* – that some portion of the sovereignty of the country, either legislative, executive or judicial, attaches, for the time being, to be exercised for the public benefit.[75]

[71] William Blackstone, *Commentaries on the Laws of England*, Vol. 2 (Clarendon Press 1766), 37; see also Norman Chester, *The English Administrative System 1780–1870* (Clarendon Press 1981), 19.

[72] Daniel Lee has explained how Roman private law models were used in the later middle ages and early modern period to craft 'public law': Daniel Lee, 'Private Law Models for Public Law Concepts: The Roman Law Theory of Dominium in the Monarchomach Doctrine of Popular Sovereignty' (2008) 70 *Review of Politics* 370, 374; Quentin Skinner, *The Foundations of Modern Political Thought*, Vol. 2 (Cambridge University Press 1978), 321.

[73] P. D. Finn, 'The Forgotten "Trust": The People and the State' in Malcolm Cope (ed.), *Equity: Issues and Trends* (Federation Press 1995), 132; William Cruise (Thomas Huntington ed.), *Digest of the Laws of England Respecting Real Property* (4th American ed., Collins and Hannay 1834), III:25.

[74] Floyd R. Mechem, *A Treatise on the Law of Public Offices and Officers* (Callaghan 1890), I, §1, §4, 4–5.

[75] Floyd R. Mechem, *A Treatise on the Law of Public Offices and Officers* (Callaghan 1890), I, §1, §4, 4–5. Emphasis mine.

An official and an employee may exercise similar powers and functions; the difference is that the acts of the official are attributable to the 'sovereign' community of which she is an organ. The *public* official will therefore be responsible to the public for actions done on its behalf – including vicarious responsibility for the acts of her employees. In this respect, perhaps less has changed than first appears. Officials still deputise official functions to employees and remain liable for their proper discharge; the method of appointing and remunerating 'deputies' has changed, and the pool of responsible officials has perhaps decreased. But similar principles of political agency still articulate the various levels of administration. Some rules attribute the acts of employees to the relevant official, while others attribute the acts of the official to the Crown. The Crown formally brings judicial review actions at the behest of an aggrieved member of the body politic.

It will never be entirely straightforward to determine who is an 'official', who is an 'employee', or what consequences will flow from that. Jean Bodin, the early modern theorist of sovereignty, wrestled with a similar question: Who should be seen as an 'officer', and who as a mere 'commissioner'? He reasoned by analogy with Roman private law. Where commissioners are delegates fully dependent upon the continuing pleasure of the *seigneur* – holding their tenure *precarium* – the officer's relationship to the sovereign is *commodatum*: 'An office is a thing borrowed, which the owner cannot demand again before the time it was lent for be expired'.[76] Of this, Daniel Lee observes that '"office" was conceptualized merely as a "legally-defined" [*lege definitum*] bundle of rights and powers which, like property, could be held and exercised by another party'.[77]

The proprietary tenure of the official's office was an essential element in Bodin's theory of limited government. The official's tenure is a check on the arbitrary will of the sovereign, who could revoke the commissioner's *precarium* arbitrarily and exercise the commission's powers personally. As McLean explains, rule by commissioner is a form of direct rule by the sovereign, which poses an ever-present threat of tyranny; the security and permanence of officials' tenure expresses a surprisingly lucid conception of the rule of law.[78]

[76] Jean Bodin (Richard Knolles trans.), *Six Bookes of a Commonweale* (London: G. Bishop 1606), 310.

[77] Daniel Lee, '"Office is a Thing Borrowed": Jean Bodin on Offices and Seigneurial Government' (2013) 41(3) *Political Theory* 409, 421.

[78] See Janet McLean, 'Between Sovereign Subject: The Constitutional Position of the Official' (2020) 70(2) *University of Toronto Law Review* 167, 172.

The distinction between 'office' and 'employment' remains a problem in modern administrative law – not least because practices such as the privatisation of certain public services are expanding. The question who is an 'employee' and who is an 'official' has vexed modern English courts under the general law and under the Human Rights Act 1998, for example. Contemporary modes of administration may call for an approach whereby a person is deemed to be an official by virtue of his property rights or contractual obligations.[79]

6.3.3 *Getting by without the Concept of Office*

The unworkability of public law without the concept of office is illustrated by some wrongful dismissal cases. The prerogative writs were traditionally available to ensure an official's tenure of her rightful office. For example, dismissal of a Constable was traditionally dealt with using the writ of *mandamus*; according to J. W. Willcock, those responsible for the appointment of a constable had power to dismiss him for misconduct, 'but if removed, the Court of King's Bench will grant a *mandamus* to show the cause of removal; and if good cause not be shewn, or if no return be made, they will aware a peremptory writ to restore him to the office'.[80] The Municipal Corporations Act 1882, on the other hand, provided that the responsible Watch Committee could 'at any time' suspend or dismiss 'any borough constable whom they think negligent in the discharge of his duty, or otherwise unfit for the same'.

The seminal decision in *Ridge* v. *Baldwin*[81] gives the impression that modern legislation displaces the traditional approach. In that case, the House of Lords considered the dismissal of a Chief Constable by the responsible Watch Committee in breach of the *audi alteram partem* rule. But this was not a straightforward employment case, either; Lord Reid identified three categories, namely 'dismissal of a servant by his master, dismissal from an office held during pleasure, and dismissal from an office where there must be something against a man to warrant his dismissal'.[82] This case fell into the third category. The various judgments differ in the extent to which they deal with the older law of offices, but the reasoning of all the Lords is 'modern' to the extent that it is based

[79] See Janet McLean, 'Between Sovereign Subject: The Constitutional Position of the Official' (2020) 70(2) *University of Toronto Law Review* 167, 181. See further Chapter 12.
[80] See J. W. Willcock, *The Office of Constable* (Litell 1840), 22.
[81] [1964] AC 40.
[82] *Ridge* v. *Baldwin* [1964] AC 40, 41 (Lord Reid).

squarely on the construction of the 1882 Act and associated Acts and Regulations.

R (Evans) v. *Chief Constable of North Wales*[83] concerned dismissal by a Chief Constable of a Probationer Constable, again in breach of the *audi alteram partem* rule. In *Ridge* v. *Baldwin*, the police officer had been content to resign, as that allowed him to retain his pension benefits. In *R (Evans)* v. *Chief Constable of North Wales*, on the other hand, the applicant sought reinstatement and did not seek monetary compensation. This left the House of Lords in an awkward position, given their finding of gross procedural unfairness against him. In the words of Lord Bridge:

> [T]he most difficult problem posed by this appeal is to decide what remedy is appropriate . . . There is no doubt in my mind that the respondent has suffered a grievous wrong. It should not be beyond the power of the courts to provide a suitable remedy. The respondent has throughout disclaimed any interest in monetary compensation. What he seeks is reinstatement. This could only be secured by an order of *mandamus* requiring the present Chief Constable of the North Wales Police to reinstate him as a probationer constable who has already completed fourteen months of his probationer service. *I have no doubt your Lordships have power to make such an order and was at one time strongly inclined to think that it should be made.* I know now that none of your Lordships favour such an order and it would therefore be an empty gesture for me to express a formal dissent on the point.[84]

The factors speaking against an order of *mandamus* were that years had passed since termination, and that the proceedings may have soured a future relationship in any case. But it is telling that a majority of the House of Lords saw the traditional remedy of *mandamus* as unavailable.

The tendency to treat offices within an employment paradigm has only intensified since the 1980s, particularly as a result of the changing modalities of administration. In *R (Walsh)* v. *East Berkshire Health Authority*,[85] for example, a senior nursing officer was dismissed, allegedly without due process. The first instance judge held that the public was concerned to see that a great public service acted lawfully and fairly to its officers, and that *certiorari* was appropriate. The Court of Appeal, in contrast, held that judicial review could not be used to enforce 'private

[83] [1982] UKHL 10.
[84] *R (Evans)* v. *Chief Constable of North Wales* [1982] UKHL 10, 6 (Lord Bridge). Emphasis mine.
[85] [1985] QB 152.

law' employee rights against a public body. May LJ referred to ordinary master and servant cases, opining that earlier decisions had to be read in light of supervening employment protection legislation.[86] Sir John Donaldson MR said:

> Employment by a public authority does not *per se* inject any element of public law. Nor does the fact that the employee is in a 'higher grade' or is an 'officer'. This only makes it more likely that there will be necessary statutory restrictions upon dismissal, or other underpinning of his employment ... It will be this [statutory] underpinning and not the seniority which injects the element of public law.[87]

It is, however, impossible to treat every official as an 'employee'; *some* civil servants must still be considered 'officials' at a conceptual level, and that this is a matter quite apart from the statutory language.[88] Robert Watt, for example, has advocated the view that civil servants are employees of HM Government, and that 'when looked at through the eyes of an employment lawyer', 'there seems to be nothing to distinguish [the Crown] from any other large employer' save that some of its employees undertake special functions. Nevertheless, Watt argues that police officers and judges should be seen as a 'secular clergy' in light of their special delegation of power from the political community to act for the public good, often in the absence of an employment contract. He does not deign, however, to mention the term 'office' in making this argument.[89]

Distinct public law considerations, however, necessarily apply to public officials. The decision of the Ontario Superior Court of Justice Divisional Court, *MacDonald* v. *Ashinabek Police Service*,[90] provides an example. In that case, a First Nations Constable was dismissed from service under circumstances which arguably lacked due process. Lane, Greer, and Lax JJ observed that, under traditional common law principles, an employee could be dismissed without a hearing unless the contract of employment provided otherwise; even where a dismissal was wrongful, the employee's recourse was an action in damages with no right to reinstatement or specific performance of the employment contract.

[86] *R (Walsh)* v. *East Berkshire Health Authority* [1985] QB 152, 167 (Donaldson MR).

[87] *R (Walsh)* v. *East Berkshire Health Authority* [1985] QB 152, 164 (Donaldson MR).

[88] Bradley Selway, 'Of Kings and Officers – The Judicial Development of Public Law' (2005) 33 *Federal Law Review* 1, 27. See also Chapter 5.

[89] Robert Watt, 'The Crown and its Employees' in Maurice Sunkin and Sebastian Payne (eds.), *The Nature of the Crown* (Oxford University Press 1999), 310, 313–314.

[90] (2006) 53 CCEL (3d) 126.

> In contrast, public office holders – even offices held at pleasure – are entitled to procedural fairness as a prelude to any dismissal and the affected person is entitled to apply to a court for judicial review of the decision. A person is a public officer where his or her employment encompasses 'some elements of a public nature' or has 'a strong statutory flavour'. Police officers have traditionally been held to be public officers.[91]

The judges cited *Attorney-General for New South Wales* v. *Perpetual Trustee Co Ltd*,[92] a Privy Council case:

> [T]here is a fundamental difference between the domestic relation of servant and master and that of the holder of a public office and the state which he is said to serve. The constable falls within the latter category. His authority is original, not delegated, and is exercised at his own discretion by virtue of his office.[93]

Admittedly, the judges noted that the Constable was a 'ministerial officer exercising statutory rights independently of contract'. However, they continued that, while a First Nations Constable appointed under the Police Services Act is not a 'police officer' as such, they have all the powers and duties of a police officer and should be treated in the same manner. In any case:

> [E]ven if Mr. McDonald is not a public officer by virtue of his status as a First Nations Constable, *he is one because his employment has considerable elements of a public nature, authority and trust*, in that his duties included enforcing the laws of Ontario and Canada. He is therefore a public office holder and a duty of fairness is owed prior to his dismissal.[94]

The court further cited the Supreme Court of Canada in *R* v. *Campbell*[95] to the effect that a police officer 'is not acting as a government functionary or as an agent of anybody' but as the occupant of a 'public office initially defined by the common law and subsequently set out in various statutes'.[96] There may be good reasons not to treat every public servant in this way. But in point of fact, it will generally be an 'official' whose action – be that as the official responsible for the actions of an employee – is the proper subject matter of a judicial review proceeding.

91 *MacDonald* v. *Ashinabek Police Service* (2006) 53 CCEL (3d) 126, [79]. Citations omitted.
92 [1955] AC 457.
93 *Attorney-General for New South Wales* v. *Perpetual Trustee Co Ltd* [1955] AC 457, 489.
94 *McDonald* v. *Ashinabek Police Service* (2006) 53 CCEL (3d) 126, [78]–[79]. Citations omitted. Emphasis mine.
95 [1999] 1 SCR 565.
96 *R* v. *Campbell* [1999] 1 SCR 565, [27].

6.3.4 *The Demise of Office in Modern Public Law Theory*

The demise of office was closely connected to the nineteenth century reforms of the administration. But they were also conceptual, epitomised in the Diceyan view of the British constitution that came to predominate English legal education – ironically – at a time when the size of the English administrative state was growing, and office was becoming more important than ever.

Antipathy towards the concept of office runs deep in the modern English outlook. Hobbes, as we have seen, combined the idea of the *universitas*, borrowed from Romano-canon private law, with a voluntaristic model of political authority. This put political organisation on a revolutionary new footing, for which Martin Loughlin credits him with the creation of a space for 'public law' autonomous from religion for the first time.[97] However, there is a legitimate and enduring concern about public law terms that are 'heuristics, or metaphors, rather than observable features of the world'.[98] This concern has also motivated the banishment of 'office' and closely related concepts such as 'corporation sole' to the periphery of modern public law.

Blackstone grafted the Hobbesian notion of the state as an artificial person onto the older idea of the King's 'two bodies', discussed in the previous chapter.[99] This exposed him to a savage critique by Jeremy Bentham. 'The constitutional branch is chiefly employed in conferring, on particular classes of persons, *powers*, to be exercised for the good of the whole society, or of considerable parts of it, and prescribing *duties* to the persons invested with those powers', argued Bentham; indulgence in fictions such as sovereigns with mystical bodies should be avoided.[100] According to McLean:

> For Bentham, what constitutes rulers is not normative and neither is it the product of political theory: it is a fact of power. He urges that we should focus on real powers and on real people, and that we should avoid abstractions, such as King and Crown, which do not do any real work.[101]

[97] Martin Loughlin, *Foundations of Public Law* (Oxford University Press 2010), 446.

[98] Edward Rubin, *Beyond Camelot: Rethinking Politics and Law for the Modern State* (Princeton University Press 2005), 15.

[99] Janet McLean, *Searching for the State in British Legal Thought* (Cambridge University Press 2012), 3; William Blackstone, *Commentaries on the Laws of England* (Clarendon Press 1765), Book I, 242; *William* v. *Berkley* (1559) Plowden 233a.

[100] Jeremy Bentham (J. H. Burns and H. L. A. Hart eds.), *An Introduction to the Principles of Morals and Legislation* (Athlone Press 1970), 307; L. J. Hume, *Bentham and Bureaucracy* (Cambridge University Press: W. Pickering 1981), 3.

[101] Janet McLean, *Searching for the State in British Legal Thought* (Cambridge University Press 2012), 4.

This aspect of Bentham's reformist agenda is echoed in Dicey's formulation of the rule of law, in which the figure of the official is stripped away, and the officeholder stands naked before the law to answer for wrongs done under the colour of office as a private individual.[102]

Bentham was an empiricist who believed that we can only have knowledge of simple, individual objects and entities: 'the only objects which have any real existence are those which are corporeal'.[103] Thus, he consistently denied the existence of collectivities, universals, and abstracts and directed his focus onto individual, tangible particulars. His favoured approach, whenever he encountered a term that referred to something other than a corporeal object (such as 'right', 'corporation', 'incorporeal hereditament' or indeed the 'Crown') was to paraphrase propositions about the fictional object in ways that reduced to a proposition about corporeal objects and their relations, to obtain a 'clear perception of the real state of things'.[104]

The problem, as L. J. Hume has explained, is that despite his basic epistemological and metaphysical commitments, Bentham still used the concept of office. Political society consists, in Bentham's account, of 'governors' and 'subjects'.[105] These two classes are differentiated insofar as subjects are in the habit of paying obedience to the governors. In his earliest work, the *Fragment on Government* (written in the late eighteenth century), Bentham conceded that 'corporate or collective forms of action in which different people have a different share in issuing commands and ideas of representation too, may require more by way of explanation' than he was able to offer.[106] Hume observes of Bentham's *Constitutional Code* (written later, in 1830):

> In his theory and his programme, [Bentham] treated the Executive and the Judiciary as both bundles of offices and masses of individual employees. He analysed the offices separately and linked them to each other through relations of command and obedience – the right to command and the duty to obey. The individuals participated in the system through their occupancy of particular offices and their possession of the relevant rights and obligations.[107]

[102] Janet McLean, 'Between Sovereign and Subject: The Constitutional Position of the Official' (2020) 70(2) *University of Toronto Law Journal* 167, 181.

[103] L. J. Hume, *Bentham and Bureaucracy* (Cambridge University Press 1988), 58, citing Jeremy Bentham (H. L. A. Hart ed.), *Of Laws in General* (Athlone Press 1970), 284.

[104] L. J. Hume, *Bentham and Bureaucracy* (Cambridge University Press 1988), 59.

[105] L. J. Hume, *Bentham and Bureaucracy* (Cambridge University Press 1988), 63.

[106] Jeremy Bentham (Ross Harrison ed.), *Fragment on Government* (Blackwell 1948), 42–43.

[107] L. J. Hume, *Bentham and Bureaucracy* (Cambridge University Press 1981), 3.

In Bentham's system, offices are not only recognised to exist, distinct from officeholders, but are *schematically important* to public law. Bentham was working 'simultaneously in two directions', elaborating general theories, on the one hand, and restating conventional principles and practices to conform to those theories, on the other.[108] By labelling abstract entities as 'fictions', Bentham attempted to use terms like 'office' without undermining his basic methodological project, especially when paired with a rigorously uniform terminology.[109] However, office remains a weak point in Bentham's intellectual legacy.

Bentham's student John Austin aggravated the error. Austin's command theory of law assumed a 'determinate body or person' able to exhibit a 'corporate character' to satisfy the logical prerequisites of a sovereign will. Austin, however, offered no proper account of how it should come to exist.[110] When he had to identify the person habitually obeyed, and habitually obeying no one, Austin feebly pointed to the King, both Houses of Parliament, and the Electors together. Dicey, for his part, pushed office to the margin and relied on the private law liability of officials rather than risking a concession of the existence of a *droit administratif*. But his neglect of administrative law is a dubious aspect of his legacy in English public law, to the extent that Dicey had clearly accepted it by the end of his career.

H. L. A. Hart duly noted that Austin's account renders sovereignty meaningless, unless we distinguish between each MP and each Elector in his 'private' and 'sovereign' (i.e., official) capacity.[111] While plausible, that solution posed a serious problem for Austin, because it implies *rules* creating a separate 'official capacity' for legislators 'contrasted with themselves as private individuals'.[112] On this basis, Hart argued that 'law' is a matter of rules, ultimately resting on a rule of recognition creating a sovereign, not just the commands of a sovereign habitually obeyed.

[108] L. J. Hume, *Bentham and Bureaucracy* (Cambridge University Press 1981), 8.

[109] L. J. Hume, *Bentham and Bureaucracy* (Cambridge University Press 1981), 247.

[110] John Austin (W. E. Rumble ed.), *The Province of Jurisprudence Determined* (Cambridge University Press 1995), 218.

[111] H. L. A. Hart, *The Concept of Law* (Rev. ed., Clarendon Press 1982), 78.

[112] H. L. A. Hart, *The Concept of Law* (Rev. ed., Clarendon Press 1982), 78.

But Hart merely refined a defective scheme. His inaugural lecture explored the questions of collective intentional action, the characterisation of communities of intentionality, and the status of individuals empowered by social practice to act on behalf of a group. He adopted Bentham's method of 'paraphrasis', arguing that we should concern ourselves 'not with anomalous or fictitious entities, but with a new and extended though analogous use of legal rules and of the expressions involved in them'.[113] As Bentham sought to discourage the use of mystical abstractions, Hart desired to break from the legal theories that had preceded him, essentially by avoiding the questions they asked.[114] Using the 'relatively minor notion' of 'status' as an example, Hart put a gloss on Austin's view.[115] Austin's discussion of 'status' revealed an apparent choice between saying that it is a 'mere collective name for a set of special rights', or that it is 'an "ideal" or "fictitious" basis for these rights', or alternatively that it is 'an "occult quality" in the person who has the status' distinct both from the rights themselves and the facts that engender them.[116] Hart did not think that any of these options were particularly attractive.

Following Hart, we would approach questions of official action not by asking 'What is the Crown?' but putting 'the Crown' in a sentence such as 'When the Crown owes me money, who has to pay?'. Legal rules, argued Hart, provide the answer to these questions. He explained these rules by analogy with games – they form the context in which statements such as 'The constable has a duty to enforce the prohibition of selling liquor to minors' have meaning.[117]

[113] H. L. A. Hart, 'Definition and Theory in Jurisprudence' in *Essays in Jurisprudence and Philosophy* (Clarendon Press 1983), 37, 39–40; Jeremy Bentham (John Bowring ed.), *The Works of Jeremy Bentham Part XV* (Tait 1841), 247.

[114] H. L. A. Hart, 'Definition and Theory in Jurisprudence' in *Essays in Jurisprudence and Philosophy* (Oxford University Press 1983), 24, referring to American Realism, Scandinavian Realism, and natural law.

[115] H. L. A. Hart, 'Definition and Theory in Jurisprudence' in *Essays in Jurisprudence and Philosophy* (Oxford University Press 1983), 24

[116] H. L. A. Hart, 'Definition and Theory in Jurisprudence' in *Essays in Jurisprudence and Philosophy* (Oxford University Press 1983), 25.

[117] H. L. A. Hart, 'Definition and Theory in Jurisprudence' in *Essays in Jurisprudence and Philosophy* (Clarendon Press 1983), 29–30.

In all this, however, Hart fell into the trap he built for Austin. First, a concept of *official capacity* is needed to distinguish official acts from private ones. Recall Hart's (rather dated) example of King Rex 'giving private orders to his mistress'.[118] Once we describe a single human being as having two 'capacities', we are ascribing invisible ('occult') properties to human beings. Secondly, for Hart, the essence of a legal system is the union of 'primary' and 'secondary rules', the former regulating behaviour and the latter empowering certain persons to make valid primary rules.[119] This union explains the essential features of a legal system, for example, the continuity of law from one sovereign to the next, and the persistence of law after the sovereign's death.[120] The transition of authority from Rex I to Rex II is possible because a 'rule of change' establishes continuity by creating an *office* connecting incumbents in *seriatim* succession:[121] 'the King is dead, long live the King'.[122] Again, the office is personified as a perpetual, ideal entity. Thirdly, it is recognition by officials (in their official capacity) that establishes secondary rules, including the ultimate 'rule of recognition'. For Hart, it was enough for the bulk of subjects to obey the law, irrespective of their motivation, but no rule of recognition could exist – and therefore no legal system – unless the relevant officials held a particular mental disposition towards it.[123] As Leslie Green has observed, this lapses into circularity. An official is someone identified as such by law; something is law only if it is identified by the rule of recognition; something is a rule of recognition only if it is practised by officials.[124] Hart, however, nowhere explained what an official is or how I might come to be one.[125]

[118] H. L. A. Hart, *The Concept of Law* (Rev. ed., Clarendon Press 1982), 68 (reminiscent of Hobbes' point that the King commands the people 'as a politic, not a natural person': Thomas Hobbes (Ferdinand Tönnies ed.), *Behemoth or the Long Parliament* (Frank Cass 1969), 51.

[119] H. L. A. Hart, *The Concept of Law* (Rev. ed., Clarendon Press 1982), 77.

[120] H. L. A. Hart, *The Concept of Law* (Rev. ed., Clarendon Press 1982), 58.

[121] Scott Shapiro, *Legality* (Belknap 2012), 87.

[122] See Ernst Kantorowicz, *The King's Two Bodies* (Princeton University Press 1997), 314.

[123] Scott Shapiro, *Legality* (Belknap 2012), 93.

[124] H. L. A. Hart (Leslie Green, Joseph Raz, and Penelope Bulloch eds.), *The Concept of Law* (3rd ed., Clarendon Press 2012), 316.

[125] M. D. Bayles, *Hart's Legal Philosophy: An Examination* (Kluwer 1992), 81.

6.3.5 Tackling the Metaphysical Problem

A common concern to avoid myth and mystery has animated judges and scholars, who all wrestle with basic questions of the ontology of legal systems and the artefacts found in them. In the end, Bentham's purported demystification left him with little to say about the state at all, beyond the observation that the notion 'can only refer to some actual body of persons in charge of some identifiable apparatus of government'.[126] But this merely restates the problem.

The way out of this mess is to accept that lawyers peddle a stock-in-trade of invisible objects all of the time. While law is not about angels dancing on pinheads, it operates with categories such as 'rights', 'corporations', 'mothers-in-law', and 'commissioners' that are not an observable part of physical reality. The sooner we accept this unavoidable truth, the sooner we can get to work in developing a robust scheme of legal ontology, that is, an explanation of the nature and mode of existence of legal institutional reality.

The Emperor's New Clothes was reportedly inspired by Hans Christian Andersen's childhood memory of standing in a crowd to see King Frederik VI of Denmark. When the king appeared, young Andersen exclaimed: 'Oh, he's nothing more than a human being!'[127] Indeed, *all* officials (high and low) are just primates wearing fancy clothes. As children, we are taught to take the institutions that shape our world as naturally existing and self-evident, according to John Searle, 'without reflecting on the special features of their ontology and without being aware that they have a special ontology'.[128] Fictions are the warp and weft of our social life.[129] Their complex structure is 'invisible'; Schools, Churches, and Parliaments 'seem as natural to us as stones and water and trees'.[130] Conversely, in the mind of someone like Bentham, the realisation that the facts of social life are conventional rather than natural

126 Quentin Skinner, 'A Genealogy of the Modern State' (2008) 162 *Proceedings of the British Academy* 325, 356.

127 For which he was scolded by his mother: see Hans Christian Andersen (Vilhelm Pedersen and Lorenz Frølich eds.), *The Stories of Hans Christian Andersen* (Granta 2004), 267.

128 John Searle, *The Construction of Social Reality* (Free Press 1995), 4.

129 See Carola Barbero, Maurizio Ferraris, and Alberto Voltolini (eds.), *From Fictionalism to Realism* (Cambridge Scholars 2013).

130 John Searle, *The Construction of Social Reality* (Free Press 1995), 4.

can provoke a violent counterreaction, especially where they are used to justify defunct social structures.[131]

The real question is whether it is possible to explain, within a coherent materialist worldview, the co-existence of offices and incumbents. The facts that make Queen Elizabeth II the daughter of King George VI can be explained by reference to natural (biological, then chemical and physical) laws. But how do we explain that she is his 'legal' daughter, his 'heir', and hence why she is 'Queen' of a thing called the 'United Kingdom'? Although undeniably a 'fiction', we can meaningfully say that it is a 'fact' that Elizabeth II is Queen of the United Kingdom because – as Hart would admonish – *rules* make it so. The fact that Queens, Crowns, and Kingdoms exist is dependent on human beliefs, intentions, and understandings in a way that the existence of rocks and trees is not. This is key. The existence of social artefacts is *epistemically objective*, but *ontologically subjective*: Things exist as a 'matter of fact', but only because a community of agents thinks they do.[132] Law is a realm of special facts, a domain in which saying something makes it so.[133] 'If law exists at all', argues Neil MacCormick, 'it exists not on the level of brute creation along with shoes and ships and sealing wax or for that matter cabbages, but rather along with kings and other paid officers of state on a plane of institutional fact'.[134]

6.4 Towards a Modern Conception of Office

This provides an analytical framework in which we can put modernist scepticism about office to rest. Offices are 'institutional facts'. The distinction between 'brute' and 'institutional' facts was described by G. E. M. Anscombe as the difference between 'delivering' and 'dumping' potatoes on a doorstep.[135] The brute acts are identical – the difference is

[131] So much is evident in Bentham's youthful recollection of the 'history of a mind perplexed by fiction': Jeremy Bentham (Ross Harrison ed.), *Fragment on Government* (Cambridge University Press 1988), 51–52. It has been speculated that Bentham was on the autistic spectrum, which might explain his penchant for categorisation and his apparent dread of the unclassified: Philip Lucas and Anne Sheeran, 'Asperger's Syndrome and the Eccentricity and Genius of Jeremy Bentham' (2006) 8 *Journal of Bentham Studies* 1.

[132] John Searle, *Freedom and Neurobiology* (Columbia University Press 2007), 82–83.

[133] See in particular Andrei Marmor, 'Law as Authoritative Fiction' (2018) 37 *Law and Philosophy* 473.

[134] Neil MacCormick, 'Law as Institutional Fact' in Neil MacCormick and Ota Weinberger (eds.), *An Institutional Theory of Law* (Springer 1986), 50.

[135] G. E. M. Anscombe, 'On Brute Facts' (1958) 18(3) *Analysis* 69.

in their context of shared understandings, intentions, and practices. Earlier, John Locke observed:

> [A] mans holding a gun in his hand & pulling downe the triger may be either Rebellion, Parricide, Murther, Homicide, Duty, Justice, Valor or recreation & be thus variously diversified when all the circumstances put together are compard to a rule, though the simple action of holding the gun & pulling the triger may be exactly the same.[136]

Or, again, Hans Kelsen used the example of a legislature: 'People assemble in a hall, they give speeches, some rise, others remain seated – this is the external event. Its meaning: that a statute is enacted'.[137]

In Searle's theory of institutional facts, a relation of *predication* explains the bridge between brute and institutional reality. An institutional fact is created when a community recognises or accepts that a certain (brute) thing 'counts as' something institutional in a particular context. For example, in the context of the United Kingdom's constitutional order, a certain woman 'counts as' Queen. This theory ties together many of the themes discussed over the previous chapters. It explains how human communities, through logico-linguistic operations (a.k.a. rules), superimpose institutional facts onto of their world.

When a rule stipulates that a person 'counts as' a Justice of the Peace, for example, that person acquires a new status within the context of the relevant society and its legal system. These rules are constitutive of the institutional fact ('Justice of the Peace') itself. This introduces a kind of quasi-formal approach to describing offices that sets the stage for thinking about judicial review. According to Searle's basic scheme, constitutive rules comprise three elements: an 'X term' (a brute fact), which counts as a 'Y term' (an institutional fact) in a given context ('C'). From these building blocks, Searle constructs a theory of *institutional power*:

> Because the creation of institutional facts is a matter of imposing a status and with it a function on some entity that does not already have that status-function, in general the creation of a status-function is a matter of

[136] John Locke, 'Draft A of the Essay' §23, cited in J. W. Yolton, *Realism and Appearances: An Essay in Ontology* (Cambridge University Press 2000), 42.

[137] Hans Kelsen (Stanley Paulson and Bonnie Litschewski Paulson trans.), *Introduction to the Problems of Legal Theory* (Clarendon Press 2002), 8.

> conferring some new *power*. There would not be much point to imposing the status-function named by the Y term if it did not confer some new power on the X term, and most (not all) creations of institutional facts are precisely conferring powers on the X term, or performing some truth functional operation such as negation and conditionalisation on the creation of the power. *In the simplest sense, the Y term names a power that the X term does not have solely in virtue of its X structure.* In cases where the X term is a person, that person acquires powers that he or she did not already have. In cases where the X term is an object, the user of that object can do things with it that he or she could not do solely in virtue of its X structure.[138]

This theory draws on Searle's work on the philosophy of consciousness and practical reason. 'Status functions' generate desire independent, non-prudential reasons for action, that is, 'deontic powers' that are a psychological consequence of recognition or acceptance by conscious agents with (the perception of) free will. Normative institutions generate complex deontologies, out of thin air as it were, and connect those deontologies real with people and objects to provide agents within the community of intentionality with reasons for action. These reasons seem peremptory even though they are, ultimately, fetishes of our own making.[139]

Social ontology is a recent branch of analytical philosophy, and has much to say of interest to law.[140] The similarities between Searle's argument for 'ontological subjectivity' and 'epistemic objectivity' resonate, for example, with Hart's 'hermeneutic' approach and the kind of distinction he drew between being 'obliged' and being 'obligated' in his classical exposition of the concept of law.[141] We can use this kind of

[138] John Searle, *The Construction of Social Reality* (Free Press 1995), 96. Emphasis mine.

[139] See W. J. Brown, 'The Personality of the Corporation and the Personality of the State' (1905) 21 *Law Quarterly Review* 365.

[140] See Neil MacCormick, *Institutions of Law* (Oxford University Press 2007); Neil MacCormick and Ota Weinberger, *An Institutional Theory of Law: New Approaches to Legal Positivism* (Springer 1986); Carlos Bernal, 'In Search of the Ontological Structure of Law' [2012] *Analisi e Diritto* 59; Carlos Bernal, 'Austin, Hart, and Shapiro: Three Variations on Law as an Entity Grounded in Social Practice' (2013) 44(2) *Rechtstheorie* 157; Carlos Bernal, 'Collective Intentionality and the Ontological Structure of Law' (2014) 45(3) *Rechtstheorie* 335; Scott Shapiro, *Legality* (Belknap 2012); Jaap Hage, 'The (Onto)logical Structure of Law: A Conceptual Toolkit for Legislators' in Michał Araszkiewicz and Krzysztof Pleszka (eds.), *Logic in the Theory and Practice of Lawmaking* (Springer 2015), 3–48; D. W. P. Ruiter, *Institutional Legal Facts* (Springer 1993); *Legal Institutions* (Springer 2010).

[141] See, for example, Neil MacCormick, *H. L. A. Hart* (Stanford University Press 1981), 27.

theory to understand the concept of office specifically. Bentham may have found it very promising and it may have soothed some of his perplexion. Speaking directly to Bentham's epistemic concerns, Searle describes a 'continuous line' from 'physics to society': 'the decisive moment' in the creation of social reality is the 'collective intentional imposition of function on *entities that cannot perform these functions without that imposition*'.[142]

Searle's 'XYC' formula perhaps even rehabilitates Blackstone, who wrote (in a passage that most likely irritated Bentham the logician):

> [A]s the logicians speak, corporeal hereditaments are the substance, which may always be seen, always handled: incorporeal hereditaments are but a sort of accidents, which inhere in and are supported by that substance; and may belong, or not belong to it, without any visible alteration therein. Their existence is merely in idea and abstracted contemplation; though their effects and profits may be frequently objects of our bodily senses.[143]

In short, Searle's basic formula does an admirable job of describing the link between Hobbes' abstract Leviathan and the mortal humans that animate it. It describes, for example, the process of investiture in an office through public rituals and the association of offices with their paraphernalia (e.g., the Great Seal).

It does not do a very good job, however, of explaining the situation where an office exists without an incumbent. Indeed, among the current disputes within social ontology is one about the necessity of a physical 'X term'. Others have opined that we can create 'free-standing Y terms', and in later works Searle has incorporated this concept into his schema.[144] Free-standing Y terms are created by a slightly different logico-linguistic operation, which quite possibly captures the essential nature of offices even better. These are created with a declaration that 'Y exists in C' and that relation 'R' exists between Y and a certain person, 'S', such that in virtue of SRY, S has the power to perform new types of action.[145] Where

142 John Searle, *The Construction of Social Reality* (Free Press 1995), 41. Emphasis mine.

143 William Blackstone, *Commentaries on the Laws of England* (Clarendon Press 1766), Book I, 20.

144 See Barry Smith and John Searle, 'The Construction of Social Reality: An Exchange' (2003) 62(2) *American Journal of Economics and Sociology* 299, 305.

145 John Searle, *Making the Social World* (Oxford University Press 2010), 101.

early offices conferred a new status on a *named* individual, usually along lines of kinship or achievement, modern bureaucratic structures are either received or else thought out in the abstract and then populated after the fact.[146]

Armed with this insight, Bentham's work on offices actually provides a worthy starting point for a modern concept of office. In broad terms, Bentham's scheme rested on a basic distinction between 'powers of contrectation' (i.e., to deal with things, including with the bodies of persons in situations like arrest and detention) and 'powers of imperation' (i.e., to command subjects to act that works on their 'active' rather than 'passive' faculties).[147] Of equal importance, however, are 'powers of accension', that is, powers to designate a person or object to a class that is the audience of a command. Hart explained the difference, taking the example of a power to appoint judges:

> When someone is given this power, certain formalities may be required by law for its exercise; generally a warrant or document must be signed of which the central operative clause would be something like '*Y* is hereby appointed to be one of Her Majesty's Judges'. When the document is signed the person becomes one of the judges and thenceforth has certain specific duties, rights and powers which constitute what Bentham calls the legal 'condition', or as we might say, the *status*, of a judge. I shall for simplicity's sake focus attention only on the duties of a judge and suppose that there are sanctions for neglect of them. The appointor by his act may be said to '*aggregate*' the new judge to an existing recognized class who have certain distinctive duties, and he may also be said to '*invest*' the new judge with those duties. So this kind of power, considered as a power to include an individual in a recognized or established class is called by Bentham 'a power of aggregation', or 'accensitive power', and

[146] Offices that they subsist even in the absence of an incumbent, although periods of vacancy represent a dangerous potential rupture in the surrounding social fabric. Historically, it is likely that many offices underwent a process of abstraction away from the mortal incumbent towards institutionalization. Paolo Selmi explained the development of *ad hoc* envoys into standing ambassadors thus: '[The office] begins to exist when one has the institution of a permanent *officium* of which the ambassador, provided with a general mandate, is the titulary during his assignment; and when the existence of such an *officium* is not diminished if it should be temporarily deprived of a titulary, such as when a vacancy creates the necessity of nominating a successor'. Paolo Selmi in D. E. Queller, *The Office of Ambassador in the Middle Ages* (Princeton University Press 1961), 76.

[147] H. L. A. Hart, 'Bentham on Legal Powers' (1972) 81(5) *Yale Law Journal* 799, 805.

> considered as a power to invest individuals with rights or duties as 'a power of investment'.[148]

The process of 'aggregation' to the judicial office is aptly explained by the Searleian scheme set out earlier. The powers, rights, and obligations of officeholders should be distinguished from those held in their personal capacity, and the continuing office should be distinguished from its temporary occupant.[149]

Bentham himself compared public offices to private 'conditions' such as 'husband' or 'company director', that is, statuses from which legal consequences follow. However, where private conditions are more or less isolated and self-contained, raising questions of invasion and protection of the rights appertaining thereto, public offices form part of a *system* and their relations within that system are crucial. The public interest requires that useful offices should be occupied and their duties performed, such that public law should pay less attention than private law to rights and the invasion of rights, and 'place more emphasis on the arrangements for the occupancy of an office, on the duties and conditions of their performance and on its relationship with other offices'.[150] Unfortunately, as we have seen, this is exactly the aspect of public law that has been neglected in modernity.

6.5 Conclusion

My discussion in this chapter has showed not only that office is an important category of public law, but that public law itself is best understood as *the law of public offices* – their creation, the distribution of powers between them, their organisation into a system, the appointment of individuals as officials, the enforcement of their duties, and the supervision of their powers.

This is significant for the law of judicial review. Elliott was more concerned with the *substantive* allocations of power between legislative and judicial branches than with the 'power-allocation *methodology*' referred to at the beginning of this chapter. That methodology is, simply, the creation and conferral of offices. Powers of

[148] H. L. A. Hart, 'Bentham on Legal Powers' (1972) 81(5) *Yale Law Journal* 799, 809.
[149] L. J. Hume, *Bentham and Bureaucracy* (Cambridge University Press 1981), 47–48.
[150] L. J. Hume, *Bentham and Bureaucracy* (Cambridge University Press 1981), 248.

commanding, rule-making, and legislation presuppose customarily constituted and observed allocations of authority, which determine the criteria of validity for such acts.[151] The rules through which this occurs are essential to understanding the legal relations in any given legal system between two or more officials and between officials and subjects. The next step will be to map the way they interact.

[151] Neil MacCormick, 'General Legal Concepts' in N. R. Whitty (ed.), *The Laws of Scotland: Stair Memorial Encyclopaedia* (Reissue, LexisNexis 19 June 2015), [2].

7

Office in Action

7.1 Introduction

The judicial review of non-statutory executive powers raises questions going to the legal nature of the Crown, the concept of office, and the logic of official action. The Crown is not a 'natural person' but a corporation sole, and the concept of office is essential for the law of judicial review. It is essential to grapple with the official mode of action, because the supervisory jurisdiction is uniquely concerned with officials acting *as officials*.

All of this underlines the need for care when making arguments about the legal position of officials, and we have seen how categories like 'residual liberties' conduce to error. This chapter sets out a schematic for analysing official empowerment, duty, and action, which in turn provides an enhanced understanding of the supervisory jurisdiction and the ultimate function of judicial review – to distinguish 'lawful' from 'unlawful' actions by officials.

Section 7.2 explains the importance of official action sets out the most important features of W. N. Hohfeld's seminal scheme of fundamental legal conceptions. Section 7.3 explains certain refinements that are necessary to avoid some types of confusion that arise in the context of non-statutory executive powers. The most important thing is to ensure separation between the 'capacitative' and 'deontic' aspects of an actor's legal position – what she is *able* to do, and what she is *permitted* to do. The scope of lawful official action is set by *rules of competence* and *rules of conduct*. These two types of rules set out the official's '*Spielraum*' and correspond to the two 'limbs' of the supervisory jurisdiction, which are concerned with action in excess of an official's jurisdiction (ultra vires in the 'narrow sense') and action in violation of a rule imposing conditions on how that jurisdiction is to be exercised (ultra vires in the 'broad sense'). Section 7.4 concludes.

7.2 Hohfeld's Fundamental Legal Conceptions

All law is a relation between legal subjects; a bearer of rights with no counterparty is incomprehensible. This is no less true of the Crown and its officials than of private persons, so public lawyers need a structured way of describing the relationship between any given official and any given subject – be it a citizen, alien, foreign diplomat, prisoner, or asylum seeker. Judicial review entails determining when one side of a legal relationship does not match the other – when, for example, my right of abode as a Belonger of a British Overseas Territory is not compatible with the action of, say, the Foreign Secretary (who has a non-statutory power of legislating for that Territory).[1]

The notion of a legal 'position' is historically and etymologically related to the idea of 'status'. The Crown, as we have seen, can only act through individuals. In his study of individual rights in public law, Georg Jellinek started with the special mode of action that is implied by official status: '[i]nsofar as the state gives an individual the competence to act for the state', he argued, 'it transposes him into a situation of heightened, qualified, *active citizenship*'.[2] The individual whose will counts, in a given context, as the will of the group is to be regarded as an organ of the group, and this person is designated by legal norms 'such that calling an individual to a position of agency can only follow on the basis of a legal order governing that calling'.[3] This makes judicial review indispensable to the very idea of lawful authority itself: 'responsibility of the organs and the way in which they express their will, the conditions under which it can claim legal validity, must be determined through legal provisions'.[4] Those provisions must, in turn, be amenable to judicial interpretation and enforcement to ensure that the official in question acts properly.

Indeed, the relational nature of legal positions differentiates brute power from lawful authority, which is the core concern of judicial review. As Jellinek argued, '[a] factual relation of control only becomes a legal one when both members, master and subject, recognise each other as

[1] See *R (Bancoult)* v. *Foreign Secretary (No 2)* [2008] UKHL 61.
[2] Georg Jellinek, *System der subjektiven öffentlichen Rechte* (Mohr 1892), 82–83. Translation mine, emphasis mine.
[3] Georg Jellinek, *System der subjektiven öffentlichen Rechte* (Mohr 1892), 83.
[4] Georg Jellinek, *Allgemeine Staatslehre* (2nd ed., Mohr 1905), 526, 529; translated in Alf Ross, 'On the Concepts "State" and "State Organs" in Constitutional Law' (1957) 5 *Scandinavian Studies in Law* 113, 126.

counterparty bearers of rights and duties'.[5] Because judicial review entails a granular analysis of the relations between 'ordinary' and 'active' citizens, it is necessary to map the legal incidents of the official position accurately.

7.2.1 *Towards a Technical Vocabulary*

We have all heard words like 'right', 'duty', 'obligation', 'liberty', and 'power' being used to mean different things, and the 'residual liberties' argument illustrates the impact this can have on theories of judicial review. We need a rigorous and consistent set of concepts to refer to relational legal positions between subjects and officials, described with a consistent terminology.

For Anglophone lawyers, the name of W. N. Hohfeld is virtually synonymous with the idea that legal relations should be modelled according to a logical scheme, and that we should only speak about legal positions and relations using a constrained vocabulary.[6] Working in the early twentieth century, Hohfeld drew on the work of nineteenth century German Pandectists as well as case studies of common law judicial language to add logical rigour to the way we speak about legal relationships.

Hohfeld claimed to describe every legal relationship as a constellation of eight fundamental legal conceptions, being 'rights', 'duties', 'privileges', 'no-rights', 'powers', 'disabilities', 'immunities', and 'liabilities'. These basic *quanta* are the 'lowest common denominators' of the law; any two legal relationships, no matter how different, can be reduced to these elements, just as incommensurable fractions can be added once expressed in terms of their lowest common denominator. Each category is *sui generis*, in the sense that formal, reductive definition is impossible; they are defined by their logical relation to one another.[7] This relation takes one of two types. Jural 'correlatives' bear a relation of logical entailment in two separate agents (for example, my right of possession entails a 'correlative' duty in you to stay off my land).[8] Jural 'opposites' bear a relation of logical negation in a single subject (for

[5] Georg Jellinek, *System der subjectiven öffentlichen Rechte* (Mohr 1892), 9. Translation mine. See also Michel Foucault, 'The Subject and Power' (1982) 8(4) *Critical Enquiry* 777, 786.

[6] W. N. Hohfeld, 'Some Fundamental Legal Conceptions as Applied in Judicial Reasoning' (1913) 23(1) *Yale Law Journal* 16; W. N. Hohfeld, 'Some Fundamental Conceptions as Applied in Judicial Reasoning' (1917) 26(1) *Yale Law Journal* 710.

[7] Lars Lindahl, *Position and Change* (Reidel 1977), 1; Gerald Postema, *A Treatise of Legal Philosophy and General Jurisprudence*, Vol. 11 (Springer 2011), 99.

[8] W. N. Hohfeld, 'Some Fundamental Legal Conceptions as Applied in Judicial Reasoning' (1913) 23(1) *Yale Law Journal* 16, 32.

example, my immunity to giving evidence against my spouse entails that I cannot be liable to give such evidence at the behest of the Crown Prosecutor). A *right* is a claim that one actor has against another, that is the correlative of a *duty* in the latter. That duty, in turn, is opposite to a *privilege* (or *liberty*[9]) to do a certain type of action (for example, where I am duty bound to assist a road accident casualty, for example, I have no privilege *not* to help her). The correlative of a privilege is a *no-right*. These four elements comprise one half of the scheme. In the other half, we find *power*, which Hohfeld defines as the ability to change an actor's legal position. A power is correlative of a *liability* in the other party to have her position changed. The opposite of a power is a *disability*. A disability is the correlative of an *immunity*, which is in turn the opposite of a *liability*.[10]

7.2.2 *Problems with the Hohfeld Scheme*

I will return to the two 'halves' of Hohfeld's scheme again further in the text, in particular to the concept of power and the need for a more developed concept of action. The usefulness of Hohfeld's schema in the public law context, however, has been questioned on the basis that it focusses on bilateral legal relations, while public law rights and duties do not always seem to be capable of the granular correlativity requirement.[11] Jellinek, however, was right that individual rights and official duties must reflect each other. Thus, although it is a point of dispute between legal theorists,[12] an official's duty to act reasonably (for example) cannot be a duty 'at large', but correlative to rights in all subjects potentially affected by her actions. The rights of one actor are always matched by the obligations of others. The reason it all works as a system is precisely *because* it is relational, as Tony Lawson explains:

> If human individuals are organised through being positioned as components of a system, and if the various positions are interrelated by way of connecting rights and obligations, it is these connections that most qualify

[9] Hohfeld spoke of 'privileges' but much of the contemporary Hohfeldian literature speaks of 'liberties': see Hillel Steiner, *An Essay on Rights* (Blackwell 1994), 59. I will use the terms synonymously.

[10] See M. H. Kramer, 'Rights without Trimmings' in M. H. Kramer, N. E. Simmonds, and Steiner Hillel (eds.), *A Debate Over Rights* (Oxford University Press 2000).

[11] See Nicholas Bamforth, 'Hohfeldian Rights and Public Law' in Matthew Kramer (ed.), *Rights, Wrongs and Responsibilities* (Macmillan 2001).

[12] See David Frydrych, 'Rights Correlativity' in Shyam Balganesh, Ted Sichleman, and Henry Smith (eds.), *The Legacy of Wesley Hohfeld: Edited Major Works, Select Personal Papers, and Original Commentaries* (Cambridge University Press 2019), §II.2, §III.2.

> as the content of the category social relation. In other words, a social relation just is (or is first and foremost) an accepted set of (matching) rights and obligations holding between, and connecting, two or more positions or occupants of positions. Social interaction can be understood as the contingent actualisations of such social relations.[13]

Describing the 'matching' of these relations is essential to understanding the structure of social relations within a given society. Constructs such as 'rights' and 'obligations' give us reasons to act in this way or another – and give other members of the community reason to encourage or compel us to do so. This says something very basic about the foundations of judicial review and its role in an organised political community. Just as the owner of Blackacre has rights 'against all the world' that only need to be stated concretely in bilateral terms whenever a property dispute arises, judicial review crystallises public law rights and duties in the context of bilateral relations between subject and officials, or between officials. Translating broadly stated public law principles to a bilateral proposition of Subject A's right and Official B's duty is the essence of judicial review.[14]

However, there are more serious issues with Hohfeld. Jeremy Bentham is credited with the first attempt to expound what he called a 'logic of imperation', which he rightly claimed was a 'branch of logic untouched by Aristotle'.[15] Bentham's deontic logic contained three modes: *obligation*, *prohibition*, and *permission*. Bentham's logic of imperation, however, languished until its revival by H. L. A. Hart (among others) in the 1970s. Thus, Hohfeld took John Austin's less sophisticated account as his departure point, relying on natural language, the use of examples, and a logic of 'correlatives' and 'opposites' rather than a modal logic.[16]

[13] Tony Lawson, 'Comparing Conceptions of Social Ontology: Emergent Social Entities and/or Institutional Facts?' (2016) 46(4) *Journal for the Theory of Social Behaviour* 359, 364–365.

[14] See Nicholas Bamforth, 'Hohfeldian Rights and Public Law' in M. H. Kramer (ed.), *Rights, Wrongs and Responsibilities* (Macmillan 2001), 1–27 ; David Frydrych, 'Rights Correlativity' in Shyam Balganesh, Ted Sichleman, and Henry Smith (eds.), *The Legacy of Wesley Hohfeld: Edited Major Works, Select Personal Papers, and Original Commentaries* (Cambridge University Press 2019), §II.2, §III.2.

[15] Jeremy Bentham (J. H. Burns and H. L. A. Hart eds.), *An Introduction to the Principles of Morals and Legislation* (Athlone Press 1970), 299. Leibniz attempted to organise relationships of legal obligation into a logical scheme in the seventeenth century, but his account remained unpublished until much later: G. W. Leibniz, *Sämtliche Schrifte und Breife 1. Band* (Preussische Akademie der Wissenschaften 1930), 465, 'Elementa Juris Naturalis'. See also Philip Mullock, 'Logic and Liberty' (1979) 35(3) *Philosophical Studies* 217.

[16] Pound described Hohfeld's logic as 'Hegelian': see Roscoe Pound, 'Fifty Years of Jurisprudence' (1937) 50(4) *Harvard Law Review* 558.

A technical revision of Hohfeld is beyond the scope of this book. For the type of legal analysis with which I am concerned, it seems best to use of the familiar Hohfeldian terminology but to couch it in a conceptual framework that incorporates two elements under-developed in the Hohfeld scheme. The first element is a *logic of action* to describe how it is that an actor can bring about changes to a certain legal state of affairs (including a change to the legal position of another actor).[17] This presents a systematic way of talking about the scope of actions that a given legal actor – in particular, a given official – is able to take. The second element is a *deontic logic.*[18] This presents a more expressive and accurate way of talking about the scope of actions an official is permitted to take (or obligated to take or prohibited from taking). The real importance of these elements appears when they are combined.

7.2.3 Hohfeldian Liberties and the Third Source Fallacy

The most serious issue with the operation of Hohfeld's scheme in the public law context relates to the category of 'liberties' or 'privileges'. The 'no-rights' to which liberties purportedly correlate are a category that Hohfeld seems to have invented to close his scheme.[19] I have never seen evidence of 'no-rights' in judicial reasoning – except, perhaps, in decisions couched in expressly Hohfeldian terms. When applied to the Crown and its officials, Hohfeldian liberties open up a grey zone in which the legal basis of official action is assumed rather than articulated.

[17] See Lennart Åqvist, 'A New Approach to the Logical Theory of Actions and Causality' in Sören Stenlund, Ann-Mari Henschen-Dahlquist, Lars Lindahl, Lennart Nordenfelt, and Jan Odelstad (eds.), *Logical Theory and Semantic Analysis* (Reidel 1974), 73–91.

[18] See Lars Lindahl, *Position and Change* (Reidel 1977), 4; Ernst Mally, *Grundsätze des Sollens. Elemente der Logik des Willens* (Leuschner & Lubensky 1926); G. H. von Wright, 'Deontic Logic' (1951) 60 *Mind* 1; G. H. von Wright, *Norm and Action* (Routledge 1963); G. H. von Wright, *An Essay in Deontic Logic and the General Theory of Action* (North-Holland 1972); Alf Ross, *Directive and Norm* (Humanities Press 1968); Alf Ross, 'Imperatives and Logic' (1944) 11(1) *Philosophy of Science* 30; Stig Kanger and Helle Kanger, 'Rights and Parliamentarism' (1966) 32 *Theoria* 85; A. R. Anderson, 'A Reduction of Deontic Logic to Alethic Modal Logic' (1958) 67(265) *Mind* 100; H. G. Bohnert, 'The Semiotic Status of Commands' (1945) 7 *Philosophy of Science* 302.

[19] Hohfeld's scheme is not entirely consistent in this regard: David Frydrych, 'Rights Correlativity' in Shyam Balganesh, Ted Sichleman, and Henry Smith (eds.), *The Legacy of Wesley Hohfeld: Edited Major Works, Select Personal Papers, and Original Commentaries* (Cambridge University Press 2019), §III.1.

Malone v. *Metropolitan Police Commissioner*[20] once again provides an illustration.[21] In *Malone*, the Police Commissioner had instructed the Post Office to tap a criminal suspect's telephone line under a warrant issued by the Home Secretary. Megarry VC distinguished the case from *Entick* v. *Carrington*[22] on the basis that Entick had a common law right against trespass by Carrington. So long as Malone had *no right* to telephonic privacy, neither the Postmaster nor the Commissioner had any *duty not* to tap his phone; they could not, therefore, have done any actionable wrong by installing one. Megarry VC based this reasoning on the proposition that 'England is not a country where everything is forbidden except for what is expressly permitted':[23]

> If the tapping of telephones by the Post Office at the request of the police can be carried out without any breach of the law, it does not require any statutory or common law power to justify it: it can lawfully be done simply because there is nothing to make it unlawful.[24]

At least as applied to the Crown and its officials, this proposition about English law should be flatly rejected. The better view was expressed by Laws LJ held in *R (Fewings)* v. *Somerset County Council*,[25] albeit in the context of a statutory body: the presumption of freedom of action that applies to private persons does not translate to public officials, whose every must be justified by positive law.[26]

Beyond this, the wisdom of denying individuals a right to telephonic privacy in the late 1970s was highly questionable. Rather than following other jurisdictions which had treated taps as searches,[27] Megarry VC

[20] (1979) 1 Ch 344.

[21] An indication that *Malone* was influenced by Hohfeld comes from Megarry VC's judgment in *McInnes* v. *Onslow-Fane* [1978] 1 WLR 1520, which concerned the High Court's private law supervisory jurisdiction over 'domestic tribunals'. Noting 'jurisprudential questions', Megarry VC preferred 'liberty to work' over 'right to work': 'I have no intention of discussing the wide variety of meanings which the protean word "right" embraces; *but if a person has a right in the strict sense of the word, then some other person or persons must be subject to a duty correlative of that right*'. *McInnes* v. *Onslow-Fane* [1978] 1 WLR 1520, 1528. Emphasis mine. On the supervisory jurisdiction over domestic tribunals, see Chapter 12.

[22] (1765) 19 How St Tr 1029.

[23] *Malone* v. *Metropolitan Police Commissioner* (1979) 1 Ch 344, 367.

[24] *Malone* v. *Metropolitan Police Commissioner* (1979) 1 Ch 344, 372.

[25] *R (Fewings)* v. *Somerset City Council* [1995] 1 All ER 513, 524 (Laws LJ).

[26] *R (Fewings)* v. *Somerset City Council* [1995] 1 All ER 513, 524; W. S. Tarnopolsky, 'Frank Scott – Civil Libertarian' (1981) 27 *McGill Law Journal* 14, 25.

[27] *Katz* v. *United States* (1967) 389 US 347 held the interception of a telephone conversation in a public phone booth subject to 4th Amendment requirements. The European Court of

extended the eighteenth century principle that 'the eye cannot by the laws of England be guilty of a trespass' to the ear.[28] This was blind and deaf to the direction of travel in the regulation of surveillance technology. The judgment was also oddly out of kilter with the established practice of treating telegraph and telephone messages as confidential in England.[29] Remarkably, however, after reviewing all the relevant history, Megarry VC held that the Commissioner needed no positive authorisation to install a tap, and that the warrant in question did not purport to be issued under the authority of any statute or of the common law.[30] It was purely optional, a belt for the Commissioner's braces; where the tapping was

Human Rights held *Malone* inconsistent with the European Convention on Human Rights in *Malone* v. *United Kingdom* (1984) 7 EHRR 14, and Parliament enacted the Interception of Communications Act 1985.

[28] *Malone* v. *Metropolitan Police Commissioner* (1979) 1 Ch 344, 369. He did, however, cite an American judge for the proposition that judicial innovation should be 'molecular rather than molar', and pointed to the legislative codification of a deserted wife's equity following denial by the courts.

[29] Breach by Post Office staff of telegraph confidentiality was an offence under the Telegraph Act 1869 and the Post Office (Protection) Act 1884. Telephone messages had been treated as analogous for other purposes since *Attorney General* v. *Edison Telephone Co of London* (1880) 6 QBD 244. For the first fifty years of telecommunications in Britain, the police had been able to request surveillance directly from the Postmaster General – then a Minister of the Crown. In 1937, it had been decided 'as a matter of policy' by the Home Secretary and the Postmaster General that a warrant from the former would be required: '[t]he view was taken that certain statutes which permitted the interception of letters and telegrams on the authority of a Secretary of State were wide enough to cover telephone tapping'. The Birkett Report of 1957 established a new framework for issuing warrants, stipulating 'strict conditions', requiring the Secretary to consider (and grant) applications personally. Monthly review by the Home Office was necessary; irrelevant material was destroyed. The Report treated the interception of communications as the 'exercise of a lawful power': *Report of the Committee of Privy Councillors appointed to inquire into the interception of communication* (Cmnd 283, October 1957), [8]. After 1937, if the Postmaster General disagreed with the Secretary, 'there would have been a disagreement between two Ministers of the Crown which ... would presumably have been determined by the Cabinet'. This changed in 1969, with the transformation of the Post Office into a corporation with greater independence of the Crown. It could no longer be assumed that the Post Office would act upon a warrant of the Home Secretary. The Post Office Act 1969 s. 80 therefore provided that a 'requirement' could be 'laid upon' the Post Office by 'designated persons holding office under the Crown' requiring interception of communications. According to Megarry VC, Parliament merely intended to provide lawful authority in the changed circumstances for what had previously been done. Mirroring the statutory defence in *Entick* v. *Carrington*, the Post Office Act 1969 provided that it would be a defence for any person charged with the offences under the nineteenth century telegraph statutes that the act constituting the offence was done in obedience to a warrant. See *Malone* v. *Metropolitan Police Commissioner* (1979) 1 Ch 344, 367–370.

[30] *Malone* v. *Metropolitan Police Commissioner* (1979) 1 Ch 344, 370.

done under warrant, the section afforded 'statutory recognition' of lawfulness of the tapping, but tapping was 'lawful without any warrant'.[31]

Assuming no right of telephonic privacy, and cast within the Hohfeldian logic, the conclusion that the Crown and its officers were 'at liberty' to tap telephone lines seems irresistible. But that illustrates the fundamental problem. It seems irresistible because it rests on an unassailable proposition: *that which is not prohibited is permitted.*[32] A tautology is definitionally true on its own terms, so it cannot be incorrect. It tells us nothing, but it conceals a tacit premise: if an official is at *liberty* to do something, then he also has the *ability* to do it.[33] Even in the absence of a duty not to do something, however, a government official may not have the ability to do a certain type of action at all. As John Howell has argued, there is little to commend the argument:

> The fact that there may be no prohibition, express or implied, on a minister doing something does not necessarily mean that he has the capacity in law to do it. Any assumption that he does, as he is the agent of the Crown, simply begs the question of what the Crown may do when acting in its public capacity.[34]

Ability does not follow from an absence of prohibition because the one refers to a *deontic* mode and the other to a *capacitative* mode.[35] *Malone* v. *Metropolitan Police Commissioner* thus obscures the very heart of the judicial review of official action.

7.3 A Revision of the Hohfeld Scheme

With two relatively simple but important modifications we can use the Hohfeldian scheme but avoid this error. The key to both is to trace out the relation between the two 'boxes' of the Hohfeld scheme. If we see Hohfeldian legal relations as propositions relating to action, then powers, liabilities, immunities, and disabilities describe what an agent is *able* do, while rights, duties, no rights, and privileges describe what an agent is *allowed* do. However, it is unclear how the two 'boxes' fit together, and this

31 *Malone* v. *Metropolitan Police Commissioner* (1979) 1 Ch 344, 370.

32 Adam Perry, 'The Crown's Administrative Powers' (2015) 131 *Law Quarterly Review* 652, 655.

33 Adam Perry, 'The Crown's Administrative Powers' (2015) 131 *Law Quarterly Review* 652, 655.

34 John Howell, 'What the Crown May Do' [2010] *Judicial Review* 36, [98].

35 See also Torben Spaak, 'Norms that Confer Competence' (2003) 16(1) *Ratio Juris* 89, 99.

lacuna encourages the derivation of ability from absence of permission instead of articulating exactly how official *duties* constrain the scope of official *powers*.

7.3.1 Action in Hohfeld, Hohfeld in Action

The first step is to incorporate a more satisfactory concept of action into Hohfeld's scheme – particularly actions by an official 'for and on behalf' of the Crown, whether legislating for a former colony as in *R (Bancoult)* v. *Foreign Secretary*,[36] or signing a lease over business premises as in *Town Investments* v. *Department of Environment*.[37] This is closely connected with the Hohfeldian concept of 'power'.

The importance of the concept of power for a theory of judicial review is difficult to overstate. Hart likened the discovery of 'enabling rules' to the invention of the wheel.[38] Law is 'both a pyramid of norms and a "cascade of powers"'.[39] Buying and selling, making gifts and wills, or getting married would be impossible in a society without power-conferring rules; these things, 'like the orders of courts and the enactments of lawmaking bodies, *just consist in* the valid exercise of legal powers'.[40] Power-conferring rules are particularly important in public law, however, as they explain the enabling and constraining roles of institutions and specify the preconditions to be met in order for officials to perform actions that they could not perform as individuals.[41] Later Hart observed that, despite that, despite their concern with the analysis of fundamental legal concepts, theorists had mostly directed the limelight onto rights and duties.[42] Hart himself did much to remedy this situation, by showing how power-conferring rules are essential to the concept of law.[43] But there is still a great amount of disagreement.[44]

[36] [2008] UKHL 61.

[37] [1978] AC 359.

[38] H. L. A. Hart, *The Concept of Law* (Clarendon Press 1961), 41.

[39] Agostino Carrino, 'Reflections on Legal Science, Law, and Power' in Stanley Paulson and Bonnie Litschewski Paulson (eds.), *Normativity and Norms* (Clarendon Press 1998), 510, citing Norberto Bobbio, 'Kelsen and Legal Power' in the same volume, 437.

[40] H. L. A. Hart, *The Concept of Law* (Clarendon Press 1982), 32. Emphasis mine.

[41] Frank Hindriks, 'Constitutive Rules, Language, and Ontology' (2009) 71 *Erkenntnis* 253, 254.

[42] H. L. A. Hart, *Essays on Bentham* (Clarendon Press 1982), 194–195.

[43] See Eugenio Bulygin, 'On Norms of Competence' (1992) 11 *Law and Philosophy* 201, 213–214 for discussion.

[44] See Joseph Raz, 'Voluntary Obligations and Normative Powers' (1972) *Proceedings of the Aristotelian Society* 79(46); Andrew Halpin, 'The Concept of a Legal Power' (1996) 16(1)

Hohfeld defined a 'power' as the ability to effect a change in a legal situation through intentional action, whether unilaterally or by agreement.[45] We have seen that Sir William Wade adopted this definition of powers to narrow down his category of 'prerogative'.[46] Hohfeld's concept of power, however, is actually overbroad. My ability to create a duty in myself (and a correlative right in you) is a Hohfeldian 'power', whether the duty arises from signing a contract or committing a tort or a crime, for example. However, these are meaningfully different types of action. Causing a legal state of affairs by exercising a legal power (i.e., making a valid will) is different to causing a legal state of affairs by a factual act to which the legal system attributes consequences (i.e., crashing my car into another).[47] Whether something effects a change in the legal situation distinguishes powers from permissions, but does not distinguish factual abilities from legal powers.[48]

Hohfeld's own thinking was inconsistent on this point. On the one hand, his definition entails that *both* the intentional exercise of a legal power *and* the volitional causation of some set of factual circumstances triggering a change in legal position are 'legal powers'.[49] Elsewhere, however, Hohfeld claimed that it is necessary to distinguish between the 'legal power' to do something and the 'physical power' to do things necessary for the *exercise* of the legal power.[50] The same term is used for both ideas. Andrew Halpin distinguishes, in this regard, between exercises of a power and fulfilment of a 'mere condition'.[51]

Oxford Journal of Legal Studies 129; Jaap Hage, 'What is a Legal Transaction?' In Maksymilian Del Mar and Zenon Bankowski (eds.), *Law as Institutional Normative Order* (Ashgate 2009), 103–124.

45 W. N. Hohfeld, 'Some Fundamental Legal Conceptions as Applied in Judicial Reasoning' (1913) 23(1) *Yale Law Journal* 16, 44.

46 See Chapter 2.

47 Lars Lindahl, *Position and Change* (Reidel 1977), 206.

48 Robert Alexy, *Theorie der Grundrechte* (7th ed., Suhrkamp 2012), 214.

49 Lars Lindahl, *Position and Change* (Reidel 1977), 206. For example, D. J. Hislop claims that 'A has the legal power by assaulting B of creating a *claim* to damages in B, but this *power* is coupled with the duty not to use it'. D. J. Hislop, 'The Hohfeldian System of Fundamental Legal Conceptions' (1967) 53(1) *Archive for Philosophy of Law and Social Philosophy* 53, 64. See also Robert Alexy, *Theorie der Grundrechte* (7th ed., Suhrkamp 2012), 214; F. B. Fitch, 'A Revision of Hohfeld's Theory of Legal Concepts' (1967) 10 *Logique et Analyse* 269, 273.

50 Lars Lindahl, *Position and Change* (Reidel 1977), 210.

51 Andrew Halpin, 'The Concept of a Legal Power' (1996) 16(1) *Oxford Journal of Legal Studies* 129.

Alongside Anglophone theorists,[52] Hohfeld drew on nineteenth century Continental legal theory,[53] where this distinction is drawn clearly. In the classical account, Alois Brinz argued that 'legal permission' [*rechtliches Dürfen*] and 'legal ability' [*rechtliches Können*] have to be distinguished, despite their overlap in everyday usage. While legal permission applies both to general and legal dealings, legal ability applies only to special acts which have 'invisible, legal effects'.[54] According to Brinz, I can perform many acts without legal ability, such as crimes and torts. Purported acts-in-the-law without legal ability, on the other hand, simply fail to have their desired effect.[55] Unlike a legally prohibited physical act, a legal act without legal ability is not an 'act' at all. It is a nullity, like an invalid move in a game.

7.3.2 Official Acts as Acts-in-the-Law

An assessment of any official action must not only affirm the absence of a (legal) prohibition and the presence of a (factual) ability; we must also describe the conjunction of (i) the factual abilities necessary to exercise (ii) a legal power with (iii) the absence of a prohibition to exercise it in the manner intended.[56] Factual actions either occur or they do not, but

[52] Roscoe Pound, 'Fifty Years of Jurisprudence' (1937) 50(4) *Harvard Law Review* 557; Anthony Dickey, 'Hohfeld's Debt to Salmond' (1971) 10 *University of Western Australia Law Review* 59; C. C. Langdell, 'Classification of Rights and Wrongs' (1900) 13 *Harvard Law Review* 659; John Salmond (C. A. W. Manning ed.), *Jurisprudence* (8th ed., Sweet & Maxwell 1930), Ch 10.

[53] See, Ernst Rudolph Bierling, *Zur Kritik der juristischen Grundbegriffe* (Berthes 1877). See the appendix to David Frydrych, 'Rights Modelling' (2017) 30(1) *Canadian Journal of Law and Jurisprudence* 125.

[54] Alois Brinz, *Lehrbuch der Pandekten Band I* (2nd ed., Deichert 1873), 211. My translation draws on Lars Lindahl, *Position and Change* (Reidel 1977), 211.

[55] Lars Lindahl, *Position and Change* (Reidel 1977), 211.

[56] Some legal theorists do ascribe to a 'reductive' conception of legal power that collapses the notion of power-conferring rules into the category of rules stipulating some form of conduct (whether by command or permission). See Eugenio Bulygin, 'On Norms of Competence' (1992) 11 *Law and Philosophy* 201. Lindahl's earlier theory adopts a negative reductive concept of power, but his later work seems to reject it. See Lars Lindahl, *Position and Change* (Reidel 1977), 211; Lars Lindahl and David Reidhav, 'Legal Power: The Basic Definition' (2017) 30(2) *Ratio Juris* 158, 163. Further examples include H. G. von Wright and Stig Kanger. Guillaume Tusseau argues that four alternate conceptions of power-conferring norms are evident in different aspects of Jeremy Bentham's theory: power-conferring dispositions as 'incomplete laws', as 'indirectly formulated obligative laws', as 'permissive laws', and as 'qualificatory dispositions'. See Guillaume Tusseau, 'Jeremy Bentham on Power-Conferring Laws' (2007) 3 *Varia* [10]–[28]. Hohfeld's conception is a non-reductive one, and should not be used to make this kind of argument. Good reductive

exercises of legal powers have an added property: they are 'invalid' or 'valid', which is determined by conformity with the relevant power-conferring rule.[57] In the context of official action, we can equate 'validity' with 'lawfulness', and this is the quality of official actions with which judicial review is ultimately concerned. Hart explained:

> Legal rules defining the ways in which valid contracts or wills or marriages are made do not require persons to act in certain ways whether they wish to or not. Such laws do not impose duties or obligations. Instead, they provide individuals with *facilities* for realising their wishes, by conferring legal powers upon them to create, *by certain specified procedures and subject to certain conditions*, structures of rights and duties within the coercive framework of the law.[58]

An analogy with magical incantation is not inaccurate; only if I get the spell right do Brinz's 'invisible, legal effects' occur,[59] which Searle would describe as the inherent suasion of deontic powers generated by subjects' own recognition or acceptance of the status functions involved.[60] This concept of power, in turn, implies – although Hart did not use the term – the concept of an 'act-in-the-law' that corresponds logically to the structure of rules conferring the power.

The idea of an act-in-the-law, more familiar in Continental legal theory (e.g., *acte juridique*, *Rechtsakt*), is increasingly familiar in Anglophone legal theory. A brief definition might run that an act-in-the-law is an act, usually a speech act, that is 'performative' in the sense of *doing* something and not just saying something,[61] in virtue of rules that connect an act with legal consequences.[62] Visa Kurki suggests that an actor holds a legal power to bring about a certain legal consequence if and

theories incorporate a more formal logic of operations and deontic relations to avoid the kind of conclusion I have criticised. I prefer 'non-reductive' approaches, such as those of Hart and Alf Ross. The most intuitive and readily applicable approach is a revision of Hohfeld that distinguishes an agent's practical ability to change legal positions from her ability to do so by performing a special type of legal act.

57 Lars Lindahl and David Reidhav, 'Legal Power: The Basic Definition' (2017) 30(2) *Ratio Juris* 158, 161.

58 H. L. A. Hart, *The Concept of Law* (Clarendon Press 1961), 27–28. Emphasis mine.

59 See, for example, D. A. Westbrook, 'Magical Contracts, Numinous Capitalism' (2016) 32 (6) *Anthropology Today* 13.

60 See John Searle, *Making the Social World* (Oxford University Press 2010), Ch 7.

61 See generally J. L. Austin, *How to Do Things with Words* (Oxford University Press 1962).

62 See, for example, H. D. S. van der Kaaij, *The Juridical Act* (Springer 2019) for a recent exploration of the concept. See also Hans Kelsen, 'Was ist ein Rechtsakt?' (1952) 4(3) *Österreichische Zeitschrift für öffentliches Recht* 263.

only if she can perform an act-in-the-law to bring about that consequence. An act-in-the-law is an act intended to bring about the stated legal consequence where that intentional action is an element of a set of 'minimally sufficient' conditions to bring about the legal consequence.[63] For example, an official has the legal competence to perform a marriage if and only if she has the ability (e.g., by uttering certain words or executing certain documents) to bring about the result that two people become 'married'. I will adopt these definitions more or less closely in my account.[64] This shows the inherent connection between 'being married', the rules that constitute that status, and the rules that empower the marriage celebrant to bring about the relevant state of affairs in the world.

We can now double back on the characterisation of third source-type powers. Are official acts just acts-in-fact by officials within the 'residual liberties' of the Crown? In truth, *attribution* to the Crown in virtue of 'official' status entails that official actions are, categorically, *acts-in-the-law*. Every act-in-the-law rests on an act-in-fact, and official actions are no different; an act-in-the-law *just is* an act-in-fact that the law treats differently because some rule states that 'act-in-fact *x*' should be counted as 'act-in-the-law *y*'. The very point of office is, after all, to conscript the factual (mental and physical) capacities of human beings, and use them to animate abstract, inanimate institutions. Lars Lindahl and David Reidhav observe a now-familiar theme:

> Legal personalities (e.g. companies, organisations, parliaments, courts) are legally constructed entities, established by legal rules. Unlike physical agents, such entities cannot perform any acts themselves, nor have any intentions themselves. Accordingly, the legal power possessed by 'impersonal' power-holders must be distinguished and explicated differently from the legal power of physical persons.[65]

The physical act of an official can only count as an act of the Crown *pursuant to rules*. Acts-in-the-law are 'artificial' (to use the language of David Hume) or 'institutional' (to use the language of John Searle), in the sense that they presuppose and are made possible by a system of rules.[66] The same point was made by Jellinek, who observed that law adds

[63] See Visa Kurki, 'Legal Competence and Legal Power' in Mark McBride (ed.), *New Essays on the Nature of Rights* (Hart 2017), 38.

[64] I use the terms 'power' and 'competence' interchangeably, however.

[65] Lars Lindahl and David Reidhav, 'Legal Power: The Basic Definition' (2017) 30(2) *Ratio Juris* 158, 164.

[66] Lars Lindahl and David Reidhav, 'Legal Power: The Basic Definition' (2017) 30(2) *Ratio Juris* 158, 161.

something to the individual's natural capacity for action, 'an ability not given to him by nature'.[67] In this way, rules quite literally create new forms of action that are impossible (indeed, *inconceivable*) in the absence of rules.

Every official action as thus an exercise of some power reposed in the office, even if its exercise presupposes and requires the factual abilities of the human official. This is a somewhat difficult point, and it has important implications for our understanding of the supervisory jurisdiction beyond negating the third source theory.

7.3.3 *The Asymmetry of Attribution and Liability*

Whenever an official takes a decision, makes a disbursement of funds, or indeed arrests a citizen, the acts-in-fact of the officeholder are being judged against a rule as potential acts of the office. What we need is a framework that explains how the legal consequences of acts performed by individuals, acting as officials, are ascribed to the Crown. The traditional view, as we have seen, was that an act ultra vires – a 'failed' act-in-the-law – stood as a naked act-in-fact, but the modern law requires an explanation of wrongdoing under colour of official authority. Considering the conjunction and disjunction of factual ability, legal ability, and legal permission allows us to refine our analysis.

Generally, an official act comprises a set of physical (including mental) actions by a human individual, that is, the incumbent of the office. These are then deemed to be the fulfilment of the necessary conditions for an act-in-the-law by the official in their official *persona*. Recall Lord Hoffmann's speech in *Meridian Global Funds Management Asia Ltd* v. *Securities Commission*[68] that any proposition about a company necessarily refers to a set of rules. There would be little sense, he continued, in deeming a corporation to exist without rules determining what acts are to count as acts of the corporation. These are 'rules of attribution'.[69] 'Primary rules of attribution' could be derived the company constitution, and 'general rules of attribution' from the law of agency. Statements about the corporation's actions and capacities were to be understood as statements about those rules. Like the Crown, a corporation 'as such'

[67] Georg Jellinek, *System der subjektiven öffentlichen Rechte* (Mohr 1892), 47. Translation mine.

[68] [1995] 3 All ER 918 (JCPC).

[69] *Meridian Global Funds Management Asia Ltd* v. *Securities Commission* [1995] 2 AC 500, 506.

cannot do anything – it must act by servants or agents. Acting through an agent, under these rules, a corporation makes itself subject to 'general rules by which liability for the acts of others can be attributed to natural persons'.[70]

Rules governing corporate liability for agents' wrongdoing reflect the general rules of attribution, but not exactly. As we saw in Chapter 5, authorisation within an organisational context to do a certain type of act does not mean that *every* wrongdoing in the course of doing that action should accrue to the organisation itself; rules of attribution and rules of liability must be tailored to the context.[71] In broad terms, the modern approach holds the Crown liable for a wider category of unlawful actions by its officers than the traditional law, namely accepting liability for some actions that cannot be fully attributed to it because they are ultra vires. The old approach is still reflected in the logical structure of the prerogative writs, in which the Crown sues the official for the maladministration of the powers reposed in her office. Today, judicial review applications are brought more or less as of right and the defendant is the office, rather than the official as an individual. Of course, there is a class of actions for which liability should always attach to the official personally – for example, gross negligence, deliberate misfeasance, or criminal behaviour.[72] But the Crown has squarely entered the 'liability calculus' in its own right.[73]

In consequence, the question of when an action should be considered 'private' or 'official' assumes even greater significance. *Hocking* v. *Director General of the National Archive*,[74] which concerned the 'official' status of documents created by a former Australian Governor General, again provides an illustration. The judgments differed on this point. The plurality judges were concerned to avoid an over-inclusive approach to 'official actions' and to preserve officeholders a mode of 'private action' (such as a judge communicating with her peers). Thus, they rejected the argument that legal title to everything created by the holder of a constitutional or statutory office in her official capacity

[70] *Meridian Global Funds Management Asia Ltd* v. *Securities Commission* [1995] 2 AC 500, 507.

[71] *Meridian Global Funds Management Asia Ltd* v. *Securities Commission* [1995] 2 AC 500, 512.

[72] See John Murphy, 'Misfeasance in Public Office: A Tort Law Misfit?' (2012) 32(1) *Oxford Journal of Legal Studies* 51, 68.

[73] P. D. Finn, *Law and Government in Colonial Australia* (Oxford University Press 1987), 145, 153.

[74] [2020] HCA 19.

automatically vested in the Commonwealth as a body.[75] They also rejected the counter-argument that things only vest in the Commonwealth as a body politic 'if the holder of the constitutional office is then acting as an "emanation of the Commonwealth"' in creating the thing.[76] But, with respect, the judgment resolves the question in a circular manner, pointing to the fact that the papers in question were always in the control of the Official Secretary to the Governor-General in his 'official capacity', and that it could not, in all the circumstances, be doubted that the documents were 'personal' to the former Governor-General.[77] This leaves us essentially where we started.

Edelman J's concurring judgment refers to various factors to determine whether the relevant actions were taken in an official capacity. In the case, (i) the former Governor-General himself always treated the exchange of correspondence as an 'official issue'; (ii) the correspondence arose from the performance of the duties and functions of the Governor-General; (iii) the documents were subsequently always treated as 'institutional, that is, part of the official establishment of the Governor-General'; and (iv) the Governor-General's Official Secretary lodged the originals with the Australian National Archive during the subsequent Governor-General's tenure. According to Edelman J, each of these matters pointed to the correspondence 'being *created or received officially and kept institutionally*'; though some of the letters might have had some personal content, it was agreed that the correspondence 'relat[ed] to the official duties and responsibilities of the Governor-General'.[78]

The notion of acting 'officially' and 'institutionally' is the right starting point, directing us towards factual enquiries into, for example, the stated functions of the office in question, the use of institutional resources, whether the relevant action was outside working hours or while 'officiating', and so forth. The necessary analysis might mirror analysis in private law concerning the scope of an employee's duty, for example, in the context of corporate agency. As in private law, each scenario will have to be examined in its circumstances. Ultimately, an act that is done 'officially' and 'institutionally' will, valid or invalid, generate some

[75] *Hocking* v. *Director General of the National Archive* [2020] HCA 19, [105] (Kiefel CJ, Bell, Gageler, and Keane JJ).
[76] *Hocking* v. *Director General of the National Archive* [2020] HCA 19, [108] (Kiefel CJ, Bell, Gageler, and Keane JJ).
[77] *Hocking* v. *Director General of the National Archive* [2020] HCA 19, [117] (Kiefel CJ, Bell, Gageler, and Keane JJ).
[78] *Hocking* v. *Director General of the National Archive* [2020] HCA 19, [249] (Edelman J).

consequences attaching to the office, and ultimately to the Crown – if only of the 'vicarious liability' type.

7.3.4 *Administrative 'Factual Powers'?*

The point of office is to conscript the factual abilities of human beings to animate institutions. The structure works, as we have seen, on the basis of a fiction whereby we count a certain act-in-fact as an act-in-the-law where certain conditions are satisfied. The relation between 'acts-in-fact by one who holds an office' and 'official acts-in-law' is essential to a proper understanding of not only the mechanics of judicial review but also the scope of non-statutory executive powers themselves. It is on this point that the third source approach goes wrong, namely by positing that the conjunction of a factual ability and a legal permission is enough.

The idea, however, is persistent. Adam Perry has rightly identified the *non sequitur* at the heart of the third source approach, and proposed an alternative category of 'administrative powers' that is a hybrid between the 'residual liberties' approach and the 'common law powers' approach. Ultimately, however, this middle ground is unstable.

Crown officials, Perry claims, possess two distinct types of non-statutory executive powers. The first are 'legal' and derive from the common law (as the 'common law powers' approach suggests). Distinct from the 'high prerogative', these powers allow the Crown, through its officials (he says 'agents') to do acts-in-the-law that ordinary legal persons can do, such as making gifts of property and entering contractual relations. The second type are 'non-legal' – they are 'factual' in nature. On this view, the act of installing a wiretap (as in *Malone* v. *Metropolitan Police Commissioner*) would be a factual, rather than a legal, act. The power to consult with officials, make lists, adopt policies and guidelines, make promises, issue apologies, communicate with foreign governments, and issue passports are all said to be 'non-legal' in nature. They affect the subject's legal position in a way analogous to a tort, not in the way that an intentional exercise of a legal power does.[79]

According to Perry, what makes it true that the Crown can do these kinds of acts is not a rule of the common law – it cannot be, he says, because it would be difficult to imagine what change in the law would make it impossible for the Crown to keep a list or make gifts. Nor is it the

[79] Adam Perry, 'The Crown's Administrative Powers' (2015) 131 *Law Quarterly Review* 652, 661, 669.

legal personality of the Crown as a corporation sole. We know that, he says, 'because non-legal entities such as natural persons have many of the same powers'.[80] What, then, is their foundation?

> Ultimately, the Crown's non-legal powers derive from our willingness as a community to attribute ordinary acts to the Crown. We are prepared to attribute to the Crown and not merely to particular officials the act of making a list, holding a meeting, or issuing an apology, to take just three examples; hence we attribute to the Crown the powers to perform these acts.[81]

Quite aside from the problematic notion that a 'natural person' is not a 'legal entity',[82] this approach collapses into the common law powers approach because it fails to incorporate an adequate theory of action.

There is some force to the argument that the act of compiling a list, for example, is not the exercise of a 'legal power'. But take the example of a 'blacklist' of individuals deemed unsafe to work with children like the list in *R (C)* v. *Secretary of State for Health.*[83] Such a list is usually compiled using the resources of a complex organisational unit within a government department, which is publicly funded and under the nominal control of a Cabinet Minister responsible to Parliament. It is done 'officially' and 'institutionally', not personally. No individuals within that apparatus of government, from social workers to police officers to heads of department, are permitted use the list for their own purposes. Presumably, the ordinary hierarchical structure of the department would determine what goes on and what stays off the list, and if a name were to be added or deleted for reasons personal to, say, a head of department or a social worker, it would be generally accepted that something had gone wrong.

The example of a list is admittedly the most difficult to assimilate to the exercise of a legal power. In my view, however, an official tasked with keeping a list would be exercising a power, because he would be keeping it not in his own right but on behalf of the Crown. He would not be able to publish the list or use the information in it for his own purposes.

80 Adam Perry, 'The Crown's Administrative Powers' (2015) 131 *Law Quarterly Review* 652, 663.

81 Adam Perry, 'The Crown's Administrative Powers' (2015) 131 *Law Quarterly Review* 652, 664.

82 The legal personality of human beings is 'is neither less nor more "juristic" than that of any other entity that the law recognises': Neil MacCormick, *Institutions of Law* (Oxford University Press 2007), 83.

83 [2000] EWCA Civ 49.

Looking at the problem in light of *Hocking* v. *Director General of the National Archive*, the list would 'belong' to the Crown in some sense, and quite possibly in the ordinary private law sense of ownership. This, in my view, is enough of a 'legal consequence' to characterise the compilation of the list as the exercise of a legal power – it creates new property rights in the Crown. The same is surely true of the audio recordings made by the Police Commissioner of Malone's private conversations. Surely, even in the absence of positive privacy norms, no one would argue that any member of the police could take that evidence with her upon retirement, or use it to make a YouTube video. A wiretap relates to the official functions of the Commissioner and is made with the institutional resources of the police force.

The compilation (and maintenance) of things like blacklists and surveillance recordings is therefore an act reliant on rules that confer competence on the officials concerned. Perry thus cannot be right to characterise them as part of the 'administrative' competence of the Crown without a 'legal' basis. According to Perry, the extent of the Crown's non-legal administrative powers 'can be determined only by the conditions under which we as a community are willing to attribute ordinary acts to the Crown'.[84] But none of Perry's three reasons really sustain his approach.

First, he argues, 'for an act to be attributed to the Crown, it must be carried out by an agent of the Crown'.[85] This is unobjectionable, but entails rules of official appointment and empowerment of the type that I have set out in this book. The Crown cannot *actually* keep a list or make an apology because it has neither hands to write with nor a mouth to speak. To the extent that it exists, it is an abstract, representative entity created by the collective imagination of a political community; to the extent that it acts at all, it acts through human organs whose physical actions are attributed to it.[86]

Secondly, he argues that 'the official agent must have had authority to carry out the act in question'.[87] Again, this is unobjectionable, but begs the question of authorisation. In the first instance, according to Perry, we

[84] Adam Perry, 'The Crown's Administrative Powers' (2015) 131 *Law Quarterly Review* 652, 666.

[85] Adam Perry, 'The Crown's Administrative Powers' (2015) 131 *Law Quarterly Review* 652, 666.

[86] See D. W. P. Ruiter, *Legal Institutions* (Kluwer 2010), 51.

[87] Adam Perry, 'The Crown's Administrative Powers' (2015) 131 *Law Quarterly Review* 652, 666.

should look to the 'internal (administrative or contractual) rules of government'; however, in cases such as a Prime Minister's official apology, we look to the 'social recognition that the Prime Minister speaks for the Crown when accepting moral responsibility for its past wrongs'.[88] Again, this is a rule; in my view there is no reason to characterise it as extra-legal rather than as a rule of customary law.[89] Thirdly, 'the act must be paid for, if necessary, with public funds, appropriately authorised'.[90] Again, the identity of the *fisc* is a matter of rules – incidentally, rules which share much of their history with the identification of the Crown as an institutional entity.[91]

Perry's lucid account draws on notions of collective intentionality, recognition, and acceptance, and has much to commend it. But, in attempting to present an alternative to a common law rule of empowerment, it in fact just describes such a rule. Institutional competence is surely a matter of 'fact', when viewed from one aspect, and just as surely a matter of 'law' when viewed form the other. This is for the fundamental reason that certain types of social facts *create* norms and normative orders. Tony Lawson gives the example of the announcement of a new public holiday. 'Such declarations . . . are only really constitutive if (eventually) they are validated by (through the conformity of the collective practices of) those implicated in the declaration'.[92] In other words, even a 'legal' act by an official rests on a 'social fact' of community recognition or acceptance that some official's declaration creates law. This should be a familiar idea, and rather describes the nature of law than points to some category of 'non-legal administrative powers'.

7.3.5 *Constitutive and Regulative Rules*

It is now possible to burrow a little deeper into the logical structure of empowering rules. The non-reductive concept of legal powers I have adopted corresponds closely to a distinction between 'constitutive' and 'regulative' rules, and this distinction is of critical importance to the structure

88 Adam Perry, 'The Crown's Administrative Powers' (2015) 131 *Law Quarterly Review* 652, 667.

89 See also Mark Walters, *A.V. Dicey and the Common Law Constitutional Tradition* (Cambridge University Press 2020), 144–145.

90 Adam Perry, 'The Crown's Administrative Powers' (2015) 131 *Law Quarterly Review* 652, 667.

91 See Ernst Kantorowicz, *The King's Two Bodies* (Princeton University Press 1997), 343 on '*terra regni*' and '*terra regis*', the former being something pertaining *ad coronam*.

92 Tony Lawson, 'Comparing Conceptions of Social Ontology: Emergent Social Entities and/or Institutional Facts?' (2016) 46(4) *Journal for the Theory of Social Behaviour* 359.

of judicial review. The classical account of constitutive rules is found in John Searle's theory of institutional facts.[93] According to Searle, constitutive rules 'do not merely regulate, they *create or define* new forms of behaviour'.[94] Concepts like 'checkmate' in chess or 'winning' in an election, for example, are not mere labels for some pre-existing state of affairs, but introduce new institutional consequences within the context of a rule-structured pattern of social interaction. So do concepts like 'legislating' or 'approving'. It is impossible to understand these actions at all except in the context of the relevant rule set. Regulative rules, on the other hand, regulate *pre-existing* forms of behaviour through the imposition of qualifications or conditions:

> There is a crucial philosophical difference between those cases where the action can be performed illegally, without benefit of the constitutive rules that provide permission, certification, and authorisation, and those that can only be performed within a system of constitutive rules, *because the constitutive rules define the act in question*. Physical acts such as driving cars or pulling teeth can be done illegally, without a license. But acts which require an institutional structure which is both the result of and the source of cooperation and recognition by others, such as passing legislation and commanding the army, cannot be done by anybody without the appropriate institutional empowerment.[95]

Constitutive and regulative rules can be difficult to distinguish,[96] and, from a certain perspective, constitutive rules inherently regulate the

[93] Particularly in John Searle, *Speech Acts* (Cambridge University Press 1969). See John Searle, 'Constitutive Rules' (2018) 4(1) *Argumenta* 51; Christopher Cherry, 'Regulative Rules and Constitutive Rules' (1973) 23(93) *The Philosophical Quarterly* 301; Frank Hindriks, 'Constitutive Rules, Language, and Ontology' (2009) 71 *Erkenntnis* 253. See also John Rawls, 'Two Concepts of Rules' (1955) 64 *Philosophical Review* 3; Georg von Wright, *Norm and Action* (Routledge 1963); Eugenio Bulygin, 'On Norms of Competence' (1992) 11 *Law and Philosophy* 201, 210. Other examples include Robert Alexy, Eugenio Bulygin, the later Alf Ross, and Aleksander Peczenick: see Torben Spaak, 'Norms that Confer Competence' (2003) 16(1) *Ratio Juris* 89, 96.

[94] John Searle, *Speech Acts* (Cambridge University Press 1969), 33–36. Emphasis mine.

[95] John Searle, 'Social Ontology: The Problem and Steps Towards a Solution' in Savas Tsohatzidis (ed.), *Intentional Acts and Institutional Facts* (Springer 2007), 27–28.

[96] Jaap Hage, 'The Deontic Furniture of the World' in Jerzy Stelmach, Bartosz Brożek, and Mateusz Hohol (eds.), *The Many Faces of Normativity* (Copernicus 2013), 80. Drug statutes, for example, schedule substances into classes, which confer a status on the relevant plant or chemical with the same effect as a directive: 'Do not consume or possess Substance X'. One this view, the criminal law (for example) appears as a plethora of constitutive rules designating objects, actions, and events as 'offences', and one single regulative rule: 'Commit no offence'. See Tony Honoré, 'Real Laws' in P. M. S. Hacker and Joseph Raz (eds.), *Law, Morality, and Society* (Clarendon Press 1977), 117.

activities they enable.[97] The matter is further complicated because regulative rules regulate institutional as well as natural behaviours; they regulate how one makes a will as well as how one slaughters animals. Constitutive rules are, however, distinct in that they provide part of the *definition of the action* they enable, and cannot be recast simply as a constraint on the performance of an action. This is especially important when considering the legality of an action from the perspective of the actor. That making a fraudulent will is an offence, for example, is irrelevant from the perspective of a person who lacks the capacity to make any will at all.

In place of constitutive and regulative rules, Alf Ross distinguished between 'rules of competence' and 'rules of conduct'.[98] I think this terminology is particularly helpful in the context of judicial review. Ross' terminology makes clear that constitutive rules grant an actor some new competence, whereas regulative rules determine the scope of her permitted conduct within the sphere of that competence. A further advantage of Ross' terminology is that it inter-operates with the revised Hohfeld scheme I have suggested: the two kinds of rules relate to different modes. Rules of competence grant the *ability* to perform acts-in-the-law with valid legal consequences; rules of conduct impinge on one's *liberty* to use that ability. In rough terms, we might say that powers are granted by constitutive rules and duties are imposed by regulative rules, that is, that there is at least a rough correlation between Ross' terms and Hart's 'power-conferring' and 'duty-imposing' rules. In many cases of judicial review, unlike conflicts in a game of chess, an official has done something admittedly within her powers, but in a *manner* or for a *purpose* that was impermissible.

7.3.6 Keeping Ability Distinct from Permission

All this underscores the importance of keeping ability and permission distinct when assessing official action. Behind whatever terminology we use (i.e., of rights, powers, duties, etc.) is a basic modal logic.[99] The core claim of this chapter is that whenever we enquire into the lawfulness of an

[97] John Searle, *Speech Acts* (Cambridge University Press 1969), 34–36; Eugenio Bulygin, 'On Norms of Competence' (1992) 11 *Law and Philosophy* 201, 212.

[98] Alf Ross, *Directive and Norm* (Humanities Press 1968), 118.

[99] See Jan Nuyts, 'Modality: Overview and Linguistic Issues' in William Frawley, Erin Eschenroeder, Sarah Mills, and Thao Nguyen (eds.), *The Expression of Modality* (De Gruyter 2006), Ch 1.

official act, we ask two questions. First, we ask the capacitative question: Is this action necessary, *possible* or *impossible* for Official A? Second, we ask the deontic question: Is this action *permitted*, *prohibited*, or *obligatory* for Official A?[100] We answer these questions by looking, first, to the physical capacities of the officeholder, then to the rules of competence that repose legal powers in the office, and then to the rules of conduct that impose conditions on the way that the officeholder has to conduct herself when exercising her official powers.

There is no convenient shorthand to express the set of possible and permissible actions open to an official in English. Lindahl has suggested the term *Spielraum*, drawing an analogy with the concept of *Entscheidungsraum* ('decision space') from decision theory.[101] A chess piece and the director of a company both have a certain *Spielraum* open to them. The *Spielraum* of the chess piece changes dynamically as other pieces on the board move. Likewise, the *Spielraum* of a company director changes when her company nears insolvency. *Spielraum* is simply the range of action possible and permissible under the relevant rule set, marked by the agent's 'ability-space' and 'liberty-space'. These spaces interact: there are things one is *at liberty* to do, though one has not the ability to do them, and there are many things one has the *ability* to do that one is not permitted to do. A further layer of complexity is added by the fact, noticed earlier, that one's ability-space has both a factual and a legal aspect. My *Spielraum*, therefore, could be said to consist of the actions which are (i) within my *factual* ability-space, (ii) within my *legal* ability-space, and (iii) within my *liberty-space* (which is inherently legal). Combining my ability-space(s) and liberty-space yields the range of actions possible and permissible *vis-à-vis* a given counterparty.

In short, a 'lawful official act' is one within the *Spielraum* of the relevant office. The value of using one shorthand term to refer to the logic of official action is that it makes clear the inherent connection – and dynamic tension – between the rules of competence and rules of conduct that enable and constrain official action. This approach is intuitive as well as logical, and should be uncontentious. In the statutory context, for example, the Australian High Court has held that, whatever the scope of executive power might otherwise be, '[a] valid law of the Commonwealth may so limit or impose conditions on the exercise of the executive power

[100] See Lars Lindahl, 'Hohfeld Relations and Spielraum for Action' (2006) 26(2) *Analisis Filosofico* 325.

[101] See Peter Gärdenfors, 'Rights, Games, and Social Choice' (1981) 15 *Noûs* 341.

that acts which would otherwise be supported by the executive power fall outside its scope'.[102] Crucially, the scope of my liberty-space restricts, but does not extend, my ability-space.

Thomas Adams has criticised the use of spatial metaphors in judicial review theory,[103] although of course the metaphor is inherent in the traditional language of 'ultra vires' itself. Such critiques have more to do with the historical ultra vires debate than with the question of metaphor use in explaining logical reasoning.[104] Nevertheless, it is legitimate to ask whether imposing conditions on the exercise of a power should be said to 'narrow' or 'restrict' the 'scope' of the power itself. While a duty to exercise a power reasonably, for example, might not restrict the *abstract* scope of the power itself, it is accurate to say that it restricts the scope of the power holder's *Spielraum*, and that is the true question in any case of judicial review.

7.3.7 *Rights Correlativity*

We can now round back on the criticism that Hohfeldian rights analysis is inappropriate in public law because certain public law duties are not correlative of any individual rights and *vice versa*. At base, judicial review involves the conjunction of A's *Spielraum* and B's *Spielraum*. We can use the familiar Hohfeldian terminology to express as bilateral relations between A and B, for example, that A has a power to sentence B to imprisonment but has a duty towards B to exercise it impartially.[105] But we must keep the logic underlying it carefully in mind. A Police

[102] *Brown* v. *West* (1990) 169 CLR 195, 202 (Mason CJ, Brennan, Deane, Dawson, and Toohey JJ).

[103] See Thomas Adams, 'Ultra Vires Revisited' [2018] *Public Law* 31. Adams' argument boils down to the idea that conditions on manner of exercise do not alter the 'scope' of a power, and that using 'spatial' language invites the misconception that they do. While the argument is elegant, it is at odds with the approach I take. See also Sir Philip Sales, 'Crown Powers, the Royal Prerogative and Fundamental Rights' in Hanna Wilberg and Mark Elliott (eds.), *The Scope and Intensity of Substantive Review* (Hart 2015), 381.

[104] See, for example, James Gasser, 'Logic and Metaphor' (1999) 20(3–4) *History and Philosophy of Logic* 227.

[105] Lindahl restates Hohfeld's eight legal conceptions to be inter-definable: The proposition 'X has a right versus Y that Y performs action A', for example, must be equivalent to 'Y has a duty versus X to perform action A'; 'Not: Y has a privilege versus X not to perform action A'; and 'Not: X has a no-right versus Y that Y performs action A'. Inter-definition is possible for every Hohfeld relation. Hohfeld's scheme thus boils down to four modes between X and Y: 'Counter-party *obligative*'; 'bearer *permissive*'; 'bearer *ability*'; and 'counter-party *disability*'.

Commissioner installing a wiretap is not like a neighbour eavesdropping. A Police Commissioner acts in a representative capacity, and must be able to point to more than the absence of a right to telephonic privacy to justify an act, taken on behalf of the whole community, that allows her to listen to the potentially incriminating conversations of an individual subject. The rule-constituted nature of official action supports the dissenting view of Elias CJ in *Hamed* v. *R*,[106] for example, that the Crown and its officials 'must point to lawful authority for all actions undertaken',[107] and the position as stated in the older editions of *Halsbury's Laws of England*:[108]

> The so-called liberties of the subject are really implications drawn from the two principles that the subject may say or do what he pleases, provided he does not transgress the substantive law, or infringe the legal rights of others, whereas public authorities (including the Crown) may do nothing but what they are authorised to do by some rule of the common law or statute.[109]

Whether or not a police officer acting as a private individual would have been at liberty to tap a suspect's phone line is nothing to the point. A Police Commissioner *categorically* needs some positive authorisation to perform such an action – in my terminology, he needs to be able to point to some *rule of competence* that empowers him to act in that way before we come to consider the rules of conduct that bind him at all.[110] T. R. S. Allan puts the point crisply:

> A public official who contravenes the ordinary law, without special authority, is accountable as if he were a private citizen. It does not follow, however, that, acting as a public official, he enjoys the same rights and liberties as a private individual, without suitable qualification. No simple analogy is available between private and government action because the latter is inherently different from the former.[111]

[106] [2012] 2 NZLR 305, [24].

[107] *Hamed* v. *R* [2012] 2 NZLR 305, [24] (Elias CJ).

[108] See *Halsbury's Laws of England* (4th ed. Reissue, Butterworths 1996), Vol. 8(2) 'Constitutional Law and Human Rights', comparing para [6] and para [101].

[109] *Halsbury's Laws of England* (2nd ed., Butterworths 1932), Vol. 6 'Constitutional Law', [436].

[110] The liberty space of individual police officers *as individuals* must be constrained by their official status – otherwise a Police Constable could engage in vigilante investigations out of hours without poisoning the evidence tree. One gives up something of one's individual freedom of action by accepting an official appointment.

[111] T. R. S. Allan, *Law, Liberty, and Justice* (Clarendon Press 1983), 157.

Granting the liberty-space of a private individual to the Crown would, by reason of the categorical imbalance of power and resources at the disposal of the latter, destroy the nominal liberty-space of the individual. Fundamentally, even though they are 'persons', corporate entities never occupy exactly the same *Spielraum* as private individuals – no matter what the treatises, statutes, and cases may say. Even where legislation (exceptionally) provides that a statutory entity 'may do anything that a natural person of full age or capacity may do',[112] it will occupy a subtly different legal position to a natural person in virtue of the fact that it is not an organism that can think and act for itself, but relies on the thoughts and actions of its human organs. *A fortiori*, common law corporations like the Crown and its Ministers and Secretaries of State occupy fundamentally different legal positions to individual human beings (and indeed to other corporations).[113]

7.4 Conclusion

This chapter has brought us closer to understanding the supervisory jurisdiction in two important respects. First, it has given some conclusive reasons to reject the major tenets of the 'third source' approach and provided a more nuanced and accurate account of third source-type powers. Secondly, and more importantly, it has laid the conceptual groundwork for a substantive doctrinal exploration of the supervisory jurisdiction as it has evolved. This enables a critical review of the ultra vires debate about the conceptual basis of the supervisory jurisdiction.

The crucial take home is the importance of incorporating a logic of action in our theory of judicial review. This includes a fine-grained analysis of how the physical capacities of individuals are treated, pursuant to rules of competence, as 'official' acts. There exist, of course, hard cases, but these are manageable if we maintain focus on *action* and do not let the principle of rights correlativity crowd out all other considerations.

The relation between rules of competence and rules of conduct is the major structural element in my theory of judicial review. A granular view of official empowerment and action tracks the two limbs of the ultra vires rule and entails certain doctrinal consequences. Where a breach of a rule of conduct results in an imperfect (voidable) act, breach of a rule of competence results in a failure to bring about the legal consequences

[112] See, for example, Crown Entities Act 2004 No. 115 (New Zealand), s. 17.

[113] See John Howell, 'What the Crown May Do' [2010] *Judicial Review* 36, [98].

intended by the actor, which has traditionally been described as void *ab initio*. This, like many other conventional ideas, has fallen out of vogue in recent decades. As we approach the supervisory jurisdiction from the perspective of office and official action, however, it becomes clear that we need to reinstate some of the law's traditional categories. In so doing, we render the supervisory jurisdiction more internally coherent and thus more capable of supporting the judicial review of executive action beyond statute.

8

Approaching Judicial Review

8.1 Introduction

We now have a conceptual framework for thinking about the typology of executive powers, the constitution of public authority through the creation of offices, the appointment of individuals as repositories of official power, and their action in that capacity (on behalf of the Crown) pursuant to rules of competence and rules of conduct. With those tools, we can embark on a critical appraisal of the law of judicial review.

Section 8.2 explores the different 'schemata' that the law of judicial review could adopt, and argues for an approach that has fallen out of favour in England and Wales, following from the concept of *jurisdiction*. Section 8.3 reviews developments in the law of judicial review in the twentieth century, against which the emergence of the modern law from the 1970s onwards can be understood. Section 8.4 explains the demise of the concept of jurisdiction in English law, particularly since the landmark case of *Anisminic* v. *Foreign Compensation Commission*,[1] and argues that jurisdiction must remain the organising concept in the law of judicial review. The point of departure is the appointment of certain individuals to a position of active citizenship that entails the exercise of powers that those individuals do not hold, and cannot exercise, in their personal capacity. The legal position of those individuals, when acting in an official capacity, is determined by the conjunction of an ability-space (derived from rules of competence) and a liberty-space (derived from rules of conduct). These rules translate into the 'narrow' and 'broad' limb of the ultra vires rule. Section 8.5 concludes.

It bears noting at this juncture that my concept of ultra vires has little to do with the so-called 'ultra vires theory'. In effect, the theory

[1] [1969] 2 AC 147.

I present here occupies a middle ground that was somehow, perhaps not even intentionally, abandoned in the ultra vires debate. The themes introduced in this chapter are followed up in Chapter 9, which explains how ultra vires follows from rules of competence and rules of conduct, and Chapter 11, which presents a 'common law theory of ultra vires'.

8.2 Taking Stock

D. R. Knight has identified four 'schemata' or approaches taken by the law of judicial review in England and Wales and in the Anglo-Commonwealth jurisdictions. These are 'scope of review', 'grounds of review', 'intensity of review', and 'contextual review'.[2] The four schemata are not mutually exclusive, and all jurisdictions adopt a hybrid approach. However, they provide a useful way of structuring analysis of the law's historical development in the jurisdictions under study. In broad terms, Australian courts tend to approach the extent and depth of the supervisory jurisdiction as a question of scope determined by reference to jurisdiction. English and New Zealand courts tend to approach it as a question of grounds and intensity. Canadian courts tend to approach it as a question of intensity and, increasingly, one that is to be answered with a fairly free rein in a broad context. The overarching feature is that modulation of the depth of scrutiny is ubiquitous; the difference is in how that modulation is achieved and justified.[3]

The scope of review schematic is the traditional approach, based on set of formal categories – notably jurisdiction and ultra vires – which determine whether judicial intervention in an administrative action is warranted. The others are, historically, departures from this schematic to achieve modulation as deemed appropriate. The need for judges to respect the constitutional role of executive officials has always been a major influence on the development of the law – as has the desire of judges to protect their constitutional role against legislative incursion, particularly in the form of statutory clauses that purport to insulate executive officials from the supervisory jurisdiction. In general, however, I am less concerned with the question of modulation and more

[2] D. R. Knight, *Vigilance and Restraint in the Common Law of Judicial Review* (Cambridge University Press 2018), 1.

[3] D. R. Knight, *Vigilance and Restraint in the Common Law of Judicial Review* (Cambridge University Press 2018), 2.

concerned with the conceptual basis of the supervisory jurisdiction. The doctrines by which judicial review is practiced and by which its intensity is modulated should follow from this, so the conceptual basis has logical priority.

8.2.1 Administrative Law's Constitutional Turn

One problem is that the major schools of thought on the conceptual basis of the supervisory jurisdiction do not map neatly onto the different schemata. The scope of review schematic tends to be favoured by formalists, who in the English context are generally adherents of the so-called ultra vires school (which Knight accurately dubs the 'legislative intent school'). Some within the legislative intent school, however, also favour the intensity of review schematic, which keeps the emphasis on parliamentary will but concedes some calibration of the depth of review, for example, in the context of common law rights. The common law school tends to favour the grounds of review schematic, which is more open to normative input from judges but ensures this is structured by the translation of substantive values into public law doctrine. The contextual review schematic, for its part, finds favour mostly with those who disavow adherence to either of these two schools of thought, although they themselves might not agree with that characterisation.[4]

As Peter Cane explains, the first stage in the historical progression was to move from a scope of review approach to a more or less formulaic set of grounds of review – classically, 'illegality, unreasonableness, and procedural impropriety'.[5] In the longer run, this led English judges to think of judicial review not in terms of a superior institution (the High Court) controlling subordinate institutions but in terms of that institution controlling the exercise of 'public' as opposed to 'private' power.[6] With the increasing importance of rights in English constitutional jurisprudence, culminating with the passage of the Human Rights Act 1998, the intensity of review model gained traction as well.

4 D. R. Knight, *Vigilance and Restraint in the Common Law of Judicial Review* (Cambridge University Press 2018), 3.

5 See *Council of Civil Service Unions* v. *Minister for the Civil Service* [1985] AC 374, 410 (Lord Diplock).

6 See Peter Cane's review of D. R. Knight in (2019) 82(1) *Modern Law Review* 200, 204; see D. R. Knight, *Vigilance and Restraint in the Common Law of Judicial Review* (Cambridge University Press 2018), 34–37.

English public lawyers in the latter twentieth century found themselves in a field cleared of traditional categories, with a clear run to develop an outcome oriented, substantive law of judicial review. But on what principles? Quite sensibly, they turned to constitutional law. The legislative intent school took A. V. Dicey's classical exposition of radical parliamentary sovereignty as their starting point and insisted that the judges' supervisory jurisdiction must rest upon implied legislative intent. The common law school took Dicey's championship of the common law as a bulwark of the rule of law as their starting point, stressing the common law basis of the supervisory jurisdiction. In this context, Mark Freedland observes that progressive jurists, who had been arguing for the autonomy of public law, stressed the continuity between administrative law and the common law as a whole, committing themselves to the inherently conservative, casuistic doctrine of the common law; conservative jurists put aside their natural antipathy for *droit administratif* and committed themselves to the distinctiveness of public law.[7]

In the end, the ultra vires debate generated 'more heat than light'[8] because most participants agreed that both statute and common law principles played a part in judicial review, that an appropriately worded statute could effectively oust judicial review in all but the most extreme cases, and that judges should have a substantial degree of independence in the constitutional balance.[9] As we have seen, it has added little to our understanding of judicial review outside the statutory context.

8.2.2 The Way Forward

Non-statutory executive powers underline the importance of starting with the logic of official action rather than with ideas like parliamentary sovereignty and the rule of law. These constitutional principles are extremely important, but they are best approached with a solid

[7] See Mark Freedland, 'The Evolving Approach to Public/Private Distinction in English Law' in Mark Freedland and Auby Jean-Bernard (eds.), *The Public Law/Private Law Divide: Une entente assez cordiale?* (Hart 2005), 95; Mark Freedland, 'Public Law and Private Finance – Placing the Private Finance Initiative in a Public Law Frame' [1998] *Public Law* 288.

[8] See C. F. Forsyth, 'Heat and Light: A Plea for Reconciliation' in C. F. Forsyth (ed.), *Judicial Review and the Constitution* (Hart 2000), 408.

[9] See Peter Cane's review of D. R. Knight in (2019) 82(1) *Modern Law Review* 200, 204; T. R. S. Allan, 'The Constitutional Foundations of Judicial Review: Conceptual Conundrum or Interpretative Enquiry' (2002) 61(1) *Cambridge Law Journal* 87.

understanding of empowerment and action. Trying to derive propositions about action from them is counterproductive.

Although he refrains from singling out the 'best' approach, stressing continuity and hybridity, Knight seems to prefer some kind of hybrid grounds of review and intensity of review approach.[10] He rates the scope of review approach poorly according to normative criteria adapted from Lon Fuller's classical *desiderata* of law.[11] Scope of review is conducive to mechanical judging; unable to suppress them, the doctrines that characterise this approach cloak normative considerations beneath a formalistic deliberative idiom.[12] Even more seriously, Knight argues that the approach is characterised by 'doctrinal morass and the lack of any organising theory'.[13] Categories implicitly determine the depth of judicial scrutiny, he says, but the distinctions often overlap and intersect. Labels such as 'jurisdictional error' are conclusive only, signalling judicial intervention but not describing the 'shape' of the underlying doctrine. He proffers Australian law as an example of the tension that arises from combining formalism with a 'bottom-up' approach to doctrinal development – that is, without reference to any overarching theory of public law.[14] The potential virtues of a rule-based system of public law are undermined by the failure of those rules to capture and express the principles of administrative justice they rest on, and by their provision of cover for the covert influence of judges' normative intuitions.[15]

This chapter seeks to rehabilitate the scope of review schematic. Modern developments in English law have not freed the supervisory jurisdiction of conceptual shackles but cut it loose from its conceptual moorings. Judicial review must begin with the logic of official action, and that logic entails the categories that organised judicial review in earlier decades. When one articulates how individuals come to exercise public authority, 'jurisdiction' (and all the categories it implies) is not

[10] D. R. Knight, *Vigilance and Restraint in the Common Law of Judicial Review* (Cambridge University Press 2018), 254.

[11] See Frank Lorett, 'Lon Fuller, *The Morality of Law*' in S. T. Levy (ed.), *Oxford Handbook of the Classics in Contemporary Political Theory* (Oxford University Press 2015), Ch 9.

[12] D. R. Knight, *Vigilance and Restraint in the Common Law of Judicial Review* (Cambridge University Press 2018), 66.

[13] D. R. Knight, *Vigilance and Restraint in the Common Law of Judicial Review* (Cambridge University Press 2018), 71.

[14] See Stephen Gageler, 'The Underpinnings of Judicial Review of Administrative Action: Common Law or Constitution?' (2000) 28 *Federal Law Review* 303.

[15] D. R. Knight, *Vigilance and Restraint in the Common Law of Judicial Review* (Cambridge University Press 2018), 74.

formalistic at all; it is the concept that must, as a matter of logical necessity, organise the exercise of executive power and the legal accountability of its repositories.[16] My approach avoids the most serious of Knight's criticisms, that is, doctrinal morass and lack of organising theory. In fact, it does a convincing job of connecting the grounds of review with the concept of jurisdiction and organising them under the two limbs of the ultra vires doctrine. Further, it explains what the consequences are of establishing any given ground of judicial review, by reference to the difference between rules of competence and rules of conduct. As I explain in Chapter 13, it also provides important insights into the concept of the rule of law and its relation to legislative supremacy within a parliamentary democracy.

Something drastic is needed. Sarah Nason, for example, has proposed a wholesale reconstruction of judicial review focussed on 'the advancement of justice and good governance' rather than the concepts of jurisdiction and ultra vires. These 'descriptive concepts', she argues, leave inadequate room for normative methods that directly address the contested nature of the values at stake.[17] Nason's proposal is based on a close analysis of how judges and advocates actually justified their position in about 500 first-instance judicial review proceedings in the mid-2010s. Use of the conventional terminology of judicial review was, according to Nason, haphazard and inconsistent. She concludes that the judges were either sloppy in their use of terminology or that 'terminological precision is not necessary to make a sound judgment in light of the issues at stake'.[18] Preferring the latter view, she proposes that the conventional

[16] My argument is not for the adoption of the Australian approach in other jurisdictions. That approach is a product of constitutional circumstances unique to Australia, in particular s. 75(v) of the Australian Constitution, and the Australian law is sometimes rightly criticised for being formalistic. Further, with its focus on statutory interpretation, it would not place us well to achieve the principled extension of the supervisory jurisdiction to non-statutory executive powers. See Will Bateman, 'The Constitution and the Substantive Principles of Judicial Review: The Full Scope of the Entrenched Minimum Provision of Judicial Review' (2011) 39 *Federal Law Review* 463; see in particular *Plaintiff S157/2002* v. *Commonwealth* (2003) 211 CLR 476 and *Kirk* v. *Industrial Court of New South Wales* (2010) 239 CLR 53; Peter Cane, 'The Making of Australian Administrative Law' (2003) 23 *Australian Bar Review* 114, 133; D. R. Knight, *Vigilance and Restraint in the Common Law of Judicial Review* (Cambridge University Press 2018), 39; Will Bateman and Leighton McDonald, 'The Normative Structure of Australian Administrative Law' (2017) 45 *Federal Law Review* 153, 172.

[17] Sarah Nason, *Reconstructing Judicial Review* (Hart 2016), 5.

[18] Sarah Nason, *Reconstructing Judicial Review* (Hart 2016), 148.

grounds of judicial review be replaced with six new grounds,[19] which she argues would do a better job of translating the purposes underlying the supervisory jurisdiction into the law-as-practiced.

While Nason's new scheme is substantively attractive, adopting such a reform agenda would be further a step further in the wrong direction. Nason identifies the purposes underlying judicial review as the values of 'upholding the constitution', 'protecting the individual', 'ordinary common law statutory interpretation', 'determining inter-institutional relationships', 'establishing general legal principles', 'structuring deliberative and administrative processes', 'core values of good governance', 'public interest litigation' and the 'elaboration and vindication of fundamental rights'.[20] Again, while none of these is objectionable, there is no convincing reason why these values should not be promoted through a scheme of judicial review that derives from a theory of official empowerment and action. It is at least worthwhile, and in my view clearly preferable, to 'clean up' the traditional concepts of judicial review, such that their application carries the narrative of judicial review complaints and judgments, and explains the different grounds of judicial review and their legal consequences. In other words, without denigrating the value of socio-legal research, there is still a legitimate and important role for doctrinal and conceptual legal scholarship, which uniquely ensures coherence between doctrine, concepts, and underlying values. Nowhere is this more important than in the context of non-statutory executive powers.

8.3 The Travails of English Administrative Law

It is difficult to move forward without considering how we got to where we are. One of the leading architects of the 'new' administrative law, Lord Diplock, declared in *Council of Civil Service Unions* v. *Minister for the Civil Service*[21] that the law had developed to a stage where one could describe the supervisory jurisdiction on the grounds of illegality,

[19] She labels the grounds 'mistake', 'procedural impropriety', 'ordinary common law statutory interpretation', 'discretionary impropriety' (which embraces 'irrelevant considerations' and 'lack of justification'), 'breach of a European Convention on Human Rights-protected right and/or equality duty', and 'significant claims based on common law constitutional values, rights, or allocation of powers and public interest claims'. Sarah Nason, *Reconstructing Judicial Review* (Hart 2016), 25.

[20] Sarah Nason, *Reconstructing Judicial Review* (Hart 2016), 79–80.

[21] [1985] AC 374.

unreasonableness, and procedural impropriety 'without reiterating any analysis of the steps by which the law has come about'.[22] This was the herald of a brave new world that had been built, by Lord Diplock and others, in the preceding years: a 'rational and comprehensive system of administrative law on the foundation of the concept of ultra vires'.[23] Incidentally, it was also a landmark case on the amenability of prerogative-type powers – in this case, managing the civil service – to judicial review.

Gaining a proper understanding of judicial review in the non-statutory context is difficult for a number of reasons, not least among them the awkward intellectual history of 'public law' in the United Kingdom and the collision of countervailing forces over the middle and second half of the twentieth century.

8.3.1 *Two Trends in English Administrative Law*

It is convenient to situate the amenability problem within the context of two broader trends. The first is the rise of an English *droit administratif.* There is, historically, some antipathy towards 'administrative law' within the English legal tradition. This is generally attributed to the Dicey's didactic sway over generations of English lawyers. The short point bears repeating that Dicey's scepticism hangs together with his insistence that officials should be – in just the same way as ordinary citizens – liable in their personal capacity for wrongs committed by way of ultra vires action.[24] Looking past Dicey's possible misreading of the French constitution, and his palpable relish in being an Englishman, a characteristic passage reads:

> Any one who considers with care the nature of the *droit administratif* of France, or the topics to which it applies, will soon discover that it rests, and always has rested, at bottom on two leading ideas alien to the conceptions of modern Englishmen. The first of these ideas is that *the government, and every servant of the government, possesses, as representative of the nation, a whole body of special rights, privileges, or prerogatives as against private citizens,* and that the extent of these rights, privileges, or prerogatives is to be determined on principles different from the considerations which fix the legal rights and duties of one citizen towards

[22] *Council of Civil Service Unions* v. *Minister for the Civil Service* [1985] AC 374, 410.

[23] *Re Racal Communications Ltd* [1981] AC 374, 382 (Lord Diplock).

[24] J. R. F. Allison, 'Variation of the View on English Legal Distinctions between Public and Private' (2007) 66(3) *Cambridge Law Journal* 698, 704.

> another. An individual in his dealings with the State does not, according to French ideas, stand on anything like the same footing as that on which he stands in dealings with his neighbour.[25]

Dicey himself later questioned whether the ordinary courts were really 'the best body for adjudicating on the offences or the errors of civil servants' after all, and speculated that a better solution might be a 'body of men who combined official experience with legal knowledge and who were independent of the government of the day'.[26]

Mark Walters has provided a nuanced revision of Dicey's 'administrative law blind spot'. Dicey was himself involved in a number of important *mandamus* applications including *R (Pemsel)* v. *Commissioners of Income Tax*,[27] and there is a curious mismatch between his work at the bar and his lectures as Vinerian Professor of English law.[28] By reference to later writing, in particular, Walters concludes that Dicey clearly recognised and endorsed the existence of specialist *droit administratif* – albeit as part of the 'ordinary law' that he insisted was necessary to ensure the rule of law.[29] Of enduring value in Dicey's account is his sensitivity to the limited scope of official action and his antagonism towards secretive, politicised tribunals. In any case, English law certain contains a distinct 'administrative law' today.

The office-based view sits uneasily with the 'classic' Diceyan view. On the one hand, there is an internal logic to the view that an ultra vires act cannot be an 'official act' and must, therefore, be an act in the official's personal capacity. On the other hand, the logic of official action implies a special capacity or official mode of action which is not completely unravelled every time the official strays outside the bounds of her *Spielraum*, and points to the need for a distinct body of law to govern that mode of action. Further, a proper understanding of the Crown and HM Government as a network of offices suggests that the Crown should

[25] See A. V. Dicey, *Introduction to the Study of the Law of the Constitution* (8th ed., Macmillan 1915), 219.

[26] See T. T. Arvind and Lindsay Stirton, 'The Curious Origins of Judicial Review' (2017) 133 *Law Quarterly Review* 91, 101, citing A. V. Dicey, *Introduction to the Study of the Law of the Constitution* (8th ed., Macmillan 1915), cxlv, 111.

[27] (1888) 22 QBD 196.

[28] Mark Walters, *A. V. Dicey and the Common Law Constitutional Tradition* (Cambridge University Press 2020), 312–313.

[29] Mark Walters, *A. V. Dicey and the Common Law Constitutional Tradition* (Cambridge University Press 2020), 326. See also J. R. F. Allison, 'Variation of the View on English Legal Distinctions between Public and Private' (2007) 66(3) *Cambridge Law Journal* 698, 711.

be liable for the wrongs of its officials in some circumstances. The severe curtailment of Crown immunity, in particular, took much of the wind out of the sails of the Dicey's classic position, placing the Crown 'squarely under the law'.[30]

Developments from the nineteenth century onwards have demanded a theory to explain the fact that HM Government is now liable in its own right to aggrieved subjects, but these efforts have not eventuated; there is still work to do.[31] Oddly enough, it is in the context of government contracting that a more 'corporate' concept of the Crown has emerged. As we have seen in *Town Investments* v. *Department of Environment*,[32] a contract made by a Minister 'for and on behalf' of the Crown presupposes a single actor in a manner antithetical to the 'disaggregating' approach instinctive to English lawyers.[33]

Either way, modern developments have definitively undermined the importance of insisting that an official wrong is an act by the official in her personal capacity. Some wrongs are so wilful or egregious that it is appropriate for the official to be liable personally, for example, in tort or under some rule of the criminal law, but in general the Crown is the liable for the wrongs of its officers, especially when they are acting regularly. The availability of injunctive and declaratory relief,[34] and the availability of damages where an appropriate head of liability exists (such as under the Human Rights Act 1998), further bolsters this view.[35] The problem then is to determine the proper ambit of 'administrative law'. Nowhere is this more difficult than in the context of non-statutory bodies that do not bear the mark of 'executive government' on their forehead.

This leads to the second trend, which I will examine in more detail in Chapter 11 and Chapter 12. The ways in which the executive government pursues policy objectives evolves continuously. The English (welfare) state expanded rapidly and considerably during and after the Second World War.[36] To a certain extent, the ground-breaking development in

30 See Lord A. T. Denning, *The Changing Law* (Stevens 1953), 20, 24.

31 See J. G. Allen, 'The Office of the Crown' (2017) 77(2) *Cambridge Law Journal* 298, 313–315.

32 [1978] AC 359.

33 See Janet McLean, 'Personality and Public Law Doctrine' (1999) 49 *University of Toronto Law Journal* 123, 138.

34 Senior Courts Act 1981 s. 31(1); Civil Procedure Rules 54.3(1).

35 Senior Courts Act 1981 s. 31(4); Civil Procedure Rules 54.3(2); J. N. E. Varuhas, *Damages and Human Rights* (Hart 2016).

36 See Derek Fraser, *The Evolution of the British Welfare State: A History of Social Policy since the Industrial Revolution* (2nd ed., Macmillan 1984), Ch 9 and 'Postscript'.

administrative law in the post-War decades was a response to this expansion. Ironically, these developments matured at an inflection point where the 'state' began to recede, or perhaps transmute, into a more complex, hybrid assembly of modalities. Functions that had just been accepted as 'governmental' were privatised or contracted-out to private (profit-oriented) service providers.

T. T. Arvind and Lindsay Stirton have offered a fairly radical redux of the development of the modern law of judicial review. First, they note an unusual, and oddly forgotten, consensus between legal minds on both sides of politics in the early to mid-twentieth century about the need for law reform and the desirability of judicial review. In particular, this 'forgotten orthodoxy' grew from the acceptance that the older system of 'private law constitutionalism' was inadequate due to the growth of new statutory powers:

> For much of the first half of the twentieth century, common law thinking about the problem had been dominated by 'private law constitutionalism'. It was thought that the law of tort, in particular, gave the courts all the tools they might need to keep administrative bodies in check. Yet it soon became apparent that tort law was not actually restraining executive overreach, not least because procedural and remedial hurdles meant that suits could in practice only succeed if the department concerned co-operated. Nor did abolishing the doctrine of Crown immunity help . . . *Ultimately, however, private law proved to lack the conceptual tools it would have required to become the central plank of legal accountability of government.* The Crichel Down affair, for example, [which concerned the compulsory purchase of agricultural land for war purposes and subsequent sale, at profit, to the Ministry of Agriculture] was almost universally seen at the time as an example of executive overreach, but neither the tort of trespass nor any other private law action would have given a remedy, because in this case – as in many others – the actions were done in purported exercise of a statutory power.[37]

The conventional story runs that judges and jurists facing the collapse of private law constitutionalism looked to modernise the supervisory jurisdiction through development of the prerogative writs. The passing of administrative functions to a professional civil service was not challenged directly; the response was to revive the older powers into a modern system of administrative law, as

[37] T. T. Arvind and Lindsay Stirton, 'The Curious Origins of Judicial Review' (2017) 133 *Law Quarterly Review* 91, 95. Emphasis mine.

described by Lord Diplock in *Council of Civil Service Unions* v. *Minister for the Civil Service.*[38]

8.4 The Demise of Jurisdiction

Modern developments, however, have not built on sound conceptual foundations. Historically, jurisdiction was the central concept that set the scope of review. As Lord Sumner observed in *R* v. *Nat Bell Liquors Ltd,*[39] one aspect of the supervisory jurisdiction is the 'area of the inferior jurisdiction and the qualifications and conditions of its exercise; the other is the observance of the law, in the course of its exercise'.[40] Jurisdiction is entailed by the distinction between rules of competence and rules of conduct. Though it is now seen as an outmoded category, it is absolutely essential and should be reinstated.

8.4.1 Jurisdiction and Judicial Review

The classical accounts of the law's early development need only be summarised here.[41] Originally, administrative wrongs were actionable collaterally in tort.[42] Collateral challenge implies a logic of action in which an incompetent act is non-existent, and can be treated as a 'nullity' and therefore as a private act.[43] This central plank of 'private law constitutionalism', however, was complemented by the writ of error of law on the face of the record. This writ offered a means to attack an official act (including, of course, a decision) directly. Officials holding inferior 'courts of record' had to maintain detailed records justifying the legal basis of their decisions; a writ of error called this record up to the King's Bench for inspection. Error had been 'perfected' by the fifteenth century as a means of rectifying judgments given according to common

[38] For an alternative account, see T. T. Arvind and Lindsay Stirton, 'The Curious Origins of Judicial Review' (2017) 133 *Law Quarterly Review* 91.

[39] [1922] AC 128.

[40] *R* v. *Nat Bell Liquors Ltd* [1922] AC 128, 156.

[41] Amnon Rubinstein, *Jurisdiction and Illegality* (Clarendon Press 1965); E. G. Henderson, *Foundations of English Administrative Law* (Harvard University Press 1963); see also Philip Murray, 'Process, Substance and the History of Error of Law Review' in John Bell, Mark Elliott, Jason Varuhas, and Philip Murray (eds.), *Public Law Adjudication in Common Law Systems: Process and Substance* (Bloomsbury 2016).

[42] *Terry* v. *Huntingdon* (1668) Hard. 480, 483; *Palmer* v. *Crone* [1927] 1 KB 804, 808.

[43] Amnon Rubinstein, *Jurisdiction and Illegality* (Clarendon Press 1965), 7; see *Rooke's Case* (1598) 5 Co Rep 99b.

law.[44] Through the early modern period, however, many official functions were put on a statutory footing,[45] leaving gaps in the system. Error applied to orders of Justices of the Peace made at Quarter Sessions (as a Court of Record), and an action could be brought for acts outside jurisdiction in the strict sense, but *intra-jurisdictional* decisions made under the Justices' new summary powers were outside the traditional forms of judicial control.[46] Error did not run to new statutory tribunals such as the Commissioners of Sewers. The King's Bench extended the writ to cover administrative powers of the Justices, and later to the administrative functions of other bodies, particularly Commissioners of Sewers in the seventeenth century. Errors of law that were non-jurisdictional but appeared on the face of the record were somewhat forgotten, then rediscovered, then overtaken by modern developments.

The 'prerogative' writs grew in importance with the emergence of the central administration. These were mechanisms for the hierarchical control of offices that work from the notion of the Crown calling its officials up to account for their actions, but it also reflects a logic of action.[47] *Certiorari* is particularly important. This writ was a 'royal demand for information' used for general governmental purposes from the thirteenth century.[48] The writ was flexible; in the early days, it was poorly distinguished from error,[49] but was also used to initiate effectively appellate proceedings. Its functions included the supervision of inferior courts of specialised jurisdiction, obtaining information for administrative purposes, bringing records into court, and removing proceedings to the King's Bench. Like the writ of error, *certiorari* called up the documentary record; decisions could be quashed, and errors amended, by the reviewing court. It thus offered a means of attacking decisions directly, rather than collaterally.

44 Amnon Rubinstein, *Jurisdiction and Illegality* (Clarendon Press 1965), 57.

45 Paul Craig, *UK, EU, and Global Administrative Law* (Cambridge University Press 2014), 68.

46 See Philip Murray, *Judicial Review for Jurisdictional Error of Law in Nineteenth-Century Certiorari and Prohibition Proceedings* (PhD Thesis, University of Cambridge 2013), 22.

47 For example, *mandamus* compels performance of an official act where she is competent to act and is not at liberty not to act: see T. J. Arnold, *A Treatise on the Law Relating to Municipal Corporations in England and Wales* (Shaw 1875), 195; J. W. Willcock, *The Law of Municipal Corporations, Together with a Brief Sketch of their History and a Treatise on Mandamus and Quo Warranto* (Benning 1827), 354.

48 S. A. de Smith, 'The Prerogative Writs' (1951) 11(1) *Cambridge Law Journal* 40, 45.

49 Amnon Rubinstein, *Jurisdiction and Illegality* (Clarendon Press 1965), 62.

8.4.2 *Inflation of the Concept*

According to Amnon Rubinstein's seminal account, the eighteenth century marked 'a general regression into confusion'.[50] *Certiorari* acquired new importance with the increasing duties of Justices out of Sessions after 1660.[51] Even as judicial review was conceptually rationalised, and increasingly associated with statutory interpretation, the relation between *certiorari* and jurisdictional error became convoluted. Here, we find opinions that the writ was available only 'where a decision was tainted by jurisdictional defects'; there we find opinions that *certiorari* could *not* be issued 'where the decision complained of was a nullity'.[52] Rubinstein argued that, although *certiorari* was originally designed to address erroneous decisions made *within* jurisdiction, Parliament's repeated attempts to oust the supervisory jurisdiction of the King's Bench lead the Court to stress the supervisory nature of *certiorari* as a remedy lying for jurisdictional defects – stimulating expansion of 'jurisdictional error' and the applicable rules of evidence.[53] Use of jurisdictional error to resist legislative incursions into the judicial supervision of official jurisdiction through 'no-*certiorari*' clauses inflated the concept of itself.

Others have challenged this view, stressing the coherence of the jurisdictional concept in the latter nineteenth century,[54] but Rubinstein's analysis is compelling. In any case, jurisdictional error has not survived modern developments. Judicial responses to the twentieth century welfare state expanded the traditional supervisory jurisdiction to form a 'specialist administrative law',[55] built on ultra vires and stressing the importance of legislative intent. Jurisdictional error and ultra vires are indeed similar doctrines. One evolved to control regional courts and inferior tribunals, while the other was used to hold local government authorities and other corporate bodies within the terms of their founding documents. Their merger purportedly enabled the rapid development of

[50] Amnon Rubinstein, *Jurisdiction and Illegality* (Clarendon Press 1965), 70, citing D. M. Gordon, 'The Relation of Facts to Jurisdiction' (1920) 45 *Law Quarterly Review* 459.

[51] S. A. de Smith, 'The Prerogative Writs' (1951) 11(1) *Cambridge Law Journal* 40, 48.

[52] Amnon Rubinstein, *Jurisdiction and Illegality* (Clarendon Press 1965), 82–83.

[53] In Australia, *mandamus* and prohibition are limited to jurisdictional errors; *certiorari* remains available for errors on the face of the record generally: John Carroll, 'The Impact of Justice Kirby on Administrative Law Jurisprudence' (2010) 63 *AIAL Forum* 54, 55.

[54] See Philip Murray, *Review for Jurisdictional Error of Law in Nineteenth-Century Certiorari and Prohibition Proceedings* (PhD Thesis, University of Cambridge 2013), 30.

[55] *R (Huddlestone)* v. *Lancashire County Council* [1986] 2 All ER 941, 945 (Donaldson MR).

a 'rational and comprehensive system of administrative law',[56] but has also raised serious questions, and has not yielded a theoretical understanding of the supervisory jurisdiction that explains the reviewability of both statutory and non-statutory executive powers.

8.4.3 *The Anisminic Revolution*

The great re-conceptualisation of English administrative law began with some 'great cases', including *Ridge* v. *Baldwin*,[57] which concerned the terminative rules governing the office of Chief Constable. These rules provided for summary dismissal *or* mandatory resignation, with consequences for pension entitlements. Following acquittal for conspiracy charges, the Watch Committee of the Brighton Municipal Corporation dismissed Ridge under the Municipal Corporations Act 1882, s. 191(4) without inviting him to make submissions. The question was whether this power could validly be exercised in violation of the principles of natural justice. The House of Lords held that breach of the *audi alterem partem* principle brought the Watch Committee outside its powers. In my terms, this approach conflates questions of *competence* and *conduct*.

Lord Reid's judgment, in particular, has been praised for embracing the review of executive action, reasserting principles that had receded into the background, and dismissing the rigid categories of older authorities. According to K. J. Keith, Lord Reid swept aside the 'conceptual baggage' governing the amenability of administrative *versus* judicial bodies, and heralded a new approach to judicial development of the law,[58] banishing the 'arid judicial gobbledegook'[59] of the old test, namely whether a body had 'legal authority to affect the rights of subjects and a duty to act judicially'.[60] The tenor of the judgment is exemplified by Lord Reid's speech in a later case: 'I would not', he said in *Haughton* v. *Smith*,[61] 'decide the matter entirely on logical argument. The life blood of the law is common sense . . . We are not applying a rule but a principle

[56] *Re Racal Communications Ltd* [1981] AC 374, 382 (Diplock LJ).

[57] [1964] AC 40; see David Feldman, 'Convention Rights and Substantive Ultra Vires' in C. F. Forsyth (ed.), *Judicial Review and the Constitution* (2000), 247.

[58] K. J. Keith, '*Ridge v Baldwin* – Twenty Years On' (1983) 13 *Victoria University of Wellington Law Review* 239, 241.

[59] K. J. Keith, '*Ridge v Baldwin* – Twenty Years On' (1983) 13 *Victoria University of Wellington Law Review* 239, 247.

[60] *R* v. *Electricity Commissioners* [1924] 1 KB 171, 205 (Lord Atkin).

[61] [1975] AC 476.

and it must be applied sensibly'.[62] Significantly, Lord Reid held that the breach of natural justice by the Watch Committee rendered its decision a nullity:

> [T]here was considerable argument whether in the result the watch committee's decision is void or merely voidable. Time and again in the cases I have cited it has been stated that a decision given without regard to the principles of natural justice is void, and that was expressly decided in *Wood v Woad.* I see no reason to doubt these authorities. The body with the power to decide cannot lawfully proceed to make a decision until it has afforded to the person affected a proper opportunity to state his case.[63]

Lord Evershed held, in dissent, that breach of natural justice rendered the Watch Committee's decision 'not void but voidable only'.[64] Unlike Lord Reid, Lord Evershed found no clear answer to the void/voidable question in the authorities, but distinguished *Wood* v. *Woad*[65] as a case in which the entire proceeding was 'wholly irregular and ineffective from first to last', likening it to another body that was held to have 'act[ed] upon a futile and frivolous cause', making the proceedings 'no more than a sham'.[66] In such cases, a declaration of nullity *ab initio* was appropriate. Wishing not to denigrate the principles of natural justice or their proper invocation in the courts, Lord Evershed nevertheless opined that jurisdictional logic could be reconciled with the practical justice of the case.[67]

Lord Reid's judgment set in train a revolution in English administrative law. Until the 1950s, *certiorari* had been available for non-jurisdictional errors of law. In *R (Shaw)* v. *Northumberland County Council*,[68] for example, a public servant who had been made redundant applied to have the matter of his compensation removed to the King's Bench to be quashed. The Tribunal admitted that an error existed on the face of its decision, but argued that *certiorari* would lie only in the case of an excess of jurisdiction. The speech of Singleton LJ gives some indication of the challenges facing mid-century judges. Much time had been spent on the question whether *certiorari* would lie for statutory powers governed by complex subordinated legislation:[69]

62 *Haughton* v. *Smith* [1975] AC 476, 500.
63 *Ridge* v. *Baldwin* [1964] AC 40, 80, referring to *Wood* v. *Woad* (1874) 9 Ex 190.
64 *Ridge* v. *Baldwin* [1964] AC 40, 86.
65 *Wood* v. *Woad* (1874) LR 9 Ex 190.
66 *Ridge* v. *Baldwin* [1964] AC 40, 92, 93, citing *Osgood* v. *Nelson* (1872) LR 5 HL 636.
67 *Ridge* v. *Baldwin* [1964] AC 40, 96.
68 [1952] 1 KB 338.
69 *R (Shaw)* v. *Northumberland CC* [1952] 1 KB 338, 346.

> The interpretation of them is left to the tribunal; there is no provision for appeal to the courts. That position arises frequently nowadays. I most earnestly wish that in such cases where difficult questions of law, and of interpretation, must arise, that there should be given some right of appeal ... Tribunals are sometimes given an unduly difficult task; there must be a feeling a dissatisfaction if it is recognised that a decision of a tribunal is wrong in law and yet there is no power to correct it; in other words, if there is no right to have the opinion of the court.[70]

Lord Reid's elegant approach effectively circumvented this problem, and subsequent cases 'enthroned' it as the modern orthodoxy.[71]

The inflection point was *Anisminic* v. *Foreign Compensation Commission*,[72] which concerned the decision of a tribunal set up under the Foreign Compensation Act 1950 to compensate British businesses whose property had been confiscated by the Egyptian government in the Suez Crisis. As David Feldman explains, this case was shaped by tactical considerations, and what the judgments actually say is quite different to what they have been taken to mean.[73] While there are differences between the judgments, on the whole the case can be taken to advance three propositions: (i) there is a strong presumption against ouster of the High Court's supervisory jurisdiction over inferior tribunals, even by clear legislative wording; (ii) there is no difference between an excess of jurisdiction at the outset, and arising in the course of, proceedings; and (iii) errors of law, whether or not 'on the face of the record', result in an excess of jurisdiction.[74] The final proposition is particularly associated with Lord Reid's judgment.

Lord Reid in fact *confirmed* the importance of jurisdictional error (resulting in nullity), observing that it would be better not to use 'jurisdiction' 'except in the narrow and original sense of the tribunal being entitled to enter on the inquiry in question'.[75] Indeed, in *R (Armah)* v. *Governor of Brixton Prison*,[76] Lord Reid had just affirmed the

70 *R (Shaw)* v. *Northumberland CC* [1952] 1 KB 338, 346.

71 K. J. Keith, '*Ridge v Baldwin* – Twenty Years On' (1983) 13 *Victoria University of Wellington Law Review* 239, 247.

72 [1969] 2 AC 147.

73 David Feldman, '*Anisminic Ltd v Foreign Compensation Commission* [1968]: In Perspective' in Satvinder Juss and Maurice Sunkin (eds.), *Landmark Cases in Public Law* (Hart 2017).

74 See *R (Privacy International)* v. *Investigative Powers Tribunal* [2019] UKSC 22, [43] (Lord Carnwath).

75 *Anisminic* v. *Foreign Compensation Commission* [1969] 2 AC 147, 171.

76 [1968] AC 192.

conventional doctrine that if an official 'has jurisdiction to go right he has jurisdiction to go wrong' and that '[n]either an error in fact nor an error in law will destroy his jurisdiction'.[77] But in *Anisminic* v. *Foreign Compensation Commission,* he held that *some* non-jurisdictional errors of law might, nonetheless, lead to invalidity *ab initio*:

> [T]here are many cases where, although the tribunal had jurisdiction to enter on the inquiry, it has done or failed to do something in the course of the inquiry which is *of such a nature that its decision is a nullity*. It may have given its decision in bad faith. It may have made a decision which it had no power to make. It may have failed in the course of the inquiry to comply with the requirements of natural justice. It may in perfect good faith have misconstrued the provisions giving it power to act so that it failed to deal with the question remitted to it and decided some question which was not remitted to it. It may have refused to take into account something which it was required to take into account. Or it may have based its decision on some matter which, under the provisions setting it up, it had no right to take into account.[78]

If a tribunal decides a question without committing any such errors, Lord Reid confirmed that it remains 'as much entitled to decide that question wrongly as it is to decide it rightly'.[79]

However, considering things like bad faith when asking whether jurisdiction *existed*, rather than whether jurisdiction had been *properly exercised*, inflated the concept. This follows Rubinstein's trend of judges blurring the lines of jurisdiction to ensure the efficacy of the supervisory jurisdiction against attempts at legislative ouster. As Lord Carnwath observed in *R (Privacy International)* v. *Investigatory Powers Tribunal*,[80] Lord Reid did not include a *simple* error of law in his illustrative list; the error must have gone to material competence, for example, 'misconstruction of the provisions giving it power to act'.[81]

Lord Reid's judgment, however, is more important for what it has been taken to say than what it actually said. It has been interpreted to abandon the concept of jurisdiction entirely – due in no small measure to

[77] *R (Armah)* v. *Governor of Brixton Prison* [1968] AC 192, 243 (Lord Reid).
[78] *Anisminic* v. *Foreign Compensation Commission* [1969] 2 AC 147, 171. Emphasis mine.
[79] *Anisminic* v. *Foreign Compensation Commission* [1969] 2 AC 147, 171.
[80] [2019] UKSC 22.
[81] *R (Privacy International)* v. *Investigatory Powers Tribunal* [2019] UKSC 22, [48] (Lord Carnwath).

a sustained campaign of *obiter dicta* from Lord Diplock.[82] In *Re Racal Communications*[83] Lord Diplock said:

> The break-through made by *Anisminic* was that, as respects administrative tribunals and authorities, the old distinction between errors of law that went to jurisdiction and errors of law that did not, was for practical purposes abolished. Any error of law that could be shown to have been made by them in the course of reaching their decision on matters of fact or of administrative policy would result in their having asked themselves the wrong question with the result that the decision they reached would be a nullity.[84]

Where Parliament confers the power to decide questions on an administrative body, as opposed to a court of law, Parliament intends to 'confine that power to answering the question as it has been so defined'.[85] If there is any doubt as to the definition of the question that body is empowered to determine, it is 'a matter for the courts of law'.[86] Because ultra vires is a matter of parliamentary intention, and parliamentary intention is a question of law, all questions of law assume a 'jurisdictional' aspect. Lord Diplock said again in *O'Reilly* v. *Mackman*,[87] which created a new procedural distinction between 'private law' actions in tort and 'public law' judicial review applications, that *Anisminic* v. *Foreign Compensation Commission* had 'liberated' English public law from the self-imposed requirement of drawing 'esoteric distinctions' between errors of law going to the jurisdiction of inferior tribunals and those committed within their jurisdiction:[88]

> The break-through that the *Anisminic* case made was the recognition … that if a tribunal whose jurisdiction was limited by statute or subordinate legislation mistook the law applicable to the facts as it had found them, it must have asked itself the wrong question, i.e. one into which it was not empowered to enquiry and so had not jurisdiction to determine. Its purported 'determination' not being 'a determination' within the meaning of the empowering legislation, was accordingly a nullity.[89]

82 See Sir Stephen Sedley, 'The Lion Behind the Throne: The Law as History' [2016] *Judicial Review* 289, [14].
83 [1981] AC 374.
84 *Re Racal Communications Ltd* [1981] AC 374, 382.
85 *Re Racal Communications Ltd* [1981] AC 374, 382.
86 *Re Racal Communications Ltd* [1981] AC 374, 382.
87 [1983] 2 AC 237.
88 *O'Reilly* v. *Mackman* [1983] 2 AC 237, 278.
89 *O'Reilly* v. *Mackman* [1983] 2 AC 237, 278.

Lord Diplock said again in *Council of Civil Service Unions* v. *Minister for the Civil Service*[90] that judicial review encompassed not only illegality in the strict sense, but irrationality and procedural impropriety as well. Although irrationality had been reviewed through the inference of an 'unidentifiable mistake of law' in earlier cases, it could 'now stand upon its own feet as an accepted ground on which a decision may be attacked by judicial review' – crucially, with the same consequences as illegality or jurisdictional error in the strict sense.[91]

This campaign was ultimately successful. The first binding decision was *R (Page)* v. *Lord President of the Privy Council*,[92] which concerned the reviewability of decisions by the Visitor of the University of Hull. Lord Browne-Wilkinson confirmed that 'in general any error of law made by an administrative tribunal or inferior court in reaching its decision will be quashed for error of law'.[93]

> In my judgment the decision in *Anisminic* ... rendered obsolete the distinction between errors of law on the face of the record and other errors of law by extending the doctrine of ultra vires. Thenceforward it was to be taken that Parliament had only conferred the decision-making power on the basis that it was to be exercised on the correct legal basis: a misdirection in law in making the decision therefore rendered the decision ultra vires.[94]

The novel proposition here is that there is no difference between (i) an official purporting to exercise powers he *does not have* and (ii) an official exercising powers he *does have* irregularly. In both cases 'he is acting ultra vires his powers and therefore unlawfully'.[95]

Boddington v. *British Transport Police*[96] concerned the use of ultra vires as a defence to prosecution under a byelaw.[97] The House of Lords rightly confirmed the availability of collateral challenge, but also endorsed the expanded category of decisions void *ab initio*. In *Director of Public Prosecutions* v. *Head*,[98] which concerned the availability of collateral challenge by way of defence, Lord Denning (in dissent) had held that an offence could be made out on the basis of an order that

90 [1985] 1 AC 374.
91 *Council of Civil Service Unions* v. *Minister for the Civil Service* [1985] AC 374, 410–411, citing *Edwards* v. *Bairstow* [1956] AC 14.
92 [1993] AC 682.
93 *R (Page)* v. *Lord President of the Privy Council* [1993] AC 682, 702.
94 *R (Page)* v. *Lord President of the Privy Council* [1993] AC 682, 701.
95 *R (Page)* v. *Lord President of the Privy Council* [1993] AC 682, 701.
96 [1999] 2 AC 143.
97 *Boddington* v. *British Transport Police* [1999] 2 AC 143, 151.
98 [1959] AC 83.

was voidable but still on foot on the date of the alleged offence.[99] This view was rejected by the majority, whose approach was then followed in *Boddington*. According to Lord Irvine LC, no-one should be sent to prison on the basis of a voidable bye-law, for it would be a 'fundamental departure from the rule of law' for a subject to be liable to conviction under a rule itself liable to be set aside as unlawful.[100]

> Lord Denning had dissented on the basis of the historic distinction between acts which were ultra vires ('outside the jurisdiction of the Secretary of State'), which he accepted were nullities and void, and errors of law on the face of the relevant record, which rendered the relevant instrument voidable rather than void. He felt able to assign the order in question to the latter category. But in 1969, the decision of your Lordships' House in [*Anisminic*] made obsolete the historic distinction between errors of law on the face of the record and other errors of law. It did so by extending the doctrine of ultra vires, so that any misdirection in law would render the relevant decision *ultra vires* and a nullity . . . Thus, today, the old distinction between void and voidable acts on which Lord Denning relied in [*Director of Public Prosecutions v Head*] no longer applies.[101]

This is, effectively, the modern position. More recently, in *R (Lumba)* v. *Home Secretary*,[102] Lord Dyson held:

> A purported lawful authority to detain may be impugned either because the defendant acted in excess of jurisdiction (in the narrow sense of jurisdiction) or because such jurisdiction was wrongly exercised. [*Anisminic*] established that both species of error render an executive act ultra vires, unlawful and a nullity. In the present context, there is in principle no difference between (i) a detention which is unlawful because there was no statutory power to detain and (ii) a detention which is unlawful because the decision to detain, although authorised by statute, was made in breach of a rule of public law. For example, if the decision to detain is unreasonable in the *Wednesbury* sense, it is unlawful and a nullity. The importance of *Anisminic* is that it established that there was a single category of errors of law, all of which rendered a decision ultra vires.[103]

As the next chapter explains, it is accurate to describe an act as 'ultra vires' both where the official has exceeded his ability-space by breaching

99 *DPP* v. *Head* [1959] AC 83, 113. In *Pearlman* v. *Keepers and Governors of Harrow School* [1979] QB 56, Lord Denning said the traditional distinction was 'very fine' and was being 'rapidly eroded'.

100 *Boddington* v. *British Transport Police* [1999] 2 AC 143, 153.

101 *Boddington* v. *British Transport Police* [1999] 2 AC 143, 153.

102 [2011] UKSC 12.

103 *R (Lumba)* v. *Home Secretary* [2011] UKSC 12, [66].

a rule of competence and where he has exceeded his liberty-space by breaching a rule of conduct. But the consequences that follow a violation of the narrow and broad limb of the ultra vires rule, respectively, are logically different.

More recently, in *R (Cart)* v. *Upper Tribunal*,[104] Baroness Hale considered that *Anisminic* v. *Foreign Compensation Commission* 'effectively removed the distinction between error of law and excess of jurisdiction'.[105] This solution to the problem of ouster clauses – that is, the proposition that a statutory provision cannot oust review of a 'decision' that is not actually a 'decision' at all and so cannot benefit from the ouster clause – has undoubtedly helped the courts to defend the supervisory jurisdiction. The problem, as Lord Carnwath noted in *R (Privacy International)* v. *Investigatory Powers Tribunal*, is that the subsequent extension of the principle may undermine its conceptual basis.[106] Although the standard reading of *Anisminic* v. *Foreign Compensation Commission* now goes unquestioned, 'its conceptual basis, 35 years on from *O'Reilly* v. *Mackman*, remains obscure'; 'the courts have not adopted a uniform approach, but have felt free to adapt or limit the scope and form of judicial review' in order to balance respect for statutory context (i.e., legislative intention) with the rule of law.[107]

The modern approach is consistent with the dominant English view of judicial review as a forum in which the competing demands of parliamentary sovereignty and the rule of law are balanced. It does not denigrate those principles, however, to say that jurisdiction is no empty concept; if we are to make sense of the judicial review of non-statutory executive powers it is necessary to examine the question of official competence and conduct with the logic of official empowerment and action in mind, even if it unwinds the '*Anisminic* revolution'.

8.5 Conclusion

The conventional view of modern developments in the law is that we have unshackled the supervisory jurisdiction from sterile technical constraints to yield a flexible jurisdiction based on grounds of review

[104] [2012] 1 AC 663.

[105] *R (Cart)* v. *Upper Tribunal* [2012] 1 AC 663, [18] (Baroness Hale).

[106] *R (Privacy International)* v. *Investigative Powers Tribunal* [2019] UKSC 22, [53] (Lord Carnwath).

[107] *R (Privacy International)* v. *Investigative Powers Tribunal* [2019] UKSC 22, [128]–[130] (Lord Carnwath).

sensitive to the context of administration and individual rights. However, judicial review is the product of a complex history, the internal structure of the supervisory jurisdiction is far from clear, and reasonable minds still differ greatly on the role of the ultra vires doctrine and the conceptual basis of judicial review.[108] Rather than liberating it, attenuation of jurisdictional logic has cut the supervisory jurisdiction loose.

At base, all judicial review is about jurisdiction, and the language of ultra vires rightly directs us to the question whether an action was within or outside the *Spielraum* of the decision-maker.[109] The task is to ensure that we articulate the grounds of review, and make arguments about the intensity and consequences of review, in a way that reflects the basic logic of action. The rule-based nature of official action and the distinction between rules of competence and rules of conduct are fundamental. Both violation of a rule of competence and a violation of a rule of conduct result in an action properly called 'ultra vires', but this rule has a broad and narrow limb. Certain legal consequences follow an excess of ability-space, others an excess of liberty-space. Thus, it is impossible to replace the concept of jurisdiction with 'principles of good administration' or individual rights, for example, because they tell only half the story. The true import of principles of good administration only becomes apparent when we translate them into duties incumbent on executive officials, and these duties must operate on a sphere of official competence. It is to the concepts of competence, conduct, and ultra vires that we now turn.

[108] See Paul Craig, 'Ultra Vires and Judicial Review' in C. F. Forsyth (ed.), *Judicial Review and the Constitution* (Hart 2000), 48, 62.

[109] See Mark Elliott and Jason Varuhas, *Administrative Law: Text and Materials* (Oxford University Press 2017), 33.

9

Competence, Conduct, and Validity

9.1 Introduction

At the heart of judicial review is the idea that powers are reposed in an office not at large but on certain terms: officials act 'validly' only within the *Spielraum* those terms trace, and the supervisory jurisdiction exists to determine whether any given action was within the complex space of 'possible and permitted' or outside it. Relevant terms are found in rules of *competence* and rules of *conduct*. They may be either statutory or non-statutory, express or implied – most often, the courts look to a combination of statutory provisions, implications from those provisions, and common law rules to determine the office's *Spielraum*. This chapter explains the supervisory jurisdiction as an expression of this core logic and explores some of the implications for legal doctrine. That sets the stage for the argument, in Chapter 11, that ultra vires should be understood as a common law doctrine that can apply to non-statutory as well as statutory executive powers.

Section 9.2 explains the concept of validity applied to official action, and introduces some of the doctrinal complexities that have arisen since the abandonment of jurisdictional error. The English law of judicial review has been conceptually confused by the desire to avoid the appearance of 'strong form' review. Though justified by a rhetoric of common sense, supposed pragmatism has sown seeds of confusion that have only made the law more difficult. Section 9.3 looks at the relation between 'facts', 'law', and 'jurisdiction', urging a rejection of the dichotomy between errors of fact and errors of law that has supposedly replaced jurisdictional error. Section 9.4 looks at the relation between official fact-finding, discretion, and subjects' rights, fleshing out the importance of the 'broad' limb of the ultra vires rule which ensures that officials respect the rules of conduct that condition their formal vires. Although this chapter is less directly concerned with the problem of non-statutory executive powers, the structure it sketches out will allow us to describe the supervisory jurisdiction over those powers.

9.2 Valid Acts-in-the-Law

'Validity' is a quality with important ramifications, whether predicated of laws, legal states of affairs, acts-in-the-law, or legal orders.[1] Different approaches exist to the concept of validity, but most of the classical theories converge on a 'systemic' one,[2] conducive to my focus on the validity of official action. Fundamentally, an act-in-the-law taken pursuant to a rule is 'valid' if the criteria in the rule have been fulfilled. A valid act-in-the-law changes institutional legal reality by altering the legal position of one or more subjects. A valid act is one that 'exists' in the context of a given legal system – participants in the relevant legal system can treat it as giving rise to legal consequences.

An act that does not conform to the conditions of validity in the relevant rule is a non-entity in the frame of reference of the system. A court that refuses to recognise a warrant, for example, treats it not as a 'warrant' but as 'a piece of scrap-paper'.[3] 'A "warrant" issued by a completely unauthorised person', argued Amnon Rubinstein, 'is non-existent in the first place'.[4] It remains a brute, and no institutional, fact. In the *Duchess of Kingston's*

[1] Torben Spaak, *The Concept of Legal Competence* (Dartmouth 1994), 50.

[2] Space precludes a detailed discussion here: see Risto Halpinen, 'Introduction II: Aspects of Eugenio Bulygin's Norm Theory' and Eugenio Bulygin, 'Valid Law and Law in Force' in Eugenio Bulygin (Carlos Bernal, Carla Huerta, Teda Mazzarese, Jose Juan Moreso, Pablo Navarro and Stanley Paulson (eds.), *Essays in Legal Philosophy* (Oxford University Press 2015), 30, 286, 291; Alf Ross, 'Validity and the Conflict between Legal Positivism and Natural Law' in S. L. Paulson and Bonnie Litschewski Paulson (eds.), *Normativity and Norms* (Oxford University Press 1999), 158; Alf Ross, *Directives and Norms* (Humanities Press 1968), 96; Alf Ross, 'On Self-Reference and a Puzzle in Constitutional Law' (1969) 78 *Mind* 1; Hans Kelsen (Anders Wedberg trans.), *General Theory of Law and State* (Harvard University Press 1945), 30; H. L. A. Hart, *The Concept of Law* (Clarendon Press 1961), 100; Stephen Munzer, *Legality and Validity* (Nijhoff 1972), 2, 23; Jaap Hage, 'The Deontic Furniture of the World: An Analysis of the Basic Concepts that Embody Normativity' in Jerzy Stelmach, Bartosz Brozek, and Mateus Hohol (eds.), *The Many Faces of Normativity* (Copernicus 2013), 79; Jerzy Wróblewski, 'Three Concepts of Validity of Law' (1982) 118 *Särtryck ur Tidskrift, utgeven av Juridiska Föreningen i Finland* 406; Torben Spaak, *The Concept of Legal Competence* (Dartmouth 1994), 51–52.

[3] Amnon Rubinstein, *Jurisdiction and Illegality* (Clarendon Press 1965), 6.

[4] Amnon Rubinstein, *Jurisdiction and Illegality* (Clarendon Press 1965), 6.

Case,[5] for example, the court considered the validity of an order issued by an ecclesiastical court. The Solicitor General argued that a 'sentence' is not just an instrument 'with a bit of wax and the seal of a court put to it', nor one 'with the signature of a person calling himself a register' nor equally 'such a quantity of ink bestowed upon such a quantity of stamped paper'; a 'sentence' is a judicial determination of a conflict between parties, in which some interest has been settled. In other words, the 'judgment' is the abstract legal concept distinct from the written instrument purporting to embody it. According to Rubinstein, '[i]f this instrument does not fulfil the juridical test of validity it is not a judgment but merely so many scribbled pages'.[6] An invalid writ was deemed a 'meaningless piece of paper' in *Holdsworth* v. *Lane*,[7] and an invalid warrant was deemed 'no more than waste-paper' in *Corrat* v. *Morley*.[8]

What about a warrant issued by a prima facie competent official irregularly – for example, based on irrational considerations, mistake, personal malice, or in breach of procedural safeguards? Traditionally, as we have seen, the two limbs of the supervisory jurisdiction entailed different legal consequences. In *Ridge* v. *Baldwin*,[9] Lord Evershed held (in dissent) that the decision of a body acting within its jurisdiction, but against the principles of natural justice, was 'only voidable and cannot properly be described as a nullity'.[10] Asking what it actually means to say that a decision is 'void', Lord Evershed based his answer on the rules of personal, formal, and material competence setting out the Watch Committee's remit. There was no question of the Watch Committee's jurisdiction to dismiss Ridge; the only question was whether, 'admitting the jurisdiction of the Watch Committee, it was properly exercised having regard to any application of the principles of natural justice to which the exercise of the jurisdiction was subject'.[11] The Committee's powers of dismissal were cabined by important duties, including duties to respect the principles of natural justice. All this notwithstanding, a competent act in breach of duty was not the same as an incompetent act.

[5] (1776) 20 St Tr 355.
[6] Amnon Rubinstein, *Jurisdiction and Illegality* (Clarendon Press 1965), 8.
[7] (1847) 10 QB 546.
[8] (1841) 1 QB 18.
[9] [1964] AC 40.
[10] *Ridge* v. *Baldwin* [1964] AC 40, 86.
[11] *Ridge* v. *Baldwin* [1964] AC 40, 87.

9.2.1 The Void/Voidable Distinction in Public Law

The distinction between an incompetent act and a prima facie competent act that violates a rule of conduct (governing, for example, manner and purpose) is important. D. M. Gordon, the doyen of jurisdictional logic, distinguished between three states – 'voidness', 'voidability', and 'impeccability': 'The distinction between the first two is that the former represents a state of nothingness from which nothing can arise, and which consequently can never acquire any different status, while the second denotes something liable to be reduced to nothingness, but which is also capable of acquiring impeccability'.[12]

The distinction is accepted in private law. In *Rolled Steel Limited* v. *British Steel Corporation*,[13] for example, Lord Browne-Wilkinson differentiated between 'acts done in excess of the capacity of the company' and 'acts done in excess or abuse of the powers of the company'; the former were null and void, while the legal effect of the latter depended on rules governing apparent authority and third-party knowledge.[14]

The distinction reflects the logic of action that also underlies public office. There are long-standing doubts, however, about the applicability of the distinction in public law. Sir Frederick Pollock called the terms 'void' and 'voidable' 'imprecise and apt to mislead'.[15] In *Director of Public Prosecutions* v. *Head*[16] Lord Somerville said the distinction was 'insufficiently clear' to determine 'whether a man should go or not go to prison'.[17] In *Durayappah* v. *Fernando*,[18] the Privy Council advised that it was appropriate in contract but not administrative law. In *Anisminic* v. *Foreign Compensation Commission*, Lord Wilberforce expressly avoided endorsing it, warning that term 'nullity' could '[draw] with it the difficult distinction between what is void, and what is voidable'.[19] Lord Diplock in *Hoffmann-La Roche* v. *Secretary of State for Trade and Industry*[20] said that it 'developed in the field of contract' and the

[12] D. M. Gordon, 'Certiorari and the Revival of Error in Fact' (1926) 42 *Law Quarterly Review* 521, 526.
[13] [1986] Ch 246.
[14] *Rolled Steel Limited* v. *British Steel Corporation* [1986] Ch 246, 304.
[15] Sir Frederick Pollock, *Principles of Contract at Law and in Equity* (8th ed., Stevens 1881), 48, cited by Lord Evershed in *Ridge* v. *Baldwin* [1963] AC 40, 92.
[16] [1959] 1 All ER 692.
[17] *DPP* v. *Head* [1959] 1 All ER 692, 104.
[18] [1967] 2 AC 337.
[19] *Anisminic* v. *Foreign Compensation Commission* [1969] 2 AC 147, 208.
[20] [1975] AC 295.

principles underlying it 'are ill-adapted to the field of public law'.[21] Textbooks warn that beneath the apparently simple dichotomy 'lurk terminological and conceptual problems of excruciating complexity'.[22] Sir John Laws has said that it serves 'no useful analytical purpose' and introduces unnecessary metaphysical concepts.[23]

Judges are said to hold discretionary powers to determine the consequences of irregularity. In *London & Clydeside Estates Ltd* v. *Aberdeen District Council*,[24] for example, Lord Hailsham considered the relevance of 'directory' and 'mandatory' conditions on the exercise of statutory powers. As the courts must determine the legal consequences of non-compliance 'in the light of a state of facts and a continuing chain of events',[25] they have not a binary choice, but a 'spectrum of possibilities' in which one compartment 'fades gradually into another'.[26] At one end are cases in which a 'fundamental obligation' has been so flagrantly ignored that the subject may 'safely ignore what has been done and treat it as having no legal consequences'.[27] Such an act may be challenged collaterally, including by way of defence. At the other end fall defects in procedure so slight that the courts will ignore the complaint of one who relies on the fault:

> [T]hough language like 'mandatory', 'directory', 'void', 'voidable', 'nullity' and so forth may be helpful in argument, it may be misleading in effect if relied on to show that the courts, in deciding the consequences of a defect in the exercise of power, are necessarily bound to fit the facts of a particular case and a developing chain of events into rigid legal categories or to stretch or cramp them on a bed of Procrustes invented by lawyers for the purposes of convenient exposition.[28]

In *R (Datafin)* v. *Take-over Panel*, Sir John Donaldson MR said that it was a 'special feature' of public law decisions that 'however wrong they may be, however lacking in jurisdiction they may be, they subsist and remain fully effective unless and until they are set aside'.[29] The court 'has

21 *Hoffmann-La Roche* v. *Secretary of State for Trade and Industry* [1975] AC 295, 356.
22 S. A. de Smith, Sir Harry Woolf, and Jeffrey Jowell, *De Smith, Woolf, and Jowell Judicial Review of Administrative Action* (5th ed., Sweet & Maxwell 1995), 257.
23 Sir John Laws, 'Illegality: The Problem of Jurisdiction' in Michael Supperstone and James Goudie (eds.), *Judicial Review* (Butterworths 1992), 57.
24 [1980] 1 WLR 182.
25 *London & Clydeside Estates Ltd* v. *Aberdeen District Council* [1980] 1 WLR 182, 189.
26 *London & Clydeside Estates Ltd* v. *Aberdeen District Council* [1980] 1 WLR 182, 189.
27 *London & Clydeside Estates Ltd* v. *Aberdeen District Council* [1980] 1 WLR 182, 189.
28 *London & Clydeside Estates Ltd* v. *Aberdeen District Council* [1980] 1 WLR 182, 189.
29 *R (Datafin)* v. *Take-over Panel* [1987] QB 815, 840.

an ultimate discretion whether to set them aside and may refuse to do so in the public interest' – even if it declares the decision ultra vires.[30]

9.2.2 *Breaching a Rule of Competence*

With respect, that approach must be rejected. Because rules of competence make a class of acts-in-the-law *possible*, their violation results in no change in the legal state of affairs. Most official acts are purely institutional. The rule of competence that says the Prime Minister can prorogue Parliament, for example, is inextricable from the concept of *prorogation itself*; any explanation of what 'prorogation' is entails the competence of an official (be it the Queen or HM Prime Minister) empowered to do the act.

This is consistent with what Lord Reid actually said in *Anisminic* v. *Foreign Compensation Commission*: 'if you seek to show that a determination is a nullity you are not questioning the purported determination – you are maintaining that it does not exist as a determination'.[31] Something that purports to the status of a determination may be 'in fact no determination at all'.[32] Only if the requirements set out in the relevant institutive rule are fulfilled does a 'determination' come into being and trigger legal consequences. The problem is that Lord Reid muddied the waters of 'competence' and 'conduct'; others have pushed the point in order to avoid directly challenging real or perceived conflict with parliamentary legislation.

Institutional legal facts are presentations of the world that have achieved the position of a state of affairs in the legal system. D.W.P. Ruiter explains that institutional legal reality is created by linguistic representations of collective intentionality. Among the most important of these utterances are declarations that create offices, which entail deontic powers governing interactions between the subjects of a legal system.[33] Validity expresses a 'juridico-causal' relationship between *operative facts* and *legal consequences*. This explains the institutional landscape we lawyers daily work in – a non-physical system populated

[30] *R (Datafin)* v. *Take-over Panel* [1987] QB 815, 840.
[31] *Anisminic Ltd* v. *Foreign Compensation Commission* [1969] 2 AC 147, 170.
[32] *Anisminic Ltd* v. *Foreign Compensation Commission* [1969] 2 AC 147, 170.
[33] Other forms of official utterance include directives and commissives, taking the form of licenses, warrants, and orders: D. W. P. Ruiter, *Legal Institutions* (Kluwer 2010), 6.

by invisible, purely conventional 'rights', 'duties', and 'powers'.[34] My lone belief that a piece of wrapping paper counts as a 'warrant' (or prorogation instrument), for example, is not sufficient to turn it into such: to be effective, recognition needs to be inter-subjective, negotiated in venues such as legislatures and courts, according to pre-existing rules.[35] Unlike actions in the 'real world', actions in the universe of institutional legal reality need not conform with the natural laws of physics; they do, however, have to conform with the rules that constitute that system. This explains why the breach of a rule of competence must result in voidness *ab initio*.

9.2.3 Voidability and Perfectibility

Violations of a rule of conduct, on the other hand, do cause prima facie changes in legal reality that are *liable* to invalidation by a competent (e.g., judicial) authority. Consider (i) a 'warrant' issued by a private individual; (ii) a 'warrant' issued by an official with no material competence to issue *that type* of warrant, or to issue a warrant over a certain geographical area or class of persons; and (iii) a warrant issued maliciously by a competent official. It is fundamental that an act clearly within the competence of an official must generate legal consequences until set aside. Where the official violates some rule governing how she has to comport herself in the discharge of her competence, the problem is slightly different to the scenario of a private 'warrant' with no legal basis at all.

Rules of competence and rules of conduct thus provide the structure of judicial evaluation of official action. In the first case, the reviewing court makes a *declaration* of the *currently existing* legal state of affairs, that is, that the act impugned was defective and never came into existence in the first place. This is an important official act, and provides much needed certainty within a legal order. It takes the form of an 'assertative' utterance. In the second case, the reviewing court does more: it actually *terminates* an *existing* state of affairs, and takes the form of a 'declarative' utterance.[36] Alternatively, of course, the judge can always declare the state of affairs to subsist by 'perfecting' an irregular action.

[34] Barry Smith, 'Searle and De Soto: The New Ontology of the Social World' in Barry Smith, D. M. Mark, and Isaac Erhlich (eds.), *The Mystery of Capital and the Construction of Social Reality* (Open Court 2008), 45.

[35] Leo Zaibert, 'Intentions, Promises, and Obligations' in Barry Smith (ed.), *John Searle* (Cambridge University Press 2003), 61; Mariano Croce and Andrea Salvatore, *The Legal Theory of Carl Schmitt* (Routledge 2013), 10.

[36] A declarative utterance asserts that a state of affairs obtains, and *makes it the case* that it obtains. The legal judgment expressed by the revocatory legal act must itself be perfect,

9.2.4 *The Two Limbs of Ultra Vires*

As official action depends on rules of competence and rules of conduct, the supervisory jurisdiction inherently comprises two limbs. In her seminal contribution to the ultra vires debate, Dawn Oliver explained that the first limb of the ultra vires rule catches actions that an official does not have the legal capacity to do, that is, excess of jurisdiction 'in the narrow, or strict sense'.[37] The second limb catches actions that are intra vires in the narrow sense, but which are done 'improperly' or 'unreasonably' in various ways: 'these ways include disregard of the rules of natural justice, unfairness, taking into account irrelevant considerations, ignoring relevant considerations, bad faith, fettering discretion, attempting to raise taxation, interfering with the free exercise of individual liberties, and so on'.[38]

D. J. Galligan had earlier argued that the modern supervisory jurisdiction could be separated into two heads, even if view then emerging saw one unified principle covering all heads of review. The court performs two tasks. The first is to settle 'jurisdictional or demarcation disputes', the second to 'enforce certain principles of good administration':[39]

> As to the first, the typical questions in issue are whether the deciding authority is properly constituted, whether it embarks on the right tasks, satisfies any conditions, and finally comes to a decision within the scope of its authority. The second task for judicial review is to maintain principles of good administration to be followed by public authorities in making decisions. Broadly speaking these principles are of two kinds: those requiring certain procedures, e.g. natural justice, and those that place constraints on the reasoning process whereby officials reach decisions, e.g. the no-fettering rule, the no-evidence rule, irrelevant considerations, improper motives, unreasonableness. These principles are concerned with what happens within the limits and only indirectly with the limits themselves. They do not stipulate the conclusionary reasons upon which any decision is to be based, but form a system of procedures and reason-guiding constraints on the process of decision-making.[40]

which may require several levels of appeal: D. W. P. Ruiter, *Legal Institutions* (Kluwer 2010), 18, 151.

37 Dawn Oliver, 'Is Ultra Vires the Basis of Judicial Review?' in C. F. Forsyth (ed.), *Judicial Review and the Constitution* (Hart 2000), 4.

38 Dawn Oliver, 'Is Ultra Vires the Basis of Judicial Review?' in C. F. Forsyth (ed.), *Judicial Review and the Constitution* (Hart 2000), 4.

39 D. J. Galligan, 'Judicial Review and Textbook Writers' (1982) 2(2) *Oxford Journal of Legal Studies* 257, 261.

40 D. J. Galligan, 'Judicial Review and Textbook Writers' (1982) 2(2) *Oxford Journal of Legal Studies* 257, 261.

Properly understood, the two limbs of ultra vires provide the doctrinal apparatus for a rational system of judicial review – all that is needed is a clear distinction between the capacitative and deontic axes of official *Spielraum*.

Again, it is essential to remember that many of the leading cases have involved a statutory clause limiting the courts' supervisory jurisdiction. The desire to circumvent no-*certiorari* clauses (without posing an open challenge to the idea that Parliament's legislative competence is unlimited) has driven the abandonment of jurisdictional logic.[41] As an alternative to Rubinstein's classical analysis, Philip Murray has pointed to review for bias and fraud as the driver for abandoning jurisdictional error.[42] Lord Denning suggested in *R (Gilmore)* v. *Medical Appeal Tribunal*,[43] for example, that no-*certiorari* clauses were generally respected by the English courts – except in cases of bias and fraud.[44] However, fraud or bias, distinct from want of jurisdiction *stricto sensu*, ought to be subject to a well-drafted ouster clause, because a fraudulent or biased decision is still a decision within the ability-space of the decision-maker. If it is to be quashed, it is for violating duties within the official's liberty-space. If that position be considered untenable, one should rather take 'strong form' review seriously.

It is possible to shoehorn bias into jurisdiction. In *R* v. *Cheltenham Commissioners*,[45] for example, counsel argued that a court with biased members was improperly constituted, and therefore without personal competence[46] – a plausible argument if the institutive rules governing personal competence disqualify a biased person.[47] But the better view is that officials who proceed to act under a reasonable apprehension of bias violate a rule of conduct – a duty to recuse when conflicted.

Fraud cases, on the other hand, are clearly non-jurisdictional. An otherwise competent official who commits a fraud straightforwardly breaches a rule of conduct regulating the exercise of his powers. As Lord Radcliffe said of a compulsory purchase order in *Smith* v. *East Elloe Rural District Council*:[48]

41 See Amnon Rubinstein, *Jurisdiction and Illegality* (Clarendon Press 1965), 60, 80, 194.
42 Philip Murray, *Review for Jurisdictional Error of Law in Ninetheenth-Century Certiorari and Prohibition Proceedings* (PhD Thesis, University of Cambridge 2013), 64.
43 [1957] 1 QB 574.
44 *R (Gilmore)* v. *Medical Appeal Tribunal* [1957] 1 QB 574, 586.
45 (1841) 1 QB 467.
46 *R* v. *Cheltenham Commissioners* (1841) 1 QB 467, 473.
47 See *Isbester* v. *Knox City Council* [2015] HCA 20; *Dickason* v. *Edwards* (1910) 10 CLR 243.
48 [1956] AC 736.

> An order, even if not made in good faith, is still an act capable of legal consequences. It bears no brand of invalidity upon its forehead. Unless the necessary proceedings are taken at law to establish the cause of invalidity and get it quashed or otherwise upset, it will remain as effective for its ostensible purpose as the most impeccable of orders.[49]

The fraud cases illustrate the unenviable situation of a judge facing a well-drafted ouster clause, and evoke some sympathy for the strategy of inflating jurisdiction. Where Parliament grants a broad (or even 'absolute') immunity from judicial review, the judge faces dilemma. Either she must challenge Parliament's competence to make such a law – that is, mount a direct challenge to parliamentary sovereignty – or she must apply the clause and accord the official a privilege to act fraudulently. The confusion of jurisdictional logic is understandable, but not tolerable.

9.2.5 *Collateral Challenge*

The void *versus* voidable/perfectible question also bears on the availability of so-called 'collateral challenge', especially by way of criminal defence. The idea that all errors of law are jurisdictional, but that voidness is always a matter of discretion, causes confusion and uncertainty here, too. The difficulty is illustrated by *Director of Public Prosecutions* v. *Head*. In that case, the fact that the victim had been designated as a 'mental defective' was a necessary ingredient of the offence of 'having carnal knowledge of a mental defective'. Designation with such a status is an official act-in-the-law; if that act was invalid, then no *actus reus* could logically exist.

On the one hand, considerations of 'practical convenience' (such as case-load and expertise) make public law collateral challenges in the Criminal Court undesirable.[50] On the other hand, it is abhorrent for an invalid act to form the basis of a criminal conviction. The traditional line was drawn on jurisdictional logic, but this too was a casualty of *Anisminic* v. *Foreign Compensation Commission*. In *Bugg* v. *Director of Public Prosecutions*,[51] Lord Woolf CJ attempted to rationalise the void/voidable distinction by linking it to the difference between 'procedural' and 'substantive' defects. A procedurally defective bye-law is valid until set aside, on this view, and must be complied with even by those who regard

49 *Smith* v. *East Elloe Rural District Council* [1956] AC 736, 769.
50 *R* v. *Wicks* [1998] AC 92, 106.
51 [1993] QB 473.

it as defective; if someone contravenes an irregular bye-law before it is revoked, 'he commits an offence and can be punished'.[52] Where the defect is 'substantive', on the other hand, subjects can treat the law as a nullity. 'No citizen is required to comply with a law which is bad on its face. If the citizen is satisfied that that is the situation, he is entitled to ignore the law'.[53] The proposed dichotomy met with academic criticism,[54] and Lord Nicholls expressed doubt about its soundness in *R* v. *Wicks*.[55] *Boddington* v. *British Transport Police*[56] held that collateral challenge was available for *any* defect, as the distinction between 'procedural' and 'substantive' defects was too difficult to maintain in practice. Lord Irvine LC opined that the distinction in *Bugg* v. *Director of Public Prosecutions* was inconsistent with post-*Anisminic* developments, which had 'freed the law from a dependency on technical distinctions between different types of illegality'.[57]

Although it can be difficult to distinguish rules of competence from rules of conduct, there is an analytical difference between them, and therefore between voidness and voidability. Our focus is generally on rules governing *remedies* rather than those governing the legal effect of a decision itself.[58] Granted, an unlawful administrative act stands until a remedy is granted by a competent authority; according to one leading textbook, it is 'hypothetically a nullity' only, whatever that means.[59] The strict logic of validity indeed seems out of touch with the functional role of the supervisory jurisdiction. This truism has been elevated, however, above logical analysis. According to S. A. de Smith, 'the problem of defining the concept of jurisdiction for the purpose of judicial review has been one of public policy rather than one of logic'.[60] In the Australian context, Mark Aronson has described the doctrine of nullity as 'a political

52 *Bugg* v. *DPP* [1993] QB 473, 500.
53 *Bugg* v. *DPP* [1993] QB 473, 500.
54 See David Feldman, 'Collateral Challenge and Judicial Review: The Boundary Dispute Continues' [1993] *Public Law* 37.
55 [1998] AC 92.
56 [1999] 2 AC 143.
57 *Boddington* v. *British Transport Police* [1999] 2 AC 143, 159.
58 J. E. Alder, *Voidness and Voidability in Administrative Law* (BCL Thesis, Durham University 1971), 3.
59 H. W. R. Wade and C. F. Forsyth, *Administrative Law* (7th ed., Oxford University Press 1994), 41; H. W. R. Wade, 'Unlawful Administrative Action: Void or Voidable?' (1967) 83 *Law Quarterly Review* 499.
60 S. A. de Smith, *Judicial Review of Administrative Action* (Stevens 1959), 67; George Sawer, 'Error of Law on the Face of an Administrative Record' (1954) 3 *University of Western Australia Law Review* 24, 34.

tool as much as a legal principle'.[61] While this rightly draws our attention to the context of administrative decisions, doctrine cannot ignore the relationship of validity to the rules that generate and constrain official power.

9.2.6 *The 'Second Actor Theory'*

Reconciling the analytical consequences of jurisdiction with the practical realities of governance has 'long taxed the ingenuity of public lawyers',[62] and a number of solutions have been tabled.[63] Christopher Forsyth has presented the most influential one, the so-called second actor theory. This starts from the premise that unlawful administrative acts are void in law, but 'clearly exist in fact', and often appear to be valid.[64] Forsyth bases his argument on Han's Kelsen's distinction between the worlds of fact and norm – of 'is and ought' or *das Sein* and *das Sollen*:

> [A]n administrative act, the writing of a decision letter in a planning appeal, say, is a fact. The piece of paper on which it is written coupled with the mental processes of the decision-maker that led up to it, are events from the realm of things that are, the *Sein*. But the meaning of that act – that certain development is permitted – is an element of the realm of norms, the *Sollen*. Now a void act – say a decision letter written for an improper purpose – is not an act *in law* but it is and remains an act *in fact* – an event from the *Sein*. And events from the *Sein* often have an effect, *directly or indirectly*, in the realm of the *Sollen*.[65]

We are obviously talking about the creation of institutional facts (the planning decision) from brute facts (documents and human mental processes). Forsyth cites Schiemann LJ's speech in *Percy* v. *Hall*[66] to the effect that even an ultra vires act has an effect on daily life, in the sense that people will have regulated their conduct in light of it. 'Where the

[61] Mark Aronson, 'Nullity' (2004) 40 *Australian Institute of Administrative Law* 19.

[62] T. R. S. Allan, 'Doctrine and Theory in Administrative Law: An Elusive Quest for the Limits of Jurisdiction' [2003] *Public Law* 429, 445.

[63] See David Feldman, 'Error of Law and Flawed Administrative Acts' (2014) 73(2) *Cambridge Law Journal* 275, 280–282.

[64] C. F. Forsyth, '"The Metaphysic of Nullity": Invalidity, Conceptual Reasoning and the Rule of Law' in C. F. Forsyth and Ivan Hare (eds.), *The Golden Metwand and the Crooked Cord* (Oxford University Press 1998), 141.

[65] C. F. Forsyth, '"The Metaphysic of Nullity": Invalidity, Conceptual Reasoning and the Rule of Law' inC. F. Forsyth and Ivan Hare (eds.), *The Golden Metwand and the Crooked Cord* (Oxford University Press 1998), 147. Emphasis mine.

[66] [1996] 4 All ER 523.

conduct has legal consequences, that is effects in the realm of the *Sollen*, those consequences flow from the legally non-existent unlawful act'.[67] Thus an invalid administrative act may, notwithstanding its non-existence, serve as the basis for another, valid, legal act by the second actor: 'Its factual existence, rather than its [legal] invalidity, is the cause of the subsequent act, but that act is valid since the existence of the first act is not a precondition for the second'.[68]

Consider two contrasting examples. *Woolwich Building Society* v. *Inland Revenue Commissioners*[69] concerned the payment of tax where the demand itself was ultra vires. The taxpayer acquired a right in restitution to repayment of the money. '[T]he simple fact that the tax was exacted unlawfully is prima facie enough to require its repayment'.[70] The tax demand was void *ab initio*, yet its factual existence had legal effects: money changed hands, and property in that money passed at private law to HM Revenue and Customs. Forsyth explains this on the basis that 'the taxpayer had the legal power to make payment notwithstanding the unlawfulness of the demand, [and] the legal right to repayment was also a consequence of the invalid demand'.[71]

In *Director of Public Prosecutions* v. *Head*, on the other hand, the validity of the second act (conviction of the accused) depended on the validity of the first act (designation of the victim). The key to understanding these two cases, Forsyth argues, is to focus on the *second actor's* legal powers. The owner of money is competent to transfer it – even in response to an unlawful request of HM Revenue and Customs or a gunman. On the other hand, the Director of Public Prosecutions is not competent to prosecute unless the accused has at least prima facie committed a crime: 'If the validity of the first act is a *jurisdictional*

[67] C. F. Forsyth, '"The Metaphysic of Nullity": Invalidity, Conceptual Reasoning and the Rule of Law' in C. F. Forsyth and Ivan Hare (eds.), *The Golden Metwand and the Crooked Cord* (Oxford University Press 1998), 147.

[68] C. F. Forsyth, '"The Metaphysic of Nullity": Invalidity, Conceptual Reasoning and the Rule of Law' in C. F. Forsyth and Ivan Hare (eds.), *The Golden Metwand and the Crooked Cord* (Oxford University Press 1998), 147.

[69] [1993] AC 70.

[70] *Woolwich Building Society* v. *Inland Revenue Commissioners* [1993] AC 70, 169 (Lord Goff).

[71] C. F. Forsyth, '"The Metaphysic of Nullity": Invalidity, Conceptual Reasoning and the Rule of Law' in C. F. Forsyth and Ivan Hare (eds.), *The Golden Metwand and the Crooked Cord* (Oxford University Press 1998), 148.

requirement for the valid exercise of the second actor's powers, then, if the first act is valid, so is the second'.[72]

This approach removes some difficulties associated with the interim validity of unlawful acts, and Forsyth claims it reconciles the traditional principles of administrative law with the effectiveness of subsequent acts taken in reliance upon unlawful administrative action.[73] The theory has been applied in a number of cases, including *Boddington* v. *British Transport Police*.[74] In effect, it stipulates that where a valid act-in-the-law by Official A is an operative fact on which the competence of Official B rests, A's error will undermine the whole chain of actions and the law must attempt to unravel the consequences insofar as possible. Where B's competence rests on an independent basis, however, this is not the case. A's invalid act-in-the-law may still generate legal consequences, in the same way a tortious or a criminal act triggers legal consequences.

The problem to be solved, however, is less acute if we just accept that there is a difference between acts that are voidable and acts that are void. The former will subsist and generate valid legal consequences until they are quashed or perfected, and the reviewing court will exercise some discretion as to whether interim legal consequences should be unwound or left on foot. A voidable act is valid until revoked, and is always liable to *perfection* by the reviewing court.

In *Director of Public Prosecutions* v. *Head*, Official A's act was a jurisdictional fact on which Official B's competence was predicated. Where A's act is void *ab initio*, on the other hand, B's act simply cannot have any legal basis. Many official decisions serving as operative facts for other another official's jurisdiction are voidable only, and the reviewing court has some discretion. A's *unreasonable* designation of the victim as a 'mental defective', for example, could be quashed *or* perfected, and the latter would create a valid operational fact on which B's competence is based. The question is whether, in the face of a collateral challenge, it is appropriate to let a faulty designation stand because the Director of

[72] C. F. Forsyth, '"The Metaphysic of Nullity": Invalidity, Conceptual Reasoning and the Rule of Law' in C. F. Forsyth and Ivan Hare (eds.), *The Golden Metwand and the Crooked Cord* (Oxford University Press 1998), 148. Emphasis mine.

[73] C. F. Forsyth, 'The Legal Effect of Unlawful Administrative Acts: The Theory of the Second Actor Explained and Developed' (2001) 35 *Amicus Curiae* 20, 21.

[74] C. F. Forsyth, 'The Legal Effect of Unlawful Administrative Acts: The Theory of the Second Actor Explained and Developed' (2001) 35 *Amicus Curiae* 20, 22; see also *R (London)* v. *Central London County Court* [1993] 3 WLR 1, *R (Evans)* v. *Governor of Blockhill Prison* [2000] 3 WLR 483.

Public Prosecutions has acted conscientiously, or because practical justice demands it in the circumstances.

Forsyth's theory seems to go further, however, claiming that a void act can have some valid legal consequences per se. David Feldman has certainly argued that that the 'interim validity' of an ultra vires act is to be determined by reference to normative and pragmatic, rather than logical, reasons:

> [T]he propositions that any error of law, broadly defined, makes a decision or rule ultra vires its maker, and that an ultra vires decision or rule is incapable of having any legal effect, are not logically linked. Saying that a decision is ultra vires does not determine the effectiveness of the decision. That calls for a separate, normative judgment: is the error sufficiently significant to merit treating the decision as wholly ineffective? If any error makes a decision ultra vires, it is likely that many of them will not have a sufficiently serious impact on those subject to the decision to merit being treated as entirely ineffective.[75]

To the extent that an invalid act-in-the-law is still an act-in-fact, and that acts-in-fact (such as torts and crimes) have legal consequences, this is trite. Beyond that, it is a bridge too far. The correct proposition is similar, but more nuanced. It is that social reliance on the *content* of an invalid act-in-the-law can be such that this content ought to be 'salvaged' by a competent authority. In effect, a legal judgment declaring an administrative act void *ab initio* confirms that the act has never existed and cannot have had legal consequences. Interim *belief* in the validity of the administrative act, however, may have elicited social conduct in reliance on its existence; in appropriate cases, the reviewing court could supplement the invalid administrative act with a retroactive declaration granting it some measure of validity from the time of its occurrence until the time of the judgment.[76] In such a case, however, it is the supplementary judgment of the court and not the invalid act itself that generates legal consequences. In any case, I do not think that such 'metaphysical' difficulties really compel the courts to treat an excess of competence and a breach of conduct as identical.

9.3 Fact, Law, and Jurisdiction

Temporal chains of 'operative facts' show that a major issue in the law of judicial review is the very relationship between facts, law, and jurisdiction.

[75] David Feldman, 'Error of Law and Flawed Administrative Acts' (2014) 73(2) *Cambridge Law Journal* 275, 312.

[76] D. W. P. Ruiter, *Legal Institutions* (Kluwer 2010), 166.

When the role of officials in interpreting and applying law to facts is understood, the concept of jurisdiction appears as a necessary category in the judicial supervision of officials. The modern approach, we have seen, is to treat all errors of law as 'jurisdictional', leaving only factual errors within an official's 'privilege to err'.[77] But the distinction between 'fact' and 'law' is slippery. Indeed, whatever the intricacies of jurisdictional logic, equally serious problems beset the error of law approach.[78]

9.3.1 *The Instability of 'Fact versus Law'*

Legal reasoning involves the application of 'mixed syllogisms' – propositions containing both empirical and legal premises that entail legal consequences. For example, the existence of a parking offence requires not only a (valid) rule designating where I may and may not park, but also the fact that I have parked in a prohibited space. It will generally (perhaps always) fall to some official to determine whether the relevant facts obtained at the relevant time to violate the legal rule. A court of supervisory jurisdiction, as opposed to an appellate court, generally accepts the official's fact-finding and does not substitute its own view.[79] This explains the conventional border between 'review' and 'appeal', but the complex nature of 'operative facts' – facts which trigger a rule and thereby entail legal consequences – and the need to rely on officials to determine the existence of facts make the border dynamic.

Questions of law 'grow down into roots of fact'; only a policy decision can determine where the line is ultimately drawn.[80] The division is 'often impossible to make without undue artificiality', which should not be surprising in a system of common law adjudication in which propositions of law are developed incrementally through decisions in particular cases.[81] Error of law is thus open to *a posteriori* decisions that an error should be one of 'law' because it is desirable for the court to interfere.[82]

[77] Amnon Rubinstein, *Jurisdiction and Illegality* (Clarendon Press 1965), 18–19; *Peat's Case* (1704) 6 Mod 228; *Anisminic* v. *Foreign Compensation Commission* [1969] 2 AC 147, 171 (Lord Reid).

[78] See Jack Beatson, 'Judicial Review for Error of Law' (1984) 4 *Oxford Journal of Legal Studies* 22, 30.

[79] See, for example, *Adan* v. *Newnham London Borough Council* [2001] EWCA Civ 916.

[80] John Dickinson, *Administrative Justice and the Supremacy of the Law in the United States* (Harvard University Press 1927), 55.

[81] Jack Beatson, 'Judicial Review for Error of Law' (1984) 4 *Oxford Journal of Legal Studies* 22, 40.

[82] T. A. O. Endicott, 'Questions of Law' (1998) 114 *Law Quarterly Review* 292, 307.

Indeed, the courts have taken radically different approaches to characterisation.[83] T. R. S. Allan argues that there is 'no analytic method' for distinguishing 'meaning and interpretation' from 'mere application'.[84] While questions of policy have their place within the law of judicial review, however, it is essential that judges exercise whatever policy discretion they have to exercise within clearly defined parameters.

The weakness of the modern orthodoxy is evident, argues Allan, in the fact that the decision establishing it actually declined to apply it.[85] The House of Lords in *R (Page)* v. *Hull University Visitor* opted for an anachronistic view of the University Visitor's jurisdiction – a *forum domesticum* based on the *dominium* of its founder not amenable to judicial review for error of law (i.e., misconstruction of the governing statutes).[86] Confusingly, however, Lord Browne-Wilkinson retreated from the logical implications of his view: 'Judicial review does lie to the visitor in cases where he has acted outside his jurisdiction (in the narrow sense) or abused his powers or acted in breach of the rules of natural justice'.[87]

9.3.2 Facts and Norms

The basic form of a legal rule stipulates that, if a certain factual state of affairs exists, a certain legal consequence follows.[88] The application of a legal provision, and therefore the review of another's application of that legal provision, always encompasses questions law *and* fact. Legal judgments, including those made in the course of administrative application of law, involve the subsumption of given facts under norms.[89] Questions of norm application are like questions of fact because they are particular,

[83] Jack Beatson, 'Judicial Review for Error of Law' (1984) 4 *Oxford Journal of Legal Studies* 22, 30–31, citing J. M. Evans (ed.), *De Smith's Judicial Review of Administrative Action* (4th ed., Sweet & Maxwell 1980), 134. Cf L. L. Jaffé, 'Judicial Review: Constitutional and Jurisdictional Fact' (1957) 70(6) *Harvard Law Review* 953.

[84] T. R. S. Allan, 'Doctrine and Theory in Administrative Law' [2003] *Public Law* 429, 444.

[85] T. R. S. Allan, 'Doctrine and Theory in Administrative Law' [2003] *Public Law* 429, 443.

[86] See *Green* v. *Rutherford* (1750) 1 Ves Sen 462, 472 (Hardwicke LC); J. W. Bridge, 'Keeping Peace in the Universities: The Role of the University Visitor' (1970) 86 *Law Quarterly Review* 531.

[87] *R (Page)* v. *Lord President of the Privy Council* [1993] AC 682, 708.

[88] See W. A. Wilson, 'A Note on Fact and Law' (1963) 26(6) *Modern Law Review* 609. The ancient Code of Hammurabi, for example, is a list of if/then provisions expressing a causal relation between an event 'in the world' and a state of affairs 'at law'.

[89] Hans Kelsen, 'Law and Logic' in Hans Kelsen (Peter Heath (trans.), *Essays in Legal and Moral Philosophy* (Reidel 1973), 246; S. L. Paulson, 'Subsumption, Derogation, and

where paradigm questions of law are general; on the other hand, they are like questions of law because they have legal consequences.[90] Judicial review combines *ex post* revision with *a priori* analytical categories: 'the decision-maker with power to bind on questions of law makes its decision *after* the other decision-maker has already given a decision'.[91] The tension inherent within a system of institutional second-guessing explains some of the law's intractability.

H. L. A. Hart's famous example of 'No vehicles in the park'[92] is typical of subordinated legislation. It is a question of 'fact' whether I have a vehicle in the park when riding a skateboard, driving an ambulance, or flying a drone. But whoever has to apply this rule must define a 'vehicle', and thereby define a *legal category* that entails propositions such as 'All skateboards are vehicles', or 'No skateboards are vehicles'.[93] Every act of norm application is an act of norm-creation at the relevant level of a hierarchically structured normative order.[94] The validity of every 'norm-as-applied' is determined by reference to a (higher-level) norm conferring competence on, say, a Park Warden. Ultimately, a rule must grant someone competence to have the final say, or to designate the one who does.

This renders the fact/law distinction radically unstable, which destabilises the distinction between review and appeal. Virtually any question can be cast as a 'question of law', and under the modern approach all errors of law are 'jurisdictional'. A judge wishing to review the Park Warden's decision will hold that the latter has made an error of law by defining a skateboard as a vehicle. A judge wishing to avoid review, on the other hand, will cast the matter as an error of fact – if the Park Warden went wrong at all, it was only in the application of the term 'vehicle' to the facts in front of him.[95] The judge must choose an approach, and her choice must be guided by extra-legal considerations.

Noncontradiction in "Legal Science"' (1981) 48(3) *University of Chicago Law Review* 802, 806.

[90] T. A. O. Endicott, 'Questions of Law' (1998) 114 *Law Quarterly Review* 292, 312, 318.

[91] T. A. O. Endicott, 'Questions of Law' (1998) 114 *Law Quarterly Review* 292, 296.

[92] H. L. A. Hart, *The Concept of Law* (Oxford University Press 1961), 123–126.

[93] W. A. Wilson, 'A Note of Fact and Law' (1963) 26(6) *Modern Law Review* 609, 614.

[94] See S. L. Paulson, 'How Merkl's *Stufenbaulehre* Informs Kelsen's Concept of Law' (2013) 21 *Revus* 29.

[95] Rebecca Williams, 'When is an Error not an Error? Reform of Jurisdictional Review Error of Law and Fact' [2007] *Public Law* 793, 793–794.

9.3.3 *Primary and Secondary Facts*

The malleability of the fact/law distinction means that the supervisory jurisdiction is inherently at risk of turning into an open-ended appellate jurisdiction that eclipses administrative decision-makers' proper competence. So much becomes apparent when we consider the different types of fact that fall to be determined when applying the law.

The application of some legal definitions is clear-cut, as some facts are readily apprehended and proved. The Dangerous Dogs Act 1995, for example, criminalises the possession of a 'dog of the type known as a pit bull terrier' in public without a muzzle. That a given dog is 'in public without a muzzle' requires evidence of 'primary facts'. Questions of 'law' thereby arise, relating to the adequacy of evidence to support the finding.[96] But subsumption of a given dog under this definition also requires inferences to be made on the evidence, and we might call these inferences 'secondary facts'.[97] The definition 'dog of the type known as a pit bull terrier'[98] is an inherently vague category that involves the application of both rules and canons of interpretation.[99] For example, do we take 'type' to refer to 'genotype or phenotype'? (A pit bull/Rottweiler cross is a different dog to a pit bull/whippet cross).

There are two possible approaches to secondary facts.[100] The 'analytic' approach characterises *every* inference drawn from a primary fact as a question of law. This approach is conceptually appealing; however, because most cases involve some secondary facts, when combined with the rule that all errors of law are jurisdictional, it eliminates administrative autonomy entirely.[101] The 'pragmatic' approach, on the other hand, accepts a 'zone of reasonable conclusions' from a given premise. Within this zone an inference is a 'matter of degree'; inferences that stray outside the pale of what is reasonable become, *ipso facto*, questions of law.[102]

96 *British Launderer's Association* v. *Borough of Hendon Rating Authority* [1949] 1 KB 462.
97 W. A. Wilson, 'A Note of Fact and Law' (1963) 26(6) *Modern Law Review* 609, 614–616.
98 See Dangerous Dogs Act 1991, s. 1(1); *R* v. *Cichon* [1994] Crim LR 918.
99 T. A. O. Endicott, 'Questions of Law' (1998) 114 *Law Quarterly Review* 292, 293.
100 See L. L. Jaffe, *Judicial Control of Administrative Action* (Little, Brown 1965), 546; Etienne Murenick, 'The Application of Rules: Law or Fact?' (1982) 98 *Law Quarterly Review* 587; *Farmer* v. *Cotton's Trustees* [1925] AC 922, 932.
101 Jack Beatson, 'Judicial Review for Error of Law' (1984) 4 *Oxford Journal of Legal Studies* 22, 41.
102 *Edwards* v. *Bairstow* [1956] AC 14, 36 (Lord Radcliffe); *Moyna* v. *Work and Pensions Secretary* [2003] 1 WLR 1929.

The consensus among both scholars and judges has settled on the pragmatic approach.[103] However, as Jack Beatson has argued, that approach implicitly denies that analytical considerations are a useful step in judicial reasoning. Judicial reasoning embraces both analytic and practical reasoning. The former does not exhaust the latter, and should not purport to; however, the robust application of logic is a useful step in reaching a practical conclusion, which may well embrace more functional or pragmatic considerations. Further, the fact/law distinction purports to distribute power between administrative and judicial officials. Abandonment of analytical reasoning undermines the rule of law as the rule of reason rather than the will of individual officials. Moreover, the pragmatic approach amplifies rather than obviates the need for a jurisdictional concept.

In my view, what the pragmatic approach effectively does is set a perimeter around the decision-maker's privilege to err – a liberty-space drawn by reference to rules of conduct.[104] To determine what that rule circumscribes, however, it first is necessary to determine the official's ability-space. *R (South Yorkshire Transport)* v. *Monopolies and Mergers Commission*[105] provides an illustration. A company sought review of a Commissioner's decision on the basis that the Commission was only empowered to investigate mergers affecting a 'substantial part' of the United Kingdom. Lord Mustill recognised that some criteria may be so imprecise that different decision-makers, all acting rationally, may disagree. A court is only entitled to substitute its own opinion for that of the person entrusted with making a decision if that decision is 'so aberrant that it cannot be classed as rational'.[106] There was no ground for interference because Commission's conclusion was 'well within the permissible field of judgment'.[107] Questions of fact boil down to questions of competence, whichever approach is taken. The court enforces rules of conduct that circumscribe the primary decision-maker's privilege to err within her sphere of competence.

Simply put, without the category of jurisdiction, judicial review faces yet another dilemma. Either judges eclipse executive officials' judgment

[103] T. A. O. Endicott, 'Questions of Law' (1998) 114 *Law Quarterly Review* 292, 308.

[104] T. A. O. Endicott, 'Questions of Law' (1998) 114 *Law Quarterly Review* 292, 308.

[105] [1993] 1 WLR 23.

[106] *R (South Yorkshire Transport)* v. *Monopolies and Mergers Commission* [1993] 1 WLR 23, 32–33.

[107] *R (South Yorkshire Transport)* v. *Monopolies and Mergers Commission* [1993] 1 WLR 23, 32–33.

or they set the bounds of their supervisory jurisdiction by reference to tacit, non-legal considerations. While the 'mixed toolbox'[108] actually used by judges usually achieves a tolerable result, the law should strive for conceptual coherence. In my view, characterising a question as one of 'fact' or 'law' is only significant *because* it determines the jurisdictional question – jurisdiction continues doing the heavy lifting out of sight. In the case of secondary facts, rules of competence stipulate who is to draw the relevant inferences, and rules of conduct then regulate that process. The integrity, reasonableness, and procedural propriety of the competent official is scrutinised by the courts, but, if she has exercised her competence properly, she is just as competent to make a wrong decision as a right one.

9.3.4 *Review and Appeal*

The traditional rule that appeal, but not review, is available for a superior court's error of law is hard to reconcile with the idea that every error of law is 'jurisdictional'. *Re Racal Communications* concerned the statutory jurisdiction of the Court of Appeal. Even while conflating error of law with jurisdictional error, Lord Diplock drew a distinction between statutory jurisdiction conferred on a 'court of law of limited jurisdiction to decide a defined question finally' and such a jurisdiction conferred on the High Court.[109] Where the words of the statute are silent, there is no basis on which to read in the intention to limit the jurisdiction of a court of unlimited jurisdiction; it is presumed empowered to 'construe the words of the statute by which the question submitted to [its] decision was defined'.[110] This left no room for error going to jurisdiction, and therefore no room for judicial review:[111]

> Judicial review is available as a remedy for mistakes of law made by inferior courts and tribunals only. Mistakes of law made by judges of the High Court acting in their capacity as such can be corrected only by means of appeal to an appellate court; and if, as in the instant case, the statute provides that the judge's decision shall not be appealable, they cannot be corrected at all.[112]

[108] T. A. O. Endicott, 'Questions of Law' (1998) 114 *Law Quarterly Review* 292, 297.
[109] *Re Racal Communications Ltd* [1981] AC 374, 384.
[110] *Re Racal Communications Ltd* [1981] AC 374, 384 (Lord Diplock).
[111] *Re Racal Communications Ltd* [1981] AC 374, 384 (Lord Diplock).
[112] *Re Racal Communications Ltd* [1981] AC 374, 384 (Lord Diplock).

Lord Diplock acknowledged the problem that, where a statute makes the decision of an inferior court final and conclusive, 'this may involve the survival of those subtle distinctions formerly drawn between errors of law which go to jurisdiction and errors of law which do not that did so much to confuse English administrative law before *Anisminic*'.[113]

The English law of judicial review, as it applies to the relationship between administrative tribunals and the courts, has evolved considerably in recent years. *R (Cart)* v. *Upper Tribunal*[114] is the leading case following the Tribunals, Courts and Enforcement Act 2007, which restructured the tribunal system into a First Tier Tribunal and Upper Tribunal. These tribunals were given more 'judicial' features, such that it became arguable to see the tribunals as a species of, not a substitute for, a court.[115] In *R (Cart)* v. *Upper Tribunal*, it was argued that the legislative designation of the Upper Tribunal as a 'superior court of record' rendered it, too, immune to the prerogative writs. In the words of Lady Hale, that argument was demolished by Laws LJ in the Divisional Court.[116]

True, *certiorari* would not run to correct errors of law made by the High Court. However, this was not because it was a 'superior court of record', but because it was a 'court of unlimited jurisdiction'.[117] The weight of learning pointed to excess of jurisdiction as the 'overriding foundation for the issue of the prerogative writs'.[118] Implicit in all the relevant authorities was that the jurisdiction of the 'subject courts' is limited, the '[edge] kept sharp by the prerogative writs'.[119] The King's Bench, on the other hand, was a court of unlimited jurisdiction and therefore was subject to appeal, not supervision.[120] Another court might be designated as a court of unlimited jurisdiction, becoming an *alter ego* of the High Court, with the consequence that it 'possesses the final power to interpret for itself the law it must apply' without the possibility of review for excess of jurisdiction.[121] This implied a conventional distinction between jurisdictional and non-jurisdictional errors – the first 'denot[ing] the case where a court travels

113 *Re Racal Communications Ltd* [1981] AC 374, 384 (Lord Diplock).

114 [2010] 2 WLR 1012 (Divisional Court); [2011] QB 120 (Court of Appeal); [2012] 1 AC 663 (Supreme Court).

115 Peter Cane, *Administrative Tribunals and Adjudication* (Oxford University Press 2010), 72.

116 *R (Cart)* v. *Upper Tribunal* [2012] 1 AC 663, 680.

117 *R (Cart)* v. *Upper Tribunal* [2012] 1 AC 663, 680.

118 *R (Cart)* v. *Upper Tribunal* [2010] 2 WLR 1012, 1036.

119 *R (Cart)* v. *Upper Tribunal* [2010] 2 WLR 1012, 1036.

120 *R (Cart)* v. *Upper Tribunal* [2010] 2 WLR 1012, 1036.

121 *R (Cart)* v. *Upper Tribunal* [2010] 2 WLR 1012, 1036.

into territory where it has no business [and the second denoting] the case where, acting within the field ascribed to it, the court gets the law wrong'.[122] Noting the complexities of applying *Anisminic* v. *Foreign Compensation Commission* to courts, Laws LJ held that while most tribunals would not qualify as *alter egos* of the High Court, the Upper Tribunal, all things considered, did.[123] Thus, while most tribunals are subject to both limbs of the ultra vires rule, the Upper Tribunal was only subject to the narrow limb (and that, apparently, in extraordinary cases only).[124]

A similar result was reached by the Court of Appeal, albeit for slightly different reasons. Sedley LJ effectively revived the old approach, holding that 'a true jurisprudential difference' exists between an error of law made in the course of an adjudication which a tribunal is authorised to conduct and the error of conducting an adjudication without lawful authority.[125] Judicial review against a finding of the Upper Tribunal should be available, where appropriate, on the 'ground of jurisdictional error in the narrow, pre-*Anisminic* sense, or procedural irregularity of such a kind as to constitute denial of the applicant's right to a fair hearing',[126] despite its designation as a superior court of record.

The Supreme Court did not endorse this approach. Instead, it emphasised the overriding need to ensure the rule of law – that is, to ensure that those exercising public authority remain within the proper bounds of their competence and exercise that competence properly. The 'rule of law', rather than jurisdictional logic, drives the judgment of the Supreme Court given by Lady Hale, and characterises the current English law on the reviewability of tribunal decisions.

According to Mark Elliott and Robert Thomas, once the amenability of tribunal decisions to the supervisory jurisdiction is accepted, there is a need to 'throttle' judicial review in order to maintain the operation of a tribunal system that runs, in parallel to the ordinary courts, to deliver a more efficient and efficacious system of adjudication. The doctrinal form of restriction suggested by the Court of Appeal was clear – the pre-*Anisminic* concept of jurisdictional error. In the Supreme Court, Lady Hale and Lord Dyson (who addressed this point most directly)

122 [2010] 2 WLR 1012, [78] (Laws LJ).
123 [2010] 2 WLR 1012, [94] (Laws LJ).
124 [2010] 2 WLR 1012, [99] (Laws LJ).
125 *R (Cart)* v. *Upper Tribunal* [2011] 2 WLR 36, [36].
126 *R (Cart)* v. *Upper Tribunal* [2011] 2 WLR 36, [4].

were both resistant to the idea of reintroducing the distinction between jurisdictional and non-jurisdictional errors of law.[127] Lady Hale opined that jurisdictional error would involve a 'return to some of the technicalities of the past' and Lord Dyson opined that it would be incompatible with the rule of law by insulating serious, but non-jurisdictional, errors of law from review.[128] On this analysis, the Upper Tribunal is not authorised to determine questions of law conclusively – it is capable of committing 'jurisdictional errors of law' like other statutory bodies. But this means that the decision to grant or deny judicial review no longer follows from the 'lawfulness' or 'unlawfulness' of the Upper Tribunal's action. The Supreme Court's analysis makes it inevitable that situations will arise in which the Upper Tribunal commits jurisdictional errors of law that cannot be challenged on either review or appeal. The Supreme Court judgment presents a 'post-jurisdictional view of administrative law' in which analysis of vires is secondary to criteria of 'proportionate dispute resolution' that limit the availability of review but do not rest on the body's legal competence. Judicial review is based on pragmatic assessment rather than any conventional doctrinal analysis.

The criteria considered in *R (Cart)* v. *Upper Tribunal* included judicial resources and tribunal expertise, informed by the overriding imperative to protect the rule of law. However, such criteria are just reasons for the Supreme Court to recognise the Upper Tribunal's competence to determine matters of law within its remit. The 'functional' considerations that drive the organisation of officials, tribunals, and courts into a system are, in fact, just reasons to recognise the material competence of one decision-maker over another.[129] These reasons inform, but do not displace, the logic of jurisdiction on which the organisation of administration is premised. There may be a number of reasonable answers from which an administrative official or lower tribunal can be left to choose. The first, narrowly jurisdictional limb of ultra vires is therefore supplemented by review of the exercise of discretion under the second, broader limb. When we reject jurisdictional error as the boundary marker of legitimate judicial interference, however, we abandon any stable division between

[127] Mark Elliott and Robert Thomas, 'Tribunal Justice and Proportional Dispute Resolution' (2012) 71(2) *Cambridge Law Journal* 297, 309.

[128] See *R (Cart)* v. *Upper Tribunal* [2011] UKSC 28, [40] (Lady Hale), [110] (Lord Dyson).

[129] T. R. S. Allan, 'Doctrine and Theory in Administrative Law' [2003] *Public Law* 429, 444; Paul Craig, 'Judicial Review and Questions of Law: A Comparative Perspective' in Susan Rose-Ackerman and P. L. Lindseth (eds.), *Comparative Administrative Law* (Edward Elgar 2010).

review and appeal.[130] Although we should not overstate *Cart's* departure from the conventional law,[131] this is a concerning development.

R (Privacy International) v. *Investigatory Powers Tribunal*[132] has entrenched English law in this rut. The leading judgment given by Lord Carnwath – one of the architects of the modern tribunals system, and a long-standing advocate of that system existing in a 'non-hierarchical' relationship with the ordinary courts[133] – provides a candid analysis of the concept of jurisdiction following *Anisminic* v. *Foreign Compensation Commission*, but also doubles down on outcomes-driven reasoning. The upshot is effectively that judicial review does whatever is necessary to balance the rule of law with the need to give effect to the expressed intention of Parliament. The direction of travel set by *R (Cart)* v. *Upper Tribunal*, he said, is 'both pragmatic and principled', and rests on the assertion that it is 'for the courts, not the legislature, to determine the limits set by the rule of law to the power to exclude judicial review'.[134] Again, we can see the importance of ouster clauses in the abandonment of jurisdictional logic in order to maintain the common law powers of the courts without openly challenging the sovereignty of Parliament:

> This proposition should be seen as based, not on such elusive concepts as jurisdiction (wide or narrow), *ultra vires*, or nullity, but rather as a *natural application of the constitutional principle of the rule of law . . . and as an essential counterpart to the power of Parliament to make law*. The constitutional roles both of Parliament, as the maker of the law, and of the High Court, and ultimately of the appellate courts, as the guardians and interpreters of that law, are thus respected. The question in any case is 'the level of scrutiny required by the rule of law', set on a basis which as stated in *Cart* is both 'principled and proportionate', [or] 'what scope of judicial review . . . is required to maintain the rule of law'; it being 'a matter for the courts to determine what that scrutiny should be'.[135]

130 T. R. S. Allan, 'Doctrine and Theory in Administrative Law' [2003] *Public Law* 429, 440.

131 See Joanna Bell, 'Rethinking the Story of *Cart v Upper Tribunal* and its Implications for Administrative Law' (2019) 39(1) *Oxford Journal of Legal Studies* 74.

132 [2019] UKSC 22.

133 See Robert Carnwath, 'Tribunal Justice – A New Start' [2009] *Public Law* 48.

134 *R (Privacy International)* v. *Investigative Powers Tribunal* [2019] UKSC 22, [131]–[132] (Lord Carnwath), citing *R (Cart)* v. *Upper Tribunal* [2011] UKSC 28, [51] (Lady Hale), [102] (Lord Clarke], [133] (Lord Dyson).

135 *R (Privacy International)* v. *Investigative Powers Tribunal* [2019] UKSC 22, [131]–[132] (Lord Carnwath), citing *R (Cart)* v. *Upper Tribunal* [2011] UKSC 28, [51] (Lady Hale), [102] (Lord Clarke], [133] (Lord Dyson). Emphasis mine.

This tendency to consider the interaction of constitutional principles – the rule of law and legislative supremacy – to the exclusion of conceptual reasoning is characteristic of most recent Supreme Court jurisprudence. I shall return to the relation between the concepts of office, jurisdiction, and the rule of law in Chapter 12. For now, it suffices to say that the concept of official competence is less 'elusive' than the rule of law or even, indeed, the sovereignty of Parliament.

9.3.5 *Operative Facts and Legal Consequences*

It is now necessary to set out the true relationship between fact, law, and jurisdiction. The starting point is that *operative facts trigger legal consequences*. As *Director of Public Prosecutions* v. *Head* shows, legal consequences *themselves* often comprise a class of operative facts from which *further* legal consequences follow. We can identify three categories of operative facts with the aid of three rules, which will help to structure analysis:[136]

(i) Ships shall not sail out of the Harbour at low tide;
(ii) Management of the Harbour and enforcement of the bye-laws shall be undertaken by the Harbour Master;
(iii) Harbour users shall berth vessels at such part of the Harbour as the Harbour Master directs.

As D. W. P. Ruiter explains, rule (i) entails a *prohibition* on sailing at low tide; rule (ii) entails legal *powers and permissions* vesting in the person occupying the office of Harbour Master from time to time; and rule (iii) entails an *obligation* incumbent on users of the Harbour to follow the commands of the Harbour Master. These rules will, in their application, reduce to a proposition regarding the Harbour Master's *Spielraum vis-à-vis* any user of the Harbour, for example, that 'The Harbour Master *can* and *may* impound a Member's vessel for non-payment of harbour dues'.

The operative facts that trigger these legal consequences belong to three separate domains. 'Low tide' belongs to the domain of physical reality; X's appointment as Harbour Master belongs to the domain of institutional legal reality; a (valid) 'command' by the Harbour Master belongs to the domain of valid acts-in-the-law, which is a sub-domain of

[136] Adapted from D. W. P. Ruiter, *Legal Institutions* (Kluwer 2010), 65.

institutional legal reality.[137] These relate, in turn, to three different types of rules. 'External rules' project a juridico-causal relation between a category of physical facts and a category of institutional legal facts. By stipulating that an event in physical reality (a change in the tide) causes a change in institutional legal reality (the activation of a prohibition on sailing out), external rules enable the law to respond to changes in the environment and endow those changes with legal meaning. 'Internal rules' project a relation between one category of institutional legal facts and another category of institutional legal facts. For example, a rule stipulating that member voting rights are suspended for breach of the byelaws allows a rule-system to be changed in response to other changes within the system itself. 'Power-conferring rules' project a relation between a category of acts-in-the-law and the validity of their purported effects, that is, stipulating that an act of type X is to have effects in the nature of new or altered institutional legal facts. These rules allow the system itself to be changed by official organs.[138]

External rules, however, are not self-executing; they must be interpreted and applied by officials. The low tide prohibition requires an official to decide what counts as a 'ship', when 'low tide' begins and ends, and when a ship is 'sailing out'. Crucially, the brute fact of low tide, which depends on the interplay of the earth, the moon, and the ocean, is not operative; the operative fact is the Harbour Master's *judgment* that it is low tide at a given time. Facts absolute cannot be operative facts, as there is no way for legal institutions to take cognisance of them except through the eyes and ears of the Harbour Master. Reviewing the Harbour Master's finding in a higher instance simply shifts the ultimate competence to make the finding of fact. It would be 'unworkable' for the binding effect of a judgment to depend on its agreement with 'facts in the absolute'; we would have to resort to a second tribunal, and 'fallibility is inherent in the fact-finding machinery of all tribunals'.[139] The result would be an infinite regress of instances – paradoxically, each more attenuated to the facts in the Harbour. A determination of a state of affairs is always, ultimately, a matter of official competence properly exercised. This brings us back to *Spielraum* set by rules of competence ringed about by rules of conduct.

137 D. W. P. Ruiter, *Legal Institutions* (Kluwer 2010), 65.

138 D. W. P. Ruiter, *Legal Institutions* (Kluwer 2010), 66.

139 D. M. Gordon, 'The Relation of Facts to Jurisdiction' (1929) 45 *Law Quarterly Review* 459, 460–461.

9.4 Facts, Discretion, and Rights

Executive officials are generally entrusted to make final determinations of fact. As the supervisory jurisdiction is concerned with review, not appeal, prima facie the reviewing court should not be concerned with the rightness or wrongness of fact determinations. But the interaction of decision-making *powers* and the *duties* of good administration is complex.[140] Traditionally, the powers engaged in the application of law to facts were categorised as falling into three kinds: 'discretionary', 'judicial', and 'ministerial'. 'Ministerial' powers were said to involve such a straightforward process of reasoning that the repository of power bears a legally enforceable duty to arrive at the one and only correct solution. 'Judicial' powers were said to involve the application of ascertainable legal rules, which direct the official to an 'objectively correct solution'; however, the rules being capable of various reasonable interpretations, she could arrive at other solutions without error. Discretionary powers were said to open up a range of alternatives to the repository of the power, none of which could be said to be objectively correct or incorrect.[141] On this view, the characterisation of the powers concerned determines the scope of judicial review:

> A ministerial function may be said to dictate the 'one and only' course of action; any but the envisaged act may be considered to be null and void. On the other hand, any grant of judicial or discretionary power embodies, by definition, a sphere in which more than one course of action is available. Within this sphere, termed 'jurisdiction', the responsible organ must be free to adopt a course of action considered erroneous by other organs, including the higher courts, without affecting the validity of the resulting acts.[142]

This 'scope of review' approach is unpopular, but it provides essential structure and keeps the reviewing judge's mind clearly on the kind of supervision she is actually imposing on the official. Each type of power involves a different class of operative facts, and implies a different relationship between the official and the court. Where the operative fact is that it is low tide, for example, the court makes its *own* determination as to the state of affairs the harbour – in this case, the Harbour Master's power is 'ministerial', and review substantially merges with appeal.

[140] See J. W. Harris, 'Trust, Power, and Duty' (1971) 87 *Law Quarterly Review* 31, 47.

[141] Amnon Rubinstein, *Jurisdiction and Illegality* (Clarendon Press 1965), 16.

[142] Amnon Rubinstein, *Jurisdiction and Illegality* (Clarendon Press 1965), 18.

A classical illustration is *Al-Khawaja* v. *Home Secretary*,[143] which concerned findings of fact by an immigration official. Lord Scarman noted 'real difficulties' with the proposition[144] that such decisions were reviewable only on the ground of *Wednesdbury* unreasonableness, preferring the view that 'where the exercise of executive power depends on the precedent establishment of an objective fact, the courts will decide whether the requirement has been satisfied'.[145]

Where the Harbour Master is given a power to permit sailing out at low tide *for cause*, on the other hand, the existence of an adequate reason is crucial. A power to derogate from a general prohibition *causaliter* is a discretionary power, and here the Harbour Master's opinion (that a reason was 'adequate') is the operative fact. In effect, discretionary powers 'lay a trust' upon the person deemed most capable of determining how his powers should be used.[146] The court respects the Harbour Master's jurisdiction – but ensures that he respects the rules of conduct that govern it. Most repositories of fact-finding power hold some judicial or discretionary power. Most errors in fact-finding, unless going to a fact by which the official's competence itself is triggered, are within her ability space and prima facie valid.

There is still scope for judicial supervision, of course. In *R (Inner London Education Authority)* v. *London Residuary Body*,[147] Buxton LJ held that a mistake of fact could be corrected by the judges where the fact was a condition precedent to the decision-maker's competence, but also where it was the only evidential basis for a decision, or where it related to a matter than had to be taken into account in exercising the relevant power.[148] The first test goes to jurisdiction, the narrow limb of ultra vires; the second and third catch a competence exercised badly, the second limb of ultra vires.

9.4.1 *An Expanded Test of Factual Error?*

The scope of factual errors leading to invalidity has also expanded in the modern cases. In *Secretary of State for Education and Science* v. *Tameside*

143 [1984] AC 74.
144 See *Zamir* v. *Home Secretary* [1980] AC 930.
145 *Al-Khawaja* v. *Home Secretary* [1984] AC 74, [61] (Lord Scarman).
146 Amnon Rubinstein, *Jurisdiction and Illegality* (Clarendon Press 1965), 18.
147 *The Times*, 24 July 1987.
148 Paul Craig, 'Judicial Review, Appeal and Factual Error' [2004] *Public Law* 788, 790.

MBC,[149] Scarman LJ held that misunderstanding or ignorance of an 'established and relevant fact' could be reviewable, suggesting a standard of rationality or reasonableness.[150] In *R (A)* v. *Criminal Injuries Compensation Board*,[151] Lord Slynn held that failure to take into account relevant factual evidence was a reviewable error, and proposed that a 'wrong factual basis' or 'mistaken fact' doctrine could be absorbed into the traditional grounds of review, suggesting a jurisdiction to quash for 'material error of fact'.[152] In *Begum* v. *Tower Hamlets London Borough Council*,[153] Lord Millet held that a decision could be quashed if it was 'based on a finding of fact or inference from the facts which is perverse or irrational; or there was no evidence to support it; or it was made by reference to irrelevant factors or without regard to relevant factors'.[154] This was said to be independent of any 'specific error of law', based on the court's inference that the decision-maker 'misunderstood or overlooked relevant evidence or misdirected itself in law'.[155]

These developments further destabilise the fact/law dichotomy, demonstrating the lack of an underlying principled approach.[156] In *E* v. *Home Secretary*,[157] Carnwath LJ effectively held that a mistake of fact giving rise to unfairness was a separate head of challenge in an appeal on a point of law.[158] *E* v. *Home Secretary* concerned an operative fact of Ruiter's second type – a prima facie competent determination by a statutory tribunal. The question on appeal was whether the Tribunal had erred by excluding evidence relevant to the question whether E faced danger if returned to Egypt. Following Lord Slynn's approach in *R (A)* v. *Criminal Injuries Compensation Board*, the authorities on factual error were posited as a separate ground of review based on unfairness.[159] This

149 [1977] AC 1012.

150 *Secretary of State for Science and Education* v. *Tameside MBC* [1977] AC 1012, 1031, 1047.

151 [1999] 2 AC 330.

152 *R (A)* v. *Criminal Injuries Compensation Board* [1999] 2 AC 330, 344.

153 [2003] UKHL 5.

154 *Begum* v. *Tower Hamlets London Borough Council* [2003] UKHL 5, [99].

155 *Begum* v. *Tower Hamlets London Borough Council* [2003] UKHL 5, [99].

156 See Paul Craig, 'Judicial Review, Appeal and Factual Error' [2004] *Public Law* 788, 794–797.

157 [2004] 2 WLR 1351.

158 *E* v. *Home Secretary* [2004] 2 WLR 1352, [66].

159 *E* v. *Home Secretary* [2004] 2 WLR 1352, [65] citing *HTV Ltd* v. *Price Commission* [1976] ICR 170 and *R (Preston)* v. *IRC* [1985] AC 835; see Paul Craig, 'Judicial Review, Appeal and Factual Error' [2004] *Public Law* 788, 791.

meant that evidence going to primary facts could support an appeal, even though statute limited appeals to 'questions of law'.[160]

This line of development just muddies the waters further. Errors of fact are not unimportant.[161] But review for unreasonable findings of fact should be clearly recognised as an instance of the second limb of ultra vires. Judicial review, distinct from appeal, is never triggered by an incorrect judgment or decision *simpliciter* – it requires either (i) an excess of jurisdiction in the strict sense or (ii) a breach of the duties framing an official competence properly characterised (in the traditional idiom) as 'judicial' or 'discretionary'.

9.4.2 The Nature of Official Discretion

From a separation of powers perspective, it is generally accepted that executive officials should be vested with certain discretionary powers, and that judges should respect officials' constitutional role. Discretion is often associated with arbitrariness; however, properly understood, discretion plays a vital role in balancing the institutional distribution of competence between the courts and executive officials that judicial review must maintain.

In a recently re-discovered essay, Hart argued that it was mistaken to identify discretion with choice: discretion is also an 'intellectual virtue', a 'near synonym for practical wisdom', the power of discerning what is appropriate to be done by reference to *applicable standards*.[162] Indulging in a whim is no exercise of discretion, nor is choosing to follow a rule that is unambiguous; discretion means a degree of normative indeterminacy properly left to the decision-maker, attended by a duty to regard the purpose of the power and its context.[163] As the proper course of action is not always fully determined by rules, officials 'holding a responsible public office' are implicitly required to 'choose responsibly having regard to their office'.[164] This recalls the language of Lord Halsbury in *Sharp*

[160] See also *R (March)* v. *Secretary of State for Health* [2010] EWHC 765, in which Holman J quashed a decision by the Secretary of State concerning the level of *ex gratia* payments made to National Health Service patients for a 'material error of fact'.

[161] There is at least 'serious doubt' whether a court can review administrative decisions for 'unreasonableness based on findings of fact' in Australia: *Pilbara Infrastructure Pty Ltd* v. *Economic Regulation Authority* [2014] WASC 346 (Edelman J).

[162] H. L. A. Hart, 'Discretion' (2013) 127 *Harvard Law Review* 652, 656.

[163] H. L. A. Hart, 'Discretion' (2013) 127 *Harvard Law Review* 652, 656, 658–659.

[164] H. L. A. Hart, 'Discretion' (2013) 127 *Harvard Law Review* 652, 657.

v. *Wakefield*,[165] for example, who held that discretion means that something 'is to be done according to the rules of reason and justice, not according to private opinion'; it is to be done 'according to law, and not humour', 'not arbitrary, vague, and fanciful, but legal and regular'; most importantly, discretion is to be exercised 'within the limit to which an honest man competent to the discharge of his office ought to confine himself'.[166]

The two-limbed nature of the ultra vires rule reflects this. 'Discretion' describes the conjunction of an ample ability-space and a constrained liberty-space. Every office implies some 'privilege to err'. Thus Gordon insisted that is illogical to say a tribunal has competence to decide a matter reasonably but no competence to decide it unreasonably.[167] The corollary of this is that 'subjective' considerations (such as reasonableness) cannot determine the scope of an office's ability-space. The vices of discretionary decision-making are caught by the grounds falling under the broad limb of ultra vires, including irrationality, improper purpose, procedural irregularity, or failure to balance the rights of those affected. Gordon's strict approach *underlines* the importance of duties constraining the manner of a power's exercise: it is clear that public powers should not be exercised unreasonably, and that an unreasonable act must be voidable.

9.4.3 *Official Duties and Individual Rights*

Judicial review provides an ultimate forum for vindicating individual rights and defining the perimeter of protection they offer. Rights protection is central to any theory of judicial review, and many believe that judicial review just is about protecting individual rights. Most 'public law rights', however, are not absolute, because individuals' rights compete with each other and with official judgments about the good of the community as a whole.[168] Subject to appropriate regard being paid to official judgments of the public interest, the nature of public law rights allows private interests to be sacrificed when the public good reasonably

165 [1891] AC 173.

166 *Sharp* v. *Wakefield* (1891) AC 173, 179.

167 D. M. Gordon, 'The Relation of Facts to Jurisdiction' (1929) 45 *Law Quarterly Review* 459, 472; *R* v. *Commissioners for Special Purposes of Income Tax* (1888) 21 QBD 313, 319 (Lord Esher).

168 T. R. S. Allan, *The Sovereignty of Law* (Oxford University Press 2013), 233.

demands it.[169] Thus, although rights provide a valuable form of protection for private interests, they are prima facie rights only: 'their content and force [is] wholly dependent on a balance of public and private interests, according to the circumstances of the particular case'.[170]

Individual rights entail limits on official powers, which the supervisory jurisdiction enforces. But where exactly do rights fit in the conceptual logic of judicial review? First, given the bilateral nature of all legal relations, Subject A's right – though it must be balanced against the rights of Subject B and Subject C – must ultimately reduce to a proposition about Subject A's legal position *vis-à-vis* the Crown. Judicial review requires us to decide how individual rights limit an official's *Spielraum*. Secondly, individual rights correlate with *official duties*. In other words, they affect the liberty-space, not the ability-space, of an official. Fundamentally, although public law duties cut across official powers, they do not correlate to an *absence* of power, but rather a *constraint* on power. As such, a rights violation cannot, without more, breach the narrow limb of ultra vires. Lest this be taken to deprecate the importance of rights, it bears stressing that one cannot exist without the other.[171] In other words, it is through the imposition of duties on officials, which constrain the manner of exercise of their competence, that rights are protected.

What about the important line of authority, stemming from *The Case of Proclamations*,[172] that the Royal Prerogative cannot be used to take away subjects' rights? It is entirely plausible argue that rights limit the scope of official powers directly, but an extra step is needed. As we have seen, some people define 'prerogative power' as something that affects rights but the *Case of Proclamations* prohibits just that. Clearly, there is something lost in translation. The proper view is that rights coupled with immunities – correlative of duties coupled with disabilities – affect an official's ability-space directly, such that an action in violation of a right could be said to be ultra vires in the narrow sense. This is what the *Case of Proclamations* lays down.

169 T. R. S. Allan, *The Sovereignty of Law* (Oxford University Press 2013), 233.

170 T. R. S. Allan, 'Doctrine and Theory in Administrative Law: An Elusive Quest for the Limits of Jurisdiction' [2003] *Public Law* 429, 453.

171 Cf *Attorney General (NSW)* v. *Quin* (1990) 170 CLR 1, 35 (Brennan J): 'the scope of judicial review must be defined in terms not of the protection of individual interests but in terms of the extent of power and the legality of its exercise'.

172 (1611) 12 Co Rep 7.

In the modern law, 'fundamental' and 'constitutional' rights are important topics of debate. In *R (Bancoult)* v. *Foreign Secretary (No 2)*,[173] for example, the House of Lords held that 'belongers' of the British Indian Ocean Territory had a right of abode, and that prerogative legislation made over dependent British Overseas Territories is, in principle, subject to judicial review on the ordinary grounds of illegality, unreasonableness, and procedural impropriety. A majority (Lord Bingham, Lord Mance, and Lord Hoffmann) agreed that a prerogative act abrogating a 'fundamental' right would be void. On the facts, Lord Hoffmann opined that the right of abode in the British Indian Ocean Territory was not fundamental enough, and was therefore liable abrogation by the prerogative legislation,[174] even though the majority (Lord Hoffmann, Lord Rodger, and Lord Carswell) held that there was basis for review under the broad limb of the ultra vires rule.[175] If the case had concerned the right of abode of a British citizen in the United Kingdom, on the other hand, an executive act to remove it would likely have been ultra vires in the narrow sense because that right is protected by an immunity.

While the violation of international human rights has generally not been regarded as a jurisdictional error in British law, Feldman has argued that under the Human Rights Act 1998 violation of a right protected by the European Convention on Human Rights should be seen as a ground of ultra vires in the narrow sense of illegality, too.[176] The language of s. 6(1) stipulates that an action incompatible with a Convention right is automatically treated as 'unlawful', which 'has the effect of turning incompatibility with Convention rights from being a possible ground for holding it to be irrational into a jurisdictional error of law'.[177] Dismissing the need to argue about whether unlawfulness 'automatically goes to jurisdiction or falls into that shadowy area in which the unlawfulness of a decision or order may not fatally flaw it', Feldman argues that

[173] [2009] 1 AC 453.

[174] *R (Bancoult)* v. *Foreign Secretary (No 2)* [2009] 1 AC 453, 485 (Lord Hoffmann), 492 (Lord Bingham).

[175] The courts below had focussed on the rules of conduct circumscribing the *purposes* for which the Foreign Secretary could make Orders in Council for the Territory: See *R (Bancoult)* v. *Foreign Secretary (No 1)* [2000] EWHC Admin 413 (Laws LJ) and *R (Bancoult)* v. *Foreign Secretary (No 2)* [2007] EWCA Civ 498 (Sedley LJ).

[176] David Feldman, 'Convention Rights and Substantive Ultra Vires' in C. F. Forsyth (ed.), *Judicial Review and the Constitution* (Hart 2000), 251–252.

[177] David Feldman, 'Convention Rights and Substantive Ultra Vires' in C. F. Forsyth (ed.), *Judicial Review and the Constitution* (Hart 2000), 251–252. Emphasis mine.

the provision is in 'absolute terms'.[178] Even an immunity against the abrogation of Convention rights, however, is usually an immunity to having rights abrogated *improperly* – in the European Convention context 'disproportionately' – so there is a procedural aspect even to 'substantive' rights. In general, we can say that rights coupled with an immunity fall under the first limb of ultra vires, and their violation constitutes a jurisdictional error that can be attacked collaterally; rights not coupled with an immunity fall under the second limb of ultra vires, and their violation constitutes a reviewable intra-jurisdictional error where the violation is unreasonable or procedurally improper.

9.4.4 Unreasonableness and Proportionality

It cannot be stressed enough that intra-jurisdictional errors – breaches of rules of conduct – are no less important for their 'non-jurisdictional' nature. Though central to the logical structure of judicial review, jurisdictional error is not substantively more important. The broad limb of ultra vires mitigates the ever-present danger of officials using their powers improperly. The courts have rightly been assiduous to avoid legislative attempts to nullify rules constraining the conduct of (admittedly) competent officials by imposing duties of reasonableness, good faith, and due process. Reasonable decision-making, in particular, is absolutely vital to the idea of a state in which law rules as opposed to a state ruled by the arbitrary will of officials.[179]

Despite the importance of the broad limb, however, there is a degree of uncertainty about the actual grounds of review governing irrational decision-making and what they entail in any given context. Lord Greene MR propounded the classical test of 'unreasonableness' in *Associated Provincial Picture Houses Ltd* v. *Wednesbury Corporation*[180] as an umbrella for various heads of review such as bad faith, dishonesty, and disregard of public policy.[181] Second-guessing the reasonableness of a decision within a local authority's remit would usurp its jurisdiction, making the court the ultimate arbiter. However, 'if a decision on

[178] David Feldman, 'Convention Rights and Substantive Ultra Vires' in C. F. Forsyth (ed.), *Judicial Review and the Constitution* (Hart 2000), 251–252. Emphasis mine.

[179] In Chapter 13, I present the idea of the rule of law as the 'rule of officials acting lawfully'.

[180] [1948] 1 KB 223.

[181] *Associated Provincial Picture Houses Ltd* v. *Wednesbury Corporation* [1948] 1 KB 223, 226.

a competent matter is so unreasonable that no reasonable authority could ever have come to it, then the courts can interfere'.[182]

'*Wednesbury* unreasonableness' is an exigent standard to prove. Lord Diplock interpreted it in *Council of Civil Service Unions* v. *Minister for the Civil Service* to require a decision 'so outrageous in its defiance of logic or accepted moral standards that no reasonable person could reach it'.[183] The test is circular: a 'reasonable decision' is defined by reference to a 'reasonable decision-maker'. Unreasonableness is entangled with process, as the requirements of due process are most frequently violated by some unreasonable act or omission, and substantively unreasonable decisions are usually reached *via* improper procedures. The relative nature of public law rights means that rights violations are difficult to distinguish from unreasonable exercises of discretion in balancing competing rights.

That raises the question whether 'reasonableness' looks different in different contexts. Unreasonableness has sometimes been interpreted to yield a 'variegated' standard of review; the applicable standard depending on the *effect* of a decision on subjective rights, rather than on the distinction between (merits-based) appeal and (legality-based) review.[184] In *Morris* v. *Beardmore*,[185] for example, Lord Scarman suggested that certain rights were 'fundamental', and that interference required greater justification. In *Bugdaycay* v. *Home Secretary*,[186] Lord Bridge held that an administrative decision that put the applicant's life at risk 'must surely call for the most anxious scrutiny'.[187] Although the House of Lords declined to adopt the principle of proportionality from European Court of Human Rights jurisprudence in *R (Brind)* v. *Home Secretary*,[188] Lord Bridge and Lord Templeman took a heightened level scrutiny to 'stretch' *Wednesbury* unreasonableness. Over a series of subsequent cases, something like substantive proportionality seems to

[182] *Associated Provincial Picture Houses Ltd* v. *Wednesbury Corporation* [1948] 1 KB 223, 229.

[183] *Council of Civil Service Unions* v. *Minister for the Civil Service* [1985] AC 374, 410.

[184] See Justice Michael Barker, 'Legal Unreasonableness: Life after Li' [2014] *Federal Judicial Scholarship* 15, [29]; see *Bugdaycay* v. *Home Secretary* [1987] 1 All ER 940, 952; *R (Mahmood)* v. *Home Secretary* [2001] 1 WLR 840, [18].

[185] [1980] AC 446; see also Lord Jonathan Sumption, 'Anxious Scrutiny' (Administrative Law Bar Association Annual Lecture, 4 November 2014), www.supremecourt.uk/docs/speech-141104.pdf (accessed 20 June 2016), 1.

[186] [1987] 1 AC 514.

[187] *Bugdaycay* v. *Home Secretary* [1987] 1 AC 514.

[188] [1991] 1 AC 696.

have been adopted under the guise of 'anxious scrutiny'.[189] Lord Kerr opined in *R (Carlile)* v. *Home Secretary*,[190] for example, that '[w]e do not ask whether the Secretary of State's view is tenable; we ask whether it is right'.[191]

Rights seem to fix a point against which an official decision can be judged objectively. Using the traditional language, the modern approach characterises the relevant power as 'judicial' rather than 'discretionary', and gives competence for the ultimate decision to the court. This position, according to Lord Sumption, entails 'a transfer to the courts of the constitutional function of the Home Secretary'.[192] As we have seen, the dispute is seldom about the primary facts, but about the weight attached to them in the balancing exercise; as Lord Sumption subsequently wrote extra-judicially, 'short of arrogating the decision-making power to itself, there is very little that the court can do to challenge the rationality of a decision based on a judgment about the significance of undisputed facts'.[193] Unlike Lord Sumption, Lord Kerr opined in *Carlile* that the Human Rights Act 1998 invested the court with a duty to 'look through' the reasons given and to decide, for itself, whether the action was justified.[194] Lord Neuberger, for his part, found neither 'right' nor 'tenable' apt to describe the quality of a decision under review; while he agreed with Lord Kerr that the ultimate decision was for the court, he conceded that, 'unless it can be shown to be based on wrong facts or law, not genuinely held, or irrational', the court could not substitute its judgment without 'strong reasons'.[195]

Perhaps to avoid the legitimacy concerns that dog substantive review in a legal culture preoccupied with parliamentary sovereignty, the Supreme Court may be developing an alternative route to the same outcome *via* an 'augmented' principle of legality.[196] The principle of

189 Lord Jonathan Sumption, 'Anxious Scrutiny' (Administrative Law Bar Association Annual Lecture, 4 November 2014), www.supremecourt.uk/docs/speech-141104.pdf (accessed 20 June 2016), 4.

190 [2014] UKSC 60.

191 *R (Carlile)* v. *Home Secretary* [2014] UKSC 60, [158].

192 *R (Carlile)* v. *Home Secretary* [2014] UKSC 60, [49].

193 Lord Jonathan Sumption, 'Anxious Scrutiny' (Administrative Law Bar Association Annual Lecture, 4 November 2014), www.supremecourt.uk/docs/speech-141104.pdf (accessed 20 June 2016), 5, citing *R (Khawaja)* v. *Home Secretary* [1984] AC 74.

194 *R (Carlile)* v. *Home Secretary* [2014] UKSC 60, [152]; see also Mark Elliott, 'Beyond the European Convention: Human Rights and the Common Law' (2015) 68 *Current Legal Problems* 85, 105.

195 *R (Carlile)* v. *Home Secretary* [2014] UKSC 60, [80].

196 See Jason Varuhas, 'The Principle of Legality' (2020) 79(3) *Cambridge Law Journal* 578, 612.

legality is an important principle of statutory interpretation, namely that Parliament should not be presumed to have derogated from common law rights and that statutory provisions appearing to do so should be construed strictly.[197] As Jason Varuhas has observed, despite the real possibility that it may eclipse substantive review, the principle of legality has been somewhat neglected by public law scholarship and is currently underdetermined, for example in relation to what 'triggers' activate the principle. Further, although the principle as such cannot logically apply outside the statutory context, there is a certain degree of cross-fertilisation evident in the judgment of Lady Hale and Lord Reed in *R (Miller)* v. *Prime Minister*,[198] which refers to the 'augmented' principle of legality set out in *R (UNISON)* v. *Lord Chancellor*[199] to guide the courts' response to prerogative action that affects constitutional principles.[200]

The way forward is to get back to basics. Despite obvious flaws, the *Wednesbury* test captures something basic about the broad limb of ultra vires: an objectively wrong decision is not reviewable unless the official acted improperly, which we implicitly define by thinking about a hypothetical decision-maker. She is duty-bound to exercise the virtues of a good decision-maker – she must be reasonable, honest, conscientious, concerned for the facts, solicitous of the subject's rights and interests.[201] These duties *define* 'reasonable action' by an official; anything 'reasonable' and/or 'proportional' is, as a matter of principle, within her privilege to err. Whatever test is adopted, the supervisory jurisdiction must be focussed on the decision-maker and her decision-making process, not the decision itself.[202]

Legal scholars reflexively appeal to utilitarian or deontological theories of justice, but tend to overlook virtue ethics.[203] This is unfortunate, because the duties constraining official discretion are not simple duties

[197] See *R (Pierson)* v. *Secretary of State for the Home Department* [1998] AC 539, 575 (Lord Wilberforce).

[198] [2019] UKSC 41.

[199] [2017] UKSC 51.

[200] Jason Varuhas, 'The Principle of Legality' (2020) 79(3) *Cambridge Law Journal* 578, 599.

[201] See Evan Fox-Decent, *Sovereignty's Promise* (Oxford University Press 2013), 204.

[202] See Sir Philip Sales, 'Crown Powers, the Royal Prerogative and Fundamental Rights' in Hanna Wilberg and Mark Elliott (eds.), *The Scope and Intensity of Substantive Review* (Hart 2015), 391–393, citing J. M. Balkin, *Constitutional Redemption: Political Faith in an Unjust World* (Harvard University Press 2011), 180.

[203] Lawrence Solum, 'Virtue Jurisprudence: A Virtue-Based Theory of Judging' (2003) 34 *Metaphilosophy* 178, 180.

to do some act, but are duties to do an act *in an appropriate manner*, or to choose whether to act or not or not as appropriate in all the circumstances. A public office lays a kind of trust on the official, and that the broad limb of ultra vires ensures that the official respects the rules of conduct that trust imposes. We speak of trusting someone to *do something*, trusting him to do it in a *certain way* (for example, carefully) and trusting him to *be* a certain way (for example, honest) when doing it.[204] Ultimately, the correctness of the decision, whether measured on a deontological or a utilitarian standard, is less important than whether the official exercised her powers as we would expect a virtuous official to do.[205] Again, the distinction between rules of competence and rules of conduct structure the practice of judicial review. The touchstone is that the court remains the ultimate arbiter of the rules of conduct circumscribing an official's liberty-space – even where the official is competent to make binding determinations of fact.

The separation of powers in the Australian Constitution implies a strict delineation between 'merits review' and 'judicial review'.[206] Unreasonableness, as we have seen, potentially undermines this distinction, and the Australian courts have engaged with the concept in recent years. In *Minister for Immigration and Citizenship* v. *Li*,[207] for example, the High Court of Australia confirmed that there is an area of 'decisional freedom' left to the official, bounded by 'rules of reason' generally derived from the statute conferring power.[208] Discretion is always subject to 'the rules of reason and justice', and this is what is meant by 'according to law', with a particular focus on fidelity to purpose.[209]

Noting that *Associated Provincial Picture Houses Ltd* v. *Wednesbury Corporation* was not the beginning and end, the Court reviewed the earlier test in *Kruse* v. *Johnson*,[210] where Lord Russell said that byelaws 'found to be partial and unequal in their operation as between different

[204] Simon Blackburn, 'Trust, Cooperation, and Human Psychology' in Simon Blackburn (ed.), *Practical Tortoise Raising and Other Philosophical Essays* (Oxford University Press 2010), 92.

[205] Lawrence Solum, 'Virtue Jurisprudence: A Virtue-Based Theory of Judging' (2003) 34 *Metaphilosophy* 178, 202.

[206] See *Re Minister for Immigration & Multicultural Affairs, Ex Parte Lam* (2003) 214 CLR 1, [76] (McHugh and Gummow JJ).

[207] [2013] HCA 18, [70].

[208] *Minister for Immigration and Citizenship* v. *Li* [2013] HCA 18, [28] (French CJ).

[209] *Minister for Immigration and Citizenship* v. *Li* [2013] HCA 18, [66] (Hayne, Kiefel, and Bell JJ).

[210] [1898] 2 QB 91.

classes', 'manifestly unjust', 'disclos[ing] bad faith', or 'involv[ing] oppressive or gratuitous interference' with subjective rights that 'could find no justifications in the minds of reasonable men' could be held ultra vires.[211] Lord Russell's extended formulation reminds us that there is a range of different ways in which an official can go wrong, and that we are concerned in all cases with the standards of conduct imposed on any repository of executive power. Likewise, in *Shrimpton* v. *Commonwealth*,[212] Latham CJ read down Regulations purporting to give the Commonwealth Treasurer an absolute discretion. Despite the broad language, this did not entitle him to take into account extraneous considerations. A discretion must always be exercised in good faith and for the purpose for which it was conferred; the Regulations did not make the Treasurer an 'autocrat free to act as he please[d]'.[213] Dixon J opined that 'absolute discretion' did not mean that the repository of power had discretion to pursue an open range of purposes; it implied an element of finality to his decision, but complete freedom from legal control was impossible for a discretion used in a manner, or for a purpose, going 'outside the power from which the law or regulation conferring the discretion derived its force'.[214]

Following *Minister for Immigration and Citizenship* v. *Li*, Australian courts should ask whether a decision 'lacks an evident and intelligible justification'.[215] That enquiry might embrace 'proportionality' as well as 'reasonableness' analysis: 'an obviously disproportionate response is one way by which a conclusion of unreasonableness may be reached'.[216] To the extent that proportionality could be seen was one of the many errors brought under the head of 'unreasonableness' by Lord Greene in *Wednesbury*, such an approach is preferable to a 'variegated' standard of unreasonableness review.

The place of 'structured proportionality' is currently being worked out in Australian law.[217] The majority of the Australian High Court

211 *Kruse* v. *Johnson* [1898] 2 QB 91, 98–100.

212 (1945) 69 CLR 613.

213 *Shrimpton* v. *Commonwealth* (1945) 69 CLR 613, 620 (Latham CJ), citing *Sharp* v. *Wakefield* (1891) AC 173, 179; *Rooke's Case* (1598) 5 Co Rep 996; *Wilson* v. *Rastall* (1792) 100 ER 1286; *R* v. *Board of Education* (1910) 2 KB 165, 179.

214 *Shrimpton* v. *Commonwealth* (1945) 69 CLR 613, 630 (Dixon J).

215 *Minister for Immigration and Citizenship* v. *Li* [2013] HCA 18, [66].

216 *Minister for Immigration and Citizenship* v. *Li* [2013] HCA 18, [66], [74].

217 See, for example, Anne Carter, 'Bridging the Divide? Proportionality and Calibrated Scrutiny' (2020) 48(1) *Federal Law Review* 282.

adopted such an approach in *McCloy* v. *New South Wales*,[218] but subsequent cases including *Murphy* v. *Electoral Commissioner*[219] and *Brown* v. *Tasmania*[220] are equivocal.[221] The choice of language, however, is less important than the logic that undergirds the doctrines it describes, in which the distinction between rules of competence and rules of conduct is primary.

The grounds falling under the broad limb of ultra vires promote credibility, transparency and accountability in official decision-making, thus legitimating the power wielded by officials.[222] In many ways, these grounds are where the heavy lifting of the supervisory jurisdiction is done. They will, therefore, remain a site for dispute and contestation. Debates about the grounds and standards of review applicable are becoming increasingly complex. In my view, a degree of discipline should be brought to bear through the clear recognition that we are concerned with rules of conduct and that the content of those rules calibrates the intensity of review but implicitly affirms the core function of executive officials to make primary decisions subject to judicial supervision.

9.5 Conclusion

This chapter has reviewed the most important doctrines of the law of judicial review and touched on some of its most important debates. In effect, it has provided an interpretative gloss on the modern law and argued for the reinstatement of jurisdictional error. Officials act in a special mode that is structured by rules of competence and rules of conduct. Judicial review exists to ensure that officials respect the rules that enable and constrain their action in that mode, and for this reason fails under a 'narrow' and a 'broad' limb.

My approach provides a conceptual basis for the various grounds of review and helps to structure debates about the applicable standards of review. Where the narrow limb of ultra vires is concerned with illegality in this strict sense, other grounds (notably unreasonableness and

[218] (2015) 257 CLR 178.
[219] (2016) 90 ALJR 1027.
[220] (2017) 261 CLR 328.
[221] Several judges have preferred to ask whether a law is 'reasonably appropriate and adapted' *versus* 'proportionate': See Ingmar Duldig and Jasmyn Tran, 'Proportionality and Protest: *Brown v Tasmania* (2017) 261 CLR 328' (2018) 39 *Adelaide Law Review* 493.
[222] Michael Barker and Alice Nagel, 'Legal Unreasonableness: Life after *Li*' (2015) 79 *AIAL Forum* 1, 4, citing D. J. Galligan, *Discretionary Powers: A Legal Study of Official Discretion* (Clarendon Press 1986), 218.

procedural impropriety) comprise the broad limb. No official is at liberty to exercise her powers in violation of the rules of conduct that govern her office. As we have seen, the grounds of judicial review have never really been argued to be either exhaustive or mutually exclusive, and the evolution of new grounds is fundamentally possible. Far from being formalistic, this approach centres our attention on what duty the official actor has violated and, by extension, why she is subject to that duty. Although a violation of the broad limb (that is, the duties of good administration) results in a voidable act only, and affords the reviewing court more latitude to quash or perfect the irregular act, the doctrines comprising the broad limb are just as important to administrative justice as the doctrine of jurisdictional error.

At the heart of the ultra vires debate was a disagreement about the role of parliamentary intention and common law principles, primarily associated with the broad limb, in the justification of judicial review. The intricacy of judicial review is, in some measure, due to legislative attempts to oust the courts' jurisdiction to control unreasonable, dishonest, and procedurally improper exercises of executive power and the courts' reticence to impose limits on Parliament's legislative competence openly. Nowhere is that complexity less useful than in the context of non-statutory executive powers. Although I have not considered the question of statutory *versus* non-statutory rules of competence and rules of conduct in this chapter, one of the virtues of this schematic is that it translates quite naturally into the non-statutory context, to which we can now turn.

10

Moving beyond the Ultra Vires Debate

10.1 Introduction

I have argued that the supervisory jurisdiction over statutory and non-statutory executive powers alike should be described with the language of ultra vires. The language of ultra vires, however, is generally associated with legislative intent in English public law. In this chapter, I argue that association should be attenuated. Simply put, the rules of competence and rules of conduct that empower and constrain official action are found *both* in statute and in the common law, so ultra vires should be recognised as a common law doctrine applicable as well to non-statutory executive powers as to powers reposed by statute.

Section 10.2 provides a redux of the ultra vires debate of the 1990s and concludes that it is of little assistance to understanding the judicial review of non-statutory executive powers. The legislative intent theories effectively concede judicial review beyond statute to the common law theories. The common law theories, for their part, fail to articulate a rigorous theory of executive power and place too much reliance on 'principles of good administration' that cut across assumed power. Section 10.3 sets out the positive features of my approach and justifies the same by reference to the doctrinal development of English law. The leading cases concerning non-statutory executive powers make it clear that the supervisory jurisdiction is a creature of the common law, but developments in the nineteenth century led to an ever-closer association of ultra vires with legislative intent. If that were ever accurate, it is no longer; the changes wrought to the practice of administration since the 1980s make the older view more appropriate.

10.2 An Ultra Vires Debate Redux

The ultra vires debate of the 1990s kicked off in the context of *R (Datafin) v. Take-over Panel*,[1] in which the Court of Appeal extended the supervisory jurisdiction to a non-statutory, nominally private body that performed a self-regulatory role in the London financial market. The Take-over Panel, as Sir John Donaldson MR observed, was a 'truly remarkable body'; perched above the City of London, it regulated an important market 'without visible means of legal support', being an 'unincorporated association without legal personality' run by twelve members appointed by leading City institutions:[2]

> Lacking any authority *de jure*, it exercised immense power *de facto* by devising, promulgating, amending and interpreting the City Code on Take-overs and Mergers, by waiving or modifying the application of the code in particular circumstances, by investigating and reporting upon alleged breaches of the code and by the application or threat of sanctions. These sanctions are no less effective because they are applied indirectly and lack a legally enforceable base.[3]

The Panel's powers could only be characterised as 'powers in the nature of public law powers' and thus, although they had no basis in any traditional source of governmental power such as statute or the Royal Prerogative, the Panel was 'without doubt performing an important public duty' and should be subject to judicial review.[4]

The conventional view at the time was that the courts performed their supervisory function as a kind of agent for Parliament. In a seminal article, Dawn Oliver observed that the extent of the Panel's powers could not be a matter of legislative intent, at least not without stretched imputations from legislative silence. *Either* the case was wrongly decided (along with all the other cases in this category), *or* the conceptual basis of the supervisory jurisdiction had to be found outside legislative intention – presumably in the common law.[5]

1 [1987] QB 815.
2 *R (Datafin)* v. *Take-over Panel* [1987] QB 815, 825 (Donaldson MR).
3 *R (Datafin)* v. *Take-over Panel* [1987] QB 815, 825 (Donaldson MR). The Panel has since been put on a statutory footing.
4 *R (Datafin)* v. *Take-over Panel* [1987] QB 815, 824–826, 828, 838 (Donaldson MR).
5 See Dawn Oliver, 'Is the Ultra Vires Rule the Basis of Judicial Review?' in Christopher Forsyth (ed.), *Judicial Review and the Constitution* (Hart 2000), 3, originally published in [1987] *Public Law* 543.

10.2.1 An Unhelpful Preoccupation

Although the debate started in the context of a non-statutory body (that was not even obviously 'governmental'), the debate almost immediately became one about parliamentary sovereignty. T.R.S. Allan has argued that substantive agreement on a radical conception of parliamentary sovereignty diverted the debate away from the central issues.[6] Indeed, most of the main protagonists in the debate agreed (i) that common law 'principles of good administration' should constrain institutional power, and (ii) that Parliament is competent to make or unmake any law whatever, even laws shielding officials who act contrary to the principles of good administration.[7] (Allan was one of the few who openly challenged the notion that Parliament has untrammelled legislative competence.) Disagreement centred on how and why this was the case and on different views of the interaction of the rule of law with parliamentary sovereignty.[8] Most of those who contributed to the debate also recognised that an explanation of judicial review resting on common law principles of good administration was more consistent with the theory and practice of the courts – the desire for 'structural coherence' with the principle of parliamentary sovereignty, however, kept some faithful to an approach based on legislative intent.[9]

Rather than delving into the debate on its terms, I will keep my focus on non-statutory executive powers and use that perspective to take stock of the debate generally. This chapter engages with a sample of the contributions to the debate only, focusing on the 'modified' legislative intent theories presented by Christopher Forsyth and Mark Elliott.[10]

[6] See T. R. S. Allan, 'The Constitutional Foundations of Judicial Review: Conceptual Conundrum or Interpretative Inquiry?' (2002) 61(1) *Cambridge Law Journal* 87; Thomas Poole, 'Back to the Future? Unearthing the Theory of Common Law Constitutionalism' (2003) 23(2) *Oxford Journal of Legal Studies* 435.

[7] According to Forsyth, the common law theorists posit: 'Unless Parliament clearly intends otherwise, the common law will require decision-makers to apply the principles of good administration as developed by the judges in making their decisions'. The legislative intent theorists posit: 'Unless Parliament clearly indicates otherwise, it is presumed to intend that decision-makers must apply the principles of good administration drawn from the common law as developed by the judges in making their decisions'. Christopher Forsyth, 'Heat and Light: A Plea for Reconciliation' in Christopher Forsyth (ed.), *Judicial Review and the Constitution* (Hart 2000), 396.

[8] See Mark Elliott, *The Constitutional Foundations of Judicial Review* (Hart 2000), 60.

[9] Mark Elliott, *The Constitutional Foundations of Judicial Review* (Hart 2000), 100, 107, 110.

[10] 'The doctrine of ultra vires is almost entirely the work of Cambridge men': Nick Barber, 'The Academic Mythologians' (2001) 21(2) *Oxford Journal of Legal Studies* 369.

10.2.2 The Problem

The core problem that *R (Datafin)* v. *Take-over Panel* presented for legislative intent theories of judicial review was that there was no obvious legislative intent to which the courts could be said to be giving effect at all. Writing shortly before the case, Sir William Wade had opined that the extension of judicial review to ministerial guidance had caused the supervisory jurisdiction to 'burst through its logical boundaries'.[11] One gets the impression, however, that Wade recognised the explanatory power of the traditional ultra vires theory being exhausted. Some years prior, Wade had observed in his Hamblin Lectures that the courts were not always acting as mere agents of Parliament:

> In their self-defensive campaign [against ouster clauses] the judges have almost given us a constitution, establishing a kind of entrenched provision to the effect that even Parliament cannot deprive them of their proper function. *They may be discovering a deeper constitutional logic than the crude absolute of statutory omnipotence.*[12]

Wade confessed to having mixed feelings over 'this latest revolution' in the law of judicial review, but remained candid about relations between the courts and Parliament. Welcoming the robust judicial control of the executive as a matter of legal policy, Wade expressed reservations on technical grounds; though welcoming the outcome in *Anisminic* v. *Foreign Compensation Commission*, Wade opined as a constitutional lawyer that 'if we are to call a spade a spade, the judges were refusing to enforce an Act of Parliament that forbad a tribunal's decisions to be challenged in the courts'.[13]

On what basis, then, were the judges were refusing to do so? In terms of *R (Datafin)* v. *Take-over Panel* itself, Wade accepted that such bodies were 'exercising power in a certain sense on behalf of the government, even though making its rules and devising [their] procedures independently', but thought expansion beyond statute could leave the courts without a compass. Administrative law should be about *law*, he argued, and confine itself to powers and duties that are genuinely based on

[11] H. W. R. Wade, 'Judicial Review of Ministerial Guidance' (1986) 102 *Law Quarterly Review* 173, 175.

[12] H. W. R. Wade, *Constitutional Fundamentals* (Stevens 1980), 68 (emphasis mine); See also Geoffrey de Q. Walker, 'The Unwritten Constitution' (2002) 27 *Australian Journal of Legal Philosophy* 144, 147.

[13] H. W. R. Wade, 'Beyond the Law: A British Innovation in Judicial Review' (1991) 43 *Administrative Law Review* 559, 567.

statutory or other legal foundations: 'Once the courts go beyond what is genuinely law, what guidelines will there be for them?'[14] A concern for ascertainable legal rules is understandable, but the notion that common law rules of conduct applicable to self-regulatory bodies are not 'law' is odd, especially given the volume of authorities on the supervisory jurisdiction over such bodies.[15]

In any case, even adherents to the legislative intent theory seemed to recognise that its lights were waning. Christopher Forsyth appears to have felt personal a calling to keep the judges on the strait and narrow, lest the supervisory jurisdiction lead an incursion into parliamentary sovereignty. Responding to Oliver's challenge, he modified the traditional theory with two related, but not wholly consistent, moves. The first was to move the 'traditional' legislative intent theory towards a 'general intent model'. The second was to find an alternative conceptual basis for cases like *R (Datafin)* v. *Take-over Panel* by arguing that the judicial review of such bodies should be seen as a modern instance of an ancient supervisory jurisdiction over economic monopolies.[16]

10.2.3 The First Move: The Interpretative Turn

Forsyth's modified legislative intent theory shifted emphasis from implication of intent from the *specific* text of a given statute to the implication (or imputation) of intent by way of *background* presumptions that guide the construction of statutes. This is, in a sense, just an extended role for the ancient principle that Parliament should be taken to legislate in a virtuous manner.[17] Importantly, however, Forsyth also adopted a particular notion of parliamentary sovereignty. For Wade, for example, sovereignty meant that Parliament is the *highest* source of law, in the sense that it can override other sources (such as the judiciary) and cannot

[14] H. W. R. Wade, 'Beyond the Law: A British Innovation in Judicial Review' (1991) 43 *Administrative Law Review* 559, 567. Emphasis mine.

[15] See further Chapter 12.

[16] Christopher Forsyth, 'Of Fig Leaves and Fairytales: The Ultra Vires Doctrine, Judicial Review and the Sovereignty of Parliament' in Christopher Forsyth (ed.), *Judicial Review and the Constitution* (Hart 2000), 32.

[17] See David Dyzenhaus, 'The Public Conscience of the Law from Hobbes to Hart' (2015) 45 *Ragion Pratica* 565. The judges must interpret the words of the sovereign by considering sovereign intent in light of equity, for it would be a 'great contumely for a judge to think otherwise of the Soveraigne': Thomas Hobbes (Richard Tuck ed.), *Leviathan* (Cambridge University Press 1997), 194.

be overridden by them.[18] But Wade accepted, and even welcomed, abandonment of the 'crude absolute' of legislative omnipotence.

Forsyth, for his part, doubled down on precisely that, adopting an Austinian conception of sovereignty by which Parliament is the *singular* source of law.[19] 'What an all-powerful Parliament does not prohibit, it must authorise either expressly or impliedly'.[20] On this view, whenever Parliament grants power to a Minister, those powers have limits and a Minister either acts within those powers or outside them. There is no grey zone. Thus, if Parliament grants the Minister the power to make an unreasonable decision, there is no basis on which the courts may limit that power (that is, by reference to principles of good administration) without implicitly mounting a 'strong' challenge to Parliament's legislative competence.

Because such a strong challenge is unthinkable within his frame of reference, Forsyth insisted that we adopt a noble lie: the courts are, *even when refusing* to apply a clearly drafted ouster clause, actually *effecting* Parliament's intention. Forsyth's theory self-consciously rests on a fiction: fig-leaves 'do not deceive anyone as to what lies beneath them', rather, like swimming costumes, they 'preserve the decencies'; the fig-leaf is necessary so that Parliament and the courts can 'interact in an appropriate manner without threatening the social order'.[21] Needless to say, I find the analogy uncompelling and resist the suggestion that courts and legislatures can interact appropriately only in some garden of innocence. We live in an obviously fallen world. Like adults, we should recognise the mixed nature of our constitution beneath the fig-leaf, namely the separation of governmental functions between mature institutions. The courts, I think, have shown themselves perfectly capable of respecting the ultimate supremacy of a democratic legislature – even while ensuring that the legislature does not grant officials arbitrary powers.

Sir John Laws criticised Forsyth's logic of omnipotence. The fact that Parliament is competent to prohibit or authorise anything at all, he said,

[18] See H. W. R. Wade, 'The Basis of Legal Sovereignty' [1955] *Cambridge Law Journal* 172.

[19] N. W. Barber, 'The Academic Mythologians' (2001) 21(2) *Oxford Journal of Legal Studies* 369, 374.

[20] Christopher Forsyth, 'Of Fig Leaves and Fairy Tales: The Ultra Vires Doctrine, the Sovereignty of Parliament and Judicial Review' in Christopher Forsyth (ed.), *Judicial Review and the Constitution* (Hart 2000), 39.

[21] Christopher Forsyth, 'Of Fig Leaves and Fairy Tales: The Ultra Vires Doctrine, the Sovereignty of Parliament and Judicial Review' in Christopher Forsyth (ed.), *Judicial Review and the Constitution* (Hart 2000), 42.

does not mean that all prohibitions and authorisations must come from Parliament.[22] According to Laws, this is a fallacy (the fallacy of the 'undistributed middle'), but the problem is rather one of premises. Before Forsyth and Austin, Bentham made the point:

> [E]very mandate that is issued within the limits of sovereignty and is not illegal, is in one sense or other the mandate of the sovereign. Take any mandate whatsoever, and either it is of the number which he allows or it is not: there is no medium: *if it is, it is his*; by adoption at least, if not by original conception: if not, it is illegal.[23]

On its terms, this approach is logically impeccable. If everything that exists within a legal system derives from this type of sovereign, then there can be no other source of law. It seems to me better to argue that the terms are wrong, i.e., that the British constitution does not recognise *this kind of sovereign* at all.

Indeed, ideas about sovereignty break down precisely where they have to explain how an omnipotent sovereign is translated into human-animated institutional structures. Once the sovereign ceases to be a single individual, there must be some sort of complex constitution in virtue of which the sovereign is to be obeyed. Austin's definition of the sovereign as the King, Parliament and the body of the Electors, for example, transfers virtually everyone to the 'sovereign' side of the equation, which alters the proposition fundamentally. As A. D. Lindsay observed in the early twentieth century, it strains credulity to say the fundamental fact about the constitution is that 'paupers, lunatics, males under twenty-one and females under thirty obey the rest of the community':[24]

> The orthodox answer to this objection is no doubt that we must distinguish between individuals in their capacity as subjects and individuals *in their capacity as part of the sovereign*. But this answer is itself enough to show that *a new theory has been introduced*, for the distinction implies a principle in virtue of which it can be drawn, *and the sovereign will be limited because constituted by that principle* . . . [T]he individual members who constitute the sovereign are obeyed as persons *only so far as their actions conform to a rule*.[25]

[22] Sir John Laws, 'Illegality: The Problem of Jurisdiction' in Christopher Forsyth (ed.), *Judicial Review and the Constitution* (Hart 2000), 78.

[23] Jeremy Bentham (H. L. A. Hart ed.), *Of Laws in General* (Athlone Press 1970), 22. Emphasis mine.

[24] A. D. Lindsay, 'Sovereignty' (1924) 24 *Proceedings of the Aristotelian Society* 235, 241.

[25] A. D. Lindsay, 'Sovereignty' (1924) 24 *Proceedings of the Aristotelian Society* 235, 243. Emphasis mine.

We might say that there is only one rule, and that is simply that Members of Parliament acting together can do whatever they like. Although standard fare, that is a pretty desperate argument. Unattractive in conceptual and normative terms, it is also wholly inconsistent with the 'campaign of self-preservation' that has kept ouster clauses from hollowing out the supervisory jurisdiction. We do not even need to consider the more obvious case of Parliament doing something blatantly improper.[26]

Whether we like it or not – most English public lawyers do *not* like it – Lindsay's reasoning leads inexorably to something like 'strong form' judicial review. For my part, I think that the most plausible solution to the conundrum is to adopt a more nuanced concept of 'legislative supremacy' in place of radical parliamentary sovereignty. I will return to this question again in Chapter 13; this chapter and the next are about the common law doctrine of ultra vires, not about the rules of competence and rules of conduct governing Parliament. It suffices to say that Forsyth's conception of parliamentary sovereignty – combined with an awareness that it is really a fiction – obscured more than it revealed about the constitutional foundations of judicial review.

Given his radical conception of sovereignty, Forsyth took an interpretative turn to ground the judges' constitutional role: judicial review is not based on Parliament's actual (specific, expressed) intention, but on a constructive (general, implied) intention, and the courts play a constitutive role in the formation of this intention. In my view, such implication is more accurately described as imputation.[27] This gives the courts the interpretative 'wiggle room' that they need to avoid the common law requirements of reasonableness and procedural propriety, for example, being ousted by Parliament.[28]

Elliott pursued this interpretative turn further still. While the details of the supervisory jurisdiction cannot be attributed to parliamentary intention, Parliament should be taken to intend that the 'judicially-created

[26] Leslie Stephen's example of a law authorising the killing of all blue-eyed babies is distinctly less hypothetical following the Holocaust than it must have in the 1880s: Leslie Stephen, *The Science of Ethics* (Cambridge University Press 2012 [1st ed. 1882]), 137.

[27] See N. W. Barber, 'The Academic Mythologians' (2001) 21(2) *Oxford Journal of Legal Studies* 369, 370.

[28] By reference to *Staatspresident* v. *United Democratic Front* 1998(4) SA 839(A), a South African case concerning vague regulations made by a Minister, Forsyth argued that, if the requirement to make clear regulations came from the common law, rather than implication from statute, clauses ousting the supervisory jurisdiction would be effective. This is only a problem if the legislature is assumed to be 'sovereign' in Forsyth's radical sense.

principles of good administration are applied' such that powers reposed by statute in executive officials are limited 'in accordance with the requirements of the rule of law'.[29] Again, the crux of the issue is really the judges' interpretative role in the case of an obvious *express* intention to, say, empower a Minister to make arbitrary decisions (for example, by granting an 'absolute discretion' that is non-reviewable in the courts). Judicial review was based on the 'vindication of the rule of law', he argued, which forms part of the bedrock of the British constitution, and 'neither constitutional propriety nor the ultra vires doctrine, properly understood, require[ed] the courts to conceal the true nature of their exercise' because the interpretative methodology of his twice-modified legislative intent theory was uniquely capable of reconciling parliamentary sovereignty with the rule of law.[30] Elliott's modification of the legislative intent theory is, however, less an explanation of the supervisory jurisdiction than a reconciliation of judicial practice with loyalty to an radical doctrine of parliamentary sovereignty.[31]

Elliott's theory is an elegant, almost Thomistic synthesis between common law reason and parliamentary will.[32] But that synthesis is only necessary if we adopt the premise of a transcendent Parliament whose revealed will takes priority to the demands of reason in the first place. Common law theorists such as Paul Craig rightly countered that if the sovereignty of Parliament can only be reconciled with judicial practice by the imputation of virtuous intentions from legislative silence, it is the canon of interpretation and not the legislative silence that carries the theory.[33] In substance, the 'general intent model' more closely resembles a common law theory of judicial review than a legislative intent theory; because the presumptions framing Parliament's intent are admittedly creatures of judicial imagination, general intent 'functions merely as

[29] Mark Elliott, *The Constitutional Foundations of Judicial Review* (Hart 2001), 110.

[30] Mark Elliott, 'The Ultra Vires Doctrine in a Constitutional Setting: Still the Central Principle of Administrative Law' in C. F. Forsyth (ed.), *Judicial Review and the Constitution* (Hart 2000), 108–109.

[31] Mark Elliott, *The Constitutional Foundations of Judicial Review* (Hart 2001), 110.

[32] Thomas Aquinas forged a synthesis between the schools of Idealism and Realism, stretching back to Plato and Aristotle, conflict between which characterised Christian (and Jewish and Islamic) thought for centuries. See Alasdair MacIntyre, *Three Rival Versions of Moral Enquiry: Encyclopaedia, Genealogy, and Tradition* (University of Notre Dame Press 1990); L. C. Kondrick, 'Thomism and Science Education: History Informs a Modern Debate' (2008) 48(2) *Integrative and Comparative Biology* 202.

[33] T. R. S. Allan, 'Constitutional Dialogue and the Justification of Judicial Review' (2003) 23 (4) *Oxford Journal of Legal Studies* 563, 564.

a *renvoi* back to the common law'.[34] Craig's is, indeed, a more parsimonious justification of judicial review: it is, after all, 'superfluous to suppose that what can be accounted for by a few principles has been produced by many'.[35]

10.2.4 The Second Move: An Alternative Basis of Review

Forsyth's vigorous propagation of his theory, however, left the actual case of *R (Datafin)* v. *Take-over Panel* unexplained. Forsyth therefore argued that the judicial review of such bodies should be seen as a modern instance of an ancient supervisory jurisdiction over economic monopolies.[36] The case was just one example of the fundamental principle that the 'law of judicial review extends to non-statutory bodies that do not exercise legal powers':[37]

> Self-evidently, it is not meaningful, when a body lacks legal power, to talk about it acting in excess of its legal powers. Thus some juridical basis, other than the doctrine of ultra vires, is needed to justify judicial intervention in such cases. Although the constitutional basis of this extension of judicial review has seldom been discussed, there is, it is submitted, ready at hand a common law root for such judicial intervention. Very usefully Paul Craig has pointed out that it has been 'almost forgotten' that the common law imposed a duty to act reasonably on those who exercised monopoly power even where that power simply existed *de facto*.[38]

I do not think that the category of '*de facto*' power is very helpful in this context, and it is certainly not meaningless to talk about a common law corporation having 'legal powers'. But there are deeper problems. Citing a number of the classical cases, which I will discuss in Chapter 11, Forsyth argued that there exists a common law power of the courts to control the

34 Paul Craig, *UK, EU and Global Administrative Law* (Cambridge University Press 2014), 129.

35 Thomas Aquinas (Dominicans of the English Province trans.), *Summa Theologica* (Benziger 1948), 1.2.3; Bertrand Russel, 'Logical Atomism' in D. F. Pears (ed.), *The Philosophy of Logical Atomism* (Open Court 1985), 160.

36 Christopher Forsyth, 'Of Fig Leaves and Fairytales: The Ultra Vires Doctrine, Judicial Review and the Sovereignty of Parliament' in Christopher Forsyth (ed.), *Judicial Review and the Constitution* (Hart 2000), 32.

37 Christopher Forsyth, 'Of Fig Leaves and Fairytales: The Ultra Vires Doctrine, Judicial Review and the Sovereignty of Parliament' in Christopher Forsyth (ed.), *Judicial Review and the Constitution* (Hart 2000), 31.

38 Christopher Forsyth, 'Of Fig Leaves and Fairytales: The Ultra Vires Doctrine, Judicial Review and the Sovereignty of Parliament' in Christopher Forsyth (ed.), *Judicial Review and the Constitution* (Hart 2000), 31.

abuse of monopolies including to subject nominally private bodies to judicial review.[39] In effect, Forsyth willingly conceded the irrelevance of the legislative intent theory for the judicial review of non-statutory powers:

> [T]he ultra vires doctrine has never been the sole justification for judicial review [but] the recognition that the common law provides the basis for judicial review in some circumstances is not an admission of the failure of ultra vires. Ultra vires remains the central position as far as decisions made under statutory powers are concerned.[40]

The move rebounds, however, against what purports to be a *general* theory of judicial review. This point was not lost on the common law theorists. Laws, for example, argued that the monopolies doctrine shows an 'abiding concern with the abuse of power' to which the legislative intent theory of was irrelevant; the monopolies doctrine is 'much closer to the fundamentals of judicial review than is [that] idea of ultra vires'.[41]

The essential problem is that Forsyth's approach bifurcates the supervisory jurisdiction arbitrarily. He effectively argued that the same *heads of review* should apply to statutory and non-statutory bodies but that the *conceptual basis* of review should be strictly distinguished:

> In relation to the former type of body, the traditional ultra vires doctrine would continue to provide that justification. In relation to the latter type of body, we would be willing to ground such controls on the common law's capacity to control public power.[42]

This dichotomy, however, is conceptually messy, not least because the dividing line between bodies that derive their powers from statute and those that is often difficult to draw.[43] Just as seriously, it begs the central question: 'if the common law is to be regarded as the legitimate basis for

[39] Christopher Forsyth, 'Of Fig Leaves and Fairytales: The Ultra Vires Doctrine, Judicial Review and the Sovereignty of Parliament' in Christopher Forsyth (ed.), *Judicial Review and the Constitution* (Hart 2000), 32.

[40] Christopher Forsyth, 'Of Fig Leaves and Fairytales: The Ultra Vires Doctrine, Judicial Review and the Sovereignty of Parliament' in Christopher Forsyth (ed.), *Judicial Review and the Constitution* (Hart 2000), 33.

[41] Sir John Laws, 'Illegality: The Problem of Jurisdiction' in Christopher Forsyth (ed.), *Judicial Review and the Constitution* (Hart 2000), 74; Paul Craig, 'Ultra Vires and the Foundations of Judicial Review' (1998) 57(1) *Cambridge Law Journal* 63, 70.

[42] Paul Craig, 'Ultra Vires and the Foundations of Judicial Review' (1998) 57(1) *Cambridge Law Journal* 63, 77.

[43] Paul Craig, 'Ultra Vires and the Foundations of Judicial Review' (1998) 57(1) *Cambridge Law Journal* 63, 78.

controls on bodies which do not depend on statute for their powers, why then cannot it be so regarded for bodies which do derive their powers from statute?'[44]

10.3 Toward a Common Law Ultra Vires Theory

My concern is to explain the supervisory jurisdiction over non-statutory executive powers in their own right and on their own terms, and to consider whether that sheds light on the supervisory jurisdiction over statutory executive powers, as well. It is clear that legislative intent theories are at their weakest in the context of non-statutory executive powers. In the central statement of his case, Elliott effectively conceded that non-statutory executive powers raise problems for his theory, because their review cannot really be explained as the courts giving effect Parliament's intent.[45] The 'essence' of the ultra vires doctrine, he wrote, is that review is based in the implied provisions of empowering legislation, so we need to look for alternative justifications for judicial review of non-statutory powers.[46] As we have seen, this causes the supervisory jurisdiction to fragment. Even if we are happy to hive off non-statutory bodies like the Take-over Panel into a separate supervisory jurisdiction, the legislative intent theory posits distinctions between the categories of executive power that are arbitrary.

For Elliott, both statutory powers and prerogative-type powers are 'legal powers' (in the Wade-Hohfeld sense). Their review, therefore, entails a 'determination that legal power is needed to support the relevant action' and an examination of whether the official actor 'remained within or trespassed beyond the limits of the power'.[47] This epitomises classical judicial review, and, given that most officials act on a statutory footing most of the time, the language of ultra vires 'accurately captures the idea that the court's role is to ensure that the state has remained within the bounds of the legal authority upon which the legality and effectiveness of its action depends'.[48] However, to the extent that ultra vires hinges on

44 Paul Craig, 'Ultra Vires and the Foundations of Judicial Review' (1998) 57(1) *Cambridge Law Journal* 63, 78.

45 Mark Elliott, *The Constitutional Foundations of Judicial Review* (Hart 2000), 127.

46 Mark Elliott, 'The Demise of Parliamentary Sovereignty? The Implications for Justifying Judicial Review' (1999) 115 *Law Quarterly Review* 119; see also T. R. S. Allan, *The Sovereignty of Law* (Oxford University Press 2013), 231.

47 Mark Elliott, *The Constitutional Foundations of Judicial Review* (Hart 2001), 167.

48 Mark Elliott, *The Constitutional Foundations of Judicial Review* (Hart 2001), 167.

legislative intention, it 'logically cannot – and does not purport to' supply a justification for the review of non-statutory executive powers. This leaves prerogative-type powers between two stools, as it were. As a set of Hohfeldian 'legal powers', the judicial review of prerogative powers should be 'vires-based'. However, because prerogative powers are non-statutory, their review must be 'rules-based'.[49]

Through it all, Elliott's approach to the review of non-statutory powers is effectively indistinguishable from the common law theory. Writing more recently, Elliott has addressed the question of third source-type powers and non-statutory bodies directly. Again, on a strict legislative intent-based approach, third source-type powers should not be reviewable at all.[50] However, such an approach would be under-inclusive, so Elliott argues that such powers should be reviewable and offers some arguments as to why this is the case. Review is usually justified by reference to (i) preventing the abuse of power, (ii) controlling the use of 'public power' or 'public law power' (what I would call 'official power'), and (iii) controlling the exercise of monopoly power.[51] Elliott replaces them with another tri-partite scheme of purposes, comprising (i) ensuring compliance with the rule of law, (ii) controlling governmental power based on the uniqueness of its position, being 'unusually powerful' and 'devoid of legitimate self-interests', and (iii) securing the 'public interest in good governance'.[52] The first limb tracks fairly closely to the concept of vires, keeping the repository of a power within the proper bounds of that power. Only by balancing these three normative considerations directly, Elliott argues, can the proper scope of the supervisory jurisdiction can be drawn across the statutory/non-statutory divide and indeed across the conventional public/private divide:

> If the purpose (and so scope) of judicial review were narrowly conceived as being concerned with the control of legal powers, judicial review would not lie in respect of decisions and actions taken by the government in exercise of its '*de facto*' or 'third source' powers.[53]

49 Mark Elliott, *The Constitutional Foundations of Judicial Review* (Hart 2001), 165, 195.

50 See Mark Elliott, 'Judicial Review's Scope, Foundations, and Purposes: Joining the Dots' [2012] [1] *New Zealand Law Review* 75, 83.

51 Mark Elliott, 'Judicial Review's Scope, Foundations, and Purposes: Joining the Dots' [2012] [1] *New Zealand Law Review* 75, 77.

52 Mark Elliott, 'Judicial Review's Scope, Foundations, and Purposes: Joining the Dots' [2012] [1] *New Zealand Law Review* 75, 79–80.

53 Mark Elliott, 'Judicial Review's Scope, Foundations, and Purposes: Joining the Dots' [2012] [1] *New Zealand Law Review* 75, 93.

The conceptual affinity of this approach with the monopolies doctrines should be kept in mind. Elliott's discussion elaborates on how these purposes play out in the context of contracted-out governmental services and other hybrid modalities of administration. He groups the cases into four categories, concerning (i) '*de facto*' or 'third source' powers (as he defines them), (ii) contractual or otherwise consensual relationships between the claimant and defendant, (iii) contracting decisions made under statutory authority, and (iv) contractual relationships between the defendant and an obviously governmental body.[54] The utility of his analysis, however, is again compromised by a ready endorsement of the 'residual liberties' approach to third source-type powers.[55]

Of more interest is what Elliott does *not* say. Beyond a passing reference to the ultra vires debate's 'focus upon the basic constitutional architecture – such as the implications of the doctrines of parliamentary sovereignty',[56] legislative intent seems irrelevant to Elliott's understanding of this domain of judicial review. Again, his could just as well be a common law theory, at least as it applies beyond statute.

When we approach the supervisory jurisdiction with non-statutory executive powers foremost in our minds, the ultra vires debate thus appears as a distraction. The underlying motive to defend the principle of parliamentary sovereignty does not arise in relation to non-statutory executive powers in the first place:

> Unlike the sovereign in Parliament, the sovereign acting alone, through the prerogative, is ultimately constrained by the rule of law. The rule of law can thus be conceptualized as a direct limit on prerogative power and intention-based reasoning need form no part of the legal basis of review in this area.[57]

In other words, non-statutory executive powers allow us to trace the contours of the supervisory jurisdiction without getting tangled up in debates about parliamentary sovereignty in the first instance. However,

[54] Mark Elliott, 'Judicial Review's Scope, Foundations, and Purposes: Joining the Dots' [2012][1] *New Zealand Law Review* 75, 93, 97, 101, 105.

[55] Mark Elliott, 'Judicial Review's Scope, Foundations, and Purposes: Joining the Dots' [2012][1] *New Zealand Law Review* 75, 83, citing B. V. Harris, 'The "Third Source" of Authority for Government Action' (1992) 108 *Law Quarterly Review* 626; B. V. Harris, 'The "Third Source" of Authority for Government Action Revisited' (2007) 123 *Law Quarterly Review* 225.

[56] Mark Elliott, 'Judicial Review's Scope, Foundations, and Purposes: Joining the Dots' [2012] *New Zealand Law Review* 75.

[57] Mark Elliott, *The Constitutional Foundations of Judicial Review* (Hart 2001), 185.

in assuming problematic categories such as '*de facto*' power and then seeing judicial review as a set of constraints that supervene on 'power', Elliott's crypto-common law theory suffers from the same conceptual weaknesses and neglects the logic inherent in the language of ultra vires.

10.3.1 Re-appropriating the Language of Ultra Vires

'Ultra vires' is used in at least three different senses. First, it refers to a 'single, self-sufficient meta-normative principle' legitimating judicial review of administrative, executive, and some types of legislative action. This principle is generally identified as the sovereignty of Parliament. Secondly, it describes the principle of legality, which forms part of a complex web of justifications for judicial review operating side-by-side with – but independently from – the first sense at a meta-normative level. Thirdly, it describes the principles applied by a court sitting in the public law supervisory jurisdiction, i.e., as an umbrella term for illegality, procedural impropriety, and irrationality.[58]

The first sense of ultra vires – the idea that legality derives from a subordinate body's compliance with the will of Parliament – was the main point of contention in the ultra vires debate. The fact that not all official powers are granted by Parliament, and that some limits are evidently imposed by judges on their own motion, explains why cases like *R (Datafin)* v. *Take-over Panel* pose such a threat to ultra vires in this first sense.[59] As observed above, both camps in the debate took this sense for granted. Oliver claimed, for example, that '*de facto* or common law powers' were impossible to analyse by reference to the intention of the donor of the powers, and therefore 'do not lend themselves to the language of ultra vires'.[60] Michael Taggart claimed that the challenges raised by the 'contracting state' have 'left the ultra vires debate somewhat high and dry'.[61] Harris has argued that judicial review 'has moved away from the concept of ultra vires' as non-statutory powers have increased in

[58] Or, in a narrower sense to distinguish illegality from the latter two: David Feldman, 'Convention Rights and Substantive Ultra Vires' in C. F. Forsyth (ed.), *Judicial Review and the Constitution* (Hart 2000), 246.

[59] See Mark Elliott, 'The Demise of Parliamentary Sovereignty? The Implications for Justifying Judicial Review' (1999) 115 *Law Quarterly Review* 119.

[60] Dawn Oliver, 'Is the Ultra Vires Rule the Basis of Judicial Review?' in C. F. Forsyth (ed.), *Judicial Review and the Constitution* (Hart 2000), 5.

[61] Michael Taggart, 'Ultra Vires as Distraction' in C. F. Forsyth (ed.), *Judicial Review and the Constitution* (Hart 2000), 428.

importance.[62] Craig argued that it was impossible to apply the ultra vires doctrine to non-statutory bodies 'without substantially altering its meaning'.[63]

Although Craig did not intentionally suggest re-appropriation of ultra vires as a common law doctrine, that is precisely what needs to be done. Used carefully, the language reminds us that the abstract grounds of review are 'not self-executing', but rather summarise the nature of legal imperfections 'whose existence must be established by close appraisal of an agency's actions and their consequences for those affected'.[64] Following the logic of official action, ultra vires is the best expression of the mechanics of judicial review. Contrary to the common law theorists, we cannot discard the language of ultra vires because we cannot determine whether power has been 'abused' without first determining the permissible scope of its proper use; without a fine-grained analysis of the vires of an office, no court can decide whether an act was a proper discharge of the office or not. In this, both rules of competence (vires in the strict sense) and rules of conduct ('duties of good administration') are integral. Ultra vires, then, is still the central principle of administrative law,[65] but not in the way we might think.

10.4 Conclusion

The ultra vires debate provided the focal point for an intense engagement by English public lawyers, and, to a lesser extent, their counterparts around the Anglo-Commonwealth, with the conceptual basis of the supervisory jurisdiction in a changing administrative context. However, on the whole, the debate really did generate more heat than light. In particular, the ultra vires debate did not prepare us well to understand the expansion of judicial review beyond statute. The 'common law camp' was compromised by abandonment of fundamental concepts (such as jurisdiction) that once structured the law, combined with an odd acquiescence to the proposition that Parliament could, if it *really* wanted to, kill all blue-eyed babies. The 'legislative intent camp', balanced

[62] B. V. Harris, 'The "Third Source" of Authority for Government Action' (1992) 109 *Law Quarterly Review* 626, 644.

[63] Paul Craig, 'Ultra Vires and the Foundations of Judicial Review' (1998) 57(1) *Cambridge Law Journal* 63, 70.

[64] T. R. S. Allan, *The Sovereignty of Law* (Oxford University Press 2013), 233.

[65] See Mark Elliott, 'The Ultra Vires Rule in a Constitutional Setting: Still the Central Principle of Administrative Law' (1999) 58(1) *Cambridge Law Journal* 129.

lip-service to a radical concept of Parliamentary sovereignty with an interpretative approach that merged, in substance, with the common law position. The debate has proved uniquely sterile over the course of decades, even as the supervisory jurisdiction over non-statutory executive powers has expanded and consolidated. Though of historical interest, it should be put behind us without hesitation or remorse.

If ultra vires were just a fig-leaf to preserve the illusion of illimitable parliamentary sovereignty, it would have to be discarded in favour of a theory of judicial review based in common law principles of good administration. However, the logic of empowerment and action behind the ultra vires rule makes it much more than that. The two limbs of the rule grow out of the logic of official action and describe the mechanics of judicial review.

The claim that an action is ultra vires may be based on rules derived from any number of sources of law, of which legislation is only one.[66] Legislative intent, as expressed in statutory language, is important, and in most cases the relevant rule of competence will be found in a statute. But in many cases the content of that rule will be determined by the common law, as well, either because statutes implicitly refer to the common law or because the common law informs the way that text is construed. Especially in the United Kingdom, with an ancient and unwritten constitution, it is to be expected that important rules are to be found in custom rather than express, formal establishment.[67] Every statutory grant of power – even grants of 'absolute discretion' fenced about with ouster clauses – are subject to judicial review under the broad limb of ultra vires, which comprises an irreducible core of common law principles of good administration reflected in rules of conduct that constrain the manner in which any competence, statutory or non-statutory, is exercised. On this basis, our analysis of the supervisory jurisdiction can advance to explore the complex interaction of statute and common law in the context of executive power in different contexts.

[66] See David Feldman, 'Convention Rights and Substantive Ultra Vires' in C. F. Forsyth (ed.), *Judicial Review and the Constitution* (Hart 2000), 248–249.

[67] See Neil MacCormick, *Institutions of Law* (Oxford University Press 2007), 161.

11

The Common Law Theory of Ultra Vires

11.1 Introduction

The ambit of the supervisory jurisdiction beyond statute has, as a matter of doctrinal law, been clear for decades. It is even tolerably clear *how* prerogative-type and third source-type powers are to be reviewed. What is not clear is *why* that is the case, and how modern judicial practice squares with the theoretical explanations of judicial review that populate the textbooks. This chapter sets out to explain the application of the common law doctrine of ultra vires to non-statutory executive powers.

Section 11.2 traces the review of non-statutory executive powers from the ancient law to the present, showing how judicial review came to be associated with legislative intent and explaining why this was, in hindsight, a wrong turning. Section 11.3 glosses the most recent Supreme Court authorities in terms of my own theory of judicial review. The judgments in *R (Miller)* v. *Secretary of State for Exiting the United Kingdom*[1] and *R (Miller)* v. *Prime Minister*[2] confirm that review of non-statutory executive powers is 'vires-based'. Although the reasoning in both cases stresses the principle of parliamentary sovereignty, I argue that they lend indirect support for abandonment of the legislative intent theory of judicial review. Further, they suggest that considerations of justiciability and deference play a modest role once the ultra vires rule itself is properly understood.

11.2 Judicial Review beyond Statute

The seminal case of *R (Lain)* v. *Criminal Injuries Compensation Board*[3] concerned a non-statutory scheme in which victims of crime

[1] [2019] UKSC 41.
[2] [2017] UKSC 5.
[3] [1967] 2 QB 864.

were to be compensated by way of *ex gratia* payment, with money provided by a grant-in-aid. Because of the non-statutory nature of the body, the question arose whether it was amenable to the supervisory jurisdiction at all. Diplock LJ observed that while *certiorari* was closely associated with legislative intent in modernity, the writ originally ran to courts 'whose authority was derived from the prerogative, Royal Charter, from franchise or custom as well as from Act of Parliament'.[4] Given the primacy of Parliament since the constitutional settlement of the seventeenth century, statutory grants of power had become the norm. Disuse of the High Court's supervisory jurisdiction did not, however, result in desuetude. Lord Parker CJ could see no reason why a body of this nature should not be amenable to the supervisory jurisdiction. *Certiorari* would run wherever a body of persons 'of a public as opposed to a purely private or domestic character' determined matters affecting subjects and was 'under a duty to act judicially', irrespective of the power's source in statute or the common law.[5] Crucially, the non-statutory basis did not make this power any less 'lawful':

> True it is not set up by statute but the fact that it is set up by executive government, i.e., under the prerogative, does not render its acts any the less lawful. Indeed, the writ of *certiorari* has issued not only to courts set up by statute but to courts whose authority is derived, *inter alia*, from the prerogative. Once the jurisdiction is extended, as it clearly has been, to tribunals as opposed to courts, there is no reason why the remedy by way of *certiorari* cannot be invoked to a body of persons set up under the prerogative.[6]

The seminal case of *Council of Civil Service Unions* v. *Minister for the Civil Service*[7] is equally clear. The case concerned an Order in Council purporting to ban employees of a department essential to national security from membership in trades unions. The House of Lords established that actions taken in reliance on prerogative-type powers are subject to the supervisory jurisdiction like their statutory counterparts. Lord Diplock could see 'no reason why simply because a decision-making power is derived from a common law and not a statutory source, it should *for that reason only* be immune from

[4] *R (Lain)* v. *Criminal Injuries Compensation Board* [1967] 2 QB 864, 884 (Diplock LJ).
[5] *R (Lain)* v. *Criminal Injuries Compensation Board* [1967] 2 QB 864, 881 (Parker LCJ).
[6] *R (Lain)* v. *Criminal Injuries Compensation Board* [1967] 2 QB 864, 881 (Parker LCJ).
[7] [1985] AC 374.

judicial review'.[8] Review would follow according to the ordinary tripartite scheme of illegality, irrationality, and procedural propriety. Lord Roskill stated the principle crisply. The traditional view was that abuse of the prerogative was subject to political, rather than legal, redress. But that position had an 'air of unreality' in the case at hand:

> [T]he right of the executive to do a lawful act affecting the rights of the citizen, whether adversely or beneficially, is founded upon the giving to the executive of a power enabling it to do that act. The giving of such a power usually carries with it legal sanctions to enable that power if necessary to be enforced by the courts. In most cases that power is derived from statute though in some cases, as indeed in the present case, it may still be derived from the prerogative. In yet other cases, as the decisions show, the two powers may coexist or the statutory power may by necessary implication have replaced the former prerogative power. If the executive in pursuance of the statutory power does an act affecting the rights of the citizen, it is beyond question that in principle the manner of the exercise of that power may today be challenged on one or more of the three [classical] grounds.[9]

The result was that exercises of prerogative-type powers were amenable to judicial review just the same as statutory powers:

> If the executive instead of acting under a statutory power acts under a prerogative power ... [I am unable to see] that there is any logical reason why the fact that the source of the power is the prerogative and not statute should today deprive the citizen of that right of challenge to the manner of its exercise which he would possess were the source of the power statutory.[10]

The short point is that no *categorical* distinction exists between statutory and non-statutory executive powers *for the purposes of judicial review*. The legislative intent theory, in other words, puts an unnecessary gloss on a simple and intuitive common law principle. Because it is appropriate to say that a body acts 'ultra vires' by taking an action outside its *Spielraum*, even outside the statutory context, the concept of ultra vires should be re-appropriated as a common law theory.

[8] *Council of Civil Service Unions* v. *Minister for the Civil Service* [1985] AC 374, 410 (Lord Diplock). Emphasis in the original.

[9] *Council of Civil Service Unions* v. *Minister for the Civil Service* [1985] AC 374, 417 (Lord Roskill).

[10] *Council of Civil Service Unions* v. *Minister for the Civil Service* [1985] AC 374, 417 (Lord Roskill).

11.2.1 The Association of Ultra Vires with Legislative Intention

Although statute remains the most important source of public authority, the supervisory jurisdiction always had a contingent relation to legislative intention. In *Groenvelt* v. *Burwell*,[11] Lord Chief Justice Holt declared that, although the relevant statute did not give authority to the King's Bench to grant *certiorari*, 'it is by the Common Law that this Court will examine if other courts exceed their jurisdiction'.[12] *Certiorari* was held to lie to every inferior jurisdiction because 'no court can be intended to be exempt from the superintendency of the King in this court' to police 'whether they keep themselves within the limits of their jurisdiction'.[13] There was no reason against that jurisdiction extending to non-statutory bodies. As we have seen, the same came to be true of the common law powers of the Crown.

Many of the cases concern decision-makers within bodies that are not part of HM Government, but play a role in public life. If we look at developments in our own time through the lens of late nineteenth and early twentieth century legal theory, this looks novel, but early modern administration involved a plethora of customary institutions, too.[14] Traditional local authorities 'flourished well into the eighteenth century' exercising some statutory powers, 'often very vaguely worded', but deriving their powers and forms of administration generally from the common law.[15] The parish, county, and borough did not owe their origins to statute until 1834; the municipal corporations were brought under statute in 1835. They held common law powers, including those held in virtue of their legal capacity as a corporation. According to Norman Chester, it was always possible to challenge the action of a public authority before the King's Bench on the ground that it had exceeded its legal powers, using the prerogative writs.[16]

[11] (1700) 1 Ld Raym 454.

[12] *Groenvelt* v. *Burwell* (1700) 1 Ld Raym 454, 469.

[13] *Groenvelt* v. *Burwell* (1700) 1 Ld Raym 454, 469; see also Amnon Rubinstein, *Jurisdiction and Illegality* (Clarendon Press 1965), 68.

[14] *R* v. *Roupell*, for example, extended *certiorari* to a presentment in the court leet of the Liberty of Savoy, a part of the Duchy of Lancaster – a baronial court with no statutory basis: Joseph Ritson, *A Digest of the Proceedings of the Court Leet and of the Manor and Liberty of Savoy* (Savoy, 1789).

[15] Norman Chester, *The English Administrative System 1780–1870* (Clarendon Press 1981), 351.

[16] Norman Chester, *The English Administrative System 1780–1870* (Clarendon Press 1981), 351.

An important line of authorities concerns Commissioners of Sewers. When Henry de Bathe travelled to Romney Marsh in 1257 to examine the sewers there, he found a 'vigorous local organisation' elected specifically to deal with the defence and drainage of the marsh, which had then existed '*a tempore quo non extat memoria*'.[17] Most Commissions were put on a statutory footing by Henry IV or Henry VIII, but many were not.[18] As the existing sewers proved inadequate, seventeenth century Commissions approved extensive new works in partnership with investors and foreign specialists, especially from the Low Countries – what we might now call a public–private partnership. All were subject to *certiorari*.[19] The famous *Case of the Isle of Ely*,[20] for example, concerned just such a non-chartered Commission.

The extension of the prerogative writs to chartered and statutory corporations, however, coupled with the statutory reform of the public service in the nineteenth century, bound the supervisory jurisdiction more closely to legislative intent in the context of statutory corporations. This brings us again to corporate theory. Jurists had long discussed the legal character and powers of a 'corporation aggregate'. According to Blackstone, such a body held capacities as a corporate agent to 'sue and be sued, implead or be impleaded, grant or receive, by its corporate name, and do all other acts as natural persons may'.[21] This approach drew on *Sutton's Hospital Case*,[22] which held that the use of a common seal enabled a corporation by Royal Charter to 'do anything that a natural person could do'. In *Attorney General* v. *Leeds*,[23] for example, Luxmoore J held that the Leeds Corporation, created by Charles I, stood on a 'different footing from a statutory corporation'; it was 'settled law' that the latter species of corporation can only do such acts as are authorised directly or indirectly by the statute creating it;

17 H. G. Richardson, 'The Early History of the Commissioners of Sewers' (1919) 34(135) *The English Historical Review* 385, 389.

18 See Daniel Chan Smith, *Sir Edward Coke and the Reformation of the Laws* (Cambridge University Press 2014), 97.

19 See generally Humphry William Woolrych, *A Treatise on the Law of Waters, and of Sewers* (Saunders & Benning 1830), 452.

20 (1609) 10 Co Rep 141a.

21 Sir Norman Chester, *The English Administrative System 1780–1870* (Clarendon Press 1981), 351, citing William Blackstone, *Commentaries on the Laws of England*, Vol. 1 (Clarendon Press 1775), 475.

22 (1612) Co Rep 1; see *Riche* v. *Ahsbury Railway Carriage and Iron Co Ltd* (1874) LR 9 Ex 224, 263.

23 See *Attorney-General* v. *Manchester Corporation* [1906] 1 Ch 643 and *Attorney-General* v. *Leeds Corporation* [1870] LR 5 Ch App 583.

whereas the former can, speaking generally, do anything that an ordinary individual can do.[24] Until the Local Government Act 1933, the spending powers of the corporation were restricted by the Municipal Corporations Act 1882, and it could be restrained from applying funds to purposes not authorised by that Act – otherwise, its powers were at large.

Another important line of authorities concerns railways, including *Coleman* v. *Eastern Counties Railways Company*.[25] Like sewers, railway construction required not only vast capital but also compulsory powers 'utterly beyond the royal prerogative to confer on any individual or association', for which legislative empowerment was required.[26] Local turnpike trusts had long borne responsibility for maintaining transportation routes.[27] The railways presented an alternative means for achieving the same public good, using modern corporate finance instead of levying local rates. Joint stock companies were created to raise private capital and invested with powers of eminent domain to carry out their projects. Soon after the companies' formation, questions began to arise regarding their legal personality, capacities, and powers. Most were still creatures of a Private Act or a Royal Charter,[28] so the notion of excess of statutory jurisdiction carried over naturally. Ultra vires in this context 'expressed the common law rule prohibiting conduct which contravened a statutory provision'.[29] According to Seward Brice, ultra vires was 'a creature of purely judicial decision', originated by the courts *proprio motu* on the grounds of public policy and commercial necessity 'to meet and provide for circumstances which called for the intervention of some strong hand, but for which the State had not yet directly provided'.[30]

[24] *Attorney General* v. *Corporation of Leicester* [1943] Ch 86, 91.

[25] (1846) 50 ER 881.

[26] Seward Brice, *A Treatise on the Doctrine of Ultra Vires* (Stevens 1874), viii, xvii.

[27] See William Foote, *Statement as to the State of the Turnpike Trusts in England and Wales* (Shaw 1847); W. T. Jackman, *The Development of Transportation in Modern England* (Cambridge University Press 1916), Ch 8.

[28] See Michael Lobban, 'Joint Stock Companies' in John Baker (ed.), *Oxford History of the Laws of England Vol XII, 1820–1914 Private Law* (Oxford University Press 2010), Part III, Ch 1.

[29] Harry Rajak, 'Judicial Control: Corporations and the Decline of Ultra Vires' (1995) 26 *Cambrian Law Review* 9, 11.

[30] Seward Brice (Ashbel Green ed.), *A Treatise on the Doctrine of Ultra Vires* (2nd American ed., Baker, Voorhis 1880), ix.

The extension of judicial review to these bodies was an appropriate response to the changes then occurring in administration and the financing of public goods. But it is mistaken to base all judicial review on this particular rationale, and to ignore the more general ambit of *certiorari* over the centuries. Effectuation of legislative intent was just not a general aim of judicial review until the nineteenth century, when Parliament began placing traditional institutions on a statutory footing.[31]

These developments signpost an important crossroad in the treatment of third source-type powers. The courts *could* have extended the traditional approach, focussed on a body's capacities and disabilities as a corporate agent, as the basic methodology of judicial review; instead, as we have seen, they 'began to draw a distinction between corporations created either by charter by virtue of the royal prerogative and those created by statute'.[32] This approach was consolidated in the legislative intent theory of judicial review that emerged as orthodoxy in the mid-twentieth century. Craig has criticised a 'temporal parochialism' following these reforms.[33] The result is that the language of ultra vires today is associated less with the basic logic of acting 'beyond one's powers' than with acting outside one's *legislative* powers.

11.2.2 Finding a Way Through

In his classical treatise, Stuart Kyd classified corporations into four types according to their creation (i) in an Act of Parliament, (ii) in a Royal Charter, (iii) by prescription, and (iv) by the common law.[34] The first two types rest on a known, express instrument; corporations by prescription are presumed to have been created in the same manner, but the record has been lost. Corporations by common law, on the other hand, 'are those to which several corporate capacities have been annexed, in virtue of their political character, by the universal assent of the community, from the most remote period which their existence can be traced'.[35] They include a number of corporations sole – Kyd named the King and numerous

[31] Paul Craig, 'Ultra Vires and the Foundations of Judicial Review' in C. F. Forsyth (ed.), *Judicial Review and the Constitution* (Hart 2000), 62.

[32] Sir Norman Chester, *The English Administrative System 1780–1870* (Clarendon Press 1981), 351.

[33] Paul Craig, 'Ultra Vires and the Foundations of Judicial Review' in C. F. Forsyth (ed.), *Judicial Review and the Constitution* (Hart 2000), 70.

[34] Stuart Kyd, *Treatise on the Law of Corporations*, Vol. 1 (Butterworths 1793), 39.

[35] Stuart Kyd, *Treatise on the Law of Corporations*, Vol. 1 (Butterworths 1793), 41.

ecclesiastical offices. When a corporation is created, 'many powers, capacities, and incapacities, are tacitly annexed to it without any express provision'.[36] These powers, capacities, and incapacities – together with any relevant legislative context – set the ability-space of the relevant office in the executive, and properly mark its 'non-statutory powers', whether of the prerogative-type or of the third source-type.

There is an element of legal history in any matter concerning non-statutory executive powers, which generally derive either from the Royal Prerogative or from the Crown's personality as a common law corporation. There is always room for a modern court to ensure that the constitution evolves with society.[37] The point is simply that there is nothing alien about searching through the ancient law to find the rules of competence of ancient offices. In the context of the powers that derive from the Royal Prerogative and capacities said to derive from the personality of the Crown as a corporation sole, this is unavoidable and provides an opportunity to demystify and modernise the office itself.

The approach taken by Lord Fraser in *Council of Civil Service Unions* v. *Minister for the Civil Service*[38] is instructive (despite his dissenting view that exercises of the prerogative were immune to judicial review). In effect, Lord Fraser read into a grant of power by Order in Council the same constrains that he would read into a parliamentary statute:[39]

> I am unable to see why the words should not bear the same meaning whatever the source of authority for the legislation in which they are contained ... Whatever the source, powers which are defined, either by reference to their object or by reference to the procedure for their exercise, or in some other way, and whether the definition is express or implied, are in my opinion normally subject to judicial control to ensure that they are not exceeded.[40]

This does not mean that we should abandon the idea of vires for a broad focus on the nature or function, rather than the source, of a power. The better approach is to look first at vires, but accept that

[36] Stuart Kyd, *Treatise on the Law of Corporations*, Vol. 1 (Butterworths 1793), 69.

[37] In *Council of Civil Service Unions* v. *Minister for the Civil Service* [1985] AC 374, 417 Lord Roskill cited a letter from F. W. Maitland to A. V. Dicey to the effect that 'the only direct utility of legal history (I say nothing of its thrilling interest) lies in the lesson that each generation has an enormous power of shaping its own law'.

[38] [1985] AC 372.

[39] *Council of Civil Service Unions* v. *Minister for the Civil Service* [1985] AC 372, 399 (Lord Fraser).

[40] *Council of Civil Service Unions* v. *Minister for the Civil Service* [1985] AC 372, 399 (Lord Fraser).

vires may have their roots in both common law and statute. If there is no difference between grants of vires by Act of Parliament and by Order in Council, I think it is arguable that the same judicial controls should operate over grants of power by prescription or the common law.

Attorney General for Canada v. *Cain*[41] was argued in *Council of Civil Service Unions* v. *Minister for the Civil Service* in support of the proposition that non-statutory delegations of power without express restrictions should not have restrictions implied into them beyond those that operate on the sovereign directly. While the thrust of this argument is dubious, it is of no consequence because the duties that bind a Minister (for example) are derivative of those binding the Crown. The operative principle is simple: the Crown cannot grant its officials any powers unencumbered by its own public character and purpose. The Ram Memorandum, for example, was interpreted by the Cabinet Office to mean that 'a department can do anything that a natural person can, provided it is not prohibited from doing so'.[42] The Memorandum itself said something quite different, namely that a Minister may, as an agent of the Crown, exercise any powers which the Crown has power to exercise, except so far as he is precluded from doing so by statute. Ignoring the relationship of delegation between the Crown and the Minister is a critical error, however, because this is the hook on which the supervisory jurisdiction hangs. Farrah Ahmed even argues that delegation provides a general theory of judicial review. Judges have the power to review official action because executive officials are delegates of Parliament (where powers are reposed by statute), the Crown (where they are not), or both. This is a neglected aspect of public theory, she argues, because it has been obscured by the ultra vires debate and because it is an assumed part of the 'furniture' of public law.[43]

11.2.3 Common Law Rules of Competence and Conduct

In the United Kingdom, Ministers are not creatures of statute, and it is *prima facie* plausible to argue that they might hold corporate capacities in their own right separate to those of the Crown. An analogous argument

41 [1906] AC 542.

42 See the Cabinet Office Report cited in Lord Anthony Lester and Matthew Weait, 'The Use of Ministerial Powers without Parliamentary Authority: The Ram Doctrine' [2003] *Public Law* 415, 421.

43 Farrah Ahmed, 'The Delegation Theory of Judicial Review' (2021), 84(4) *Modern Law Review*, 72, 74.

was made in *Hazell* v. *Hammersmith & Fulham LBC*,[44] which concerned the incidental powers of an incorporated local authority. The Council had entered into swap agreements to hedge its risk under infrastructure loans. These agreements were challenged as ultra vires the corporation because they were on a scale unrelated to the corporation's actual risk exposure.[45] Generally, anything not expressly permitted to a statutory corporation is prohibited, except for a range of incidental powers.[46] The creditor banks argued that, although the powers of the Council were limited by the Local Government Act 1972, the Borough itself had all the powers of a natural person; the Borough, acting by the Council, was therefore free of the limitations imposed by the Act.[47] Lord Templeman observed that *Sutton's Hospital* was 'largely incomprehensible in 1990', and that the submission was arcane and absurd.[48] Although several authorities have applied this rule to corporations created by the prerogative, Lord Templeman held that it did not apply to the Council which was a 'hybrid' (statutory and non-statutory) corporation.

This raises an important point about the nature of corporate capacity that is essential to a proper understanding of the supervisory jurisdiction over non-statutory executive powers. The cases that established this interpretation of *Sutton's Hospital* mainly concerned corporations. Generally, incorporation was liberalised over the nineteenth century. Over time, the *quid pro quo* of easy incorporation through registration under modern companies legislation was the requirement that corporate purposes be set out clearly in a Memorandum and Articles of Association.[49] The absence of an express declaration of purposes for corporations created by Royal Charter was then taken to mean that they retained open-ended powers. In *Pharmaceutical Society of Great Britain* v. *Dickson*,[50] for example, Lord Upjohn applied this approach to hold that a chartered corporation was not subject to ultra vires in the normal sense – only its members could challenge an action as ultra vires internally, to prevent the corporation from having its charter stripped by

44 [1992] 2 AC 1.

45 See Ewan McKendrick, 'Local Authorities and Swaps: Undermining the Market?' in Ross Cranston (ed.), *Making Commercial Law* (Clarendon Press 1997), 209.

46 See *Attorney General* v. *Great Eastern Railway Co* (1880) 5 App Cas 473; *Attorney General* v. *Mersey Railway Co* [1907] AC 415.

47 *Hazell* v. *Hammersmith & Fulham LBC* [1992] 2 AC 1, 39.

48 *Hazell* v. *Hammersmith & Fulham LBC* [1992] 2 AC 1, 39.

49 See Companies Act 1862 s. 8(3); Harry Rajak, 'Judicial Control: Corporations and the Demise of *Ultra Vires*' (1995) 26 *Cambrian Law Review* 9, 11.

50 [1970] AC 403.

scire facias. That background is one reason for Dawn Oliver's rejection of ultra vires as an expression of the basis of judicial review.[51] But this must not obscure the core logic of ultra vires. A corporation – including the Crown – is 'merely a political institution' and can have no capacities other than those necessary to give effect to the purposes for which it was created.[52] *All corporations*, of whatever type, are subject to limitations in the form of duties and disabilities.[53]

The claim that corporations 'may do all other acts as natural persons may' was always 'manifestly wrong if taken in its full sense'.[54] Corporations inherently have definite limitations and may not act outside those limitations. According to Seward Brice, '[t]his is but the germ of the doctrine of ultra vires'.[55] The language of a 'common law ultra vires doctrine' was recently suggested by Sir Philip Sales:

> The Crown enjoys the private law rights it holds as tools which may only be employed by it for the purposes for which the common law recognises it as having special legal personality as a corporation sole, that is, for the public good. This suggested model is one of a sort of common-law *ultra vires* doctrine, where certain attempts at action by the Crown would be found to be unlawful and ineffective (for example, where acting for improper purposes – such as if bribed – or in a capricious or arbitrary manner; or where the Crown's power to act as corporation sole is regarded as conditional on ministerial advice being given, and that advice is itself open to legal challenge on such grounds).[56]

The suggested approach incorporates standards of fairness to be applied and enforced in respect of action by the Crown to utilise its powers, simply tracking the way that fairness standards are implied into the powers of statutory corporations wielding public authority, as implied conditions for the lawful exercise by them of their powers, including private law powers.[57] Adopting it, we would look to the written *and* unwritten sources of law setting out the rules of competence and rules of

[51] See Dawn Oliver, 'Is the Ultra Vires Rule the Basis of Judicial Review?' in Christopher Forsyth (ed.), *Judicial Review and the Constitution* (Hart 2000), 10.
[52] Stuart Kyd, *Treatise on the Law of Corporations*, Vol. 1 (Butterworths 1793), 70.
[53] Stuart Kyd, *Treatise on the Law of Corporations*, Vol. 1 (Butterworths 1793), 71.
[54] Seward Brice, *A Treatise on the Doctrine of Ultra Vires* (Stevens & Haynes 1874), 10.
[55] Seward Brice, *A Treatise on the Doctrine of Ultra Vires* (Stevens & Haynes 1874), 10.
[56] Sir Philip Sales, 'Crown Powers, the Royal Prerogative and Fundamental Rights' in Hanna Wilberg and Mark Elliott (eds.), *The Scope and Intensity of Substantive Review* (Hart 2015), 383.
[57] Sir Philip Sales, 'Crown Powers, the Royal Prerogative and Fundamental Rights' in Hanna Wilberg and Mark Elliott (eds.), *The Scope and Intensity of Substantive Review* (Hart 2015), 383.

conduct governing the office in question. We would apply the usual canons of interpretation to all of these sources; it is generally accepted that the courts do not approach statutory grants of power in a vacuum. Even the fiercest advocates of parliamentary sovereignty accept that legislative intention looks quite different once the judges are done with it. Unwritten grants of power would not be any different. The common law always imposes duties on powers to ensure fidelity to purpose, procedural fairness, and rationality.

11.3 Judicial Review in the Modern Supreme Court

Recent United Kingdom Supreme Court authorities on the judicial review of non-statutory executive powers also support, albeit indirectly, my approach. *R (Miller)* v. *Prime Minister*[58] was clearly about the *competence* of the Prime Minister, not about common law rules constraining his *conduct*. Lady Hale and Lord Reed (giving the judgment of the court) held that the purported prorogation of Parliament was ineffective because the Prime Minister's advice to HM the Queen, on which the prorogation was based, was unlawful. Early in the substantive analysis, they confirmed the fundamental reviewability of non-statutory executive powers:

> In principle, if not always in practice, it is relatively straightforward to determine the limits of a statutory power, since the power is defined by the text of the statute. Since a prerogative power is not constituted by any document, determining its limits is less straightforward. Nevertheless, every prerogative power has its limits, and it is the function of the court to determine, when necessary, where they lie.[59]

Those limits were to be determined, first and foremost, by reference to the inter-institutional arrangements between Parliament and the courts, and other constitutional principles. The principle of parliamentary sovereignty thus frames the decision expressly. However, no categorical distinction could be drawn between statutory and non-statutory executive powers: 'In their application to the exercise of governmental powers, constitutional principles do not apply only to powers conferred by statute, but also extend to prerogative powers'.[60] The purported exercise

58 [2019] UKSC 41.

59 *R (Miller)* v. *Prime Minister* [2019] UKSC 41, [35] (Lady Hale and Lord Reed).

60 *R (Miller)* v. *Prime Minister* [2019] UKSC 41, [39]–[40] (Lady Hale and Lord Reed).

of a power that does not conform with the rules on which it rests is invalid in the eyes of the law:

> The logical approach [to the prorogation's validity] is to start at the beginning, with the advice that led to it. That advice was unlawful. It was outside the powers of the Prime Minister to give it. This means that it was null and of no effect . . . It led to the Order in Council which, being founded on unlawful advice, was likewise unlawful, null and of no effect and should be quashed. This led to the actual prorogation, which was as if the Commissioners had walked into Parliament with a blank piece of paper. It too was unlawful, null and of no effect. It follows that Parliament has not been prorogued and that this court should make declarations to that effect.[61]

This passage sets out a chain of official actions, each providing an operative fact for the next action in the chain, with the result that the purported prorogation was a non-entity. Translated into my terms, Lady Hale and Lord Reed's judgment implicitly claims that the Prime Minister exceeded his competence in the strict sense and did not merely exercise his competence badly. The judgment posits that certain fundamental principles of parliamentary democracy exist, and then posits that an official action interfering with those principles must rest on *some kind* of reason. In the total absence of any reason, the decision to prorogue was unlawful in the strict sense and void *ab initio*.[62] With respect, this reasoning probably conflates the two limbs of the ultra vires rule – that is, treats the question of whether the Prime Minister had *adequate reasons* on which to base his decision as one going to the scope of his competence, rather than the manner of its exercise, by analogy on the notion of a 'fundamental constitutional principle' that triggered something like the principle of legality.[63] The Prime Minister's wrongdoing in proroguing Parliament could also be seen as a breach of a rule of conduct. Be this as it may, the judgment indirectly supports the distinction I have drawn between actions outside the ability-space of the office and actions that are *prima facie* within that ability-space but violate some rule of conduct,[64] all based on common law rules.

61 *R (Miller)* v. *Prime Minister* [2019] UKSC 41, [69]–[70] (Lady Hale and Lord Reed).

62 *R (Miller)* v. *Prime Minister* [2019] UKSC 41, [58] (Lady Hale and Lord Reed).

63 See J. N. E. Varuhas, 'The Principle of Legality' (2020) 79(3) *Cambridge Law Journal* 578, 585.

64 This distinction is also expressly relied on in the speech of Lord Reed in *R (UNISON)* v. *Lord Chancellor* [2017] UKSC 51, [199] to which the judgment refers.

11.3.1 The Limited Relevance of Justiciability and Deference

The Supreme Court was assiduous to avoid examining the Prime Minister's motivations for deciding to prorogue Parliament.[65] *R (Miller)* v. *Prime Minister* concerned a matter of high politics – indeed, one of the most controversial political issues of our generation. Discussion of justiciability and deference has been conspicuously scant in this book. Without denigrating the importance of modulating the standard of judicial review according to context,[66] this is for the simple reason that, once ultra vires is properly understood, justiciability and deference have less work to do than the conventional wisdom suggests.

Again, jurisdictional logic and the two-limbed structure of ultra vires review provides some guidance. No question of justiciability ever arises under the narrow limb of ultra vires.[67] There is a basic tension between non-justiciability itself and the basic judicial imperative to adjudicate.[68] So long as officials have limited powers, there is a justiciable question irrespective of context. This is almost definitional in the case of the narrow limb of the ultra vires rule, but T. R. S. Allan is right that the judges retain an inherent power to adjudicate questions concerning officials' legal duties to exercise their vires reasonably, for example, under the broad limb. A finding of 'non-justiciability' is, in substance, just a finding that the official was not subject to any *legally enforceable* limits. As we are concerned with judicial review, and not any other mechanisms of official accountability, it is one and the same to say that an issue is 'non-justiciable' and that no legal limits exist.

In *R (Miller)* v. *Prime Minister*, for example, the Divisional Court had held that the matter of prorogation was non-justiciable. Lady Hale and Lord Reed noted that although the courts should steer clear of political questions, the fact that a legal dispute concerns the political process cannot make it *ipso facto* non-justiciable as a political question: 'Many if not most of the constitutional cases in our legal history have been concerned with politics in that sense'.[69] If an issue is justiciable, deciding it will not disrupt the constitutional separation of powers but promote them.[70] This

65 *R (Miller)* v. *Prime Minister* [2019] UKSC 41, [58] (Lady Hale and Lord Reed).

66 See generally D. R. Knight, *Vigilance and Restraint in the Common Law of Judicial Review* (Cambridge University Press 2018), Ch 4.

67 See, for example, Chris Finn, 'The Justiciability of Administrative Decisions: A Redundant Concept?' (2002) 30(2) *Federal Law Review* 239.

68 T. R. S. Allan, *The Sovereignty of Law* (Oxford University Press 2013), 274.

69 *R (Miller)* v. *Prime Minister* [2019] UKSC 41, [31] (Lady Hale and Lord Reed).

70 *R (Miller)* v. *Prime Minister* [2019] UKSC 41, [34] (Lady Hale and Lord Reed).

reasoning supports the idea of legislative supremacy, but also confirms the distinction between rules of competence and rules of conduct, and in so doing supports my argument that the scope of an official's ability-space is inherently a justiciable question.

It is only in relation to the broad limb that justiciability and deference issues arise, that is, where a power exists and was exercised intra vires in the strict sense but appears 'challengeable in the courts on the basis of one or more of the recognised grounds of judicial review'.[71] By reference to *Council of Civil Service Unions* v. *Minister for the Civil Service*, Lady Hale and Lord Reed said that the answer to that question would depend on the nature of the power in question. In this case, which went to the Prime Minister's motive for requesting a prorogation from HM the Queen, questions of justiciability would arise.[72] That ground did not need to be considered, however, given that the case could be determined on the narrow basis.

In any case, it is fair to say that the category of non-justiciable questions is narrow because the courts are, by their nature, responsible for policing the ability-space *and* liberty-space of executive officials. There is a certain preserve of action proper to the executive that should not be second-guessed by judges. However, as we have seen, even grants of 'absolute discretion' are subject to legally enforceable duties of reasonableness and proper purpose. To the extent that differs from justiciability, judicial deference does not affect this analysis. Jurisdictional logic sets out executive officials' 'privilege to err', ringed about by rules of conduct. Deference only operates where no legally enforceable duty has been breached. Thus, judicial deference should be seen as 'baked in' to the structure of the supervisory jurisdiction itself rather than operating as a limiting factor in the second instance.

The limits of deference are set by the scope of the duties owed by the official in the exercise of his powers. Judicial deference is quite simply a function of (i) proper characterisation of the official duties in question and (ii) proper judicial determination of what those duties are. As Allan claims, 'deference' merely marks the situation where an administrative decision is accepted by the courts as 'fall[ing] within the proper scope of the relevant powers'.[73] *True* deference only arises where there is a range

[71] *R (Miller)* v. *Prime Minister* [2019] UKSC 41, [35] (Lady Hale and Lord Reed). Emphasis mine.

[72] *R (Miller)* v. *Prime Minister* [2019] UKSC 41, [54] (Lady Hale and Lord Reed).

[73] T. R. S. Allan, *The Sovereignty of Law* (Oxford University Press 2013), 269; see D. R. Knight, *Vigilance and Restraint in the Common Law of Judicial Review* (Cambridge University Press 2018), 215.

of outcomes that all meet the test of justification; only in those circumstances is it legitimate for a court to defer on constitutional or expertise grounds to the executive's preference for one or the other of two lawful options. While important, this is a limited set of circumstances – even in the realm of non-statutory executive powers.

11.3.2 Separation of Powers and the Common Law Protection of Vested Rights

R (Miller) v. *Brexit Secretary*[74] is more complex. Despite the non-statutory nature of the power concerned, the frame of analysis adopted by the Supreme Court was (again) squarely on parliamentary sovereignty. According to Mark Elliott, the case *could* be painted as an affirmation of English constitutional orthodoxy – the executive was put in its place, and Parliament was put squarely in the drivers' seat, as it were, 'free from the competing claims represented by (on the one had) the Government's innate prerogative authority and (on the other hand) the devolved legislature's asserted rights of constitutional participation'.[75] Unfortunately, in his view, the reasoning that drove the majority's judgment to these outcomes 'reflects an understanding of the Constitution that is inadequately subtle'.[76]

The central tension in *R (Miller)* v. *Brexit Secretary* arises from the fact that making treaties is clearly the regular business of the Crown, being a classical prerogative-type power.[77] However, under the dualist approach of British law to international law,[78] treaties are not self-executing and must be incorporated by legislation in order to become part of the law of the United Kingdom.[79] The dynamic of interaction between the non-statutory treaty-making power and a treaty system incorporated by parliamentary legislation thus set the stage for the key question. Was the Prime Minister, in reliance on the common law powers

[74] [2017] UKSC 5.

[75] Mark Elliott, 'The Supreme Court's Judgment in *Miller*: In Search of Constitutional Principle' (2017) 76(2) *Cambridge Law Journal* 257, 259.

[76] Mark Elliott, 'The Supreme Court's Judgment in *Miller*: In Search of Constitutional Principle' (2017) 76(2) *Cambridge Law Journal* 257, 259.

[77] See, for example, *Blackburn* v. *Attorney General* [1971] 1 WLR 1037, 1040 (Lord Denning MR); see generally Campbell McLachlan, *Foreign Relations Law* (Cambridge University Press 2014).

[78] See further Chapter 4.

[79] See James Crawford, *Brownlie's Principles of Public International Law* (8th ed., Oxford University Press 2012), Ch 3.

inuring in that office, competent to trigger the United Kingdom's exit from the European Union under Article 50 of the Treaty on the Functioning of the European Union, or did she need parliamentary authorisation to do that? Again, the case turned on a question of competence, rather than conduct, in the exercise of non-statutory executive powers.

Nick Barber, Tom Hickman, and Jeff King identify two strands of argument, both at first instance and in the Supreme Court.[80] The first strand is a 'frustration argument', which tracks the principle identified with cases such as *Attorney General* v. *De Keyser's Royal Hotel Ltd*,[81] *Laker Airways Ltd* v. *Department of Trade*,[82] and *R (Fire Brigades Union)* v. *Home Secretary*.[83] In *Attorney General* v. *De Keyser's Royal Hotel Ltd*, officers of the Crown had taken possession of a hotel in wartime; the dispute turned on the compensation payable for compulsory use. That in turn depended on whether the taking power relied on was statutory or non-statutory.[84] The House of Lords held that the passage of certain statutes and regulations put the prerogative power of taking into abeyance (so long as the statutory regime existed). *Laker Airways Ltd* v. *Department of Trade* turned on the interaction between a statutory scheme and non-statutory policy guidance given to the Civil Aviation Authority. The later guidance effectively cut across the policy of the statute, and was for this reason ultra vires.[85]

In *R (Fire Brigades Union)* v. *Home Secretary*, Parliament had enacted a statutory scheme to replace a non-statutory compensation scheme. However, the Secretary of State decided to delay its coming into force *sine die* and to create a new non-statutory scheme to replace the old one. The House of Lords affirmed the *De Keyser* principle, but, 'since the statutory provisions were not [yet] in force they could not have excluded the pre-existing prerogative powers', strictly speaking that principle could not apply.[86] Reflecting the two limbed nature of the ultra vires rule, the court examined whether there had been an abuse of those

80 N. W. Barber, Tom Hickman, and Jeff King, 'Reflections on Miller' [2016–2017] 8 *UK Supreme Court Yearbook* 212, 214.

81 [1920] AC 508.

82 [1977] 2 All ER 182.

83 [1995] UKHL 3.

84 See *Attorney General* v. *De Keyser's Royal Hotel Ltd* [1920] AC 508, 523 (Lord Dunedin); see *The Zamora* [1916] 2 AC 77 (Privy Council).

85 See *Laker Airways Ltd* v. *Department of Trade* [1977] QB 643, 704 (Lord Denning).

86 *R (Fire Brigades Union)* v. *Home Secretary* [1995] 2 AC 513, 553 (Lord Browne-Wilkinson).

prerogative powers. In the Court of Appeal, Hobhouse LJ had opined that the existence of a dormant statutory scheme had no bearing on the question. In the House of Lords, Lord Browne-Wilkinson held that it was 'directly relevant' to the lawful exercise of the prerogative power; the decision to enact a new non-statutory scheme just before a statutory scheme was due to come into force, for example, would constitute an abuse of the prerogative power.[87]

The second strand of the judgments is a 'rights argument'. Since at least the *Case of Proclamations*[88] it has been accepted that 'the King hath no prerogative, but that which the law of the land allows him';[89] in particular, 'the King by his proclamation of other ways cannot change any part of the common law, or statute law, or the customs of the realm' and 'proclamations shall not alter the law, statutes, or customs of the realm, or impeach any [subject] in his inheritance, goods, body, life, etc.'[90] The claimants' argument in *R (Miller)* v. *Brexit Secretary* was simply that the United Kingdom's membership in the European Union vested rights in United Kingdom subjects. Because demission of the European treaties would take at least some of those rights away, giving notice to leave the European Union without statutory authorisation would be ultra vires the Prime Minister under the *Case of Proclamations* principle.

The strands run together in the judgments – at first instance, and especially on appeal – and the frustration argument appears to carry the reasoning.[91] The central holding of the majority in the Supreme Court (Lord Neuberger, Lady Hale, Lord Mance, Lord Kerr, Lord Clarke, Lord Wilson, Lord Sumption, and Lord Hodge) was that giving notice without statutory authorisation would be inconsistent with the European Communities Act 1972 because that Act 'endorsed and gave effect to the United Kingdom's membership of what is now the European Union under the EU Treaties *in a way* which is inconsistent with the future exercise by ministers of any prerogative power to withdraw from such Treaties'.[92] Withdrawal from the EU would constitute a significant

[87] *R (Fire Brigades Union)* v. *Home Secretary* [1995] 2 AC 513, 554 (Lord Browne-Wilkinson).

[88] (1610) 77 ER 1352.

[89] *The Case of Proclamations* (1610) 77 ER 1352, 1354.

[90] *The Case of Proclamations* (1610) 77 ER 1352, 1354.

[91] See *R (Miller)* v. *Brexit Secretary* [2017] UKSC 5, [69].

[92] *R (Miller)* v. *Brexit Secretary* [2017] UKSC 5, [77] (Lord Neuberger, Lady Hale, Lord Mance, Lord Kerr, Lord Clarke, Lord Wilson, Lord Sumption, and Lord Hodge). Emphasis mine.

constitutional change which, considering the background of constitutional principle and the European Communities Act 1972, required parliamentary legislation.

Viewed as a proposition relating to official action, the implicit ruling is that the act of demitting from the European treaties, notwithstanding the traditional prerogative-type power of treaty demission, would change the law in virtue of the European treaties constituting a special type of legal system over and above a normal treaty framework.[93] That was an action that the majority held to be ultra vires in the narrow sense.

The dissenting judgment of Lord Reed, by way of contrast, characterised the act of demission not as an act-in-the-law to change the law applicable in the United Kingdom but as a kind of act-in-fact with the effect of changing the facts on which the European Communities Act 1972 operated. This was based on Lord Reed's interpretation of s. 2(1) of the European Communities Act 1972, in particular the reference to rights 'from time to time created or arising under the Treaties'. The demission of the treaty was an act-at-international-law (an act-in-fact for domestic legal purposes) with the consequence that the set of rights referred to in s. 2(1) was empty. No act-in-the-domestic-law existed to violate the principle in the *Case of Proclamations*.[94]

Elliott has criticised the majority's reasoning in strident terms: 'to the extent that [it] can lay claim to intellectual coherence', he argues, it rests on a notion of 'scale' or 'constitutional importance' that is too vague.[95] The power to demit from a treaty is not put into abeyance by just any statute, only by a 'constitutional statute'[96] of adequate calibre, such as the European Communities Act 1972. According to the majority, the special status of this statute relates to the unique effect it had as a kind of 'direct conduit' of international law into domestic law, a point on which the approach of the majority and Lord Reed differed.[97] But the majority judges failed to articulate a robust test of 'constitutional importance'.

93 This was European law at the time the European Communities Act 1972 was passed. See *Van Gend en Loos* (Case C-26/62) [1963] ECR 1; *Costa* v. *ENEL* (Case C-6/64) [1964] ECR 585.

94 See *R (Miller)* v. *Brexit Secretary* [2017] UKSC 5, [186] (Lord Reed).

95 Mark Elliott, 'The Supreme Court's Judgment in *Miller*: In Search of Constitutional Principle' (2017) 76(2) *Cambridge Law Journal* 257, 263.

96 See *R (HS2 Action Alliance Ltd)* v. *Secretary of State for Transport* [2014] UKSC 3, [207] (Lord Neuberger and Lord Mance, with whom Lady Hale, Lord Kerr, Lord Sumption, Lord Reed, and Lord Carnwath agreed).

97 See *R (Miller)* v. *Brexit Secretary* [2017] UKSC 5, [61].

While there is credence to Elliott's critique, the real problem is that *R (Miller)* v. *Brexit Secretary* became, once again, prematurely concerned with parliamentary sovereignty in a debate about non-statutory executive powers. Granted, the separation of powers between Parliament and the Crown (acting in reliance on its traditional prerogative-type powers) is important. But at base, the case is about imposing common law limits on the ambit of non-statutory executive powers in order to protect a common law constitutional principle. Even where that common law principle prevents the Crown from pre-empting a statutory scheme, its roots are in the common law rules of competence that draw the Crown's non-statutory ability-space. In other words, although the intention of Parliament in passing the European Communities Act 1972 determines *where* the line is to be drawn, the Supreme Court could not, in my view, be said to be acting as the agent of Parliament in drawing it.

The true importance of *R (Miller)* v. *Brexit Secretary* therefore does not appear on the face of the case at all. Indeed, there was a subtle but important shift in how *R (Miller)* v. *Brexit Secretary* was argued and decided. At first instance, argument centred on the 'rights strand'. Rights were argued to be protected by a common law immunity deriving from the principle in the *Case of Proclamations*. The tabloid press at the time ran a brazen campaign, including a scandalous denunciation of Lord Thomas CJ, Sir Terence Etherton MR, and Sales LJ (sitting in the Divisional Court) as 'enemies of the people'.[98] Perhaps this context explains the importance of the 'frustration strand' in the Supreme Court.[99] In the midst of a tense constitutional moment, one might forgive the judges for emphasising the courts' role in protecting the sovereignty of Parliament in a system of representative democracy, rather than policing the common law borders of a populist government's non-statutory executive powers. That the common law protects the supremacy of the legislature by preventing the pre-emption of statutes, however, supports rather than undermines the argument that judicial review rests on the common law ultra vires doctrine.

There are sometimes good reasons for judges to avoid calling a spade a spade. Will Bateman and Leighton McDonald have described the drift of Australian High Court jurisprudence towards an approach focussed on statutory language, and the grafting of the concept of jurisdictional

98 See *Daily Mail*, 4 November 2016.

99 This conclusion is based on my objective analysis of the Supreme Court judgments, and does not purport to draw on my experience as a Judicial Assistant to the Divisional Court.

error to the exercise of statutory interpretation, from the 1980s onwards. Each step in this trajectory was geared towards providing a buffer against the pressure mounting on the judiciary to curb its role as the scrutineer of executive action in politically controversial areas:

> Justice Brennan was at his most vocal in expounding the constitutional virtues of legislative purpose when the judiciary was being asked to act adventurously . . . In the prominent immigration cases of [the early 2000s] the High Court was moving in politically fraught territory, and it was under those conditions that legislative purpose mutated from an intellectual framework to an operative test of legality. Set against the broader political landscape, the choice to move . . . to the statutory approach can be understood as an attempt to lose the battle and win the war. In the short term, the Court was attempting to persuade that judicial review does not involve the court in political judgments – that when it invalidates an administrator's decision it is simply enforcing the letter or spirit of a statutory power and thereby acting as parliament's proxy.[100]

In any case, *R (Miller)* v. *Brexit Secretary* establishes that the judicial review of non-statutory executive powers follows a scheme which is most accurately described by the language of ultra vires and by the logic of official empowerment and action set out in this book.

11.4 Conclusion

Reviewing the judicial review of non-statutory executive powers, I have often felt a sense of bewilderment that the notion of ultra vires beyond statute is controversial. To me, it has always seemed obvious that the language of ultra vires, and the concept of 'acting outside one's powers' that it implies, is the natural expression to encapsulate the procedure at the heart of judicial review. If we trace it step by step, the logic of official empowerment and action lays out a straightforward path by which we first look for the rules of competence that repose powers in an office – be they in the written or unwritten law. We then ask what rules of conduct constrain the exercise of the powers reposed in the office, by reference both to general standards and to the purpose inherent within any public office – be they in the written or unwritten law. We follow a simple and intuitive method of measuring the actual conduct of the official against these rules. That, in a word, is the common law doctrines of ultra vires.

[100] Will Bateman and Leighton McDonald, 'The Normative Structure of Australian Administrative Law' (2017) 45 *Federal Law Review* 153, 172.

12

The Borders of the Supervisory Jurisdiction

12.1 Introduction

The non-statutory executive powers of the Crown and its officials are amenable to judicial review under the common law theory of ultra vires. This chapter turns, by way of comparison, to the parallel supervisory jurisdiction over the powers of bodies that are not obviously 'official' or even obviously 'public' at all. As mentioned, these bodies bear certain parallels to third source-type executive powers, so it is instructive to discuss the issues they raise together.

The common law challenge to the legislative intent theory of judicial review rode on the back of 'pluralist and corporatist realities' changing the face of governance in the latter decades of the twentieth century,[1] particularly following the decision of the Court of Appeal in *R (Datafin)* v. *Take-over Panel.*[2] The modern doctrinal position is that the substantive grounds of judicial apply to a range of bodies that fall, at best, into the penumbra of public law. Some of them fall closer, some further, from the core of HM Government. Exploring the border between the 'core' supervisory jurisdiction and its cognates, such as the monopolies doctrine, will help us to understand the logical structure and conceptual foundations of both.

The extension of judicial review beyond statute not only unleashed disagreement about the rationale for judicial review, it was generally taken to mark a shift of focus from the source of a power to its 'nature' or 'function'. The 'public' *versus* 'private' nature of a body's function, of course, assumed even greater importance following the

[1] T. R. S. Allan, 'Doctrine and Theory in Administrative Law: An Elusive Quest for the Limits to Jurisdiction' [2003] *Public Law* 429, 431; Paul Craig, *Administrative Law* (4th ed., Sweet & Maxwell 1999), Ch 1.

[2] [1987] QB 815.

reform of the Supreme Court Rules and the ruling in *O'Reilly* v. *Mackman*[3] that proceeding with a private law claim in parallel to a judicial review application constituted an abuse of process. However, no stable border has yet been drawn around the public law supervisory jurisdiction, and the trend towards increased hybridisation rather works against the idea that public law represents a coherent and self-contained system.[4]

Section 12.2 surveys the supervisory jurisdictions in private law to see what light they shed on the domain of 'judicial review'. This section also examines the complicating factors, including debates about the nature of 'public law' and the rise of new modalities of 'governance' including market-based activities by the Crown, which have borne negatively on our ability to determine what is and what is not amenable to the supervisory jurisdiction. Section 12.3 then turns to the question whether the office-based approach is helpful in this context, too. It argues that there is a meaningful sense in which a nominally private actor might be said to occupy an 'office of public trust' and be, on that basis, amenable to the supervisory jurisdiction. Section 12.4 concludes.

12.2 One Supervisory Jurisdiction or Many?

A common bedrock of principle supports the supervisory jurisdiction over non-statutory executive powers. The type of power with which the supervisory jurisdiction is concerned is, for the most part, exercised by an individual who acts in a capacity other than her personal capacity in virtue of some position within an institution. Typically, that institution is straightforwardly 'public', has a clear historical and organisational connection to the Crown and the broader network of offices that make up HM Government, and might even bear a name like 'HM Prison Service'.

R (Datafin) v. *Take-over Panel*[5] admittedly pushed the envelope of the supervisory jurisdiction; not only was it a non-statutory body, it was not obviously a 'governmental' body at all. Beyond the Panel, the substantive grounds of judicial review have been applied to bodies including the London Stock Exchange,[6] self-regulatory bodies in industries including

3 [1983] 2 AC 237.

4 See John Alder, 'Hunting the Chimera – the End of *O'Reilly v Mackman*?' (1993) 13 *Legal Studies* 183.

5 [1987] QB 815.

6 *Weinberger* v. *Inglis* [1919] AC 606.

advertising,[7] pharmaceuticals,[8] media,[9] and insurance trusts,[10] the Office of the Independent Adjudicator for Higher Education,[11] self-described ombudsman schemes in the commercial context,[12] sporting organisations including those regulating horse racing,[13] football,[14] and greyhound racing,[15] University Visitors,[16] the Inns of Court,[17] the Showmen's Guild,[18] the 'Film Artistes Association',[19] and many others. A similar supervisory jurisdiction has also been asserted, from the early modern period at least, over de jure and de facto economic monopolies. Commentators have further noticed parallels between judicial review and the control of contractual discretions,[20] contracts in restraint of trade, and the older doctrine of 'common callings'.[21]

This raises the valid question of how far the common law theory of ultra vires can take us in explaining the courts' various supervisory jurisdictions. The question has become more, rather than less, important with the passage of time: we have seen that both the legislative intent theorists and the common law theorists accept that a sub-set of these bodies, at least, should be amenable to judicial review.

[7] *R (Advertising Services plc)* v. *Advertising Standards Authority Ltd* [1990] COD 42.

[8] *R (Professional Counselling Aids)* v. *Code of Practice Committee of the Association of the British Pharmaceutical Industry* [1991] COD 228.

[9] *R (Stewart-Brady)* v. *Press Complaints Commission* (1997) 9 Admin LR 247.

[10] *R (Ross)* v. *Life Assurance Unit Trust Regulatory Organisation* [1993] QB 17.

[11] *R (Siborurema)* v. *Office of the Independent Adjudicator* [2007] EWCA Civ 1365.

[12] *R (Aegon Life Assurance Ltd)* v. *Insurance Ombudsman* [1994] COD 426; *R (Kubis)* v. *Panel of the Federation of Communication Services Ltd* [1998] COD 56; *R (Sunspell Ltd)* v. *Association of British Travel Agents* [2001] ACD 16; *R (Briggs)* v. *Lloyd's of London* [1993] 1 Lloyd's Rep 176; *R (West)* v. *Lloyds of London* [2004] EWCA Civ 506; *R (Mooyer)* v. *Personal Investment Authority Ombudsman Bureau Ltd* [2001] EWHC Admin 247.

[13] *Mullins* v. *The Board of Appeal of the Jockey Club* [2005] EWHC Admin 2197; *R (Massingberd-Mundy)* v. *Disciplinary Committee of the Jockey Club* [1993] 2 All ER 207; *R (RAM Racecourses Ltd)* v. *Jockey Club* [1993] 2 All ER 225; *R (Aga Khan)* v. *Disciplinary Committee of the Jockey Club* [1993] 1 WLR 909.

[14] See *R (Football League Ltd)* v. *Football Association Ltd* [1993] 12 All ER 833; *Modahl* v. *British Athletic Federation Ltd* [2002] 1 WLR 1192; *Newport Association Football Club Ltd* v. *Football Association of Wales Ltd* [1995] 2 All ER 87; *Stevenage Borough Football Club Ltd* v. *Football League* [1996] WLUK 36.

[15] *Law* v. *National Greyhound Racing Club* [1983] 1 WLR 1302.

[16] *R (Page)* v. *Hull University Visitor* [1993] AC 682.

[17] *R (Wooller)* v. *The Benchers of Lincoln's Inn* (1825) 107 ER 1277.

[18] *Lee* v. *Showmen's Guild* (1952) 2 QB 329.

[19] *Faramis* v. *Film Artistes Association* [1963] AC 925.

[20] See T. C. Daintith, 'Contractual Discretion and Administrative Discretion: A Unified Analysis' (2005) 68 *Modern Law Review* 554.

[21] See D. S. Bogen, 'The Inkeeper's Tale: The Legal Development of a Public Calling' [1996] 1 *Utah Law Review* 51.

My position is generally consistent with the common law theories of judicial review, but suggests some important refinements. Dawn Oliver, for example, argued that the extension of the supervisory jurisdiction beyond statute showed judicial review's true colours. By reference to prerogative-type powers, third source-type powers, chartered corporations, nominally private bodies, and various other cases at the margin, Oliver argued that legislative intent could not explain judicial review at all:

> In place of the ultra vires rule a doctrine is emerging that, in the public sphere, the courts in exercising a supervisory jurisdiction are concerned both with the vires of public authorities in the strict or narrow sense referred to above, *and with abuse of power.* If abuse of power is established, the courts may properly intervene. If no abuse is established, the courts should leave to the political process the function of dealing with complaints about the exercise of power.[22]

One problem with this approach is that it acquiesces in the identification of ultra vires with legislative intent – an unnecessary concession that has done much to hamper progress towards a rational view of the supervisory jurisdiction. Another, more serious problem is that it moves on too quickly, without developing an adequate concept of official power. Despite some engagement with the different forms that power can take, Oliver settled on a sociological concept of 'power' rather than a juridical one: it is on 'power, not powers' that 'broad principles of good administration' supervene.

12.2.1 Still a Matter of Vires Amenable to Review

In the context of non-statutory bodies, the first step is always to set out the vires of the body within the relevant context. Only on that basis is it possible to ask whether that context makes those powers approximate 'public law powers'. Oliver's argument rightly highlighted the changing nature of public administration at the time. Just as the courts were striving to separate 'public' from 'private' law, the two were converging:

> An awareness of the nature of power, and of the 'interpenetration of state and society', is leading the courts towards a willingness to supervise public and private power. The weakness of [legislative intent] as the basis for judicial review, and of the doctrines of separation of powers and

22 Dawn Oliver, 'Is the Ultra Vires Rule the Basis of Judicial Review?' in Christopher Forsyth (ed.), *Judicial Review and the Constitution* (Hart 2000), 25. Emphasis mine.

> parliamentary sovereignty on which [it] rests, is symptomatic of the absence of workable concepts and of a framework of theory about the nature of power, whether public or private, upon which to build the supervisory jurisdictions of the courts.[23]

There is merit in searching for a unified explanation of the supervisory jurisdiction over non-statutory executive powers *stricto sensu* as well as over institutions in the penumbra of public law. The question is how to describe this supervisory jurisdiction – in its full ambit – as a coherent whole, rather than as a set of discrete jurisdictions that just happen to share identical grounds.

The problem is generally couched in terms of a choice between a test of amenability based on the *source* of the power in question and one based on the *nature or function* of the power in question. *R (Datafin)* v. *Take-over Panel* famously rejected the traditional source-based test. Sir John Donaldson MR observed that, while the cases yielded indicative factors, it would be an error to take a rigid formulaic approach to amenability; the crucial factors were a 'public element' which would take different forms, and the exclusion of bodies whose sole source of power was consensual submission to their jurisdiction.[24] Though 'non-legal', the Take-over Panel's powers were not 'private' or 'contractual' and operated as part of a government-sanctioned framework for regulating corporate mergers. Lloyd LJ opined that 'if the duty is a public duty, then the body in question is subject to public law'.[25]

English public law jurisprudence has not yet developed a positive replacement for the source test, however.[26] Three approaches can be observed. A power has been held to be 'public' if exercised (i) by a private body performing a function that the Crown would otherwise carry out directly (sometimes known as the 'but for' test),[27] (ii) by a private body performing a function that is somehow underpinned by statute (sometimes known as the 'statutory underpinning' test),[28] and (iii) by a private body performing a function 'enmeshed' in the activities of a public body.[29] Factors held to speak against amenability include

23 Dawn Oliver, 'Is the Ultra Vires Rule the Basis of Judicial Review?' in Christopher Forsyth (ed.), *Judicial Review and the Constitution* (Hart 2000), 26.
24 *R (Datafin)* v. *Take-over Panel* [1987] QB 815, 839 (Sir John Donaldson MR).
25 *R (Datafin)* v. *Take-over Panel* [1987] QB 815, 848 (Lloyd LJ).
26 C. D. Campbell, 'Monopoly Power as Public Power for the Purposes of Judicial Review' (2009) 125 *Law Quarterly Review* 491, 521.
27 See *R (Aga Khan)* v. *Disciplinary Committee of the Jockey Club* [1993] 1 WLR 909.
28 See *R (Datafin)* v. *Take-over Panel* [1987] QB 815.
29 See *Hampshire County Council* v. *Beer* [2003] EWCA Civ 1056.

a contract or other consensual relationship between the subject and the repository of power,[30] and (perhaps) the existence of an alternative remedy such as a private law remedy.[31]

In the wash, the 'multi-factorial' approach that emerges from the cases lacks both legal certainty and logical coherence. Judges themselves have described the question as being as much 'a matter of feel' as a one of 'whether any particular criteria are met',[32] and have described bodies having a sufficient 'public law flavour'[33] to render them amenable. While the courts purport to apply the functional approach, the cases themselves give significant weight to institutional and source-based considerations.[34] The law is 'largely incoherent' or at least 'inadequately elaborated'.[35]

This is a serious problem for judicial review beyond statute because, although most of the entities immediately subject to review are not part of HM Government in the strict sense, they are bound up in the business of modern administration. Looking at their amenability to review – the question of grounds and standards being fairly moot – not only sheds light on the core cases of prerogative-type and third source-type powers, but is itself an important context for 'administrative accountability' broadly defined.

12.2.2 *The Supervisory Jurisdiction over 'Domestic Tribunals'*

R (Lain) v. *Criminal Injuries Compensation Commission*[36] marked the commencement of judicial review over prerogative-type powers in the modern law, harking expressly back to the availability of the prerogative writs against all kinds of non-statutory bodies in the ancient and early-modern law. Yet Lord Diplock in that case also held that so-called 'private

30 See *R (Goldsmith)* v. *Servite Houses* (2001) 33 HLR 35, [89] (Moses J).

31 *R (Aegon Life Assurance Ltd)* v. *Insurance Ombudsman Bureau* [1994] CLC 88, 93 (Rose LJ); Cf *R (Aga Khan)* v. *Disciplinary Committee of the Jockey Club* [1993] 1 WLR 909, 933 (Hoffmann LJ).

32 *R (Tucker)* v. *Director General of the National Crime Squad* [2003] EWCA Civ 57, [13] (Scott Baker LJ).

33 *R (Holmcroft Properties)* v. *KPMG LLP* [2016] EWHC Admin 323, [31] (Elias and Mitting LJJ).

34 Alex Williams, 'Public Functions and Amenability: Recent Trends' (2017) 22(1) *Judicial Review* 15, 26.

35 Mark Elliott, 'Judicial Review's Scope, Foundations and Purposes: Joining the Dots' [2012] [1] *New Zealand Law Review* 75.

36 2 AC 330.

or domestic tribunals' remained outside the scope of *certiorari*, because their authority was 'derived solely from contract' between the parties concerned.[37]

This position reflects the shifting emphasis from 'private law constitutionalism' (in which an official acting ultra vires was tantamount to a private defendant who happened to be indemnified by HM Government), to the new system of public law based around the prerogative writs. However, there is also a rich – if not entirely consistent – jurisprudence concerning a parallel supervisory jurisdiction over domestic tribunals. In my view, that jurisprudence is a valuable resource as the modalities of government again change – and as private entities are increasingly involved in the formulation of policy and delivery of services. If this jurisdiction marks the outer bound of the (core) public law supervisory jurisdiction, exploring its ambit should help to determine the scope of judicial review.

But the picture that emerges is anything but clear. Originally, a property right was necessary to enliven the supervisory jurisdiction over domestic tribunals.[38] From the mid-nineteenth century, the borders of this supervisory jurisdiction were extended. First, contract was established as an alternative to property rights.[39] Later, a confederation of notions of 'public policy' – including restraint of trade, 'right to work', and the control of economic monopoly power – were established as an alternative to contract.[40]

Here we can observe some familiar tensions. For example, cases like *Abbott* v. *Sullivan*[41] and *Lee* v. *Showmen's Guild*[42] concerned an error of law by a domestic tribunal. The Court of Appeal held that an express or implied contract between the parties would suffice to enliven the supervisory jurisdiction over domestic tribunals, and that no proprietary interest was necessary. However, the relation of the sub-categories within this supervisory jurisdiction was already unclear. Some judges opined

[37] *R (Lain)* v. *Criminal Injuries Compensation Board* [1967] 2 QB 864, 882 (Lord Diplock).

[38] See *R (Wooller)* v. *The Benchers of Lincoln's Inn* (1825) 107 ER 1277.

[39] See, for contemporary, commentary Denis Lloyd, 'The Disciplinary Powers of Professional Bodies' (1950) 13(3) *Modern Law Review* 281; Denis Lloyd, 'Judicial Review of Expulsion by a Domestic Tribunal' (1952) 15(4) *Modern Law Review* 27.

[40] This move was broadly reflective of labour relations at the time: see R. W. Rideout, 'Admission to Non-Statutory Associations Controlling Employment' (1967) 30(4) *Modern Law Review* 389; Patrick Elias, 'Trade Unions – Expulsion – Damages – Right to Work' (1971) 29(1) *Modern Law Review* 15.

[41] (1951) 1 KB 189.

[42] (1952) 2 QB 329.

that the 'social club' cases and the 'medical cases' (concerning statutory self-regulatory tribunals) should be distinguished from the 'right to work cases',[43] while the chief proponent of the right to work jurisdiction, Denning LJ, took a more holistic approach.[44]

An important line of authorities concerns horseracing. The year before *R (Lain)* v. *Criminal Injuries Compensation Board* was decided, the Court of Appeal had held that the Jockey Club was amenable to judicial review in *Nagle* v. *Feilden.*[45] The case concerned arbitrary refusal of a license application by the Jockey Club on the basis that the applicant was a woman. At first instance, Nagle's claim was struck out for lacking a cause of action: she had no contract with the club. Lord Denning MR granted the appeal, however. Had the case concerned a 'social club', the members could have done as they liked. But this association 'exercise[d] a virtual monopoly in an important field of human activity' whose Stewards 'could put a man out of business' by refusing a license.[46] That placed the Jockey Club under a duty of non-discrimination. Citing the supervision of bodies such as the Stock Exchange,[47] trade unions,[48] and drawing analogies to the self-regulatory guilds of earlier centuries,[49] the law protected the right to work.[50]

A few years later, in *Enderby Town Football Club Ltd* v. *Football Association Ltd*,[51] Lord Denning MR summarised the development of the law. Though it originally relied on the fiction of a contract between the members, 'the truth is that the rules are nothing more nor less than a legislative code – a set of regulations laid down by the governing body to be observed by all who are, or become, members of the association'.[52] Such regulations were subject to the control of the courts. Again citing authorities on restraint of trade, invalid ouster of the supervisory jurisdiction, right to work, and violation of natural justice, '[a]ll these are

43 See *Abbott* v. *Sullivan* (1951) 1 KB 189, 196 (Baron Evershed MR); *Lee* v. *Showmen's Guild* (1952) 2 QB 329, 351 (Romer LJ).

44 See e.g., *Abbott* v. *Sullivan* (1951) 1 KB 189, 201 (Denning LJ).

45 [1966] 2 QB 633.

46 *Nagle* v. *Feilden* [1966] 2 QB 633, 644 (Lord Denning MR).

47 *Weinberger* v. *Inglis* [1919] AC 606.

48 *Faramis* v. *Film Artistes Association* [1964] 1 All ER 25.

49 See *Tailors of Ipswich* (1614) 11 Co Rep 53a and *R* v. *Surgeons Company (Master)* (1759) 2 Burr 892.

50 *Nagle* v. *Feilden* [1966] 2 QB 633, 646 (Lord Denning MR).

51 [1971] Ch 591.

52 *Enderby Town Football Club Ltd* v. *Football Association Ltd* [1971] Ch 591, 606 (Lord Denning MR).

cases where the judges have decided, avowedly or not, according to what is best for the public good'.[53]

It is difficult to say in *which* supervisory jurisdiction such cases should fall – whether they comprise part of 'the' supervisory jurisdiction or a separate one. At the time, the need to classify them was not acute. It became so, however, in the 1980s. *O'Reilly* v. *Mackman*[54] drew a bright line between 'public law' and 'private law' actions against official decision-makers, and made it an abuse of process to pursue a private law action where judicial review was available.[55] In this new landscape, which route was appropriate in the context of domestic tribunals? In *Law* v. *National Greyhound Racing Club Ltd*,[56] for example, a body argued that judicial review was the proper avenue for a challenge to its decision. The Court of Appeal disagreed, holding that the claimant had acted rightly by bringing his action based on contract. However, it remains difficult to draw a bright line between that case and *R (Datafin)* v. *Takeover Panel*.

Obviously, a private law supervisory jurisdiction exists alongside the public law supervisory jurisdiction, and the border between them must mark their respective outer bound of 'judicial review'.[57] But that border is not easily traced. In *Modahl* v. *British Athletic Federation Ltd*,[58] the Court of Appeal further split the jurisdiction over domestic tribunals. The case was based squarely on breach of contract. Previously, *Newport Association Football Club Ltd* v. *Football Association of Wales Ltd*[59] had held that an injunction was available to prevent unreasonable restraints of trade, and *Stevenage Borough Football Club Ltd* v. *Football League*[60] had held that a jurisdiction existed to grant declarations even in the absence of a contract. Mance LJ observed that the availability of declaratory and injunctive relief to assist claimants where (public

[53] *Enderby Town Football Club Ltd* v. *Football Association Ltd* [1971] Ch 591, 607 (Lord Denning MR), citing *Dickson* v. *Pharmaceutical Society of Great Britain* [1967] Ch 708, *Scott* v. *Avery* (1856) 5 HL Cas 811, *Nagle* v. *Feilden* [1966] 2 QB 633, *Edwards* v. *Society of Graphical and Allied Trades* [1971] Ch 354, and *Faramis* v. *Film Artistes Association* [1964] AC 925.

[54] [1983] 2 AC 237.

[55] The traditional position was that an official acting ultra vires was subject to an action in tort: *Abbott* v. *Sullivan* (1951) 1 KB 189, 201 (Denning LJ).

[56] [1983] 1 WLR 1302.

[57] See *Wilander* v. *Tobin* [1997] 2 Lloyd's Rep 293, 299 (Lord Woolf CJ).

[58] [2002] 1 WLR 1192.

[59] [1995] 2 All ER 87.

[60] [1996] WLUK 369.

law) judicial review is not available *and* there is no contract cannot prevent the inference of a contract where one exists; this inference was the preferable route to establishing jurisdiction. Lord Denning MR's 'more general preference for a public over a private law approach in this field' in *Nagle* v. *Feilden*, he said, had not found higher endorsement.[61]

A kind of '*Nagle* hangover' remains, however, for several reasons. First, it is sometimes necessary to decide cases where no contractual basis exists. In such cases, the analysis necessarily proceeds on principles of public policy that are uncomfortably close to public law principles. Secondly, the contractual basis only obliquely expresses the real concern in these cases, which always touch on matters of public policy. This suggests that the border will continue to be difficult to define, and potentially porous. Finally, this leaves a very fragmented taxonomy of supervisory jurisdictions.

In *Bradley* v. *Jockey Club*,[62] Richards J held that the private law supervisory jurisdiction over domestic tribunals had a 'contractual' and a 'non-contractual' limb – both distinct from the public law supervisory jurisdiction. However, the substantive principles of review were essentially the same – both between the contractual and non-contractual limbs of the private law supervisory jurisdiction, and between private law and public law.[63] With respect, I doubt the private law supervisory jurisdiction cleaves so neatly, and *Bradley* v. *Jockey Club* leaves the conceptual basis and scope of the private law supervisory jurisdiction tacit.[64] Again, the modern cases consider the two supervisory jurisdictions to be isomorphic, and use the same language and concepts in both, even while insisting on their conceptual distinctiveness.[65]

61 *Stevenage Borough Football Club Ltd* v. *Football League* [1996] WLUK 369, [109] (Mance LJ).

62 [2004] EWHC 2164 (QB).

63 *Bradley* v. *Jockey Club* [2004] EWHC 2164 (QB), [29]–[35] (Richards J).

64 See further Simon Boyes, 'Sport in Court: Assessing Judicial Scrutiny of Sports Governing Bodies' [2017] *Public Law* 363.

65 *Fallon* v. *Horseracing Regulatory Authority* [2006] EWHC 2030 (QB), [12] (Davis J): 'It is well established that the decision of a body such as the [Horseracing Regulatory Authority] cannot be challenged by judicial review proceedings. But it is equally well established that the High Court retains a supervisory jurisdiction over such decisions, and the approach to be adopted is essentially that which the Administrative Court would adopt in public law cases'.

12.2.3 Tests of 'Publicness'

Various tests have been used to identify the 'public law factor' that renders a body amenable to the public law supervisory jurisdiction, but here, too, the law is unsatisfactory. In *R (Aga Khan)* v. *Disciplinary Committee of the Jockey Club*,[66] the Court of Appeal turned its face against *Nagle* v. *Feilden* and returned to the contractual basis of the supervisory jurisdiction over domestic tribunals. Sir Thomas Bingham MR said that *Nagle* v. *Feilden* lacked a clear foundation in principle, and Hoffmann LJ whiffed an 'improvisatory air' about it.[67] Drawing a bright line between private associations based on contract and public bodies, the decisions of the Disciplinary Committee were not amenable to judicial review because they were binding decisions of a private association to whose authority members had submitted consensually. While 'private power may affect the public interest and the livelihoods of many individuals', that fact alone did 'not subject it to the rules of public law' and redress should be sought through alternative routes such as contract, the restraint of trade doctrine, applicable statutes, European law, and 'all the other instruments available in law for curbing the excesses of private power'.[68] In addition to the presence of a contractual relationship between the parties, Hoffmann LJ and Farquharson LJ adopted the approach that the Jockey Club was not amenable to judicial review because, had the Jockey Club not existed, the government would not necessarily have created a public body to perform its functions. The case was distinguished from *R (Datafin)* v. *Take-over Panel* on the basis that the latter was 'integrated into a system of statutory regulation' and 'constituted a privatisation of the business of government itself'.[69]

With respect, Hoffmann LJ's reasoning sits uneasily with the fact that the Jockey Club regulated a nationally significant industry, exercising powers in the public interest, operated under a Royal Charter, and exercised power over every person who wanted to participate in the racing industry. Indeed, Sir Thomas Bingham MR accepted that, 'if the

[66] [1993] 2 All ER 853.

[67] *R (Aga Khan)* v. *Disciplinary Committee of the Jockey Club* [1993] 2 All ER 853, 916 (Sir Thomas Bingham MR), 933 (Hoffmann LJ).

[68] *R (Aga Khan)* v. *Disciplinary Committee of the Jockey Club* [1993] 2 All ER 853, 933 (Hoffmann LJ).

[69] *R (Aga Khan)* v. *Disciplinary Committee of the Jockey Club* [1993] 2 All ER 853, 932 (Hoffmann LJ).

Jockey Club did not regulate this activity, the government probably would have been driven to create a public body to do so'.[70]

Subsequent cases suggest that the approach taken in *R (Aga Khan)* v. *Disciplinary Committee of the Jockey Club* was too strict. As we have seen, in *Bradley* v. *The Jockey Club*,[71] the High Court accepted that the standard of review is similar in the private law and public law supervisory jurisdictions, suggesting that the significance of the distinction may be receding. In *Mullins* v. *Appeal Board of the Jockey Club*,[72] the High Court considered a claim for unlawfulness outside of judicial review, and held that the courts could interfere in a sporting tribunal's decision where it is arbitrary, capricious, or based on an obvious misinterpretation of its governing rules. Again, if the two supervisory jurisdictions are doing similar things on identical grounds, it is worthwhile to consider how they might fit together in the bigger picture.

12.2.4 'Governmental' instead of 'Public'?

One possible alternative to looking for a 'public' element is to look for a 'governmental' element. In *R (The Insurance Service plc)* v. *Advertising Standards Authority*,[73] for example, a self-regulatory body was held amenable to judicial review, despite having no apparent statutory or common law powers, because it was clearly exercising a function that would otherwise be performed by the Director General of Fair Trading.[74] In the leading case of *R (Wachmann)* v. *Chief Rabbi of the United Hebrew Congregations of Great Britain and the Commonwealth*,[75] Simon Brown LJ said:

> To attract the court's supervisory jurisdiction there must be not merely a public but potentially a *governmental interest* in the decision-making power in question. And, indeed, generally the exercise of the power in question involves not merely voluntary regulation of some important area of public life ... [W]here non-governmental bodies have hitherto been held reviewable, they have generally been operating as an integral part of

[70] *R (Aga Khan)* v. *Disciplinary Committee of the Jockey Club* [1993] 2 All ER 853, 866 (Sir Thomas Bingham MR).
[71] [2004] EWHC 2164.
[72] [2006] EWHC 986.
[73] (1990) 2 Admin LR 77.
[74] See *R (The Insurance Service plc)* v. *Advertising Standards Authority* (1990) 2 Admin LR 77, 86 (Glidewell J); *R (Professional Counselling Aids Ltd)* v. *British Pharmaceutical Industry Association Code of Practice Committee* [1991] COD 228.
[75] [1992] 1 WLR 1035.

> a regulatory system which, although it is itself non-statutory, is nevertheless supported by statutory powers and penalties clearly indicative of a government concern.[76]

HM Government would not perform the Chief Rabbi's spiritual functions were he to abdicate, so the office was not amenable to judicial review.

While the ruling is unobjectionable on that basis, the test it lays down requires judges to speculate on what the government *would* do in a counterfactual state of affairs.[77] This is a legally vacuous test that rather turns on one's theory of what the proper role of government is.[78] It is a generally recognised in the academic commentary that, depending on one's politics, a 'potentially governmental interest' inheres in *every* decision-making power.[79] Distinctions between the public and the private realm are the object of historical, contextual, and evaluative disagreement,[80] and there is an ebb and flow in the realms of life that we identify as public and private over time.[81] A test might instead turn on whether the government *has in fact* assumed a certain type of activity, but that looks more like a 'statutory underpinning' or 'enmeshment' test, which rest on different considerations. As Alex Williams observes, few functions will be universally agreed to be public or private by their nature alone:

> At the heart of the issue lies the essentially political matter of which functions the state should perform, of the proper role of the state. To have the greatest chance of persuading, the definition of publicness must therefore be derived, as far as possible, from settled considerations about the nature and role of the state. After all, it is the existence of a state, as distinct from the individual, that gives rise to a certain ineradicable

[76] *R (Wachmann)* v. *Chief Rabbi of the United Hebrew Congregations of Great Britain and the Commonwealth* [1992] 1 WLR 1035, 1041 (Simon Brown LJ). Emphasis mine.

[77] See Murray Hunt, 'Constitutionalism and the Contractualisation of Government in the United Kingdom' in Michael Taggart (ed.), *The Province of Administrative Law* (Hart 1997), 33; see also David Pannick, 'Who is Subject to Judicial Review and in Respect of What?' [1992] *Public Law* 1, 5. The same approach was followed in *R (Suleiman Ali)* v. *Imam of Bury Park James Masjid Luton* [1992] COD 132.

[78] Mark Elliott, 'Judicial Review's Scope, Foundations and Purposes: Joining the Dots'" [2012] [1] *New Zealand Law Review* 75, 96.

[79] Mark Elliott, 'Judicial Review's Scope, Foundations and Purposes: Joining the Dots' [2012] *New Zealand Law Review* 75, 89.

[80] J. W. F. Allison, 'Variation of View on English Legal Distinctions between Public and Private' (2007) 66 *Cambridge Law Journal* 698, 704.

[81] See Philip Walsh, 'Hannah Arendt on the Social' in Patrick Hayden (ed.), *Hannah Arendt: Key Concepts* (Routledge 2014), 128.

distinction between public and private, however intractable the more abstract question of the 'correct' meaning of a public function may be.[82]

According to Williams, this points to the need to go back to the 'source' test and develop it from first principles rather than abandoning it for an ultimately hollow 'nature of function' test.[83] However, he has not yet presented such a revised test and the direction of travel seems to be in the opposite direction.

12.2.5 The Human Rights Act 1998 Jurisprudence

If we try to describe a function not merely as 'public' but as 'governmental', we face the very problem we sought to avoid – defining the 'state' and then working deductively from that premise. This entails abandonment of the 'nature of function' test for a source-based test. Such a regression can actually be seen in the Human Rights Act 1998 jurisprudence. Section 6 of the Act defines a 'public authority' as 'any person certain of whose functions are functions of a public nature' – a tautological (and clearly 'nature of function') definition.

Again, the cases often concern penumbral public bodies. *Poplar Housing and Regeneration Community Association Ltd* v. *Donaghue*[84] concerned a provider of social housing in receipt of public money. According to Lord Woolf CJ, the purpose of s. 6 was to 'deal with hybrid bodies which have both private and public functions'.[85] While the activities of the body did not necessary entail public functions, it was closely associated with the local council. Where the *particular* function of the body was a 'public as opposed to a private act', it could be considered a 'functional, or hybrid, public authority' under the Act.[86] This test was refined in a judicial review case in which *Poplar Housing and Regeneration Community Association Ltd* v. *Donaghue* was distinguished, *R (Heather)* v. *Leonard Cheshire Foundation*.[87] In that case, Lord Woolf CJ, Laws and Dyson LJJ held that a charity's actions were not 'public'

82 Alexander Williams, 'Judicial Review and Monopoly Power: Some Sceptical Thoughts' (2017) 133 *Law Quarterly Review* 656, 661.

83 He provides a critical discussion of Mark Elliott, 'Judicial Review's Scope, Foundations and Purposes: Joining the Dots' [2012] [1] *New Zealand Law Review* 75, 83–90.

84 [2002] QB 48.

85 *Poplar Housing and Regeneration Community Association Ltd* v. *Donaghue* [2002] QB 48, 66 (Lord Woolf CJ).

86 *Poplar Housing and Regeneration Community Association Ltd* v. *Donaghue* [2002] QB 48, 66 (Lord Woolf CJ).

87 [2002] All ER 936.

despite a high degree of public funding. Tellingly, the court asked instead whether the charity was 'standing in the shoes of the state' when exercising its functions.[88] 'Standing in the shoes of the state', however, begs the very question at the heart of the source test under the guise of a functional analysis.

YL v. *Birmingham City Council*[89] illustrates the difficulty of determining amenability in the context of services contracted-out by local authorities. The House of Lords applied a factor-based approach to whether a private body was subject to Convention duties, embracing the role of public funding, the presence of coercive statutory powers, the relationship between the contractor and the public body contracting-out, and the nature of the service provided. Even when all factors were addressed, however, the decision came down to an inherently contestable definition of the public realm. The majority (Lord Neuberger, Lord Mance, and Lord Scott) held that the private law contractual relation between the Council and the accommodation provider broke the necessary public connection. According to Lord Scott, the contractor exercised its powers for a commercial motive, and entered into 'private law contracts with the residents in its care homes and with the local authorities with whom it does business'; in short, it was 'simply carrying on its private business with a customer who happens to be a public authority'.[90]

Lord Bingham characterised things differently. It was 'very clear' that the company should be subject to the duties of a public authority: 'the performance by private body A by arrangement with public body B, and perhaps at the expense of B, of what would undoubtedly be a public function if carried out by B' was precisely the sort of by intended to be caught by the definition in s. 6.[91] Baroness Hale opined that the relevant contrast was between 'what is "public" in the sense of being done for or by or on behalf of the people as a whole and what is "private" in the sense of being done for one's own purposes'.[92] All things considered, the 'inexorable' conclusion was that the body was subject to Convention duties.[93] *YL* thus not only illustrates disagreement at the highest level on the operative

88 *R (Heather)* v. *Leonard Cheshire Foundation* [2002] All ER 936, [55] (Loord Woolf CJ, Laws and Dyson LJJ).

89 [2007] UKHL 27.

90 *YL* v. *Birmingham City Council* [2008] 1 AC 95, 108–109.

91 *YL* v. *Birmingham City Council* [2008] 1 AC 95, 104, 107.

92 *YL* v. *Birmingham City Council* [2008] 1 AC 95, 118.

93 *YL* v. *Birmingham City Council* [2008] 1 AC 95, 120.

question; it suggests that the judges are working with dichotomies that are not particularly helpful.

The intuitive opposition between public and private interest is an idea that is anachronistic to the mid-twentieth century. Today, the profit motive is often harnessed in the pursuit of public sector efficiency. This is not novel. In *Kruse* v. *Johnston*,[94] a case dealing with the byelaws of the Kent County Council, Lord Russel CJ observed:

> The great majority of cases in which the question of by-laws has been discussed are not cases of by-laws of bodies of a public representative character entrusted by Parliament with delegated authority, but are for the most part railway companies, dock companies, or other like companies which carry on their business *for their own profit, although incidentally for the advantage of the public*. In this class of case it is right that the Courts should jealously watch the exercise of these powers, and guard against their unnecessary or unreasonable exercise to the public disadvantage.[95]

The assumption underlying such arrangements was that the public advantage could be sought by harnessing private interests. The provision of public goods by private speculators is, indeed, a trend whose arc we can trace from Elizabethan society to the twenty-first century (and probably much longer).[96] Thus, the presence of a commercial motive really cannot be that indicative one way or the other. Judicial supervision is necessary to ensure that the entities concerned act fairly and reasonably – especially where they are exempted from the ordinary market processes that would govern them, such as the discipline of competition (for example, a statutory monopoly) or the need to operate in a free market (for example, powers of compulsory acquisition over private property). This is especially the case where the contracting party is the Crown. Janet McLean has recently argued that liberal contract theory itself – that branch of contract theory perhaps most hostile to public law values – compels the special treatment of contracts with the government as a party.[97]

[94] [1898] 2 QB 91.

[95] *Kruse* v. *Johnston* [1898] 2 QB 91, 98–99 (Lord Russel CJ). Emphasis mine.

[96] See G. G. Harris, *Trinity House of Deptford 1516–1660* (Athlone Press 1969), 180, cited in Ronald Coase, 'The Lighthouse in Economics' (1974) 17(2) *The Journal of Law & Economics* 357, 364. Harris (at 264) cites Sir Edward Coke before Parliament in 1661: 'Proioectours like watermen looke one waye and rowe another: they pretend publique profit, intend private'.

[97] See Janet McLean, 'For a Law of Public Contract *Per Se*: An Intervention from Liberal Contract Theory' (2019) 39(4) *Oxford Journal of Legal Studies* 856, 857–858.

12.3 An Office-Based Approach to Amenability

If the traditional source test has little to say in the context of non-statutory executive powers, and the modern 'function' tests designed to replace it are confused, perhaps it is helpful to frame the question of amenability in terms of office, too. Prima facie, it should be possible to determine who is an 'official' – including a 'deemed official' or even a 'shadow' official – beyond statute and the prerogative.

Kirsten Rundle has recently observed that the law struggles to frame contracted-out public sector functions, and suggested that the concept of office might help.[98] She turns by way of example to the Australian High Court case of *Plaintiff M61/2010E* v. *Commonwealth of Australia*,[99] which concerned the 'offshore processing' of asylum seeker claims. The case is significant to the judicial review of non-statutory executive power in its own right, as the Commonwealth argued that the relevant actions were taken under the prerogative-type powers provided in s. 61 of the Australian Constitution and were, for that reason, not subject to a duty of procedural fairness. The High Court unanimously held that rules of conduct do impose due process requirements on this kind of power.[100] The other interesting aspect of the case, however, was that (for complex reasons) the assessments (on the basis of which the relevant officials made their decisions) were performed by employees of a private company. Section 75(v) of the Australian Constitution vests original jurisdiction in the Australian High Court to issue the writs of prohibition, *mandamus* and injunction against 'Officer[s] of the Commonwealth'. The Commonwealth submitted that the employees of the outsourcing company were not Officers of the Commonwealth. The case thus provided a perfect opportunity to determine who is an official in Australian law. The High Court declined to do so, however, as there existed an alternative gateway to jurisdiction in s. 75(iii): 'Accordingly, it is appropriate to leave, for another day, the question whether a party identified as "an independent contractor" nevertheless may fall within the expression "an officer of the Commonwealth" in s 75(v) in circumstances where some aspect of the

98 Kirsten Rundle, 'Office and Contracting-Out: An Analysis' (2020) 70(2) *University of Toronto Law Journal* 183.

99 [2010] HCA 41.

100 See *Plaintiff M61/2010E* v. *Commonwealth of Australia* [2010] HCA 41, [75], [105] (French CJ, Gummow, Hayne, Heydon, Crennan, Kiefel, and Bell JJ).

exercise of statutory or executive authority of the Commonwealth has been "contracted out"'.[101]

Rundle concludes that the idea of office cannot survive the contracting-out process, as contract and office are inimical forms of social relation.[102] With respect, I do not think that the existence of a contractual relationship between the Crown and a nominally private party necessarily undermines the 'official' nature of the latter's role. Indeed, I think that such an approach is conceptually flawed and historically problematic. Unfortunately, again, the absence of a developed office concept renders this task more difficult. The older cases, as we have seen, were preoccupied with the traditional immunities of the sovereign and approach the concept of office *via* the notion of an 'emanation of the Crown'. In *Gilbert* v. *Corporation of Trinity House*,[103] for example, Day J held that a statutory aggregation of various local lighthouse authorities did not attract Crown immunity. 'It is a corporation with great powers vested in it by statute, but in no possible sense can it be deemed to represent the Crown'; 'all great officers of the state [are] emanations of the Crown' in the sense of 'delegations by the Crown of its authority to particular individuals'.[104] Lord Luxmoore gave the 'emanation of the Crown' short shrift in *International Railway Company* v. *Niagara Parks Commission*,[105] equating 'emanation' with 'agent or servant' and rightly holding that the company was not an agent of the Crown to which Crown immunities should attach.[106]

Such authorities are of limited value today because the question of Crown immunity is oblique to the question of amenability. The present question is not one of immunity but of attribution. In that respect, the monopolies doctrine and certain other ancient doctrines constraining the action of private actors offers a fresh perspective in terms of the amenability of contractual acts by public officials.

Certain social positions – which may not be strictly 'legal' but are underpinned by legal structures such contract and property rights – put their occupant into something that could be described as an 'office of

[101] *Plaintiff M61/2010E* v. *Commonwealth of Australia* [2010] HCA 41, [51] (French CJ, Gummow, Hayne, Heydon, Crennan, Kiefel, and Bell JJ).

[102] Kirsten Rundle, 'Office and Contracting-Out: An Analysis' (2020) 70(2) *University of Toronto Law Journal* 183, 196.

[103] (1886) 1 QB 795.

[104] *Gilbert* v. *Corporation of Trinity House* (1886) 1 QB 795, 801 (Day J).

[105] [1941] AC 328.

[106] See *International Railway Company* v. *Niagara Parks Commission* [1941] AC 328, 343 (Lord Luxmoore).

trust and confidence concerning the public'.[107] While we cannot make too much of the point, it is relevant that offices were conventionally seen as a form of private property,[108] and that the accountability of officials was achieved, in the seventeenth and eighteenth centuries especially, through the principle that 'property in an office would be subject to certain restrictions if the office constituted an implied trust'.[109] The holders of such offices were prevented from delegating discretion in the performance of office to a deputy, and could forfeit the office for certain types of misfeasance, nonfeasance or refusal to exercise an office.[110] 'Public law' accountability was achieved through a process of impressing private property rights with public duties. This might be the baby of 'private law constitutionalism' that has been thrown out with the bathwater.

While the institutional context is obviously important, couching the enquiry in terms of whether the relevant position is, or should be deemed to be, an 'office of public trust' subtly shifts the task from defining the nature of the body in question to determining whether the relevant actor – if not a public official, then often an employee or official within a corporate body – should be held to owe duties to the public that limit the way that she exercises her legal capacities, whatever they are and whatever their source. Of course, the inference that a given legal actor occupies an 'office of public trust' follows more naturally in circumstances where that actor is an official within some kind of institution or association than in the case where she is a private actor acting *suo jure* for profit. The best example is probably the capacity to make quasi-judicial determinations within some non-state association such as a 'domestic tribunal'. The institutional connections between the association and the Crown would also seem to be important as a factor relevant to the latter question. (Incidentally, where these connections are contractual, the notion of third source-type powers is incredibly important.)

One of the leading ancient cases, *R* v. *Bembridge*,[111] for example, concerned the liability of an accountant in the office of the Receiver

[107] *R* v. *Bembridge* (1783) 22 How St Tr 1, 155 (Lord Mansfield).

[108] See Koenraad Wolter Swart, *Sale of Offices in the Seventeenth Century* (Martinus Nijhoff 1949), 47.

[109] E. Mabry Rogers and Stephen B. Young, 'Public Office as a Public Trust: A Suggestion that Impeachment for High Crimes and Misdemeanors Implies a Fiduciary Standard' (1975) 63 *Georgetown Law Journal* 1025, 1028.

[110] See *Sir George Reynel's Case* (1612) 77 Eng Rep 871; see also *Earl of Shrewsbury Case* (1611) 77 Eng Rep 798 and *Bennet* v. *Easedale* (1626) 79 Eng Rep 821.

[111] (1783) 22 How St Tr 1.

and Paymaster General of the Forces for fraudulent record keeping. During the relevant time, the office of Receiver and Paymaster General moved from one Lord Holland to one Lord Sondes, and the accountant was responsible for making up the final account of Lord Holland 'to be adjusted, settled, and passed, according to the ancient course of the Exchequer'. He omitted to do so, to the detriment of the *fisc*, and the case turned *inter alia* on whether he himself occupied an 'office of trust'. Lord Mansfield observed that no money actually passed through his hands, as the office concerned the accounts of another. Further, there was no written constitution of the office – 'what his duty is can only be learned from what he has always done'.[112] All things considered, however, the defendant was '[obviously] a trustee for the public and the paymaster'.[113]

This approach is instructive because it looks at the relationship between the relevant actor, any obviously public official, and the public directly. The question is whether his position in that constellation gives rise to an expectation of public duty, whatever that entails in the circumstances.[114]A broadly similar approach could be read from the monopolies doctrine itself. In *De Portibus Maris*, Lord Hale CJ opined that, all else being equal, a person could set up a piece of infrastructure such as a wharf and demand the highest rates he could get 'for his private advantage' – he was merely doing what was lawful by 'mak[ing] the most of his own'.[115] Yet his legal position changed where that wharf was the only game in town:

> [I]f the King or a subject have a public wharf unto which all persons who come to that port must come and unlade their goods . . . because there is no other wharf in that port as it may fall out where a port is newly erected; in that case there may not be any arbitrary or excessive duties for cranage, wharfage, pesage, etc . . . the duties must be reasonable and moderate, though settled by the King's license or charter. For now the wharf, and crane and other conveniences are affected with a public interest, and they cease to be *ius privati* only.[116]

[112] (1783) 22 How St Tr 1 (Lord Mansfield).
[113] (1783) 22 How St Tr 1 (Lord Mansfield).
[114] Similar problems arise in the context of the tort of misfeasance in public office. Despite an apparently long history, the tort is reasonably modern, but 'not modern enough' to have determined who might be a public officer, and what might be a public power: 'we have yet to learn how far it extends into the outsourced state, and how far it might apply to abuse of dominant position as opposed to power'. Mark Aronson, 'Misfeasance in Public Office: Some Unfinished Business' (2016) 132 *Law Quarterly Review* 427, 444.
[115] *De Portibus Maris* (1787) 1 Harg Tr 78 (Lord Hale CJ).
[116] *De Portibus Maris* (1787) 1 Harg Tr 78 (Lord Hale CJ).

The principle cuts across situations where the monopoly is de facto or de jure – the existence of 'the King's license or charter' is neither the conceptual basis for the court to impose public duties, nor an obstacle to imposing them. Secondly, the principle applies to the Crown as it does to any private infrastructure provider. It would seem therefore to be a principle that is well equipped to deal with the Crown's third source-type powers, for example, as a property owner or contracting partner. Lord Ellenbourough CJ applied this principle in *Allnut* v. *Inglis.*[117] This case concerned a monopoly to provide warehouse storage of wine. This position made the property an 'instrument of the general benefit' and constrained the warehouse owner in the kinds of fees he could levy.[118]

All of these cases dance around a common set of themes, but have somehow failed to crystallise into a coherent body of doctrine. Indeed, the monopolies doctrine belongs to a broader family of doctrines regulating the interface between private (or quasi-public) interests and the public. The doctrine of 'common callings', for example, imposed duties on those carrying on socially important businesses. The normal remedy was an action on the case rather than judicial review, but those engaged in common callings were often subject to a self-regulatory body that was itself, in turn, amenable to judicial review.[119] In the United States, the doctrine is used in the modern context to prevent racially discriminatory market behaviour by utilities companies, for example.[120] The 'rising tide of liberalism' in England left the doctrine stranded in a 'sea of *laissez-faire* thinking',[121] but the doctrine of 'quasi-public trust' does something similar by encumbering private property with public duties. K. J. Gray has argued that the common law doctrine of 'quasi-public trust' generally reflects an older code of marketplace morality, which emphasises the relation between commercial privilege and social obligation.[122] In a similar vein, Larissa Katz has argued that private property rights

[117] (1810) 12 East 527.

[118] (1810) 12 East 527, 538 (Lord Ellenborough CJ).

[119] See Dawn Oliver, *Common Values and the Public-Private Divide* (Butterworths 1999), 86. *Certiorari* was held to run, for example, to a company 'existing from time out of mind' and incorporated by Royal Charter in 1638 in *The Case of the Company of Horners in London* (1642) 2 Roll Rep 481.

[120] Duncan Fairgrieve, *Judicial Review in International Perspective* (Kluwer 2000), 328; Dawn Oliver, *Common Values and the Public-Private Divide* (Butterworths 1999), 203.

[121] Michael Taggart, 'The Province of Administrative Law Determined?' in Michael Taggart (ed.), *The Province of Administrative Law* (Hart 1997), 8.

[122] K. J. Gray, 'Regulatory Property and the Jurisprudence of the Quasi-Public Trust' (2010) 32 *Sydney Law Review* 221.

themselves constitute a 'network of offices' through which states allocate responsibility for certain tasks to private individuals, including sometimes 'core governance functions'.[123]

12.3.1 *A Unified Normative Foundation for Judicial Review?*

Both common law theorists and legislative intent theorists have recognised the existence and importance of parallels between public law judicial review and its cognates, but their interpretation and implications for the doctrinal, conceptual, and normative basis of judicial review are contested. C. D. Campbell has pushed the commonalities to the conclusion that *all* judicial review (including over public officials) is based on monopoly power. Campbell's concept of 'monopoly power' is broader the concept of an economic monopoly within a market; it simply means 'only one person or body in fact performs the function pursuant to which the power is exercised'.[124] In Campbell's terms, 'statutory power, prerogative power, and non-statutory regulatory power'[125] all meet the definition. Statutory power is, in fact, archetypically monopolistic in his sense: '[i]t is invariably the case that where the permission of a statutory body must be obtained, so as to enable a person legally to partake in an activity, the relevant legislation makes it clear that permission may *only* be granted by the statutory body'.[126] In particular, he argues that the monopolies principle cuts across the idea, applied in *Aga Khan* v. *Disciplinary Committee of the Jockey Club*, that consensual submission to a body's administrative powers should not be taken to preclude judicial review, and that this yields a more coherent picture of the authorities across the statutory/non-statutory divide.[127]

[123] Larissa Katz, '"Governing through Owners": How and Why Formal Property Rights Enhance State Power' (2012) 160 *University of Pennsylvania Law Review* 2029; see also Larissa Katz, 'It's Not Personal: Social Obligations in the Office of Ownership' (2020) *Cornell Journal of Law and Public Policy* (forthcoming).

[124] C. D. Campbell, 'Monopoly Power as Public Power for the Purposes of Judicial Review' (2009) 125 *Law Quarterly Review* 491, 493.

[125] C. D. Campbell, 'Monopoly Power as Public Power for the Purposes of Judicial Review' (2009) 125 *Law Quarterly Review* 491, 496.

[126] C. D. Campbell, 'Monopoly Power as Public Power for the Purposes of Judicial Review' (2009) 125 *Law Quarterly Review* 491, 496.

[127] C. D. Campbell, 'Monopoly Power as Public Power for the Purposes of Judicial Review' (2009) 125 *Law Quarterly Review* 491, 503.

By way of example, Campbell cites a number of cases including *Associated Provincial Picture Houses Ltd* v. *Wednesbury Corporation.*[128] Essentially, the 'consensuality objection' is met by the argument that the activity in question is generally subject to prohibition absent some license or permission, and the body empowered to grant or withhold that permission is a monopolist in the relevant sense. The touchstone seems to be that the function performed by the body is essential, or at least important, and that the subject adversely affected by the exercise of the power in question is 'unable to choose to deal with an alternate decision-maker'.[129] As there is no alternate body that may exercise the function of (for example) granting a racing license, that power is monopolistic in nature.

In Campbell's analysis, 'high' prerogative-type powers are archetypically monopolistic.[130] While non-statutory executive powers more broadly are not *necessarily* monopolistic,[131] most cases of review concern situations where the power in question was, in fact, monopolistic in the circumstances. Finally, he argues that most cases of judicial review of (what he calls) 'non-statutory regulatory powers' involve bodies that are the only regulators of the relevant sphere of activity.[132] The religious cases constitute somewhat of an exception, which he suggests should be bracketed out on the basis that the activities in question are not a proper subject matter for judicial review at all.[133] As for the good number of cases which the monopoly rationale cannot explain, Campbell argues simply that they were wrongly decided.[134]

128 [1948] KB 223 CA. He also cites *Schmidt* v. *Secretary of State for Home Affairs* [1969] 2 Ch 149 CA and *Lavender & Son* v. *Minister of Housing and Local Government* [1970] 3 All ER 871 QBD.

129 C. D. Campbell, 'The Nature of Power as Public in English Judicial Review' (2009) 68(1) *Cambridge Law Journal* 90, 116.

130 C. D. Campbell, 'Monopoly Power as Public Power for the Purposes of Judicial Review' (2009) 125 *Law Quarterly Review* 491, 499.

131 C. D. Campbell, 'Monopoly Power as Public Power for the Purposes of Judicial Review' (2009) 125 *Law Quarterly Review* 491, 499.

132 C. D. Campbell, 'Monopoly Power as Public Power for the Purposes of Judicial Review' (2009) 125 *Law Quarterly Review* 491, 501.

133 C. D. Campbell, 'Monopoly Power as Public Power for the Purposes of Judicial Review' (2009) 125 *Law Quarterly Review* 491, 504.

134 C. D. Campbell, 'Monopoly Power as Public Power for the Purposes of Judicial Review' (2009) 125 *Law Quarterly Review* 491, 503, citing *R (Williams)* v. *Provincial Court of the Church in Wales* [1999] COD 163 QBD; *R (Bloom)* v. *London Beth Din (Court of the Chief Rabbi)* [1998] COD 131 QBD; *R (Aga Khan)* v. *Disciplinary Committee of the Jockey Club* [1993] 1 WLR 909 CA; *R (Football League)* v. *Football Association* [1993] 2 All ER 833 QBD; *R (Wachmann)* v. *Chief Rabbi of the United Hebrew Congregations of Great Britain*

Campbell draws indirect support for his argument from the various supervisory jurisdictions that operate in private law, including 'businesses affected with a public interest', domestic tribunals, and the supervisory jurisdiction over trustees. All of these jurisdictions track the broad ultra vires grounds of review.[135] The combined effect of this jurisprudence, he argues, is to bolster his proposed test for the characterisation of a power as 'public'. This is further underlined by the desirability for power to be exercised rationally and in accordance with the rule of law, that is, not arbitrarily, which speaks for the extension of the public law supervisory jurisdiction beyond the 'organs of the state' narrowly defined.

This is surely correct, as far as it goes. Someone concerned with the elimination of arbitrary power can make 'no clear-cut distinction between the state and other "quasi-public" bodies, or even private associations that exercise significant power over their own members'.[136] In my view, however, Campbell places more weight on the monopoly concept than it can safely bear. The monopolies doctrine points us in the right direction, but it is not our final destination. The deeper question is why monopoly powers *themselves* attract 'public law' duties.

The true principle is that the more powerful a private body becomes – whether through the accretion of property rights or through de facto or de jure monopoly – the more it affects the interests of the public at large, and the more general becomes the courts' scrutiny of its actions. Judicial supervision – public or private – is never really concerned with individuals; to the extent individuals are amenable to judicial review, they are either expressly or implicitly enmeshed in some kind of associational structure, be it a football club or the *res publica* itself. In other words, the more willing the courts become to look through an aggregation of individuals as an *expression* of individual autonomy and see it as a *constraint* on individual autonomy. This, I think, explains the judicial concern with economic monopolies and with the rule-based administrative procedures of associations organised under the private law (for example, as unincorporated associations, corporations, or trusts).

[1992] 1 WLR 1036 QBD; *R (RAM Racecourses Ltd)* v. *Jockey Club* [1993] 2 All ER 225 QBD; *R (Flint Town United Football Club)* v. *Football Association of Wales* [1991] COD 44 QBD; *Law* v. *National Greyhound Racing Club Ltd* [1983] 1 WLR 1302 CA.

135 C. D. Campbell, 'Monopoly Power as Public Power for the Purposes of Judicial Review' (2009) 125 *Law Quarterly Review* 491, 505. See generally Daniel Clarry, *The Supervisory Jurisdiction over Trust Administration* (Oxford University Press 2018).

136 T. R. S. Allan, *Constitutional Justice: A Liberal Theory of the Rule of Law* (Oxford University Press 2001), 11.

This sort of approach fits well in the context of contracted-out public services because, just as these entities in question are at the *margins of the state*, so they are at the *margins of the market*, too. This is certainly true of health care under a universal, single payer system, social housing, or self-regulation of strictly limited professions and trades. The 'private' bodies subject to judicial review are ones in which the normal 'discipline' of the marketplace does not, for one reason or another, work. And where no market operates – for example, because a service provider holds a de jure monopoly – there the power of a 'private' *versus* a 'public' body fades into a similar shade of grey.

However, this points to the need to articulate a deeper normative principle that determines when something affects the 'public interest' and why this should trigger judicial review. In his critique of Campbell's proposal, Williams points to the question whether the candidate for judicial review is expected to act in an *other-regarding manner*, that is, whether it can interact with (other) subjects in the pursuit of its own interests or not.[137] It is generally accepted that the Crown has no legitimate self-interest. To the extent it exists, it exists to serve the public it governs. Elliot, too, fixes on the notion that certain 'public' actors have no legitimate self-interest to promote in the use of their powers as one of the anchor points for the supervisory jurisdiction beyond statute. Recognising that legislative intent is not necessarily relevant in this context and that existing tests of amenability are deficient, Elliott argues that the amenability of non-statutory executive powers is based on three related purposes: (i) ensuring compliance with the rule of law; (ii) controlling governmental power, based on the unique extent of the government's power and the fact that the government is devoid of self-interests; and (iii) securing the public interest in 'good governance'.[138] These factors all run together, in Elliott's analysis, and determine on balance whether any given body ought to be subject to judicial review. Their relative importance will depend on the context. For example, securing the interest in good governance will be especially relevant in cases like *R (Datafin)* v. *Take-over Panel*, because the idea of 'good governance' is agnostic in terms of the institutional set-up involved. Cases concerning third source-type powers exercised by government officials, on the other hand, presumably rest on the need to control

[137] Alex Williams, 'Judicial Review and Monopoly Power: Some Sceptical Thoughts' (2017) 133 *Law Quarterly Review* 656, 666.

[138] Mark Elliott, 'Judicial Review's Scope, Foundations, and Purposes: Joining the Dots' [2012] [1] *New Zealand Law Review* 75, 79–80.

governmental power and ensure that public officials are not abusing their special role.

Despite my general critique of Elliott's approach, and in particular his fragmentation of the supervisory jurisdiction into so many clones, Elliott is right to point to the importance of these factors. In my view, however, rather than just providing three (or more) factors to be weighed, they are actually context-sensitive expressions of the same principle which is best articulated in terms of the office concept and the essentially other-regarding nature of official powers. The upshot of all of this is that the two limbs of ultra vires should apply to nominally private actors that exercise a power of the kind that, in all the circumstances, should be seen as touching the public interest. In all cases, the reviewing court assesses the ability-space of the relevant actor – whether based on a grant of 'public power' or on private law rights and powers such as the power to contract – and then assesses the liberty-space of that actor. Where a monopolist's ability and prima facie liberty to set market prices conflicts with a right against discrimination, for example, the court imposes duties into the liberty-space of the monopolist to constrain the manner of their exercise.

12.4 Conclusion

The scope of the public law supervisory jurisdiction is, to say the least, blurry at the margins. The modern tests of amenability are not satisfactorily clear; there is a suggestive set of parallels between the public law supervisory jurisdiction and cognates like that over economic monopolies, domestic tribunals, and other bodies, but no overarching theory along which to draw bright lines. In my view, however, the same logic of official empowerment and action structures not only the doctrines applied to reviewable decision-making bodies, but suggests fruitful lines of development for a unified understanding of their conceptual basis.

The scope of the 'state', and what it is appropriate for the government to provide directly, indirectly, or leave completely alone, is a question of political economy on which reasonable minds always differ and on which consensus shifts over time. The important thing is to ensure that the law is not too much out of phase with the current modalities of governance. The breakout of a distinct public law appears, in hindsight, to have occurred at just the wrong moment in twentieth century history – at the dawn of the 'contracting state'. It was a response to the expansion of the welfare state following the Second World War, but the solution to that state's problems are ill-matched to the neo-liberal governance of the Thatcher Era and all that has followed. The absence of a clearly articulated office concept has left the law less coherent, and calls for further theoretical work. As Sir Stephen Sedley observes, the point is not that 'the state is just another corporation' nor that ministers should still be liable as private individuals for torts committed in office: 'It is that the rule of law has to embrace state, corporation, and individual alike'.[139]

When facing this task, the courts should not shy away from the conceptual analysis needed to frame the normative questions that give the supervisory jurisdiction its ultimate content. In particular, it is essential to remember that any supervisory jurisdiction comprises both the scope of a power in the strict sense and the duties constraining it. A constitution is a 'compendiously instituting-and-empowering set of interlocking norms'.[140] These are usually in the form of explicit rules but are often found in the unwritten law as well. They rest on inherently contestable normative foundations that we articulate as 'constitutional principles' and 'values'.[141] The common law powers of the Crown are a particularly apt illustration of the way in which these principles and values percolate to the surface when the courts articulate legal rules. It is impossible and undesirable to isolate the doctrinal questions of judicial review from these more basic questions of legitimacy. But it is equally important to frame normative disagreements in the context of rigorous analytical arguments about the way that public authority is constituted and bestowed on individuals – especially in our complex, historical tradition of public law.

[139] Sir Stephen Sedley, 'Public Power and Private Power' in Christopher Forsyth (ed.), *Judicial Review and the Constitution* (Hart 2000), 306.

[140] Neil MacCormick, *Institutions of Law* (Oxford University Press 2007), 287.

[141] Neil MacCormick, *Institutions of Law* (Oxford University Press 2007), 287.

13

The Normative Foundations of Judicial Review

13.1 Introduction

In England, the law of judicial review is generally framed by the two grand pillars of the British constitutional tradition: the rule of law and the sovereignty of Parliament. Although there are important differences of emphasis, and disagreements as to the content of these principles, the majority of public lawyers ascribe to a rough consensus on their relation: the principles stand at odds with one another,[1] and the major question is how they should be reconciled in the facts of an instant case. Consider, by way of example, a statute that grants a Minister 'absolute discretion'[2] or makes her decision unreviewable in the courts. On its face, such a statutory empowerment is broad enough to be construed as granting her the power to act arbitrarily or for an improper purpose. So seen, such statutory language sets up an inherent tension between the values of democracy (the expressed will of a democratic legislature) and the rule of law (judge-made principles of good administration such as reasonableness and procedural propriety).

The stakes thus set are high, and the debate they have stimulated has produced some heat. As we have seen, however, the supervisory jurisdiction over *non-statutory* executive powers has been collateral in that debate. Further, while the practice of reviewing prerogative-type powers, third source-type powers, *and* the powers of non-governmental bodies that exercise 'governmental' functions is clearly established, the theoretical explanation of this practice is thin. The relative neglect of non-statutory executive powers in administrative law theory is, frankly, bizarre given that so many of the leading cases have actually concerned non-statutory executive powers.

[1] See Jeffrey Goldsworthy, *Parliamentary Sovereignty: Contemporary Debates* (Cambridge University Press 2010), 60–61.

[2] See Hanna Wilberg, '"Absolute Discretion": Are NZ's Parliament and Courts Compromising the Rule of Law?' (2019) 45(4) *Federal Law Review* 541.

My approach in this book has been to take a step back and look, in the first instance, at the problem of *official action* in the non-statutory context. This yielded a novel and useful analytical framework for looking at the supervisory jurisdiction over executive officials generally. On this view, individuals exercise reviewable powers in virtue of some official status (usually formal, but sometimes ad hoc or even deemed). These powers are granted in statutory *and* common law rules of competence and circumscribed by statutory *and* common law rules of conduct. The former set the actor's ability-space, or vires in the narrow sense, while the latter set the actor's liberty-space, which constrains the scope of those vires, typically by limiting the manner and purpose of their exercise. These rules correspond to the two limbs of the ultra vires rule, which is a common law doctrine that applies across the statutory/non-statutory and indeed the public/private divide.

This simple theory goes some way towards explaining the conceptual basis of the supervisory jurisdiction – inverting the usual order of enquiry by starting with non-statutory executive powers and working back to the general case of statutory powers. It goes against the direction of travel in English law – for example, urging the reinstatement of jurisdictional error. However, it does a better job of explaining the law as it is applied. It is especially valuable because it provides a framework for connecting the conceptual basis of review with the doctrines of review (particularly the grounds of review).

Beyond providing the resources for a kind of doctrinal clean-up of the supervisory jurisdiction, however, the office-based approach provides a basis from which to explore the *normative* basis of the supervisory jurisdiction, as well. Officials are subject to judicial supervision in the exercise of their powers because they hold those powers in a special capacity and are accountable to the public, including *via* the courts in appropriate cases, for their exercise.

The most natural expression of that normative basis is found in the simple concept of an 'office of public trust'. There is nothing revolutionary about this idea; it is conventional. Theories of government based on the concept of a fiduciary relationship between the government and the people were a commonplace of constitutional theory during the formative period from the seventeenth to nineteenth centuries.[3] P.D. Finn has described the relationship between

[3] See John Gough, *John Locke's Political Philosophy: Eight Studies* (Oxford University Press 1964), 138

government and the people as 'the most fundamental of fiduciary relationships in our society' that stamped its mark on common law political thought for over 300 years.[4]

The idea is unpopular, however, today – perhaps especially in England. As described in Chapter 6, reforms in the latter nineteenth century consolidated and formalised governmental practice into the institutions of Westminster-style government that we now take for granted. In that process, the democratic principle retained prominence but both the concept of office and the doctrine of public trust fell under what P.D. Finn calls a 'collective amnesia'.[5] Modern judges are generally critical of the notion that fiduciary principles operate in public law,[6] and most modern cases that have adopted a 'public trust' approach are not good illustrations of the principle.[7]

In the past decade, however, there has been a resurgence of scholarly interest in both the concepts of office and 'public trust' to ground and structure public law, including the law of judicial review.[8] Calling public officials 'fiduciaries' is, at base, an expression of popular sovereignty that recognises the need for professional, institutionalised administration.[9] In short, the sovereign right of the people is protected by imposing 'trust-like' duties upon those involved in the business of government. These individuals are necessarily separate from the body politic, even if they are

[4] Paul Finn, 'The Forgotten "Trust": The People and the State' in Malcolm Cope (ed.), *Equity: Issues and Trends* (Federation Press 1995), 131; *R* v. *Boston* (1923) 33 CLR 386, 410 (Higgins J); *R* v. *White* (1875) 13 SCR (NSW) L 322.

[5] Paul Finn, 'The Forgotten "Trust": The People and the State' in Malcolm Cope (ed.), *Equity: Issues and Trends* (Federation Press 1995), 131.

[6] See, for example, *Pitt* v. *Holt; Futter* v. *Futter* [2012] Ch 132, 204–205 (Mummery LJ). This position accepts some common standards of decision-making, for example *Wednesbury* reasonableness, but contests whether public law duties are meaningfully described as 'fiduciary'. On the related question whether public law standards of rationality should operate in private law more broadly, for example in the context of discretionary contractual powers that are not fiduciary, see *IBM United Kingdom Holdings Ltd* v. *Dalgleish* [2017] EWCA Civ 1212; Lord Philip Sales, 'Public Law Perspectives on the *IBM Case*' in Sinéad Agnew, P. S. Davies, and Charles Mitchell (eds.), *Pensions: Law, Policy and Practice* (Bloomsbury 2020), 209.

[7] See, for example, *Bromley London Borough Council* v. *Greater London Authority* [1982] 2 WLR 62; John Griffiths, 'Fares Fair or Fiduciary Foul?' (1982) 41(2) *Cambridge Law Journal* 216. Cf *Magill* v. *Porter* [2002] 2 WLR 37 (Lord Bingham) and *Scott* v. *National Trust* [1998] 2 AER 705, 717 (Walker LJ).

[8] See, in particular, the recent anthology by Evan J. Criddle, Evan Fox-Decent, Andrew S. Gold, Sung Hiu Kim, and Paul B. Miller (eds.), *Fiduciary Government* (Oxford University Press 2019) and the symposium on 'The Idea of Office' in (2020) 70(2) *University of Toronto Law Journal*, 163–314

[9] Evan J. Criddle, Evan Fox-Decent, Andrew S. Gold, Sung Hiu Kim, and Paul B. Miller (eds.), *Fiduciary Government* (Oxford University Press 2019), 4.

drawn from and comprise a subset within it. These duties require them to use their powers *virtute officii* in the service of the public exclusively. The office-based approach to judicial review thus suggests a notion of the rule of law as the *rule of officials acting lawfully*. This provides a powerful way of connecting the theory of judicial review, from its normative basis to its conceptual structure and doctrinal manifestation.

The vires of public officials are always circumscribed by common law as well as statutory rules. It is common for a common law rule of conduct to limit an ability-space granted by statutory rules of competence. In such cases, rather than some grand collision between parliamentary sovereignty and the rule of law, the proper point of reference is the fact that Parliament is a collegiate body inhabited by officials whose only claim to power is derivative of their claim to represent the political community.[10] If we accept that premise, the notion that Parliament's *Spielraum* has some outer bounds is not really controversial. Approaching the question of parliamentary sovereignty from this perspective is, I think, more conducive to a more sober discussion of the twin pillars of British constitutionalism.

13.2 Towards a Law of Public Fiduciaries

A challenge for administrative law theory today is to connect the particular grounds of judicial review with the constitutional values on which the supervisory jurisdiction rests. Adam Perry argues that the bridge between abstract claims of value (i.e., the rule of law and parliamentary sovereignty) and the specific legal doctrines of judicial review (such as *Wednesbury* unreasonableness or fettering discretions) is insufficiently developed.[11] In my view, neither of the dominant camps in the ultra vires debate did an adequate job of explaining how we get from one to the other. The major accounts within the common law camp, in which I would place my own theory, start from constitutional values such as the rule of law, human dignity, fairness, equality, and then posit

[10] See Lael Weis, 'The Constitutional Office of the Legislature' (2020) 70(2) *University of Toronto Law Journal* 214.

[11] See Adam Perry, 'Plan B: A Theory of Judicial Review' (Oxford Legal Studies Research Paper No. 66/2017, 22 November 2017), https://ssrn.com/abstract=3075886, 5–6. For arguments that existing theories do not do this well enough, see Farrah Ahmed, 'The Delegation Theory of Judicial Review' (2021) 84(4) *Modern Law Review* 772; Jason Varuhas, 'The Reformation of English Administrative Law? "Rights", Rhetoric, and Reality' [2013] 72(2) *Cambridge Law Journal* 369.

a supervisory jurisdiction that cuts across all forms of 'power' independently of the traditional concept of 'powers' as vires. The legislative intent theorists, for their part, were so eager to defend a radical idea of parliamentary sovereignty that they preferred to divide the supervisory jurisdiction into identical twins rather than accept that common law values directly inform common law rules that supervene on parliamentary intention. Through it all, Perry argues that there is a general failure for any coherent theory to bind these abstract principles and their doctrinal manifestations together. A broadly similar concern was expressed by Finn in the early 1990s, in the context of public sector corruption.[12]

In my view, the idea of the 'office of public trust' spans that bridge. Officials are entrusted with public powers by the political community. Those powers are limited in scope, not least in that they are cabined by duties. The most important of those duties ensure that official powers are exercised in a manner, and for a purpose, that is legitimately directed towards public ends. The fiduciary principle, in the public setting, helps to explain how officials ought to act.[13] In other words, the 'principles of good administration' reflect and express the terms on which officials are entrusted with power, and the supervisory jurisdiction is a mechanism to enforce that trust. If an official fails to discharge his trust properly, the court will quash his decision and instruct him to make it again in a manner that conforms with the conditions on which it was granted.

13.2.1 Why a Law of 'Public Fiduciaries'?

What value is added by the 'fiduciary' label in the public law context? In their introduction to a recent anthology on the subject, Evan J. Criddle, Evan Fox-Decent, Andrew S. Gold, Sung Hiu Kim, and Paul B. Miller identify two strands of 'public fiduciary theory'.[14] The first strand takes

[12] '[L]egal, constitutional and political thought in this century in particular has not made the adaptations necessary to enable us to use "the public trust," *or for that matter any other normative idea*, in a principled way to explain and justify the standards we may now wish to demand of officials'. Paul Finn, 'Integrity in Government' (1992) 3 *Public Law Review* 243, 245. Emphasis mine.

[13] See Timothy Endicott, 'The Public Trust' in Evan J. Criddle, Evan Fox-Decent, Andrew S. Gold, Sung Hiu Kim, and Paul B. Miller (eds.), *Fiduciary Government* (Oxford University Press 2019), 306.

[14] Evan J. Criddle, Evan Fox-Decent, Andrew S. Gold, Sung Hiu Kim, and Paul B. Miller (eds.), *Fiduciary Government* (Oxford University Press 2019), 2.

a *metaphorical* approach, arguing that public offices involve the exercise of other-regarding powers like private fiduciary roles, and are susceptible of many of the same evils. The fiduciary metaphor provides a fruitful counterpoint to social contract theories of the state, in particular, that offers new conceptual, interpretative, and normative aspects. Perhaps most importantly, the metaphor moves the debate from one about consent and agreement to one about power, vulnerability and trust.[15] The second strand of theory is *interpretative*. This strand, in turn, comprises two approaches. One interpretative approach argues that the relationship between the public and the state is *analogous* to (private law) fiduciary relationships on the basis of shared characteristics – both depend on trust, implicate power, engender dependence and vulnerability, and are open to abuse. Another interpretative approach argues that the authority of public officials *actually is fiduciary* because it mirrors constitutive properties of fiduciary relationships in general.

Both strands share a concern for bridging the normative foundations of liberal democracies (i.e., some kind of republican theory of popular sovereignty) with the importance and value of organised administration. This is what I have called the problem of official action – the unavoidable need for public power to be exercised by individuals – and it has been front and centre throughout this book. The latter, interpretative strand of theory is the most consistent with my account of office.

This chapter argues that the position of a public official is meaningfully described as 'fiduciary' without analogy or metaphor. There is a fundamental similarity in the logical structure of the *Spielraum* of private law fiduciaries and public officials – the conjunction or 'coupling' of wide-ranging powers with duties that regulate the exercise of those powers by reference to manner and purpose. This does not invite the simple transplantation of private law fiduciary principles in public law. A major theme of the immediate prior chapters is, of course, that the public/private divide is more porous than the stylised notions of the textbook writers allows. But rather than arguing all public fiduciaries are (more or less) 'like' private fiduciaries, we need an intentional and careful development of 'natively' public law fiduciary principles. A major site for the expression of these principles is surely to be found in the law of judicial review.

[15] See J. G. Allen, *Trust and Consent as Bases of Political Legitimacy* (Research Master Thesis, University of Tasmania January 2013), an early effort on which this Chapter draws.

13.2.2 The Cornerstone: Other-regarding Use of Official Vires

The Crown, as a common law corporation, has no legitimate interests of its own. It exists to serve the public weal and, as the traditional doctrine ran at least, could neither perform any action contrary to that interest nor authorise any contrary action.[16] The Crown's officials are therefore obligated to exercise whatever powers have been reposed in them in pursuit of legitimate public purposes.[17] The same goes for every other person occupying a position that gives rise to the expectation that the position will be used to promote public rather than private interests – whether in virtue of cooperation with HM Government or, allowing for the complexities of that question, any other factor.

The essentially other-regarding nature of public authority was recognised in the seminal case of *R (Fewings)* v. *Somerset County Council.*[18] That case concerned the exercise of private law property rights by a local government authority. In pursuit of a policy against cruelty to animals, the Somerset County Council resolved to ban the hunting of deer with hounds over certain of its land. This was challenged by hunting groups who argued that the resolution was unlawful because based on irrelevant considerations. At first instance, Laws LJ held that the resolution was unlawful. Both public bodies and private persons are subject to the rule of law, but they are subject to very different principles:

> A public body has no heritage of legal rights which it enjoys for its own sake; at every turn, all of its dealings constitute the fulfilment of duties which it owes to others; indeed it exists for no other purpose. I would say that a public body enjoys no rights properly so called … [I]n every instance … where a public body asserts claims or defences in court, it does so, if it acts in good faith, only to vindicate the better performance of its duties for whose fulfilment it exists. It is in this sense that it has no rights of its own, no axe to grind beyond its public responsibility: a responsibility which defines its purpose and justifies its existence. Under our law, this is true of every public body.[19]

[16] For discussion of the 'public service principle', see Dawn Oliver, 'Psychological Constitutionalism' (2010) 69(3) *Cambridge Law Journal* 639.

[17] See also Evan Fox-Decent, 'The Fiduciary Nature of State Legal Authority' (2005) 31 *Queen's Law Journal* 259.

[18] [1995] 1 All ER 513.

[19] *R (Fewings)* v. *Somerset County Council* [1995] 1 All ER 513, 523 (Laws LJ).

Laws LJ's judgement was affirmed on appeal.[20] Sir Thomas Bingham MR held that it was essential to distinguish between the legal position of the private landowner and that of a land-owning local authority:

> To the famous question asked by the owner of the vineyard ('Is it not lawful for me to do what I will with mine own?' St Matthew, chapter 20, verse 15) the modern answer would be clear: 'Yes, subject to such regulatory and other constraints as the law imposes'. But if the same question were posed by a local authority the answer would be different. It would be: 'No, it is not lawful for you to do anything save what the law expressly or impliedly authorises. You enjoy no unfettered discretions'.[21]

R (Fewings) v. *Somerset County Council* is in some respects an odd case, and has been criticised as over-broad, based on historical distinctions between the powers of different types of corporation. However, the above-mentioned speeches make a more basic point: the Crown cannot be at liberty to do any act unconstrained by duties to the public it exists to serve, and neither can the officials who act on its behalf. This highlights the crucial feature of the 'public fiduciary' concept, which in my view is the implicit connection between a public body's *ability to act* and the *duties* it owes to the public. There should, on this view, be a fundamental symmetry between the body's actions and its duties: a public body should only use its competences in the discharge of its duties.

The question then becomes how this duty of self-less action translates in the relevant context – for example, in the context of (private law) landowner's rights or in the context of non-statutory executive powers. The first observation to make is that the legal position of a public official is at least analogous to the legal position of a trustee. As Walker LJ held in *Scott* v. *National Trust*,[22] a case that arguably falls into the 'penumbra of public law' described in Chapter 12,[23] trustees, 'in the exercise of their fiduciary discretions', are under constraints which do not apply to adult individuals disposing of their own property, and these constraints closely mirror the substance of those rules of conduct that comprise the broad

[20] *R (Fewings)* v. *Somerset County Council* [1995] 3 All ER 20.

[21] *R (Fewings)* v. *Somerset County Council* [1995] 3 All ER 20, [3] (Sir Thomas Bingham MR).

[22] [1998] 2 All ER 705.

[23] See Sir Robert Walker, 'The Limits of the Rule in *Hastings-Bass*' (2002) 13 *King's College Law Journal* 173, 174.

limb of the ultra vires rule (including reasonableness, proper purpose, and fettering discretions).[24]

The notion that these duties *in public law* rest on something accurately described as a 'fiduciary principle' is contentious. Timothy Endicott, for example, has argued that the duty to act 'altruistically' in the context of private fiduciary law is something quite different to the duty to act in the 'public interest' in the context of public law. His argument boils down to the proposition that private law fiduciaries are duty bound to act in the interests of *specific* beneficiaries, and that the main focus of fiduciary law is to prevent conflicts of duty and personal interest. The duty of public officials, on the other hand, is to act in the *general* public interest, and the main conflict is between duties owed to different segments of the public.[25] This gives rise to a 'responsible government principle' rather than a 'fiduciary principle'. A broadly similar argument has been made by John Glover, who categorically rejects the fiduciary principle in the public law context. Government, he says, must act in the general interest and not in some sectional interest, and all must be equal before the law. On Glover's view, this precludes 'particular loyalty' to any given class of beneficiaries:

> Fiduciary obligations attributed to governments and public officials are radically inconsistent with these principles. *The opposite of impartiality is mandated.* Undivided loyalty amounting to positive discrimination must be shown in favour of the persons to whom fiduciary duties are owed. Interests of other persons and of fiduciaries themselves must be subordinated to the trust invested in fiduciaries, or which they have assumed to act. Owing conflicting duties to two or more persons is prohibited by first principles of fiduciary law. [. . .] *Persons whose duties continually conflict must be regulated by some other and presumably a public law code.*[26]

Such arguments, however, assume the private law sense of 'fiduciary' and are really arguments against the direct application of private fiduciary duties (and remedies) to public officials, or perhaps the reliance on analogies with private fiduciary law. That is not what I am suggesting. The basic 'fiduciary principle' in public law is that the public fiduciary must act in the general, public interest; the 'public law code' expresses the

[24] *Scott* v. *National Trust* [1998] 2 All ER 705, 717–718 (Walker LJ).

[25] See Timothy Endicott, 'The Public Trust' in Evan J. Criddle, Evan Fox-Decent, Andrew S. Gold, Sung Hiu Kim, and Paul B. Miller (eds.), *Fiduciary Government* (Oxford University Press 2019), 312.

[26] John Glover, 'Public Officials, Public Trusts and Fiduciary Duties' in Ken Coghill, Charles Sampford, and Tim Smith (eds.), *Fiduciary Duty and the Atmospheric Trust* (Federation Press 2012), 78.

public law fiduciary principle. In short, much of the literature critical of public fiduciary law simply talks past the actual argument.

There is, again, an overlap between private and public law in any case, which cases concerning bodies like the National Trust aptly illustrate. The operation of the duty of loyalty in a large body of beneficiaries changes – even in a purely 'private' context. Following Finn, it is uncontroversial that, 'where a fiduciary serves classes of beneficiaries possessing different rights, though obliged to act in the interests of the beneficiaries as a whole, the fiduciary is nonetheless required to act *fairly* as between the different classes of beneficiary in taking decisions which affect the rights and interests of the classes *inter se*'.[27] Fox-Decent has observed that a trustee of a large discretionary trust may favour the interests of one beneficiary (or group of beneficiaries) over those of another, but may not do so on an improper basis. In cases of multiple beneficiaries with competing interests, trustees must exercise their discretion with fairness and reasonableness as between the classes. This might arise in the context of trusts for charitable purposes, as well in private trusts for persons where the beneficiaries' interests diverge:[28]

> [I]n such contexts the duty of loyalty has to manifest itself as fairness and reasonableness because the fiduciary principle can authorise the use of fiduciary power only to the extent that such respects each person's co-equal status as a beneficiary ... If a fiduciary were to favour one party arbitrarily at the expense of another to whom she owed the same duty she would necessarily violate her duty to the party suffering the relative disadvantage.[29]

In other words, we should not put the (private fiduciary law) cart before the (public fiduciary law) horse. Rather, we should start from the premise of office, which straddles the public/private divide, and then look at how an official faithfully discharges his official vires in the relevant context, be it public or private.

27 Paul Finn, 'The Forgotten "Trust": The People and the State' in Malcolm Cope (ed.), *Equity: Issues and Trends* (Federation Press 1995), 138; see also Paul Finn, *Fiduciary Obligations* (Federation Press 1977), Ch 2.

28 See *Howe* v. *Lord Dartmouth* (1802) 7 Ves 137, concerning conversion of assets in a will and apportioning income between life interest and remainder beneficiaries.

29 Evan Fox-Decent, *Sovereignty's Promise: The State as Fiduciary* (Oxford University Press 2011), 35–36. See also Evan J. Criddle and Evan Fox-Decent, 'Guardians of the Legal Order: The Dual Commissions of Public Fiduciaries' in Evan J. Criddle, Evan Fox-Decent, Andrew S. Gold, Sung Hiu Kim, and Paul B. Miller (eds.), *Fiduciary Government* (Oxford University Press 2019), 67–95.

13.2.3 *The Indeterminacy of 'Fiduciary Law'*

A more serious problem is that the 'constitutive properties of fiduciary relationships in general' are not always clear. Sir Anthony Mason famously described the fiduciary relationship as a 'concept in search of a principle'.[30] A considerable literature has resulted from the attempt to find the principle that organises the various instances of legal relations that are accepted, in doctrinal private law, to have a 'fiduciary' character. Reflecting on the four decades of fiduciary scholarship that followed from his landmark text on the law governing fiduciary offices, Finn has launched a serious indictment of the burgeoning field:

> For all the construction and demolition that has gone on across the common law world, I question whether we are any closer to agreeing upon a simple, intelligible and coherent account of the law [of fiduciaries] and its rationale. My own impression is that we are heading, unnecessarily, in exactly the opposite direction.[31]

Often, fiduciary relationships are defined (tautologically) as relationships in which fiduciary *obligations* inure; indeed, many theorists prefer to speak of 'fiduciary obligations' rather than 'fiduciary relationships'. There is longstanding disagreement as to whether it is an obligation or a relationship that is 'fiduciary', and whether the character is impressed upon that obligation or relationship on the basis of undertakings made by the fiduciary or imposed *ex lege* on the basis of the relationship's indicia. Much of the literature approaches the fiduciary principle inductively, through examination of cases in which the courts have held it to operate, rather than from any broad principle.[32] Fiduciary law's incremental development has, for the most part, been based on an ad hoc justification of particular equitable remedies in the case at hand. Private law fiduciary scholarship has, by and large, also left the concept of office undeveloped.[33]

[30] Sir Anthony Mason, 'Themes and Prospect' in P. D. Finn (ed.), *Essays in Equity* (Law Book 1985), 246.

[31] P. D. Finn, *Fiduciary Obligations: 40th Anniversary Republication with Additional Essays* (Federation Press 2016), [756].

[32] Courts of equity imposed a broad discretionary remedy to 'breaches of confidence' such as those between a trustee and his or her beneficiary. As the term 'trust' crystallised, 'fiduciary' was used to cover relationships which bore hallmarks of the relationship between trustee and *cestui que trust* but which lacked its proprietary features: Leonard Sealy, 'Fiduciary Relationships' [1962] 20(1) *Cambridge Law Journal* 69, 70–71.

[33] Exceptions include Finn's *Fiduciary Obligations* itself, whose first part deals with 'Fiduciary Offices and the Fiduciary's Duty to Act Honestly in What he Alone

This makes general assertions about the 'fiduciary principle' prima facie fraught,[34] and it may seem ill-advised to ground the public law supervisory jurisdiction in such a vague principle. However, the principle is poorly understood precisely *because* the existing scholarship has ignored (i) the concept of office in the conceptual scheme of fiduciary law and (ii) fiduciary offices outside of private law. Perhaps counterintuitively, by examining the fiduciary principle as something that operates in relationships predominantly structured by public law as well as in its more familiar, more private contexts, we might make more sense of fiduciary law more generally.

13.2.4 The Coupling of Powers and Duties

At its simplest, the idea that spans the law of private fiduciaries and public law is that an individual is appointed to a certain office, and reposed with powers in that office, so that she can exercise those powers to promote interests other than her own. Similar duties are coupled with, and control, the powers of any office – whatever the vires the office happens to hold. An office has, in my conceptual scheme, a particular type of *Spielraum*, namely one with an open-ended ability-space and a tightly cabined liberty-space. (In contrast to private individuals who lack legal powers to compel others but are, for that reason, unbound by duties to promote interests other than their own.)

The open-ended nature of the officials' ability-space makes it appropriate to describe the office as one in which 'discretionary' powers are reposed, regardless of the 'public' or 'private' context, and a similar catalogue of duties constraining the liberty-space spans the public/private divide, as is generally acknowledged. The 'fiduciary' label attaches to this type of *Spielraum*, rather than to the context in which the *Spielraum* operates – be it the law of trusts, corporations law, or public law. In fact, in the *longue durée* at least, these three areas of law have co-evolved to a significant degree and have actively cross-pollinated each other. Consider a case like *Sutton's Hospital*,[35] which concerned an 'almshouse for the old'. The principles applicable to charitable trustees were set out in this case, which have formed the basis of modern 'corporate governance law'.

Considers to be the Interests of his Beneficiaries'. The concept of office is also central to Daniel Clarry's trust scholarship, including D. C. Clarry, *The Irreducible Core of the Trust* (Hart 2018) and D. C. Clarry, *The Supervisory Jurisdiction over Trust Administration* (Oxford University Press 2018).

[34] See John Glover, *Commercial Equity – Fiduciary Relationships* (Butterworths 1995), 41–43.

[35] (1612) 77 Eng Rep 960.

There is less *technical* difference between public law powers and private law powers than is often assumed.[36] Alf Ross, for example, distinguished between 'public authority' and powers based on 'private autonomy'. The former are qualified in certain ways – they must be exercised by designated persons, they are heteronomous and unilateral, they must be exercised in the public interest, and they are non-transferable to their repository of power's personal successors. Powers based in private autonomy, on the other hand, are generally held by all adults, are autonomous, generally exercisable for one's own sake, and they may be transferred to one's personal heirs.[37] These hallmarks of 'public authority', however, could be applied just as well to any *official* role, and indeed any fiduciary office, as well. For example, a trustee, guardian, executor, company director, is a 'designated person' that exercises powers that are 'heteronomous and unilateral' (within their proper sphere), must be exercised in the interest of the person or association that is their proper beneficiary, and they are non-transferable to the repository of powers' personal successors.

This bolsters Dawn Oliver's view that common values undergird the public/private divide and that we should not be surprised to see similar principles being worked into common law rules in the contexts of public officials, on the one hand, and repositories of fiduciary powers such as trustees and company directors, on the other. The principles of legality, rationality, and procedural propriety, she argues, are not unique public law principles derived from legislative intention, but in fact represent principles of virtuous decision-making developed by the common law and applied to discretionary powers, including those exercised by public bodies.[38] Fundamentally similar principles are applied to decisions in public law cases and in cases concerning company law, trusts, and private licensing organisations, self-regulated professions, and other private bodies, as we have seen.[39] In all of these constellations, we see the conjunction of unilateral administrative power with the duty to act for another's benefit:

> The origin of the trust is the need to prevent trustees from abusing their powers as legal owners of trust property by applying it for their own

[36] See Eugenio Bulygin, 'On Norms of Competence' in Eugenio Bulygin (Carlos Bernal, Carla Huerta, Tecla Mazzarese, José Juan Moreso, Pablo E. Navarro, and Stanley L. Paulson (eds.), *Essays in Legal Philosophy* (Oxford University Press 2015), 27.

[37] Alf Ross, *Directives and Norms* (Humanities Press 1968), 130.

[38] Dawn Oliver, 'Review of (Non-statutory) Discretions' in C. F. Forsyth (ed.), *Judicial Review and the Constitution* (Hart 2000), 307.

[39] Dawn Oliver, 'Is the Ultra Vires Rule the Basis of Judicial Review?' in C. F. Forsyth (ed.), *Judicial Review and the Constitution* (Hart 2000), 3; see also Chapter 12.

> benefit. This is similar in constitutional theory and public law that ministers and other public officials should not abuse their powers by acting in their own interests, but must be altruistic. In both trusts and judicial review, decision-makers are under duties of selflessness and altruism.[40]

Of course, the application of a shared principle in different context demands the formulation of context-specific rules. We are all familiar with the dangers of direct transplantation of private law fiduciary remedies in public law.[41] Indeed, Leib, Ponet, and Serota argue that 'something gets lost in translation' when we attempt to transplant private law fiduciary doctrines into the public law context. In particular, they argue that judicial enforcement of the fiduciary duty of loyalty is not always the most appropriate remedy for official misconduct.[42] While that is undoubtedly true, it does not mean that where judicial enforcement is appropriate, it is not accurately described as the judicial enforcement of the 'public trust'. Care is necessary to tailor existing public law remedies to maintain the trust reposed in public officials; however, this should prompt the concerted development of a public fiduciary law, not the denial of its existence.

In my analytical terms, the fiduciary principle is expressed as a conjunction of a certain, limited liberty-space with a certain, more expansive ability-space. It is less important what the relevant powers actually pertain to – the important element is that they put their holder in a position where she can unilaterally affect the interests of whoever is subject to them. The decisive 'fiduciary' feature is that the powers are coupled with the raft of duties described by Oliver, earlier, which recurs again and again in apparently different contexts. In other words, 'fiduciary' is a label that can only be applied to a certain type of official *Spielraum*. As Finn explains:

> First, but by no means uniquely, fiduciary law's concern is to impose standards of acceptable conduct on one party to a relationship for the benefit of the other where the one has responsibility for the preservation of the other's interests. Secondly, again in common with other bodies of

[40] Dawn Oliver, 'Review of (Non-statutory) Discretions' in C. F. Forsyth (ed.), *Judicial Review and the Constitution* (Hart 2000), 310.

[41] See *Bromley LBC* v. *Greater London Council* [1983] 1 AC 768; J. A. G. Griffiths, 'Fares Fair or Fiduciary Foul?' (1982) 41(2) *Cambridge Law Journal* 216, 218; John Glover, 'Public Officials, Public Trusts, and Fiduciary Duties' in Ken Coghill, Tim Smith, and Charles Sampford (eds.), *Fiduciary Duty and the Atmospheric Trust* (Ashgate 2012), 69.

[42] E. J. Leib, D. L. Ponet, and Michael Serota, 'Translating Fiduciary Principles into Public Law' (2013) 126 *Harvard Law Review Forum* 91, 93, criticizing see D. Theodore Rave, 'Politicians as Fiduciaries' (2013) 126 *Harvard Law Review* 671.

> law, it does this by proscribing one party's possible use of the power and of the opportunities his position gives, or has given, him to act inconsistently with that responsibility ... *The fiduciary duty originates in public policy*, a view of desired social behaviour ... A fiduciary relationship, ultimately, *is an imposed not an accepted one.*[43]

Arthur Ripstein has argued that the structure of an official role parallels the structure of a private relationship of status. From his formulation, a picture of the rule of law as the rule of officials acting lawfully begins to emerge. An official is legally empowered to make arrangements for others, and is thereby prohibited from using his or her office for private purposes:

> An official is permitted only to act for the purposes defined by [her] mandate. The concept of an official role thus introduces a distinction between the mandate created by the office and the private purposes of the officeholder. That distinction shows what it is for laws rather than people to rule, even though the actual ruling is done by people.[44]

While the details of the restrictions differ, their broad structure is clear. Offices are for public purposes, and any power of choice they confer is public, not private. Officials in the legislature, executive, and judiciary change the normative situation of private persons, and through the exercise of their powers, render them vulnerable to coercion.[45] On this view, a society achieves a 'rightful condition' when officials act within the scope allotted to them by the law. The law of judicial review is to maintain the rule of law by ensuring that officials act always within their *Spielraum*.

13.3 Parliamentary Sovereignty and the Rule of Law

The conventional mode of debate about the conceptual and normative basis of judicial review turns, as we have seen, on an apparent tension between the principles of parliamentary sovereignty and the rule of law. This was particularly influential in the ultra vires debate. The 'modified' legislative intent theories represented a kind of synthesis between the postulates of illimitable power of a sovereign Parliament, on the one hand, and the principles of good administration required by the rule of law, on the other.[46] As Mark Elliott has recognised, however, an account

[43] P. D. Finn, 'The Fiduciary Principle' in T. G. Youdan (ed.), *Equity, Fiduciaries, and Trusts* (Carswell 1989), 2. Emphasis mine.
[44] Arthur Ripstein, *Force and Freedom* (Harvard University Press 2009), 192.
[45] Arthur Ripstein, *Force and Freedom* (Harvard University Press 2009), 194.
[46] Mark Elliott, *The Constitutional Foundations of Judicial Review* (Hart 2001), 100.

of judicial review based on the rule of law is more internally coherent with the theory and practice of the courts; considerations of structural coherence with the sovereignty of Parliament, however, pull towards an approach based on the construction of legislative intent.[47] As we have seen, such theories are not well adapted to the specific problem of non-statutory executive powers. I have argued instead for a theory that is based on the common law power of the judges to enforce the rules of competence and rules of conduct governing an office, regardless of their base in statute or in the common law. Again, approaching the question from the perspective of official action provides some fresh insight into the nature of and interaction between the principles in question.

13.3.1 Naturalising Legislative Supremacy

It should be uncontroversial, as a basic proposition, that Parliament is an institution created by rules found in the unwritten constitution of the United Kingdom. As Edmund Burke said in his 1782 speech on the reform of the House of Commons, Parliament is a corporate body whose existence is to be explained by reference to prescriptive rules, that is, based on existence from 'time out of mind':

> Your King, your Lords, your Judges, your Juries, grand and little, all are prescriptive; and what proves it, is, the disputes not yet concluded, and never near becoming so, when any of them first originated . . . Now, if the Crown and the Lords, and the Judicatures, are all prescriptive, so is the House of Commons of the very same origin, and of no other. The House of Commons is a legislative body corporate by prescription, not made upon any given theory, but existing prescriptively . . . for at least five hundred years.[48]

Naturalising Parliament in this way sets the stage for a sober discussion of the ability-space and liberty-space of the legislature, and the interaction of the relevant common law (i.e., prescriptive) rules of competence and conduct with those governing the executive and the judiciary. For the most part, we can determine the ability-space and liberty-space of executive officials without a detour to legislative intent.

I have tried to steer clear of the 'weak' *versus* 'strong' form judicial review debate. Here, my argument is a little more controversial. It is that the courts, pursuant to their proper common law rules of competence and rules of conduct, exist in a relationship with Parliament that allows

[47] Mark Elliott, *The Constitutional Foundations of Judicial Review* (Hart 2001), 107.
[48] Edmund Burke, *Select Works of Edmund Burke*, Vol. 4 (Liberty Fund 1999), 20–23.

some scope to supervise the acts (i.e., Acts) of Parliament. So much is clear, albeit on the limited basis of a written constitutional text, in Australia and Canada. However, my argument is a broader one in the 'common law constitutionalist' vein, that would justify constitutional judicial review beyond the minimum entrenched judicial review in those jurisdictions.[49]

The ancient notion that fundamental principles of the common law constrain Parliament's legislative power has been interpreted in modernity as a principle of legality, that is, that Parliament does not intend to overthrow fundamental common law principles without a clearly expressed intention.[50] A certain line of modern authorities including *Jackson* v. *Attorney General*,[51] *AXA Insurance Ltd* v. *Lord Advocate*[52] and *Moohan* v. *Lord Advocate*[53] suggest that radical concept of Parliamentary sovereignty may be waning. More recent authorities on the other hand, have stressed the sovereignty of Parliament in their rhetorical justification of judicial review even in the non-statutory context – not least *R (Miller)* v. *Brexit Secretary*.[54] Be that as it may, the notion that Parliament is truly beyond any legally enforceable limits is inconsistent with the notion that Parliament itself, and its Members, derive their authority from the political community they serve.

In Locke's theory of government, for example, the right to resist an unjust government is predicated on a theory of trust:

> [T]he Legislative [despite being the supreme power in a constituted commonwealth] only being a Fiduciary Power to act for certain ends, there remains still *in the People a Supream Power* to remove or *alter the Legislative*, when they find the *Legislative* act contrary to the trust reposed in them. For all *Power given with trust* for the attaining an *end*, being limited by that end, whenever that *end* is manifestly neglected, or opposed, the *trust* must necessarily be *forfeited*, and the Power devolve into the hands of those that gave it.[55]

49 See Will Bateman, 'The *Constitution* and the Substantive Principles of Judicial Review: The Full Scope of the Entrenched Minimum Provision of Judicial Review' (2011) 39 *Federal Law Review* 463.

50 See *R (Simms)* v. *Home Secretary* [2000] 2 AC 115 (HL) 131; see also Anne Twomey, 'Fundamental Common Law Principles as Limitations Upon Legislative Power' (University of Sydney Law School Legal Studies Research Paper No. 10/29, February 2010), 4.

51 [2005] UKHL 56.

52 [2011] UKSC 46.

53 [2014] UKSC 67.

54 [2017] UKSC 5.

55 John Locke (Peter Laslett ed.), *Two Treatises of Government* (Cambridge University Press 1960), II §149, 384–345.

Locke held resistance to be justified in four circumstances, and thereby identified four concrete 'bounds' which limit the exercise of governmental power by all its branches, and which justify resistance when they are transgressed.[56] These bounds include (i) the requirement to govern by promulgated laws, respecting the principle of equality before the law; (ii) the requirement that laws must be aimed exclusively towards the 'good of the people'; (iii) the requirement of consent to taxation; and (iv) the requirement that the legislative body actually exercise legislative power and not transfer it to any other body.[57]

The question is, of course, how Parliament's 'trust' is to be enforced – particularly, whether the judicial branch plays any role in keeping Parliament within its constitutional *Spielraum*. Many would agree with Locke that the courts should not play any role here, and I have already said that the remedies of private trust law are not really an appropriate avenue to address breaches of the public trust.[58] For the most part, the legislature is accountable to the political community primarily through regular elections, and, if one follows Locke, Parliament is subject to armed resistance *in extremis*.

I think that the courts today both can and should play a limited role in enforcing the trust reposed in Parliament – not least to avoid the situation where storming Parliament appears necessary. As Sir William Wade observed, the judges have for centuries 'firmly set their faces' against clauses purporting to make executive action unreviewable in the courts by refusing to apply them.[59] This is rightly so, because to exempt a public authority from the jurisdiction of the courts would be 'an abuse of the power of Parliament, speaking constitutionally'.[60] This justified the rebellious stand taken by judges against Acts of Parliament attempting to 'create pockets of uncontrollable power in violation of the rule of law'.[61] I think there is a good interpretative argument to be made that the judges have, in so doing, implicitly taken it upon themselves to enforce Parliament's trust *legally* in certain circumstances, at least.

56 John Locke (Peter Laslett ed.), *Two Treatises of Government* (Cambridge University Press 1960), II §142, 381.

57 John Locke (Peter Laslett ed.), *Two Treatises of Government* (Cambridge University Press 1960), II §142, 381.

58 See, for example, *Tito* v. *Waddell (No 2)* [1977] Ch 106; *Kinloch* v. *Secretary of State for India* (1882) 7 App Cas 619 for modern examples of 'trusts' in a 'higher sense' that are not subject to legal enforcement.

59 *The Times*, 1 February 1969.

60 H. W. R. Wade, *Constitutional Fundamentals* (Stephens 1980), 66.

61 H. W. R. Wade, *Constitutional Fundamentals* (Stephens 1980), 66.

13.3.2 *Sovereignty as a Theological Concept*

The idea that 'sovereignty' is a secularised theological concept is familiar, for example, the classical argument to that effect by Carl Schmitt.[62] The intellectual history of the idea has an important, and unfortunate, corollary. The conventional concept of 'sovereignty' is not helpful for reasoning about relations between institutions manned by human beings. Its paradoxical nature peeks through in the conundrum of 'continuing' *versus* 'self-embracing' sovereignty. If Parliament is 'sovereign' in the sense of having illimitable competence, it must be able to pass any Act – including an Act limiting its competence. If Parliament (today) has this competence, it might not be 'sovereign' tomorrow; however, if it does not have the competence to limit itself, it is not truly sovereign.[63] Thus truly a sovereign Parliament can bind itself, but only a Parliament that cannot be bound by a predecessor is truly sovereign.

This reminds me rather too much of the Christian theodicy, or the paradox of pantheism in non-dualist *kabbalah*.[64] It does not, in my view, provide a very good basis for approaching practical problems such as whether Parliament can grant a subordinate official the vires to exceed his vires. If we accept that Parliament is 'sovereign' in the conventional sense, it is arguable that Parliament can delegate such a *Kompetenz-Kompetenz* on a subordinate official, but this is not a very edifying kind of debate. A grant of power in terms to exceed the terms of the grant is incoherent. Alternatively, to the extent that we give the courts the role of interpreting that grant of power, we have moved towards a concept of

[62] See Carl Schmitt (George Schwab trans.), *Political Theology: Four Essays on the Concept of Sovereignty* (University of Chicago Press 2005), Ch 2. I prefer Michael Wilks, *The Problem of Sovereignty in the Later Middle Ages: The Papal Monarchy with Augustinus Triumphus and the Publicists* (Cambridge University Press 1963).

[63] See George Winterton, 'The British *Grundnorm*: Parliamentary Sovereignty Re-Examined' (1976) 92 *Law Quarterly Review* 591; 'continuing' and 'self-embracing' are from H. L. A. Hart, *The Concept of Law* (Clarendon Press 1961), 164.

[64] The theodicy is the problem posed by the existence of evil in a universe created by an *omnipotent* and *benevolent* God. As stated by David Hume: 'Is he willing to prevent evil, but not able? Then he is impotent. Is he able, but not willing? Then he is malevolent. Is he both able and willing? Whence then is the evil?' See Kenneth Surin, 'Theodicy?' (1983) 76 (2) *Harvard Theological Review* 47, citing David Hume's 'Dialogues Concerning Natural Religion'. The pantheist problem is similar. In Lurianic *kabbalah*, the Infinite (*Ein Sof*) Creator 'withdraws' to make room for creation. But if the *Ein Sof* is without limitation, it cannot have been changed through that withdrawal, and so is paradoxically both 'outside' and 'within' creation. See E. R. Wolfson, 'Negative Theology and Positive Assertion in the Early Kabbalah' (1994) 32/33 *Daat: A Journal of Jewish Philosophy and Kabbalah* 5.

relative supremacy between institutions in a mixed constitution.[65] More controversially, perhaps, I think that a power granted to an official in clear terms to behave in an irrational or bad faith manner could not be tolerated by any court worthy of the name. The fact that judges generally agree is evident from the ouster clause cases.[66]

At its most general, authority is generated when individuals are organised into a group around a shared set of representational beliefs. In its external aspect, 'sovereignty' means that this group (represented by its official organs) does not recognise itself to be subject to the organs of any other group. It is a further step to say, however, that the powers of those official organs *within* the group are logically illimitable. Freedom from suzerainty, for example, was never said to entail this kind of internal 'sovereignty' in the political philosophy of the classical civilisations. Sovereignty is a late medieval concept developed in the context of the Pope's claims to transcendent power as *vicarius dei* that was later (partially) securalised in a succession of doctrinal wars – first between the Pope and the Emperor, then between the Emperor and his rebellious princes, and later between those princes and the emerging 'nations' they ruled.[67] Throughout, the 'juristic *desideratum*' of the omnicompetent sovereign gained traction against both the classical traditions of mixed government and the medieval traditions of fundamental law.[68] In particular, the waning ability of the papacy to control European monarchs in the thirteenth and fourteenth centuries was counterbalanced by the elaboration of fanciful and extreme doctrines of papal sovereignty; these eventually passed into the political thought of the secular state in the seventeenth and eighteenth centuries.

The frustrating thing is that not even the advocates of parliamentary sovereignty really ascribe to the full implications of their view. This tension between grand statements of principle and sensible intuitive understandings of the operation of legal and constitutional institutions threatens the coherence of English public law.[69] 'Although a majority of British jurists continues to endorse a largely formal conception of the rule

[65] See Alison Young, 'Sovereignty: Demise, Afterlife, or Partial Resurrection?' (2011) 9(1) *International Journal of Constitutional Law* 163.

[66] See David Dyzenhaus, 'Formalism's Hollow Victory [2002] [4] *New Zealand Law Review* 525, 554.

[67] See Carl Schmitt (George Schwab trans.), *Political Theology: Four Chapters on the Concept of Sovereignty* (University of Chicago Press 1985).

[68] Michael Wilks, *The Problem of Sovereignty in the Later Middle Ages* (Cambridge University Press 1964), 184.

[69] T. R. S. Allan, 'Questions of Legality and Legitimacy: Form and Substance in British Constitutionalism' (2011) 9(1) *International Journal of Constitutional Law* 155.

of law, as a matter of descriptive analysis, judicial practice demonstrates adherence to a more substantive understanding, embracing the protection of common law constitutional rights'.[70] This is evident both in Dicey's more nuanced understanding of the role of the courts, and in the legislative intent theorists' modification of their theory that reduces parliamentary sovereignty to a kind of *shibboleth* that signals loyalty to a polite consensus. Elliott, as we have seen, effectively abandons the hard-line position.[71] His interpretative modification of the legislative intent theory very nearly squares the circle, but one may ask whether the circle exists all, or whether the more parsimonious approach might be to abandon radical parliamentary sovereignty for something more easily reconciled with the rule of law.

13.3.3 *Legislative Supremacy and the Public Trust*

In my view, the basis of the principle of legislative supremacy is the 'simple and inexorable logic'[72] that sovereign power resides in the people, and is devolved onto the executive, legislative and judicial branches of government to be exercised by their various officials. To that extent, it rests on the self-same principle as the rule of law itself. Seeing things in this way allows a greater constitutional role for the courts than parliamentary 'sovereignty' admits. No dichotomy between 'legal' and 'political' sovereignty, and no doctrine of legislative supremacy *vis-à-vis* the other branches of government, can 'extinguish our sovereignty or the obligation of our parliamentarians to us'.[73] Nobody can give or be given the jurisdiction to act in ways that flout the condition on which legitimate public authority itself depends – not even Parliament.[74]

This approach is consistent with Allan's argument for a different interpretation of Dicey's classical theory of parliamentary sovereignty itself. As parliamentary sovereignty can only be a consequence of popular

70 T. R. S. Allan, 'Questions of Legality and Legitimacy: Form and Substance in British Constitutionalism' (2011) 9(1) *International Journal of Constitutional Law* 155, 158.

71 Mark Elliott, 'The Ultra Vires Doctrine in a Constitutional Setting: Still the Central Principle of Administrative Law' in Christopher Forsyth (ed.), *Judicial Review and the Constitution* (Hart 2000), 108–109.

72 Paul Finn, 'The Abuse of Public Power in Australia: Making Our Governors Our Servants' (1994) 5 *Public Law Review* 43, 45.

73 Paul Finn, 'The Abuse of Public Power in Australia: Making Our Governors Our Servants' (1994) 5 *Public Law Review* 43, 45.

74 See T. R. S. Allan, *The Sovereignty of Law* (Oxford University Press 2013), 219.

sovereignty, the rule of law limits the sovereignty of parliament to its purpose, and this limitation is enforced by the courts.[75] Modern reinterpretations of Dicey, for example, by Mark Walters, stress that even Dicey recognised that the law defines what Parliament is, that Parliament's sovereign power is, itself, 'legal', and that Parliament can only act by legislation, and in no other way.[76] These three features hold implications for the nature of legislative authority, and undermine the type of claims usually made with an invocation of Dicey's name.

David Dyzenhaus has presented compelling arguments to similar effect. Dyzenhaus shares with Allan a desire to escape the long shadow cast by parliamentary sovereignty over debates about the constitutional underpinnings of judicial review.[77] Describing the sterility of the ultra vires debate as a consequence of faulty premises, Dyzenhaus argues that we need to move beyond the formalist opposition of courts and legislative and cast the question as one of 'consubstantiality'[78] rather than supremacy: 'a view in which both Parliament and the judiciary are engaged in the same task of using reason to given expression to a common set of fundamental values'.[79]

If that be a bridge too far, it is at least necessary to recognise that constitutional order depends on mutual respect between institutions in an effective, if not rigid, separation of powers.[80] According to John Searle, the conventional notion of 'sovereignty' rests on a false notion of transitivity. In a transitive relation, if A has power over B and B has power over C, A has power over C as well.[81] The relation between the branches of our government is not transitive as a matter of institutional reality or constitutional theory, and it is unhelpful to pay lip-service to a caricature of the British constitution. Indeed, accounts of sovereignty that see the rule of

[75] See T. R. S. Allan, *Law, Liberty and Justice: The Legal Foundations of British Constitutionalism* (Oxford University Press 1993), 12; T. R. S. Allan, *Constitutional Justice: A Liberal Theory of the Rule of Law* (Oxford University Press 2001), 25.

[76] See Mark Walters, *A. V. Dicey and the Common Law Constitutional Tradition* (Cambridge University Press 2020), 165, 269.

[77] D. R. Knight, *Vigilance and Restraint in the Common Law of Judicial Review* (Cambridge University Press 2018), 226.

[78] Another loan from Christology, this time *via* J. G. A. Pocock, *The Ancient Constitution and the Feudal Law: A Reissue with Prospect* (Cambridge University Press 1987), 271.

[79] David Dyzenhaus, 'Formalism's Hollow Victory' [2002][4] *New Zealand Law Review* 525, 555.

[80] See Neil MacCormick, 'General Legal Concepts' in N. R. Whitty (ed.), *The Laws of Scotland: Stair Memorial Encyclopaedia* (Reissue, Lexis Nexis 19 June 2015), [2].

[81] John Searle, *Making the Social World* (Oxford University Press 2010), 163.

law as a *precondition* to sovereign power are not only normatively more attractive, they are also empirically more plausible. As Allan argues:

> As one institution among others that together comprise the governmental machinery of a firmly established liberal democracy, Parliament holds its legislative power in trust to secure the general good. To contemplate the existence of 'absolute' power for other ends, inimical to a broadly defensible common good, is not political realism but rather formalist abstraction.[82]

The judicial review of parliamentary legislation is not the subject matter of this book, which is focussed on non-statutory executive powers. But in passing I would mention that 'strong form' judicial review would follow the same logical structure as the rest of the supervisory jurisdiction. Parliament's ability-space is unlimited by reference to subject matter, and on any account would have to be more or less open-ended. However, we have noted that purported ouster of the supervisory jurisdiction over executive officials perhaps should be accepted to fall outside Parliament's ability-space. As for Parliament's liberty-space, this would be constrained by the same duties of rationality and proper purpose as any other institution. Ancient authorities such as *Dr Bonham's Case*[83] that assert the judicial power to 'control' Acts of Parliament that are 'against common right and reason, or repugnant, or impossible to be performed'.[84]

Leslie Stephen's Act authorising the killing all blue-eyed babies might fall into this category. I hope that it would be generally agreed, following events in twentieth century Europe, that an Act of Parliament authorising the killing of all Jewish babies, for example, would be denounced by the courts today.[85] In more quotidian circumstances, despite the modest role played by justiciability and deference in my account of the judicial review of non-statutory executive powers, the proper role of the legislature as the body most directly expressive of popular sovereignty should inform the more nuanced inter-institutional relation I am suggesting.

13.3.4 The Rule of Law as the Rule of Officials Acting Lawfully

The notion that even a 'sovereign' office is subject to legal limits because it is a creature of law is not new. Bracton wrote that the King, 'though

[82] T. R. S. Allan, 'The Constitutional Foundations of Judicial Review: Conceptual Conundrum or Interpretative Inquiry?' (2002) 61 *Cambridge Law Journal* 87, 104.

[83] (1609) 8 Co Rep 107, 118a.

[84] *Dr Bonham's Case* (1609) 8 Co Rep 107, 118a (Lord Coke).

[85] See Kirsten Rundle, 'The Impossibility of an Exterminatory Legality: Law and the Holocaust' (2009) 59(1) *University of Toronto Law Journal* 65.

above the subject, should be subject to the law, for without the law there could be no King'.[86] The very *concept* of official power implies limitations, which play out in the context of bi-lateral legal relations between official and subject.[87] Ultra vires shares much common ground with the 'rule of law, not of men' strand of rule of law thinking, both conceptually and historically.[88] It is thus no surprise that the office-based account of authority sustained in this book offers a powerful expression the rule of law: *the rule of law as the rule of officials acting lawfully*, that is, intra vires. The common law theory of ultra vires is thus an essential reflection of the rule of law itself. Noting that the rule of law is a contested concept, Jeremy Waldron identifies this as the cornerstone of rule of law theory:

> The most important demand of the Rule of Law is that people in positions of authority should exercise their power within a constraining framework of well-established public norms rather than in an arbitrary, *ad hoc*, or purely discretionary manner on the basis of their own preferences or ideology. It insists that the government should operate within a framework of law in everything it does, and that it should be accountable through law when there is a suggestion of unauthorized action by those in power.[89]

As Bracton argued, if law confers power, it must restrict it implicitly.[90] The point is made pithily in Georg Jellinek's concept of 'self-limitation'. The manner in which legal authority is *generated* – that is, through the attribution of a status of 'active citizenship' to officials – necessarily limits that power:

> A power to rule becomes legal by being limited. *Law is legally limited power*. The potential power of the ruling commonwealth is greater than its actual power. Through auto-limitation it gains the character of legal power. Such auto-limitation is not arbitrary, i.e., whether the state actually wants to cultivate this is not something that lies at the state's pleasure. The limitation is, in type and extent, disclosed through the entire antecedent process of history. *Staatsgewalt* is thus not power [*Gewalt*] *per se*, but

86 Henry de Bracton (G. E. Woodbine and S. E. Thorne eds.), *On the Laws and Customs of England*, Vol. 2 (Hein 1997), 33.

87 See Evan Fox-Decent, 'Democratising Common Law Constitutionalism' (2010) 55(3) *McGill Law Journal/Revue de Droit de McGill* 511.

88 Michael Taggart, 'Ultra Vires as a Distraction' in Christopher Forsyth (ed.), *Judicial Review and the Constitution* (Hart 2000), 427.

89 Jeremy Waldron, 'The Rule of Law' in E. N. Zalta (ed.), *Stanford Encyclopaedia of Philosophy* (Summer 2020 ed.), https://plato.stanford.edu/archives/sum2020/entries/rule-of-law/.

90 See Neil MacCormick, *Institutions of Law* (Oxford University Press 2007), 166.

> power exercised within internal legal limits, and hence legal power. Consequently, *all governmental actions are subject to legal evaluation.*[91]

The entire activity of the state, argued Jellinek, must be performed in the interests of its subjects.[92] This grounds official power in the normative basis of the constitution itself, namely the common weal of the political community. The state can only act through individuals appointed to an official status, and the action of those officials is inherently limited by reference to the interests of the social arrangement within which they hold that status. In most cases, they will be subject to the court of public opinion and internal (e.g., managerial or parliamentary) controls; in appropriate cases, however, judicial supervision is necessary and the courts' mandate to exercise a supervisory jurisdiction is implicit in the notion that all governmental actions are subject to 'legal evaluation'. In short, the rule of law obtains where officials act within, and not beyond, the prescribed limits of their vires. To the extent that executive officials are accepted to act lawfully without statutory authorisation, therefore, the rule of law demands that their actions be subject to evaluation to determine whether they have acted intra vires or ultra vires, according to the approach set out in this book.

[91] Georg Jellinek, *Allgemeine Staatslehre* (3rd ed., Springer 1932), 386, translated in Martin Loughlin, *Foundations of Public Law* (Oxford University Press 2012), 217. Emphasis mine.

[92] George Jellinek, *System der subjektiven öffentlichen Rechte* (Mohr 1892), 82.

INDEX

For EU product safety concerns, contact us at Calle de José Abascal, 56–1°, 28003 Madrid, Spain or eugpsr@cambridge.org.

www.ingramcontent.com/pod-product-compliance
Ingram Content Group UK Ltd.
Pitfield, Milton Keynes, MK11 3LW, UK
UKHW021840170526
471087UK00010B/593
* 9 7 8 1 0 0 9 0 1 7 7 2 5 *